TRIUMPH ON THE WESTERN FRONT

TRIUMPH ON THE WESTERN FRONT

Diary of a Despatch Rider
1915–1919

Oswald Harcourt Davis MM R.E.
compiled by Philip Holdway-Davis

FIRESTEP
Press

FireStep Press
An imprint of FireStep Publishing

Gemini House
136-140 Old Shoreham Road
Brighton
BN3 7BD

www.firesteppublishing.com

First published in Great Britain by
FireStep Publishing, 2015

ISBN 978-1-908487-56-8

Cover design by Ryan Gearing Typeset by Vivian Foster
@ Bookscribe

Printed and bound in Great Britain

CONTENTS

FOREWORD

WHEN I READ OSWALD DAVIS'S DIARY IN THE IMPERIAL WAR
Museum I was impressed by two things: the value of his account and the difficulty of reading it on microfilm. It really was hard work.

Yet its value quickly was evident. Oswald was a writer, and an admirer of other writers, a biographer of some in years to come and a published poet in his own right already. I often wished I could have read him with greater ease and at greater leisure.

So to learn that his diary is to be published was a most welcome surprise.

Oswald was a despatch rider, and the importance of the DR in the Great War has been for too long lost sight of. By the time Oswald enlisted, 'Don R' no longer served in the crucial role he had in 1914, but he was still a vital cog in the machinery of war, and Oswald's descriptions of the DR's interaction with the Corps Pigeon Service is, to my knowledge, unique. That fact alone makes this an important book.

But Oswald's account is of much more far-ranging value. He tells us a great deal of what war was like on the Home Front. He delays enlisting out of the honesty and strength of character that marks him – and out of loyalty to his family's firm. "It seemed best in my deepest self that I should not go at present, but wait until I felt absolutely certain that I ought. In a sense it is difficult not to go. Hard to resist the subtle, strong pressure of public opinion. To yield to this pressure is weakness – that was how I decided for the present." When he does go he gives much detail of enlisting and training.

The main attraction of Oswald's account is of course what he tells of despatch riding and the pigeon service, but, as he describes life on the Home Front, he also gives a rich portrayal of everyday life as a soldier, the companionship and exhilaration, the snobbery and degradation: "our own humble Tommies were treated as often as not with the most disgusting disdain and humiliating brusqueness" by officers with "the manners of a railway porter and the brains of a toy dog." The military details that he gives on the Pigeon Service, the travails of the DR he describes, are no less important than the social and military complexities that he explores. Observing field punishment leaves him appalled. He reports the bitterness of an Old Sweat: "They can do anything in the army with yer, bar put you in the family way."

Despite some louts and 'shits' he encounters, Oswald enjoys army life: "All the soldiers I have seen seem twice as happy and careless as civilians"; but soon, "in the lives of most of us, great as it is, the war has passed into secondary importance and, as of yore, we are preoccupied by our private affairs. This is nature's medicinal way."

Yet never so 'preoccupied' does he become that he is blind to the brutality and ugliness: "all the Somme hatefulness – mud or dust, Machonocies and bully, sluttish inimical peasants and the strategic dominance of the Hun." Nor is he unaware of how making the best of things can distort recollection: "Looking back, the life does not seem unpleasant, and I suppose, with familiarity and confidence and interest in pushing my work to success, the misery of it must have thinned like mist and gradually gained colour and warmth."

A telling side of this observation is that "interest in pushing my work to success": Oswald's work ethic is splendid. His home leave he spends in the family business and off his own bat he overhauls the slovenly management he finds in the pigeon service at the Somme. Both here and at Ypres his sense of responsibility is so stern that he is taken advantage of by others, yet while he is aware of this and sometimes resents it he disdains "swinging the lead" himself. When towards the end he feels "the army had almost converted me into a shirker" he is "rather ashamed". Really he is a sterling example of duty: "I like being relied on."

Oswald was a writer and a sensitive soul, in many ways out of place in the rough-and-tumble of army life, yet he stands up for himself when he has to: "though I'd rather face shells than quarrel with a man, I felt I was right in this case," so he takes on a bully in a boxing ring and beats him – and then feels pity for the man's humiliation.

The quality of Oswald's character runs through his account and it's his character that gives his diary a good deal of its value. Initially he comes across as a self-conscious, rather 'Victorian' figure, with a good deal of Puritanism seeping through – even something of a prig. Here we find a man whom we might not seek out for a night on the town, but who we soon feel certain would guard our confidences. Here is a man to rely on. His honesty can be disconcerting at times. He ponders with distaste: "why are young married people so demonstrative? Rather embarrassing for a squeamish chap like myself." But any initially-unattractive prudery is counterbalanced by refreshing, if occasionally alarming, frankness: he is utterly unabashed by his virginal status – if anything indignant at the doctor who "looked as if he didn't believe me". Anyone who could say all this would hardly dissemble on less personal matters.

"The past is a foreign country," L. P. Hartley observes; "they do things differently there". There, then, a 'respectable' 32-year-old man might pride himself on his purity (for Oswald's attitude to premarital celibacy was hardly remarkable in that 'foreign country'); today he'd be embarrassed by his 'innocence'. Oswald recreates for us this foreign country of the past. As the strength of his character emerges, our trust in his descriptions, his statements, indeed his judgement, is reinforced. His diary is as vivid in its details as it is honest in its reflections on the horror and complexity of war. That both revisionists and anti-revisionists will find much in here to cheer them as well as dismay them is testament to its objectivity and value.

The diary also is as well-written as might be expected of a poet. Much of it is in clipped sentence-fragments, but frequently the lyricist gains the upper hand of the gazetteer: "On my way to Shrapnel Corner, ten Gothas steered white and stately, like pieces of pale Gothic masonry loosed from some cathedral roof, each floated, scorning earth against the silver blue of the sky."

That such an original, intelligent, well-written, valuable account could not find a publisher in the 1970s says a great deal about the poisoned attitudes that persisted until recently. For far too long the historiography of the Great War was dominated by the politicised partisan views of AJP Taylor and Basil Liddell Hart and their ilk, and there was a leftist fashion for "snigger[ing] at patriotism and physical courage", as George Orwell put it – exactly what Oswald Davis and his chums exemplified.

Though simplistic attitudes survive in the public mind, in recent decades scholarship has challenged them, and continues to do so with greater confidence. Publication of his diary, long after his death, allows Oswald Davis once again to "do his bit", this time for the historical record.

MICHAEL CARRAGHER
BLACKROCK
CO DUBLIN
AUGUST 2013

PREFACE

THIS IS THE GUTS OF THE GREAT WAR DIARY OF OSWALD Harcourt Davis (civilian) and 148768 Corporal Davis, O H (soldier). Being an avid writer, motorcyclist and adventurer, Oswald takes us on a unique and in-depth journey through his war years. We join him in July 1915 when he provides us with a taste of life in Britain at war. The thoughts, challenges and fears of ordinary folk on the Home Front braving Zeppelin raids and sad news from the trenches of loved ones lost. He takes us through the joining-up process and his early days in uniform and in training. From there we are landed at the R.E. Depot at Abbeville, France in July 1916. As a corporal in the Royal Engineers Signals Corps he is provided with a 'Trusty Triumph H' motorcycle and supports 1 ANZAC Corps on the Somme as a despatch rider taking pigeons up the line. He is then posted to the Ypres Salient where he is attached to the ANZAC Corps as pigeon DR. We hear about the battle of Messines during which he is awarded the Military Medal. Ever facing the danger of being 'bumped' and 'knocked' he rose to duty's call and made sure the pigeons got through. Oswald admits he was scared and on the brink of cowardice, yet he was brave enough for decoration. Shortly after the Armistice is signed he is sent to Cologne in Germany.

It is fascinating to observe that he mingles and chats with the local German soldiers and civilians as if the war had never happened! He stays with the Corps until his departure at Dunkirk in February 1919 and subsequent demob.

Oswald wanted to capture the language of the soldiers in the trenches and preserve an in-depth eye-witness account of what was said and what actually happened.

This War Diary is essential reading for a diverse group of people interested in:

- World War I
- The ANZAC Corps
- Royal Engineers & Signals Corps
- Social commentaries on Great War Britain
- Old Brum & Birmingham
- Northern France & Flanders
- Germany after the war
- Motorcycles
- Family ancestry research
- Exciting true stories. Oswald's War Diary certainly captures the imagination.

This work is much more than a war diary. These are the happiest days of Oswald's life. He thrives on the job. It is an adrenalin-fuelled, petrol-headed, fast and furious life. Duty and danger mixed with comradeship and romance. He frequents the estaminets in search of innocent romance, refreshment and gay times with his comrades. In his army role he is someone, but as a civilian he is nobody. He covets the idea of staying in the army as sergeant in charge of pigeons for the second army. His romantic feelings towards Adrienne seem to be reciprocated. Life is looking rosy. But news from Birmingham that sister Ettie is on the verge of a nervous breakdown and running the family drapery business into potential bankruptcy, moves Oswald to apply for demob and return to Blighty.

You can't help but feel sorry for him. Oswald's fourth 'Ardencester' novel, *This Great City*, reflects these galling lost opportunities more as a biography rather than a novel.

PROLOGUE

RAY DAVIS FAMILY PERSPECTIVE

I never knew my Great Uncle Oswald as I was only two years old when he died in 1962, but most likely he would have heard about me. I was the second born to his eldest nephew, Raymond Davis. Oswald always got on very well with Ray's father – Oswald's brother Wilfred. My father recalled that he had never heard a bad word spoken between them. Because of their close friendship, Oswald consequently spent much time with Ray and the other three nephews – Donald, Oswald and Paul.

My mother wrote the following memoir about him a few months before she died:

> "Ray got on particularly well with Oswald. He spent a lot of time with him and his brother Wilfred (Ray's Father). They all used to play tennis together and Ray remembers playing on Oswald's backhand because that was his weakness. They went ice skating together and played bridge into the early hours. Ray recalls that at 3 am in the morning Oswald would state, 'Well, I must have a couple of hours between the sheets'. Don made up the tennis fours, but being four years younger than Ray, did not spend the same amount of time with Oswald or his father. Ray talked about Oswald a lot. He also loved his father Wilfred a great deal. Ray was Wilfred's favourite son and is buried with him in the cemetery. Oswald also wrote several books and a war diary which Ray and Don tried to get published posthumously."

SHIRLEY JUNE DAVIS, 26 JANUARY 2010.

Whilst my mother may (understandably) have been a little biased in favour of her husband, there is no doubt that all four of Oswald's nephews liked their uncle immensely. All four worked together to have his latter three books, *The Master*, *George Gissing* and *This Great City*, published posthumously.

My father did talk about Oswald a lot. He often mentioned the *War Diary* and how he had tried to get it published posthumously. He said that Oswald was keen to capture the 'language of the trenches'. I still have the letters from the Imperial War Museum sent in the late 1960s. They declined to pay for the diary's publication but were keen to record it on microfilm, which is exactly what they did. Ray, Don and Oswald put in a lot of time and effort to get the *War Diary* published and it is fitting to acknowledge them for their hard work accordingly. It appears that Paul was away at the time. He was serving his country as the British Vice Consul to Rhodesia (latterly Zimbabwe). Because of his high British profile, Paul was in constant danger in Rhodesia and on at least one occasion survived an assassination attempt. My father once rushed over to visit him on news that he had been shot at.

Naturally I grew up being aware of Great Uncle Oswald, his *War Diary*, and the other books he wrote. My father died in 2001. He was the first of the four nephews to come into this world and sadly the last to leave it. As there was no uncle left alive to approach about re-kindling the mission, I chose to take up my father's mantle and strive to have the *War Diary* published myself. I shared this passion with my mother who somewhat dampened the enthusiasm by asking me to wait for a few more years. It was not until we were nearing the end of the decade that she finally granted me her consent and blessing to complete the mission.

My first course of action was to actually read the *War Diary*. I had decided not to read it until I embarked on the mission to have it published. How pleasantly surprised I was to discover that Oswald Harcourt Davis had joined the Royal Engineers – the Sappers. I too had joined the Sappers for three years from 1979–1982. As 'Ubique' brothers of the Corps we had more in common than I had thought. We had both volunteered out of a sense of duty to defend our country against the aggressor. We had both served for three years. Oswald was attached to the ANZAC Corps and I have lived in New Zealand since 1991. Fate and destiny display their peculiar fashion.

The second step was to follow in Oswald's tyre treads and visit Northern France and Flanders on a brief reconnaissance mission. My long time English friend, and fellow Great War enthusiast, joined me as navigation officer. The French maps were very difficult to read. We began the 'Oswald's Triumph' part of our journey at Abbeville. This R.E. depot is where his diary in Northern France begins on 18 July 1916. It ends at Dunkirk on 16 February 1919.

We stuck to a basic outline of Oswald's movements from the Somme to Flanders, Albert to Ypres, intending to follow them more precisely in a future visit. Battlefield visits were a high priority. Our first battlefield stop was at La Boisselle (on the road to Bapaume) and its Lochnagar Crater, an impressive mine hole 100 metres across and 30 metres deep, the remaining mark of the series of explosions on 1 July 1916 (my birthday!). Here, at 7.28 am, it marked the launching of the Battle of the Somme by the British troops. Sappers of the Royal Engineers had tunnelled it.

So excited were we at having successfully navigated the roads to find our first battlefield gem, we focused our attention on the next site instead of which side of the road to drive on. Murphy's Law came into effect and we had a head-on collision with another car. Both cars were write-offs but nobody was hurt, thanks to seatbelt and airbag technology. It could have been worse, but at least I knew how Oswald must have felt when he nearly got 'bumped' and 'knocked' at the Somme.... another co-incidence meant-to-be I wonder?

Rather than tire the reader with more modern tales from the Western Front, I will return to the exploits of Oswald and leave the battlefield descriptions for another book another time.

You cannot judge a book by its cover, and neither can you judge Oswald Harcourt Davis. Oswald joined the army in his early thirties, was 5 foot 6 inches tall, weighed 120 pounds and owned seven teeth. This may not have seemed very impressive but inside that cover was a man who was quite extraordinary. By reading his diary, along with his other books, you will get to know him rather well. He clearly expresses his opinion on numerous subjects and puts his, and others', points of view across in a direct manner. He writes honestly as he sees it and shares with the reader his frailties and humanity. Oswald was a decent, fair-minded, polite, intelligent, adventurous, hard-working and dutiful man with an eye for a pretty girl. He was also fit, strong and brave. His writing style paints a lucid picture for the reader. I can easily imagine this small figure pushing his heavy metal (no plastic parts those days) motorcycle miles through mud whenever it broke down. I can see him taking pigeons up the line when others were too afraid because of fear of being 'bumped' and 'knocked'. He was awarded the Military Medal for Valour (bravery in the face of danger) at Messines. I can also clearly see the barrack-room fist fight that he won against a larger opponent. In summary, Oswald was a 'Real Hero'.

Oswald was born in 1882 and educated at Camp Hill School, Birmingham. His first book of poems was published when he was eighteen. His novels were based on Birmingham and the Black Country. His mother, Sarah Davis, appreciated his literary talent and helped support him financially in his writing, research and travels. An inveterate traveller, as time permitted, Oswald visited every country in Europe, except for Russia, by motorcycle and travelled in this fashion even into his sixties. Sarah was an astute business woman and did not suffer fools gladly. Her life was tinged with sadness as she saw both her husband and son drown off the south-west coast of England. Oswald's father had tried to save Oswald's brother Frank who was caught in a current whilst swimming. Frank was survived by Wilfred, Oswald and sister Ettie. Neither Oswald, Frank nor Ettie had children.

Oswald was an occasional contributor to the literary and drama columns of *Birmingham Post and Mail* and of articles to *The Times*, the *Daily Mail* and *Punch* amongst others. Such was Oswald's command of the English language that upon reading his books, my father would say, "you need to read his books with a dictionary in the other hand". My mother always felt a little intimidated, not because of any physical threat, but that she would have to guess what some of the words meant that Oswald naturally used in conversation.

Oswald has now had thirteen of his books published including *Triumph On The Western Front*. Details of these appear on the 'Other Works of Oswald H. Davis' page towards the back of this book.

Triumph On The Western Front now supercedes *This Great City* as the last of Oswald's posthumous works. But this may in-turn be replaced by another novel which I only discovered after my mother's death in 2010. A long lost novel forgotten about and never mentioned. The fifth 'Ardencester' novel: *Gold in Bethel*. This is a mystery. I will have much pleasure in embarking on yet another mission to publish this new discovery and ensure the legacy and memory of my great Great Uncle Oswald marches on.

Philip Holdway-Davis (nee Davis) and Adrian Davis (brother and supporter but no longer with us):

OSWALD DAVIS FAMILY PERSPECTIVE
OUR GREAT UNCLE OSWALD | THE UNCLE OF OUR FATHER

Oswald H Davis was our great uncle, a man we were brought up to revere, to emulate and to hear about in anecdotes. His memory was kept very much alive by our father who, himself a man of books and languages and who later went on to serve in World War II, had a profound respect for his Uncle Oswald. Our father, Oswald, was the third born of four nephews and was named after his literary uncle. Our father's perspective is the gauze through which we were taught to see the man O. H. Davis, his writing career and his experiences of the First World War. A love of books permeated the shelves of our house and so Great Uncle Oswald was something of a hero in our home, an awe-inspiring presence. A character frequently referred to but unseen.

Maybe it was this backdrop and the constant, enthusiastic urging of our father to read Uncle Oswald's novels that led us as children to leave those books to collect dust on our bookshelves as we grew up to follow our own interests and to delve into other, less familiar books. His novels were always there, waiting to be read. Now they help us to navigate the landscape of our past and to answer some of the questions about our family members that can no longer be answered personally. They serve now as a precious window to the boyhood of our father, a boisterous childhood as one of four sons born and raised in a Birmingham suburb where a drapery shop guaranteed the family income and where tennis and bridge became family passions. For some of us they still are. This family drapery shop is the setting for Uncle Oswald's *Soft Goods* novel, while *This Great City* serves as his tribute to Birmingham.

Our father, together with his brothers Raymond, Donald and Paul, made a huge effort to publish Uncle Oswald's diary in the 1970s, but the time was not right.

Characteristics and experiences in families often repeat themselves and our family is no different. A generation later, our father Oswald Wilfred Davis, was forced to interrupt his studies of German and French at Birmingham University and was called up to serve in the Second World War. He too wrote a diary, a detailed account of his experiences in Persia (now Iran) and Iraq where he served as an intelligence officer. During this time he learned to speak Arabic. Later our father was sent to the British allied zone on the frontier between Austria and what is today Slovenia. He was responsible for gathering information from prisoners of war who were returning home in and from all directions, at a time when people were crossing all over Europe in search of their families and the life they had lived before the war.

It was during this time that our father met our Austrian born mother, returning to England with her to resume and complete his studies at Birmingham University and to start his own family.

Our Great Uncle Oswald showed our mother great kindness at a time when post-war England was still cold-shouldering German speakers. This kindness remains unforgotten. Maybe it was the mark of a man who was different, some lovingly insisted that he was eccentric. Maybe it was because he had first-hand experience of what it feels like to be caught up in the challenges and cruelties of war. Maybe one day we will be able to place a version of our own father's World War II diaries on a bookshelf alongside the detailed account written by the man who was our Great Uncle Oswald and for whose publication it is an honour that we be asked to write a brief piece.

BY HIS GREAT NEPHEWS AND NIECE
WILFRID DAVIS
ERWIN DAVIS
KARIN ERTL (NEE DAVIS)

THROUGH ENGLAND IN WAR TIME

REPRODUCED FROM *THE ACADEMY AND LITERATURE, 1914–1916*
(ISSUE 2261, 2 SEPTEMBER 1915)

OF THE IMPERTURBABILITY OF WEST AND MID-ENGLAND I
had heard so much that I determined to traverse the area North to South and
see for myself how this section of our country contrasted with Eastern shires set
agog by the sinister imminence of the Great War.

In midsummer I rode out of Birmingham as the night-shift of a great ordnance works streamed forth from the factory gates. First stragglers for the day
shift were collecting in dark rivulets on arid suburban streets. Except for recruit
musters and Home Defence Corps marchings, lighting restrictions, long pro-
cessions of Army motor lorries, and a manufacturing boom, there has been so
far in the Midlands little momentous sign of war. My trusty motorcycle fluttered
her way through affluent suburbs of the city, and then braked sharply down as
she encountered drove after drove of workers scouring along the high road on
cycles from Bromsgrove and outlying villages to the city factories. Droitwich
was unchanged in her pictorial beauty. Worcester, with her cathedral planted
plumb in the centre as if to insist on a passing plaudit, was calm and patrician
as ever, feeling no indignity in her use of women conductors for the trams. The
road to Tewkesbury runs close between brown shadows of the Malvern and
Cotswold hills, over smiling meads odorous with bloom and damascened with
gold and white of flowers. The noble bulk of the Abbey looked down on an old-
world town serenely unconscious of war. Gloucester had an urban stir but the
military note was not prominent.

In Bristol the Saturday afternoon was just starting with the holiday air gen-
erated by young people spreading themselves abroad in sports suits. It took

nearly an hour to get through the clogged city to the Bridewater road, yet the sole tokens of war I noticed were a few Red Cross automobiles and War Department wagons, plus the usual percentage of khaki figures. Bristol, in the wide trough of her river valley, and throughout her high broad downs and cliff-like ridges and crests of houses, seemed only peacefully brisk. Perhaps the echo of war was found more truly beside the white inns, the flint cottages, the grey churches, that brooded upon the fine road between Bristol and Taunton. For the sand-coloured uniforms teemed in these plain villages that look out here upon the green commons, brown sedge, shadowy pool, and floor of yellow wildflower, about the Mendip gap. Taunton, that languorous town of the dusky Somerset race, was full of the military.

By evening I was in Devonshire; and thereafter chiefly what I saw as I pushed to the coast was the sun flashing and fading in ambush behind the tremendous beacon-shapes of the North Devon hills. Wiveliscombe, dainty Bampton and its superb valley-gorge, South Moulton, were steeped in profound peace. The clocks were near midnight when I slackened to cross Barnstaple Bridge, and my only untoward incidents had been vicious swerves in the dark on the country cart-tracks over the moors, and once when a policeman darted his neck forward and back like a swan to see that my front and rear lights were correct. A similar scrutiny awaited me on the Bideford road; then, as the moon heaved up her saffron globe to peer upon my engine's sighing transit through the pallid roads, blue river-glimmer and ghostly villages, I touched the far West Coast at Westward Ho! In an eighteen-hour journey I had not been barred or challenged once.

Next day there was in Bideford a recruiting meeting for North Devon regiments. I rode along England's western limb as far as Bude, and down and up the Devon and Cornish coast saw, in the way of service officials, not so much as a coastguardsman. The Bude rocks dozed in russet quiet on their spits of fawn sand and blue sea. Vessels went by as continuously as ever along that viewless horizontal wire upon which they appear to be perpetually sliding when seen in motion from a coast. Inland the landscapes were faultless pictures of rich-coloured tranquility. A stay in Devon and my tour back to the Midlands by road did not appreciably add to these impressions.

By way of varying the angle of vision I next went north from Birmingham by rail. The stations and trains were, of course, alive with soldiers. In Preston, with its suites of flat mills and tapering stacks, every sixth man seemed in khaki. Again many of the trams were piquantly graced by girl conductors. At Lancaster we met a troop train, its occupants singing, cheering, taking gifts from our train on the next set of rails. The shrouded cannon, the packed horses uneasy in their trucks, made the mind miserable. Then at Windermere I shouldered my rucksack, hearing as I started a Belgian refugee conversing with an English officer. For over a week I walked and climbed in Cumberland, two days' post from home, and out of reach of newspapers.

"That's a fine horse," I said one morning to a carter. "They'll be wanting that for the war!"

"Na, na. They will not. There's good news come through at last."

"What's that? It's days since I saw a paper."

"They're through the Dardanelles, they say. The flags are out at Whitehaven. I had it from the engine-driver at Ravenglass."

And Lord Muncaster's gardener, as he stroked his stalwart horse in the grandiose foliage of Muncaster Park, beamed at me with candid joy. Barring casual conversations, the rather pointed advertisements in a village public building, and the shooting practice of half-a-dozen red-badged volunteers in Coniston, this was the single repercussion I heard of the impact of war on this north-west corner of England.

The trains, crammed with soldiers, had to be duplicated as I returned at midnight. At the buffets haughty waitresses rebutted wily Tommies who sought by feigning innocence to coax out a nut-brown draught long past the stipulated hour. The station of Preston, Crewe, Stafford, Wolverhampton, were chill and desolate, and grudged any comfort for fighters. Soldiers and sailors, suffering the pangs of being reft from relatives who clustered on the foreboard, quitted a malodorous and high-priced "refreshment room" only to step into a train that could provide nothing better than standing room in a freezing corridor. The Black Country was busier than usual at night, and through the deep corn-flower blue of breaking dawn pierced the gold-dust plumes of chimney flares. Factories rode the dark hung with tinted lights like a ship in full illumination at sea. The slag banks went by like waves, and at last the arcs of Birmingham stretched in crescent like a curved harbour front.

No matter what the havoc and sensation of this war, there are still in England beautiful tracts where the stunned beholder may bathe and recover as in a lake of healing. These domestic facts do not make so loud and vivid an appeal as the clash of events at the front; yet how much would the future historians of England give to know them intimately as we can!

OSWALD H. DAVIS

THE DIARIES OF OSWALD HARCOURT DAVIS

1915

SATURDAY 10 JULY

In afternoon with Pinnock Memorial Class on outing to Marston Green on the 2.55, and then by field path that I have often jumped over and walked on when a schoolboy, to Coleshill. At the Swan Hotel we had a splendid tea for a shilling – lovely thin bread and butter, but anaemic cake. While waiting for tea we watched tennis players in the hill by church over river. English girls playing athletically do give one a fine idea of life.

We walked to Maxstoke, talking about the war and the new loan, and the foulness of the *Daily Mail's* attack on Kitchener, Haldane, Von Donop, etc, and the dirty turn done by the Liberals in forsaking Winston Churchill, because he appears to have made mistakes over the Dardanelles policy. We agreed that he and Grey were the only men with any imagination in the government. Funny how all the Tory press, especially the Mail, are kow-towing to Lloyd George as Munitions Minister – the man whom they spewed at a dozen years ago, and whom, in Birmingham during the South African war, they pelted with stones and would have killed.

SUNDAY 11 JULY

Mr Lymath and Dolly to tea, after which I played the piano (Beethoven) for three-quarters of an hour. I left at 8.15 to get my motorbike from Coventry

Road and ride home to Wylde Green. At Hodge Hill Common there was quite a dense parade of girls and fellows. Although about four miles out of Birmingham, the road was as thick with young folk for the length of half a mile as at church parade.

MONDAY 12 JULY

To biz by motorbike at 8.45. Finally corrected 'The Boomerang' – Arthur's and my play written in collaboration. Last week we had a record week, but this week things got quieter, owing perhaps to town sales and the weather having broken after a long very fine and dry spell lasting perhaps two months.

Evening to Red Cross meeting at Marston.

TUESDAY 13 JULY

At biz made ready 'Boomerang' for dispatch to Miss Horniman's theatre, Manchester, and Arthur posted it in the afternoon.

WEDNESDAY 14 JULY

A lot of manuscripts received back which had to be sent off. This week I have had copies of my new book of verse, *London Pastels*, returned from J M Dent's, Smith, Elder and Co, Elkin Matthews – all rather favourable, but intimating that, owing to causes related to the war, they were unable to publish at their expense. Dent's would probably otherwise have published for me, and possibly Matthews.

Amazing how inopportunely I contrive to get my literary work done. I have practically no luck. Just as I was beginning to get articles and long poems in *The Strand* and in *The Englishwoman*, and the receipt of favourable letters from *Poetry and Drama* (now suspended owing to the war), the war came along.

I have had *The Granite City* and *Norman Gale* held over by Everyman[1], and two probables of Arthur's and mine rejected respectively by the *Birmingham Daily Mail* and *The Academy*. Of course, until now I haven't had much opportunity to work regularly, and now, when I could have got a volume published in the ordinary way, events have coopered[2] that too. But such misfortunes are slight compared to what thousands or millions are suffering – and I have learned to be satisfied with life itself, apart from artistic success, although it has taken a long time to learn. 'Gratified' is a better word than 'satisfied'. I am quite hardened to failure and don't at all feel disappointed. I have confidence in myself and know I have written good work, and am pleased because I have done such work apart from desire for success – although of course it is nice to be watered with a little recognition. Anyhow, it was a triumph to get 'A London Tube Railway' in

Country Life. Such an unconventional poem, in such a staid paper! I am simply one of those who have to keep pegging away. I have no intellectual power of brilliance, but only vivid imagination and emotion, and 'the gift of the gab'.

In the afternoon played tennis with Arthur Hougham, and discussed with him the miracle of South Africa coming to our aid and conquering the rebellion there. What a blessing was Campbell Bannerman's power to give self-government – as if Africa hadn't had it, the country might have rebelled successfully, and that first disruption of the Empire might have been the beginning of the end. Instead of which, the victory of Botha is an augury for the success of our Empire (I never used to talk like that about 'our Empire', but since the war we have learned that we have a real empire, knit together by fast thongs of affection). Yet it was a near go with Bannerman – the Tory papers were preaching repression of Africa and what folly to give the states their liberty. They would have had us 'Prussianise' them, but by a miracle, a higher morality prevailed, and perhaps it meant the salvation of the Empire. I said to Arthur that virtue and evil are always waging thus their fight, and the balance of good is perpetually hinging on our private and national deeds. It is always felt to be a miracle when the right prevails, because always the wrong is so near to being on top.

At Marston found that Maurice had joined the University Officers' Training Corps, and was flushed with his experience of the first day's drilling. He showed us what he did and how Sergeant Major Moran swore at them. Moran is the most original swearer in the Midlands – so it's an irony that he should have been chosen to drill gentlemen.

We argued about the war, I saying it seemed ironic how each nation was fighting with the idea that it was doing so for pure patriotism. We reviled the Germans, yet with them it was undoubtedly largely a holy war. Though ironical, this made the contest sublime – we are fighting for a moral idea and not for pelf. Of course, Mammon was behind the war because civilisation has been frankly materialistic for the last fifty years, but in the war, men have changed and the bulk of people in my station, have gone simply from a sense of duty and patriotism, and to help Belgium. Yet I can't help seeing all the time that there is a German side to the question, though undoubtedly they are fighting on the wrong side.

In the *Lusitania* case they answer that we are trying to starve their civil population by blockade, which they say is as bad. But of course in blockading, an attacked government can always give way before their women and children get killed – the *Lusitania* had no alternative offered. On the other hand, the ship was carrying ammunition and some say this was a sort of insurance of ship and cargo by the passengers, the Cunard directors thinking the Germans would not dare to sink a ship thus freighted with human life.

IN 1915 THE LUSITANIA WAS TORPEDOED AND SUNK BY A GERMAN U-BOAT, WITH HEAVY LOSS OF LIFE.

Another thing about fighting, I said, was that men who were fighting for England were still fighting for a country that had not yet learnt to give them a noble birthright. Is there any exulting impulse to fight for your home when that home is a slum in Digbeth? Think how people could rush gloriously to fight for England if she really gave loveliness and liberty to the people. Maurice said, 'You're talking as if you lived in Utopia. We're living in the present and have got to fight in the present!' I said, 'It's horrible to fight to destroy. One wouldn't mind fighting to create – yet people never offered to help with their lives to construct fine social conditions. Strange they should be so finely willing to sacrifice their lives for a destructive code.' Maurice said 'But this is constructive. We can't build better until we've destroyed the bad.' And so we argued and neither could convince and neither could glimpse the truth. But, thinking it over, I am not disappointed, because these great questions are too big to decide off-hand. Life, being so various, is so big that we can't see all round, and it is this infinity that makes life's interest. So I don't feel irritated when I can't settle a point of philosophy or judgement.

FRIDAY 15 JULY

Ettie is working at W and R's, after their first having refused to entertain the idea. Mother persisted and I wrote a conciliatory letter, and after all they started her on wholesale work at a good salary. Strange what persistence, confidence and tact will do!

SUNDAY 18 JULY

Undecided whether to take down the bike engine or not, but mother having told me how father damaged a fender he had tried to repair, I curbed my zest and revised the second poem – 'Saturday and Sunday'.

Home from a full class by 5.15, but in the usual way, trifles drag on and it was six o'clock before I had taken the bike round to John Loache's and 6.10 before I was there myself with bag of appliances. After slight delays in which John conquered problems, we got the cylinder down to find that it was not heavily carbonised, but that the top piston-ring was carbonised in, and looked as if it would never come out. However, coaxed with paraffin, it began to move and John soon worked both rings off, and we cleaned and replaced them. I was very interested in thus seeing the workings of the cylinder. The piston was hollow with perforations – I had expected it solid. I then rode it home and it seemed to go all right – so we were delighted and proud to have done it.

MONDAY 19 JULY

Worked at despatching manuscripts until insurance representative called, and we got talking about the war. He said he and several others would go to fight like a shot, but what about provision for their wives who had been used to comforts?

A customer came in the shop in black, and another customer told me with that morbid lusciousness they affect, 'Her husband was shot and left her with four little ones, the very day she got a letter from him about a parcel she was sending. He was a tram-man and "off benefits".' 'What does that mean?' I asked. 'He hadn't paid up.' He was not a reservist, but had probably been indirectly forced to by Tramways Department to join early in the war.

In the evening paid a long-deferred visit to Grindle at Central Library, but found that Grindle was on his holidays. So I went upstairs and in *The Athenaeum* saw a three-column review of John Drinkwater. In my unbiased opinion, Drinkwater is overpraised at present. He is a fine, careful craftsman with only just a suspicion of affectation, but he lacks masculinity of creation and achievement. He is in a compartment – he is not in touch with the great outside universe, though he thinks he is. I may be unfair to him, but I always have the impression he is condescending to us lesser fry. He is always gassing in his verse and in public about universal brotherhood, etc, and yet he is a bitter snob to those who have no influence to help him in his career.

Home by tramcar, when old fool, fussy with self-importance, said to me, 'Now, you're a likely enough young fellow for a recruit. Let me persuade you to enlist. I'm not speaking without authority – I'm on war work.' And he exhibited some badge or other on the lapel of his coat. Of course, this attempted dictation enraged me. I asked him, blushing a little, what business it was of his. I never interfered with other people's business, I said, and expected my own to be left alone. Three girls opposite murmured, 'Everybody can't go.' After a minute's pause, the old chap joined in a conversation opposite about the strike of the Welsh miners. He shouted out his opinion in such loud tones that the conductor had to call, 'No shouting in the car!' and the other man refused to argue with him. He created quite a scene and the three girls giggled and joked continuously. I was glad I had not continued recriminations with the man, or he might have followed me out instead of the other man, which he did when his opponent got up to go.

As regards the Welsh coal strike, I personally think that the fact that this strike has been allowed is a sign of England's true greatness. In that, even in a time of universal crisis like this, there is such a traditional respect for the 'other' point of view, that neither the government nor public have loudly or unanimously cried, 'Down with the miners'. Of course there is the usual minority of the public that always cries, 'They ought to be shot!' But most of us know that huge profits have been made out of war prices by the coal-owners, and that the men are entitled to benefit. A section of the public and the press seek to make this war an occasion to ride rough-shod over every constitutional right of Englishmen. Why should the men consent to be treated like dogs? It is for individual liberty we are fighting, and how can we fight for it if we kill it at home by refusing justice to our own nation? I respect the miners for having the pluck to stand out against public opinion. That is the most difficult thing to do. Of course I am taking it for granted that they are in the right and are acting decently. I don't know the exact facts, and they may be in the wrong – but that is how I feel.

TUESDAY 20 JULY

Shaved in double-quick time, despatched a hasty breakfast and caught train to town. Bought at the warehouse of W and R's and found that ribbons were very scarce, and delivered slowly, so had to arrange to send on a season's order to cover over the Xmas trade. I managed to book a few more woollen gloves, but whether they will be delivered or not is another thing.

WEDNESDAY 21 JULY

Off by 8.15 on bike, which ran splendidly. Strange, I thought on Monday that our work was in vain, and it seemed too good to hope for that the bike would get better – yet undoubtedly a small miracle has happened, and it works grat-ifyingly. Perhaps it was the engine grease that made the piston rings a bit stiff, and they have now worked soft.

At work, sending off 'London Pastels', and writing to *Country Life* in answer to letter from Editor, saying my 'Holborn' too long, but they would be glad to consider short pieces.

After lunch worked at typing 'A London Day', then Arthur came round, and as it was dull, we decided to work and reconstructed a poem he had written, which we called 'Wafted'. It was a job. I felt a little tired and could then have done with fresh air and tennis, but we went on with our play, 'The Tattlers', and did a very good page. Later worked very happily at typing 'A London Day'.

THURSDAY 22 JULY

Busy in the shop although it was such a rainy day. The weather has definitely broken and for the last three weeks has been uncertain and rainy. Typed 'A London Day' and got off three manuscripts.

FRIDAY 23 JULY

Rose at 6.30 and made cocoa, then watched the cat with her kitten. Three-quarters of an hour's work typing second 'Saturday and Sunday', then to busi-ness. Typed 'Wafted' and got off three manuscripts.

SATURDAY 24 JULY

It was raining, so I caught the 8.17 train and at business prepared lesson on Solomon's dedication of the temple for the Pinnock Memorial Class.

SUNDAY 25 JULY

Class attentive but small. Finished at 4.00 prompt. I got home at 6.30 and started work on the bike at once, being rather rude in omitting to see Miss Clarke, who was visiting us. In my haste and zest, I clean forgot our guest. I was up until 12.30, scraping the cylinder and fitting paper washer to same, but I felt I had done the job well.

MONDAY 26 JULY

Rose at eight, and from 8.45 finished work on the bike. I was dreading that my toil would be to no avail, but instead the bike started promptly and gave an al-together new, bell-like distinct explosion – clean and succinct. Naturally I was delighted, taking this for good compression, although when I started out there seemed little compression.

Very busy during the day – rushed at times. Night very busy with shop full of clients. At 8.20 rode off to Marston, but at Maurice's found there was no Red Cross class until after the holidays. He was busy studying signalling for his OTC work. I took a dozen yards of Herden[3] for soldiers' sandbags and rode away at 9.30, just as it was raining. Bike went splendidly all this time.

TUESDAY 27 JULY

To business by bike on damp roads, arriving by 8.45. Looked at the house Wilf thought of renting for his approaching marriage – very nice. Right up to this point the bike had gone splendidly, but I noticed now, the last half mile, while the explosion was good, the engine was noisy and half powerless. What does this mean? We shall see. Probably just a fleeting mood.

THURSDAY 29 JULY

Started to prepare the bike for long three- or four-day tour at August Bank Holiday. The bike not running particularly well, so I tightened the belt twice with shorter links. Home through stained horizons with trees pictorially black at Hodge Hill Common… very beautiful.

FRIDAY 30 JULY

Busy, but not so much with clients as with sorting and buying in new stocks, which we had to get against expected shortages owing to the war.

The note prevailing with the war lately has been one of more optimism. Despite the *Daily Mail*, there is no fear or prepossessing thought of the war abroad now. In the *Birmingham District Post* today I noticed a column by its military correspondent, Edgar Wallace, foretelling that there would be no winter campaign owing to the wastage of German troops that must have taken place. I wonder what will become of this prophecy.

Rumours are current that the Russians are evacuating Warsaw. I didn't expect this, and according to the papers – *The Western Gazette*, *The News*, etc, nobody really did. And yet now it is really taking place, the papers talk as if it had been half expected and ignore the importance of the blow. There is some truth in the *Daily Mail* calling some papers 'Hide and Truth' papers. What a sickening game this glossing over of defeats is. If we are whacked now and then, as we were when the first 'gassing' took place, why don't we say we're whacked? It's like election times when a loss is always explained away as if it were a gain. I should think if a paper had the pluck to state facts plainly, it ought to be well supported… but is Bernard Shaw right? Do the British public refuse to admit the truth? I know the better part does not, and I believe in the democracy.

SATURDAY 31 JULY

To business by bike in my new heavy motor overalls, which are fine. Owing to their colour and curly shape, Arthur christened me 'the Gherkin'. Finished greasing and fettling the bike by 11.15. Not extra busy in the shop – people seem to have gone away early this year. There has been a great exodus from Birmingham, but mostly to the country. They must have bought the stuff they needed earlier. Rather different from this time last year. Now is all calm and routine again. People have got quite used to the war, as Arnold Bennett in *The Old Wives' Tale* prophesied they would.

SUNDAY 1 AUGUST

I woke at four o'clock and dozed, listening to the lovely sounds of life – of steps and voices in husky conversation, 'How ye going, Jack?' and then a postman's grumbling response floated up.

Had a nice breakfast with aunt and uncle, then I copied out 'Saturday and Sunday' poem. There are so many interesting sights going on outside that I am not concentrating easily, but rather am enjoying the pageant of the commencing holiday. The weather appears to be clearing towards sunshine.

Left Birmingham at 2.15 and the bike ran only fairly. I noticed the carburettor flooding, so I gave the bike a rest, then after Coventry it began to fly with splendid compression and I raced along to Daventry – old and quaint and startlingly picturesque. Stony Chalford, Stony Stratford – Hockliffe brisk and beautiful. Dunstable spacious, then on to Hitchin via Luton, from there to Letchworth – a fine specimen of inclusive Garden City. Rode around in dusk. The Fox, like the Wheatsheaf, was full up and in Baldock the Rosemount and White Hart were full, but got good digs at Stevenage.

MONDAY 2 AUGUST

A rare, radiant beautiful Bishops Stortford and Braintree and Colchester. The scenery flatter towards Thorpe and Comarques. I imagined one particular house was Arnold Bennett's.

Had tea at Nags Head – a well-spoken stranger told me that that was indeed Arnold Bennett's house and I called in, but AB was playing tennis, so I rode to Clacton – a flat but very busy seaside place. Back to Comarques by 6.45 and waited.

* * *

On 2 August 1915 Oswald Davis rode through Colchester and resolved to call, unannounced, on his literary hero, Arnold Bennett. Despite finding him out at first, Davis returned later and was invited in.

ARNOLD BENNETT (1867–1931).

As he wrote later in his diary, he spent a lot of time committing a verbatim account of their conversation to paper, and these notes and further articles on Bennett's work were published in The Master – a study of Arnold Bennett. *The full account is long and very detailed, but a short summary shows the impact this meeting had on Davis, and the influence it had on his literary future:*

'Ask him into my study,' came a mellow, quietly masterful, deliberate voice.'

Following the maid, Davis was shown into a large room. 'I sat down in a big chair, remote from the door. I was in too tense a state of vibration to observe with method the appointments of the room.'

Bennett appeared. 'A man smaller than myself… entered the room and closed the door. He had an air of extreme detachment, a detachment even mystical, but not cold. Clad in white flannel trousers and grey lounge jacket, he seemed more absorbed in some inner topic of thought than *concerned with his entrance or my attitude as I got on my feet. He had a good head of wavy hair which was just brindling into grey, as if powdered. His was an undecided young middle-age. He constantly carried the well-shaped head slightly backward on the nape. Thus the chin was lifted alertly and a little defiantly, as I have often seen held the chin of a girl challenging the world with her superb youth. This carriage, adding to the thrusting of one hand in the trouser pocket till the coat-tails jutted out behind, gave him an appearance pleasantly jaunty.'*

Davis explained that two years before he had sent him a book of his verse – The Night Ride – and reminded him that he had acknowledged it warmly, saying 'that it possessed an original note.' He had the letter with him. Davis warmed to his task. 'What I really came about… I've no axe to grind, and I thought you'd like to know that you're influencing strongly young fellows like myself. We're enthused and we admire your work. Such a disinterested tribute, it has often seemed to me, must be as much to an author, or even more than, a formal and public success like yours has become.'

They went on to discuss art, music, fiction, other authors – and Bennett's own works. 'I thought you would be gratified to know that many of us don't overlook the earlier and lesser known stuff. We find a charm in nearly everything you write. And I think we're doing a service. After all, it is we young fellows, the unknown readers, who count. You yourself, in Literary Taste, say an author's enduring fame is made by those devotees who keep ardently discussing and recommending a writer.' At this Oswald noticed, 'He had become more practical, more easy, and he kindled to my talk.' When Bennett asked if he liked Literary Taste, he replies, 'Like it! I should think so. It's most useful as a touchstone. One can often help new readers. I give them Literary Taste and see at once if they have the germ of the grand passion.'

Based on Oswald's enormous admiration for Bennett's style they found much in common. They touched on Thomas Hardy – "You read Hardy?" he enquired. "He was my first love," I said simply. "I always read him," replied Bennett, with equal simplicity and adoration.'

By half way through their meeting, Oswald already referred to Bennett as 'my friend', and Bennett, for his part, gave the novice respect for his opinions, 'What do you think of Synge?', encouraging him to have confidence in his replies. However, when Oswald mentioned 'our own man Drinkwater', he was not too conciliatory to snap, 'Distinctly third rate.'

The subject matter became more ethical and spiritual, in the context of GK Chesterton's articles for democracy and against conscription, which had much moved Davis – 'made my pulses beat'. To write and achieve this effect, he said, was surely 'something to have lived for'. 'That's all art's for,' stated Bennett. 'If so, then art is moral.' 'It is,' he remarked in a tone unerring. 'How can anyone doubt it?' 'Then art and morality are indissolubly blended?' 'Yes, certainly,' said my oracle.

With a warming rapport, albeit between master and aspiring writer, hours passed. Eventually, as Davis rose to leave, Bennett offered him a book. What would he like? He chose Journalism for Woman, which he had never managed to acquire. Bennett agreed it was a rarity, but he had three volumes, one of which he signed.

'To Oswald H Davis,
with kind regards from
Arnold Bennett (formerly known as E A Bennett)   2. 8. 15'

They shook hands outside in the dark and Davis recorded, 'I hugged myself all the way back to the hotel. To celebrate the occasion I asked the hostess for some port wine, but it was long after hours. I lay in bed too excited to sleep. I had not made a note, but I kept recapitulating the interview and remembering smart things I had left unsaid and authors unmentioned.' His final impression, he concluded, was that Bennett was 'to no small extent a spiritual mystic. I had discerned the marks of this occult trait both in the Commonsense treatises and in the novels. Now I found it verified by actual contact.'

This meeting was one of the most influential episodes of Davis' pre-service life, and coloured his literary career for the rest of his life.

* * *

TUESDAY 3 AUGUST

Off about ten – weather uncertain and towards Frinton it rained. Then to Walton – a much older place and more pictorial – not unlike Swanage in some respects. Off to Ipswich after pausing at Thorpe to buy postcards from a private house. The daughter, in the absence of father photographer, sold me postcards of Comarques cottages and typical East-Anglian studies. I had omitted to get photos as mementos of my tour, as I usually do when touring, so I left some money for some to be forwarded, as they were at present out of them owing to soldiers having bought up their stock.

Arnold Bennett had said Ipswich was worth a visit, and it was very quaint and unusual as you approached it, and from a fine bay-windowed inn saw across the River Orwell estuary the town lined up with ships in front. Ipswich much larger than I had thought, with many old and gabled houses – but perhaps not as beautiful as I had expected.

Then to Woodbridge, and on by-roads, muddy and curly, to Aldeburgh, where my plug got sooted up. A very quaint old place, not unlike a fishing village. I should have liked to stop there, but as I had got to get home next day, thought I had better push on. After leaving, turned back to get a few postcards, and as I was about to go, a police officer asked me if I had registered. I said that I didn't know I ought to, as I was not staying, but I would be pleased to if he wished it. I therefore registered in his office. He thought I had been there all day, and mistook my overalls for military attire. I explained I was only touring on holiday, and had come from Thorpe that morning. I must say the constabulary are very courteous and reasonable, as this was the first time I had been met with any such request.

I whipped along to Saxmundham – an old medieval place – with the dusk growing. I decided to push on so as to relieve the journey the next day, but it was dark before I got to Framlingham, and then in the murk and rambling tortuousness of the place I found all the hotels were full up with officers and even a private lodging recommended by the hotel could not spare a room. So, in the dark and mud, feeling disconsolate, I had to push on through by-roads.

Passed one inviting inn, alight on the road, but expected they didn't have beds. On to Debenham, just on closing time. At the Cherry Tree there was the sound of dancing or some hilarity, and a girl waiting in the road outside told me the way to the Red Lion.

Here I didn't look very presentable in my mud-stained garb, but my face must have reassured mine host, who told the old ostler to 'horse' my motor-bike. I went in and as the 'missus' would be back soon from a concert given by

Framlingham soldiers in the village hall, I sat down in the pleasant commercial room and read the first part of *Journalism for Women* given me by Arnold Bennett. It was most delightful. The hostess gave me a fine supper, then I went to my bed in a very large room.

WEDNESDAY 4 AUGUST

Up at about 8.30 and talked with the hostess, who said she wished they had soldiers there, as things were very quiet now so many men had joined the army, and their billets had departed. She, like the others, and like the girl at Thorpe at the postcard house, took the air-raids rather as jokes, and the chance of them happening had become quite a part of normal life. Strange how we get used to the most extraordinary developments.

It was 10.30 before I got away – again forgetting until after starting out to get picture postcards of Debenham. There is so much to see to on a motorbike that one forgets the usual details of a tour. The bike had been running very well, and after all my uncertainty and distress, it is evident that when the engine has been cleaned and top piston-ring removed and decarbonised, the bike is as good as new. The experience I have gained on my two tours will be very useful if I join the Royal Naval Air Service as despatch rider. Before these tours, and before I had to do it, I did not know how to take down the cylinder, and as for removing a piston-ring – why, the very name was enough to frighten me. But now I feel quite confident, and I am glad at being so self-reliant over mechanical jobs, for this kind of work is not the thing a chap of artistic temperament usually excels in. I want to get as much practice as possible, so that if I join, I can join as motorbike rider. I want to serve my country if I feel I ought, but I would like to do it in the way I feel I can be most useful. My tours have made me love England more than ever. In what other country can one have so much freedom and meet such loveable people and such exquisite landscapes?

It was a lovely run to Bury St Edmunds. At Ostock I paused by the tremendous village green, and two dark-eyed comely girls working in front of their cottage with their mother passed the time of day jokingly. 'I should like to come with you on the carrier,' said the prettier of the two, laughing. 'Won't you let me?' she queried, while her mother smiled as if this was an everyday request to a stranger. I rode on, exultant in the variety and adventure of life.

The road to Newmarket and Cambridge was the flattest I have ever travelled, and not very interesting. A storm at Newmarket, so I cleaned my plugs. Cambridge beautiful in the afternoon sun, though it won't compare with

Oxford. Looked into two beautiful colleges. How marvellous those swards are against the hoary walls and gates.

Off again to Bedford in the rain, the road glistening under a strange eastern effect of orange and reds un, like a faint impressionist picture. For the first time saw soldiers with red gorgets – staff orderlies, I believe. Scenery fine and the bike raced along on practically no gas into Northampton, running better than ever.

Lit up my lamps at Northants at about nine. Then on to Weedon in the dark – but after that my road home was straight. Strange, riding in the dark – the telegraph poles seemed friendly as I could tell the right road by them being on each side in the dark – but the trees seemed hostile. Moths fluttered into my lamp and the mist thickened my beam. After riding like this for hours, the hands got rigid as if they were holding on to rigging, and I rode half-dazed.

Blowed if just after Meriden the bike didn't stop suddenly. I tested it and once it ran for a minute – and then stopped dead. In the dark I couldn't see what was wrong, so after much fiddling while my lamps threatened to die down, I decided to walk it for the present.

At first a horribly desolate feeling pervaded me as I surveyed the erring bike, but I got over it. Three fellows passed me on the start of a night-ride, but they did not offer to help, and I didn't like to stop them, but was glad for their momentary companionship. I pushed and wheeled and as I got near to Stone Bridge, saw two lights like those of a cottage. It was a huge lorry of two parts in the turn of the Coleshill Road, and it had lamps hung low on it. I woke the man asleep inside and asked permission to use his lamps. Soon there was I, feeling quite cheery, philosophical and leisurely now with companionship, getting out my cigs and tool-bag and spreading myself over the road, endeavouring to take my carburettor to pieces.

For three mortal hours I wrestled with the thing, until the dawn began to bloom in the east. Lovely scents arose from the earth and the birds began to strike up, and despite my weariness and annoyance, I could not help marvelling over the recurrent beauty of dawn and the untireable earth. She is so impassive and independent of us, going on with her loveliness as if that is the only thing that mattered. This did me good, but it didn't undo my carburettor, which I couldn't see how to unloose.

At last I sought the logbook and there found 'If bike stops suddenly after running a minute, it is probably due to dirt or water in the carburettor. If so, unscrew hexagonal nut beneath jet and lean bike well over, allowing petrol to run through.' How simple! I did it in a minute or so and off went the bike like a two-year-old! Such is life. If I had only known that wrinkle I should have been in bed by then, but I should have missed that dawn. Soon I was off, shooting through the cold, misty, bare dawn and on through the still, lamp-lit streets to Wylde Green, where I ate a meal and got into bed as a beautiful cloud effect tangerined in the east.

THURSDAY 5 AUGUST

A lot of work to do, but Arthur called at dinner-time and as we walked in the park I told him the details of the Arnold Bennett interview. This he much relished and informed me I had got a xxxxx cheek!

SUNDAY 8 AUGUST

Worked at recording the Bennett visit – three hours in the morning and three at night. Total for the week, a lot of uncorrected notes and writing.

TUESDAY 10 AUGUST

I believe there was another air raid this week, rumoured at Goole.

After business I went down to library to see Grindle, but he was out on National Registration work, so I went upstairs to see if *The Academy* had become defunct or changed address. I turned the sheets and suddenly seemed to recognise a sentence as trite, homely, familiar – and mine. I could not at first believe my eyes – but it was so. There was the first part of the 'Mark Rutherford' article, submitted ten days ago. *The Academy* was the last publication I thought would have accepted it. It has always been so with my acceptances. The only worm in the bud is, will they pay? Not that my literary aspirations are mercenary, but it will be more of a conquest if the paper is one that commands a sale and can choose, loftily, its contributors because it can afford the best writers. I don't mind if I'm not paid, though the work I've spent on that paper would surprise some. The class thought nothing of it and ridiculed it, but I knew it was a good piece of work – the first time Rutherford's work has been presented in an organic body as novelist and his philosophy compressed to manageable form.

I didn't read the article through, but left it until I could procure copies. It seemed miraculous. Exultant, but not with quite the bursting exhilaration I used to have (the worst of success). Then home, where mother was glad but my sister uninterested.

SUNDAY 14 AUGUST

Started at ten this morning to take down cylinder and clean it in anticipation of a new tour to the Highlands, last week in August.

It took me until noon next morning fixing it up, but was proud when I had done it. It ran splendidly and I had fixed the cable after removing twice and learning its tricks.

MONDAY 16 AUGUST

In the evening told Maurice Hirst of *The Academy* success and of the Bennett meeting. He was delighted and my recital made their faces light up. He was in the midst of patterns for his officer's uniform. He had been out practising signalling. He's a fine chap – I wonder if the Germans can produce a better…

TUESDAY 17 AUGUST

Tried to get copy of *The Academy*, which was not on sale anywhere, even at Smith's. That doesn't look well for the paper's circulation, I thought. Ordered nine at Booth's and three of August 14 issue, when I presumed the second article would be out. Our kid, Wilf, read the article and liked it.

WEDNESDAY 18 AUGUST

In the paper this morning news of another air raid on the east coast, but it did not state where, and bad rumours were current. In the coffee house, Joe Hogg said it was London and railway stations and a number of churches had been damaged. He said, that he had been told early that morning by railway men who know. It transpired later, I believe, that it was at Leytonstone, and the damage or loss of life, while very regrettable, was not considerable. It seems very dirty work, this bombing of civilians from the air. I don't think our people would engage in such a game – it is not the British way.

Working at Bennett interview until 8.15 in the evening, then ran down to Skinner's. Millie was in and I showed her the photos of my tour. Millie showed me a letter from George Burgoyne at the Alexandria depot en route for the Dardanelles. He said he had had a glorious voyage and enjoyed it so keenly that he was sorry when it was over. The conditions of living were bad as regards climate, sand, heat, scorpions and flies and insects. Leave had been refused at Alexandria, so he as an NCO had had to invent excuses to get on land to see the sights, and then he and the others had been very severely reprimanded by the officers and refused all leave henceforth. The officers still don't understand the new type of British soldier. George Burgoyne is the soul of honour, and as for getting drunk on leave or doing anything discreditable, a chap from his stratum of society in Brum would as soon think of eating paving stones. Of course they can't see this. Men are mere units without character for the purposes of discipline.

THURSDAY 19 AUGUST

Copies of *The Academy* came and I was pleased. A slight religious argument with Aunt Margaret, which I regretted entering as, while each should respect each other's religious convictions, it is hard to do so in practice, and one easily gets stirred and supercilious of opposing views. Showed her *The Academy* article as a fair partial expression of my views – those of Mark Rutherford, with the exception that I don't think we are 'crushed into indistinguishable dust without hope of record' and also his Pantheistic conception of the deity is not satisfactory. I incline to a mystical conception of a spiritual force behind life, of which we can at present gain little conception.

SATURDAY 21 AUGUST

Mother admitted she would be glad if I would go away with her for a week in September, as if I had to go away to the war, it might be the last holiday we should have together, and I acquiesced with pleasure.

Today the glass is gradually going up and it is evidently going to be a fine week. I don't mind spending it at home, as it is Wilf's last full week here before he gets married, and I have plenty of work to do.

MONDAY 23 AUGUST

This morning there was great news of a nasty smack to the Germans in the Gulf of Riga. They lost a dreadnought, a cruiser, several smaller boats, some barques and the men they were trying to land from them, and had to retire. There is some mystery about the news and exact details are not to hand, but it is stated that it was a British submarine that sank the *Von Moltke*.

WEDNESDAY 25 AUGUST

Dispatched two copies of 'London Pastels', of which one came back immediately from Mills and Boon – 'not in their line'. The other I sent to John Lane – and I also sent 'The Boomerang' to the Liverpool Repertory Company. It was nicely acknowledged.

Got ready to go to the Triumph works, having written out a typed form for them to sign if necessary re cable and carburettor. After fine ride in lovely weather arrived at two lofty red buildings facing each other. One large ornamented door was marked 'Offices', and no other could I see open – but a girl went into a wide, double-gated passage, and I followed her in. I wheeled the bike in and went over to the man inside. He rushed to the door as if to bar it – as if I were an interloper. I said, 'I just want to discuss a few points about my new Triumph. Where should I go?'

OSWALD IS ON THE THIRD BIKE ON THE RIGHT.

I was directed to Dale Street, where I sloped swiftly down to a large entrance, like a magnified garage. As I slid in, I noticed a uniformed official. 'Ah – you're on the wrong spot there. Bring her over here.' He motioned toward his office behind him, to the left of the entrance. He was courteous and humorously twinkly, and yet kept, by means of a hinted formality, the dignity of his uniform. 'If you'd wait a minute, a gentleman will see you.' Just then, a youngish fellow with smart grey flannel trousers and well-cut green coat, passed him. The door-keeper addressed him, then said to me. 'That young man who's just passed will see you in a minute.'

I explained all the points to him. Of course, he explained away nearly everything. Re carb, 'Have you tried three parts gas and no air to start?' he asked.

'I've tried every mixture, I expect,' I said. 'But that might do it now.'

'Your belt's too loose,' he said. 'It's slipping. You want to keep your belt tight. It's hard to notice on a two-stroke. You might do it a lot of harm.'

'I'm most particular,' I said. 'I'm going to take that in, but you don't want to be always messing at them. I reckon about two hundred miles first.'

'Some belts stretch more than others,' he said. (An example of how the expert, no matter what you say, brings some unexpected and fertile argument to confuse you.)

He listened gravely to all my remarks, then went to the large repair shed. A young mechanic came forward and I found his look unprepossessing. 'Just see to the spring of that cable and the magneto slide.'

'Wait a minute,' I said.

'I'll have that belt off and tighten it while I'm waiting. It won't take me a minute,' said the mechanic, and took it away.

I waited, intensely interested. The two rooms to the right were large and long – lofty and immaculately clean as a milliner's, and very brightly lit. In the one farther from the door were ranged a hundred bikes, finished and awaiting odds and ends. Frames were suspended from the ceiling, and the next room had crates and large cases full of articles such as crank cases and cranks, etc. It too was widely glistening and clean. From time to time a weary, pottering, elderly man wheeled a case of parts into the room on a truck. This room at the far end was busier, and men appeared to be actually working. In the repairing shop they were busy. Out in the street, youths clad in rubber jumpers were testing the four-horse-power bikes that leant against the wall. They would give the kick-start a kick and let the engine run, then screw up the nuts over the carburettor. Then they'd blow up the tyres… then off with a great noise.

Everyone in the place seemed agreeable, laughing and playing rather than working. Considering that bike factories are supposed to be busy helping with Government work, I was surprised to see things so slack, but at home, over at Woodgate's the chap told me it is their boast there that they never rush anything, no matter what the hurry.

At last the mechanic brought my bike back, and said he had done the belt. I asked a few other questions, then away and had an enjoyable ride.

FRIDAY 27 AUGUST

Heard about the death of young Gibbons, shot at the front by a stray bullet while returning from sniping duty. It seems unreal. Little over a year ago I was meeting him with his chubby young face at dances, along with his two sisters – and now he is dead.

SUNDAY 29 AUGUST

As this was Wilf's last Sunday at home, and he was staying here all day instead of visiting his fiancée, I lounged about, gassing and drinking tea, and got late for class. Two hymns had already been sung, but the third was beautiful and quite melted me. It made me think of all the old Sundays and the passage of youth, and life seemed pathetic and some joys irrecoverable. There was a full class singing heartily, and it was most exhilarating.

After the lesson, we gathered round in animated chat and I said to Dowler what a good time I had that Bank Holiday, and what a pity it was that we hadn't fixed up a tour together. We discussed the prospects of a tour in the future, only as he is at the BSA, he gets no time off from tool-making for munitions workers. I left the class with emotions crowding in on me – a sense of pleasant experiences so thick that they could not be digested.

I walked down to town with Teddy and got him to explain what they were doing in the town hall in the National Registration work. He said trestle tables were fixed up in the Town Hall, and there workers were codifying the information gained, thus each street and name and trade had a number, and the information was sorted under these numbers and put on a stiff card attached to each person's case. These cards were punched into holes in columns and then put in a mechanical sorter. Teddy controlled some such codifying department of trade – he said that his knowledge was useful in this connection, as the enumerators had failed to ensure that workmen entered what metal they worked in. For instance, a man might put down 'lathe-hand' but not state 'in brass-working' and then Teddy had to learn by turning up his employers.

Home by tramcar, reading *Whom God Hath Joined*[4], which I keenly enjoyed, this being a wonderful piece of construction and of imaginative writing. It made me feel anew the beauty of existence, and again I felt that I was full of aesthetic sensations, which thronged too thickly to be appreciated.

MONDAY 30 AUGUST

Stayed after the shop closed and finished typing an article on Lawrence, just catching the 10.30 post to send it to *The Academy*. I wasn't altogether satisfied with the piece, though it has some good descriptive phrasing. Saw that I hadn't sufficiently mapped out the strict form it should take, but will now try to remember this lesson, which is so hard to learn, as form does not come to me by instinct. It should have been based on the fact of Lawrence trying new techniques, and should have been kept on those lines, instead of diverging into his philosophy – or lack of it.

The last night with Wilf at home. It will be a big loss to me. This is the anniversary of Frank's and father's deaths by drowning.

TUESDAY 31 AUGUST

Shop busy and could not get in a good smack of work, so typed and revised Arthur Hougham's poem to the 'Men of the RAMC' and sent it to *The Times*.

In the afternoon the insurance man called, urging Aircraft Insurance. This Wilf and I agreed to take on. The Government rates are high (as admitted by the official of the Drapers' Mutual Fire Insurance Company) and it seems over cute the way they have you unless you insure to full value. Still, it helps the east-coast people by spreading the premiums, and of course, there is a slight risk here on the direct London Road, so we plumped.

Tonight I went to see the town hall while engaged in National Registration work. I went to the door where the policeman was. He first barred the way, but when I said I wanted to see Mr Lymath, who had mentioned to the constable on duty that I should call, he told me which way to go.

The floor of the hall was filled with about six long rows of green cloth-covered tables on trestles. Here were seated a lot of girls, young ladies and older women with about the third the number of youths and men. I wandered up and down rather shyly, as usual not liking to push. As I was walking past the big entrance doors, about which a big barred-in counter had been fixed, I saw Will Pinnock behind the barrier. On the counter were piles of slips and forms, and on the floor were two-feet crates.

'I've come for Teddy to show me round. How do you get up to the Great Gallery?' I asked him.

'I can show you,' said Will, and he led the way.

I went into the Great Gallery where Ted was bending over the velvet seats. On seats here and there were filled-in registration forms, made into piles. 'What are they doing down there?' I asked. 'Filling up certificates,' said Ted, 'according to districts.'

I noticed that hung about the floor over the tables were large letters of the alphabet, indicating districts. Ted showed me a punched code-form. At the right of this small form, the size of a pocket-case, were parallel columns with numbers from 1 to 26, running down in columns of twos or threes. There were perhaps six columns of such numbers, and some of the figures were punched. Each figure, or set of figures, in each column represented the code-number of a district or trade or age, etc. Then Ted took me down to the orchestra stalls and seats, where was a line of Gas-Office operators, punching the cards with little machines like baby Blick typewriters. Ted took me down into the room under the orchestra, where there were three tabulating machines. One machine sorted 200,000 forms in a day.

From the top of this machine a wire ran to the electric bulb and drove a small motor at the bottom of the machine. This was not unlike the knife-grinders that itinerant grinders bring round to your door.

At the side away from the operator, who stood up as at a desk, a tin device like a miniature, elongated mill-wheel, ran round. The machine went rat-rat-rat-rat, very quickly, and as cards from the top slipped down the race, they dropped according to the holes punched into them, into compartments fixed alongside the race. As the pile in each little letterbox grew, it was taken out and ranged with others on the counter until stacks grew. The operator was dealing with single females, and we noticed that the stack at the age of 25 grew apace, while that at 26 was small. Evidently the age of 25 was crucial and that was the age when girls mostly got married. Behind the counter were empty boxes like bullion crates in which the filled-in registration forms were being stored. Ted and I were much interested, and we stood for some minutes before he showed me out.

WEDNESDAY 1 SEPTEMBER

Up at 7.30, agog for the wedding. The scenery was very beautiful this morning and after the wet and in the sun it looked like pictures just painted, on which the paint was still heavy and wet.

Mr Sanby called in the morning and told us how his eldest son, a fine lad, had been shot by shrapnel in the trenches. 'He never ought to have gone through the ranks, as he did, refusing commission,' said Sanby, with catches in his voice. 'Still, that was his spirit. What he endured has been terrible. If I wasn't a husband, I'd go myself, old as I am. That man, the Kaiser, will have to pay for this.' I felt very sorry for him in his great loss. 'Still,' he said, 'what is life? It seems only a few years since I was a youngster. It's just a dream.'

We were busy in the shop – farmer's hosiery man called and I had to buy, as values were rising so and stuff was scarce. While I was trying to fix up final things, a woman came in for eight yards of two-and-a-half brown calico, and down into the cellar I had to go, with buttonhole in best coat, and Wilf's ring in my pocket.

Back at home I pottered about, helping Wilf. We sorted out buttonholes for aunt and uncle and mother, and Wilf waited until 12.20 precisely before he started out. Through Garrison Lane to the Registry Office, rain slightly spitting, to the Registry Office at the decent end of Vauxhall Road.

At the Registrar's we waited, dusting the heavily leather-moulded seats, of which there were two, and a few chairs – otherwise it looked not unlike the waiting room for a dentist. I went out and the other taxi came up, with Mr Jones' family and the bride. We introduced all round and sat somewhat awkwardly. Soon a dowdy lady came out and asked, 'Come in, please.' We filed in, bride and bridegroom first.

'Have you the certificate?' asked the clerk. I produced it and handed it to Wilf, who handed it over, pursing his mouth a little in the way of a boxer preparing to receive and give back a blow. The clerk perused it and said, 'Is your father still living?' 'No.' 'Was he a draper too?' 'Er… yes.' 'What was his full name?' 'Edward James Davis,' took up mother, while Wilf kept silent and we all held our breath. 'I expect, Mr Hastings, it's a well-known Aston family. His father used to keep a draper's shop at Six Ways. He knew your father, Mr Hastings. You remember them I expect?' 'By Greenforth's the grocer's, wasn't it? Mmm, yes. I think I do.'

The registrar had a brave, senatorial aspect, though of medium stature. He looked like a king of gnomes – but benign. 'Am I wrong in thinking your father kept a tailor's at Aston, near Mr Davis?' The registrar looked a little taken aback. 'Eh?' 'Your people were tailors, weren't they?' mother continued. 'Yes, that is so,' the registrar admitted slowly, but without reluctance. 'They had a shop near Six Ways.' 'I thought so.' And her point gained, mother subsided and the bridegroom was allowed once more to come into prominence.

'Frid?' said the clerk enigmatically. 'You spell 'Wilfred' Wilfird?' 'W-i-l-f-r-i-d,' said Wilf. 'Eva May Jones. Is your father still living? Asked the clerk. 'I hope so,' laughed Mr Jones. 'Very much so. I'm here.'

The clerk with his mild but persistent seriousness discountenanced levity, and said, 'What is your vocation?' 'Engineer.' 'But what sort of engineer?' 'Mechanical,' whipped out Mr Jones cavalierly.

The clerk re-entered his atmosphere of priestly gravity, and the registrar on the other side of the table beckoned the prime couple forward. We all stood.

'I do solemnly declare,' chanted the old man of the grey-tinged auburn beard and hair, 'before these witnesses here present assembled, that I, W M Davis know of no lawful impediment why I should not be joined in matrimony with Eva May Jones.'

And Wilf repeated the above, with slightly challenging air and yet an overtone of excitement aroused by the occasion and the registrar's druidical manner, as the official chanted in thick, deliberate speech. Then the Druid went over the formula with the bride, laying particular stress on the careful pronunciation of 'impediment', as if he had found that his female flock stumbled over the big word.

I gave the ring and Wilf, with an eloquent look, wriggled it gradually on, and I paid 7/7 in exact money – and it was all over.

I signed as witness in a big book after Wilf and Eva and mother. The pair drove off, then the parents got in and the taxi driver motioned for me to get in, but I said I want to see the young ones in. We were soon home, and they were waiting in the hall to welcome. At the health, Mr Jones proposed a toast to the health of the couple, advising them not to take life too seriously, and to appreciate money without abusing it. Wilf responded without hesitation, and with another telling glance at his bride, confessed it was love at first sight.

The parting was somewhat pathetic, with Eva almost crying. Arthur and I went to the station with them, I paid the taximan, and got back about four. There was some singing, with Grandpa giving us 'The Guardship' without music, to a tune I couldn't trace. He worked hard vocally, with sterterous pauses after lines, but it was a fine accomplishment and very unique for a naval-looking man of 74.

Then Aunt told tales. She said that when she was a teacher, 'I asked a girl why she came to school "smelling so loud", and the next day an irate lady – an Irishwoman – appeared and said, "What do you mean by telling my daughter she's was loud? Her's a gel – her aren't a rose, and I didn't send her to be smelt but larned."' She continued, 'In those days girls used to bring their little sisters to be minded at the school with them. One day I noticed a girl with one of these little Molochs and I said, "Sarah, Lucinda, Jemima, Jane, couldn't you contrive to leave that baby of yours alone for once?!" "Her ain't a baby, her's my aunt," was the reply.'

After tea there was more singing, and I was having such a good time I couldn't drag myself away for class, and time went on so mother kindly suggested I should stay at Coventry Road.

FRIDAY 3 SEPTEMBER

So busy in the shop that I couldn't do anything but serve. The postman had dropped among other letters, one with 'Academy' on it, on the counter. I served first, though eager to open it. I tore off the wrapper. Can it be possible they have printed something again, as they keep sending me the paper every week? I looked first down the contents and saw three or four alien titles – then 'Through England in Wartime'! They had accepted and printed an article, which though well written, I should not have thought would suit them. I was so glad it made the evening happy, and I was often thinking of opportunities conjured up by the second acceptance, rather than working and concentrating on business. Is *The Academy* on the rocks, or are they stable and think my work good? I think it good, but not often do other people in literary circles coincide with that view. Mother was delighted and I read her the article over supper.

SATURDAY 4 SEPTEMBER

It is lonely with Wilf away after all our fun and liveliness, but I am standing it better than I thought I should. Mother seems quite cheerful and well.

SUNDAY 5 SEPTEMBER

Sat down to correct 'Fleet Street' in the sun. Since *The Academy* acceptances, I don't care so much now if I do have to go away to the war. I have demonstrated that I can write decent stuff, and I feel I have justified my existence and endeavours.

Grindle is coming today, and we are both looking forward to a long talk about Bennett. I meant to get away to meet Grindle by 4.15, but it was this time before I got away from school.

When I got to Steelhouse Lane it was 4.29 and no Grindle. Just like me trying to crowd too much in and spoiling all. However, I finished *Whom God Hath Joined* – a fine piece of work. Ettie came to meet me, saying Grindle had arrived. At tea I felt, as usual, how impulsive I am in conversation, and how I express only one side of a thing and am unfair to my own views. Contrasted with Grindle's stately and comprehensive style of enunciating a view, I feel ineffective. He is so balanced in view and holds the scales impartially, so you feel that he has so unerringly seized the essentials.

After tea we were in the garden with mother, and again Grindle illustrated his sang-froid. I was saying what made the idea of conscription odious was that it was allied with the detestable Northcliffe press; he cut me short with, 'Ah – there you are'. I hold no brief for these, but if it had not been for the *Daily Mail* and *The Times*, and the revelations made by Colonel Repington who was the guest of General French, that shell question would never have been raised.' 'How was it,' I asked, 'that General French didn't complain, instead of leaving it to Repington?' 'Ah, there you raise delicate questions of military etiquette.' He said an officer had informed him that some of the guns had been limited to two shells a day! Can this be true? If so, what chance did our army stand while the Germans were hurling thousands of shells per day? Grindle further pointed out the contradictions issued officially by Asquith and Kitchener over the shells. He also attributed the fall of the Ministry and the rise of the coalition to the shell exposé. When I said it might be merely coincidence, he asked if so, how was it that a week before, the Prime Minister had said that the Government had no intention of changing? He silenced my arguments.

Despite the stress on the Western front, our soldiers and officers come home frequently on leave, except for some of the Mons veterans. VC winners have an ovation in their native villages and receive purses of gold presented by the men they saved. Another astonishing thing is that in the midst of war there should be this Charlie Chaplin craze. CC is the new comedian representing the 'dopey' man on the cinema stage, and adults and children swarm to see him. CC is in the very air. A friend of mine looks like him and wherever he goes they often call 'Charlie Chaplin' after him.

When this war is over and, I hope, won by Britain, it will seem as if the issue was never in doubt and that we were certain to win. I desire to place on record that there have been and are now, days when we feel no such certainty. When Paris was first attacked it looked as if real disaster was here – we could not believe it, but we felt its nearness, and several times during the Ypres struggle, although we have this incurable belief in our ultimate triumph, we felt it was really touch and go. There was a time when we really feared actual invasion – not much, it is true, but a little. Now that has quite disappeared – but looked at materially, the facts in Europe are still against us. The Russians have been overwhelmingly driven back. Since the Battle of the Marne we have gained no ground, yet here we all take it as a matter of course that we shall win – but we know we may not.

A man in the shop the other day said he thought the *Daily Mail* was making a mistake with its conscription campaign, which would, if executed, only disorganise the industry of the country. Where is the money to come from? Already labour is acutely short. In answer to three adverts in *The Post* for two girls, we got only one answer, when we usually had a dozen. This army is marvellous. I can say definitely that Ralphs, Allen, Eliot, Hirst, Eltree – five acquaintances of mine – joined purely from the wish to scotch militarism, and from altruistic motives. They are all cultured and sensitive men. Three of my cousins have joined up from love of adventure and three friends and parents have had hard work to keep their younger sons from going.

MONDAY 6 SEPTEMBER

After a very busy day in the shop I went through the fragrant September gloom to see Maurice, who has joined the OAC. He didn't believe Grindle's story of the two shells per gun. He dislikes soldiering and is working merely to smash German atrocity.

Another thing to record is the astonishing credulousness not only of the uneducated, but also of the educated public. People seriously discuss the most cock-and-bull yarns – about nets right across the Channel and floating magnets, and spy scares. I don't think I am unduly sceptical – I merely want direct evidence, knowing how prone human nature is to gossip and magnify an occurrence - and this war has proved more than anything to me how rumours grow into tradition and legend. People are willing to believe anything if the papers say it. Yet I would not wish to misunderstand or misrepresent the public, because I love it and am a democrat. Beneath all this there is really a fund of common sense and virtue. The best of our nation is inarticulate. Does *The Daily News* represent me, although I read it for its literature? Does the *Daily Mail* represent me because I read it for its factual articles? No – I laugh at both of them because they are tied to their circulations. That brings me to another contrast between us and Germany. As regards ultimate victory and rightness of cause, both nations seem to believe they are right, though I believe posterity must impartially award the verdict of justice to Britain. A main difference between the nations is that Germany boasts and Britain does not. We are by nature and by wish, mute. I have never heard a single boast from soldier or civilian. Everyone is apparently casual but underneath is a grim purpose. This, in my opinion, will win for us. I distrust boasters. I have in life seen them fail so often, and then slink away, expecting you to overlook their folly.

TUESDAY SEPTEMBER 7

Bought hosiery at Larkins' – the place was full of girls instead of fellows. At Oliver's typewriting office I saw one girl where there used to be a dozen – now all engaged doing men's work, I suppose. When the war is over, how will this problem be settled, of men's places being taken so extensively by women? Will employers be fair?

WEDNESDAY 8 SEPTEMBER

A lovely day again, with warm sunshine and mild air, the light intensifying all. For the last three weeks the weather has been beautiful. Today it is fairylike – the leaves are late on the trees and only just starting to go, owing to the wet weather before this fine spell. Early this morning the air was misty, fresh and fragrant. It was so new and pregnant, it was as if some of the earth had been drawn off into the mist and you could draw it in through your senses as you felt the air, and as you draw in the savour of a woman.

I notice that the Press has been very loyal to the censorship, but the censorship has not been loyal to the Press. The censors have allowed an American journalist, Palmer, to see and describe our Grand Fleet in the North Sea, and his descriptions have been copied into English newspapers, but the censorship has never allowed English pressmen to see those sights. This seems to me grossly unfair, and an instance of superfluous official disdain, as if the Government had a grudge against our own press.

Harry Fletcher's sister told me my old school pal, her brother, had joined up and was now driving and interpreting for a major. He would have stayed with the Austin had he known business would have continued so well and what was going to happen at home. He had sent for candles, as they were sleeping in a cellar of an unfinished house. Since going he had never been home, having no luck when they had balloted for leave. She thinks he has had about enough of it now. He is the last man in the world I should have thought would have gone, being in delicate health, yet now he says he can't sleep in a bed, and when he gets home they will have to make him up a bed under the kitchen table.

THURSDAY 9 SEPTEMBER

Heard that Walter Elliot has been wounded in the Dardanelles, and they haven't told the old man because he's in a nursing home after an operation. How it brings back that week in LOS camp, when young Walter was a mere joyous schoolboy, larking about! Also Cleaver has been killed – a brother of one of our old Sunday school fellows. Grindle's brother is in hospital in Alexandria from a horse kick.

A short time ago there were three Small Heath fellows killed – now we are beginning to feel the shocks. Last night the newsman was calling out 'Figures of last night's air raid in London'. It gave me a pang of gloom – sixteen killed and 86 injured, I believe. Yet here in Birmingham the streets seem so normal and the crowds light-hearted. The two things don't seem possible together.

THE LZ 38 ZEPPELIN DROPPED HIGH EXPLOSIVES AND INCENDIARY BOMBS DURING WORLD WAR I CAUSING MUCH DEVASTATION.

SUNDAY 12 SEPTEMBER

Miss Pickin's fiancé from next door told me about the Zepp raid in London. He had seen the Zepps – they looked like big silver cigars. He was somewhat scared and says he's coming back to Birmingham from Enfield if this sort of thing continues. He says it's all nonsense about there being no panic – women were walking down into the underground stations in nightwear in a kind of trance.

In afternoon to tea with Mr Nodder, who said he was in Ravenglass and Partington shortly after the submarine attack. He said that the natives told him the accounts printed in the papers were largely false, that the sub attacked only the benzene factory at Partington; that many people watched the attack, and could easily have been shot at, but the enemy refrained. Also that we made a flare of oil to deceive the enemy, who then disappeared. If this is so, why do the press find it necessary to tell lies? Still, it is only hearsay.

MONDAY 13 SEPTEMBER

Dinner at Joe Hogg's – splendid – hot beef, boiled and roast potatoes, cabbage, milk pudding for 9d. Joe had been down to London and had seen the air raid. He said the talk about Fleet Street being smashed was false, there being only plate glass windows damaged.

[Oswald Davis recorded his diary for the next fortnight in longhand – and it is sadly now illegible. He set out by bike for a tour of the south coast – his story picks up in typed script on 26 September.]

SUNDAY 26 SEPTEMBER

At Brighton I saw an airship – the first I have seen. It was impressive in its slow, yet quick stately undeviating gliding motion – yet in its shape it looked like a somewhat ugly grey-blue fish of the mullet variety. Aeroplanes were common down there.

MONDAY 27 SEPTEMBER

Went to see Guildford and next door was the Abbot's Hospital, 296 years old, and kept in usage similar to that of the day it was established. I entered and in the oak-panelled common room saw a medieval scene – a curved, pew-backed oak bench sat at the left of the old chimney nook. Before the open fireplace were real fire-dogs with pokers etc, plain-topped longish tables with heavy carved-claw wood legs stood in the centre. A brother who came in with a black flowing gown and white flowing whiskers and healthy face of aquiline, yeomanly aspect, explained the tools hanging on the wall. 'Tha's the old-fashioned shepherd's crook. That there's a water bottle or beer bottle. They had those when I was a boy. They had no glass in those days. Tha's a cow-bell and that there's a flail. You see this part, of ash? It works on a swivel, and the end stick, of crab-apple wood – very tough – flails the corn. Tha's the old fashioned flail to thresh wheat with as they used to in the barns. Them? They are modern – fire-extinguishers, though they do look ancient. If there was a fire now I'd up to 'en and slap that at it. Now this lock – here's the date on him – 1636. He might be older than that, but that's when he was placed here. Now you don't understand about corn – you see that's a dibble (pointing to a stick with a rounded end). They used to have them instead of drills that they use now, that drills and drops the seed at the same time.'

Upstairs he showed me the floor and said it must have been several hundreds of years old, as the wood must have been well matured before laying, otherwise it wouldn't have kept the grain so perfectly. The boards were laid just as cut from the tree, the broad base end of one fitting to the slender, tapering end of the other. Down in the chapel he explained to me all the stories of the stained glass windows. It was the first time I had seen the beauty and marvel of stained glass-work, but it now struck me, explained by this simple Sussex yeoman. He went on into history of England – facts which I didn't know – for instance, that Charles I came of the House of Hanover[5]. That the fact of there being German blood in our reigning house was one of the reasons why the Kaiser had pretensions to England. 'Now we've got this here Prussian customer at us,' and, 'You wouldn't believe I've had no education. Well, I haven't.'

A limping, bent figure with black whiskers about him and a pale flabby face, went by. 'That's the master.' He spoke with affection. This is the only almshouse I have met where the inmates are not corrupted by the tipping system which is in vogue. Here you put your tip in a box for the general fund, which is regularly divided. The fellow was so nice and disinterested, I gave double what I should have done.

I went out into the street and bought postcards. Strange that the people in a beautiful city like this seem oblivious of their town's beauty. Guildford was not more seemly or fine in character because of its beauty. It seemed full of youth, frivolous and slangy and irreverent. The best part of the denizens seemed the soldiers – well set up and cheerful and frank and manly. They were on for sport but in an open, jocund cavalierish way, instead of furtively or in nervously stimulated flippancy.

Kingston, close against the stately river, was interesting and graceful. I met a company of soldiers marching and another resting on the green, all healthy and gay. An elderly territorial guarded the river with drawn bayonet. Between here and London Army Vet Stables, London Division Engineers' quarters, I passed a string of ambulance motorcars and other motor vehicles, and the entrance to a military hospital. Here and there, as frequently along the road, wounded soldiers in their boyish blue cotton uniforms, with white reverse collar and red trimmings, being taken for motor drives or hobbling on the road. It seemed strange to see all these things accepted as matter of course after only fourteen months of war.

London was the same as ever, except for slight tokens of war, such as a soldier addressing a non-descript crowd in favour of recruiting, I presumed. The army adverts for recruits on the walls and the arrows pointing the way to the nearest recruiting office. How lovely it was to me to be in London again.

I savoured every sight and sound like the presence of a lover. The grim grey flux of buildings and street-life were magical and reinvigorating. I wandered up and down Jermyn Street to find St James' Market – it led from 51 Haymarket, and up a narrow passage I went. Facing me as I went in, was a building which might have been a laundry, a printing press or a photographer's studio, there being much glass about it. I had seen on the two upper windows of the cowshed *The Gipsy*, *The Pomegranate Press*, and *The Academy*.

I mounted a narrow spiral of low-roofed stairs like the belfry of a cathedral, and emerged in a dingy room, and fronting me was a counter piled with stacks of *The Academy* of varying dates. Near it was an elderly man of the coachman appearance variety, with ginger whiskers and bent knees.

'Is the Editor in?' I asked. The old man turned to a younger man with marble-shaped face, of dark hair, and tanned but dissipated face. 'They're out,' said this individual facing me. 'Are you a contributor?' 'Yes.' 'Recent?' 'Yes. Davis. Oswald H is my name. When do you expect either of them in?' 'They should be in this afternoon.' 'I'll go and have some lunch and come back about 2.30.'

After a meal of roast mutton, back to *The Academy*, up the stairs and round partition. The old man didn't know me.

'Anyone in now?' I asked. 'They're not back yet. I'm sorry.' 'Oh, I'll wait a little.' 'You know we're only publishing monthly?' he asked me at last.

After waiting some half hour and hoping the editor didn't come because I didn't want to state my wishes in that confined room with all those people about, and the girl in the next room. I decided to wait no longer.

'I think I'll hook it,' I said, 'else I'll have the rain catching me before I get to Birmingham.' 'Right,' he said. 'I'm sorry they're out. I haven't seen the editor today.' I left and walked self-consciously through the square.

That morning had come through news of a fine British and French victory on the Western Front. The London papers, with their usual sentimental gush, said every face was wreathed in smiles, the sole topic of conversation being the first great victory. This was an immense lie. I was in the heart of London, and no-one mentioned the victory to me and nobody smiled more than usual. The only thing remarkable was the gusto of the newsvendors and the placards of the various papers which tried to outdo each other in giving a new and piquant setting to the same news.

The fact is that by now, in the lives of most of us, great as it is, the war has passed into secondary importance and, as of yore, we are preoccupied by our private affairs. This is nature's medicinal way. Of what avail would it be to pore over and lament the war and grow morbid over its brutalities and terrors and lies? We do not forget the sublime heroisms of the war. The revelation of human courage and pluck, of our continuing willingness to sacrifice Mammon for ideals, of this incredible spirituality in our century when we thought spirituality was dead – this recognition is with us like a song, chanting bird-like in our hearts. Otherwise, except for scraps of conversation in which drift through the news of slaughtered relatives and friends, the war is only in the background of our consciousness.

I was soon on the St Albans road, with the bike going only moderately well. Dunstable had a great fair in it, glaring in the middle of the wide road. I rode on and a few miles out, the moon emerged most beautifully from a shaggy great cloud – the cloud-edge turned sulphur colour and the sky below was of miraculous lily-blue. Stars sang out and the lovely landscape shone like a stage scene. I stopped for some time to witness it.

Riding at night, the first thing to notice is the moths that keep fluttering blindly into the lamp-beam and against the glass. Then the telegraph poles that are so friendly late at night, and the trees that assume strange shapes and are inimical. It is a strain continually groping with your eyes, and you often seem to be moving in a daze or dream, your hands clamped to the handlebars as if they were a vertical tiller or halyard. The road and the sky converge palely to a horizontal point like two funnels meeting at the narrow end.

At Coventry lights were low except for one pub that blazed out over the road. At the lower end, the coffee house was open, and perished with cold, I went in for tea. I noticed some 'swaddies' and others having bread and cheese, and by the side of each, a saucer full of delicious shallots. I said I'd have this, and they were a treat with nice cheese – just warmed me up. Outside a man telling me the way to the Birmingham road said, 'If you hurry up, you'll just have time to get a drink at the Stone Bridge Hotel, half way, before they close.' Evidently in his opinion people only posted from place to place to get drinks.

He represents a large portion of the community, but he was amiable and well-wishing. Strange world – still it is no more strange frequently to desire whisky than frequently to desire tea, I suppose.

TUESDAY 28 SEPTEMBER

Work and the shop seemed dull and drab at first after my freedom. However, trade good – weather fine. We have had a lovely Indian summer this September.

WEDNESDAY 29 SEPTEMBER

Arthur and I had a most lovely walk to Sheldon in glorious sun with autumn tinting. He was in a gay mood, telling me all the details of his first lesson in English composition with Frank Jones.

Walking alone later, I met Ralphs who said that the Turks are mutilating our men's penises and castrating them – or so he had been told by army men. He was of the opinion that we had got the Germans on toast and they were 'nailed'.

FRIDAY 1 OCTOBER

Tonight a session of the Pinnock Memorial Class opened. I started with a debate paper (against my principles) advocating secret diplomacy, then had to leave to see mother in at the station from Brighton and London. The station was packed – soldiers in a great group were singing gaily. How happy they all seem. All the soldiers I have seen seem twice as happy and careless as civilians. The train came pompously in, having all its old poetry for me. It was packed with soldiers who streamed out in a long, pressing, surging stream.

Off to class again, where Percy Glendon was much in earnest about the anti-democratic qualities of secret diplomacy, and he moved us considerably. Enjoyed it.

SUNDAY 3 OCTOBER

Got to school at 3.25. This was our first open Sunday, and we had twenty-five present – it was a great success. I enjoyed the review lesson of early Israelite history. This biblical history is beginning to grow dear through association with youthful days when I have had it dinned into me at Sunday School. It has taken all these years of steady penetration to pierce me with its curious charm.

MONDAY 4 OCTOBER

Busy in shop – worked at writing the Bennett interview.

Aunt Marge spoke of Uncle Will's clients who had been making shells, and the acid burnt holes in their shirts and made them sick. This client asked to be sent to the war, though over age, preferring to be shot rather than nauseated by shell-making at home.

WEDNESDAY 6 OCTOBER

Busy in the shop. Though we have had a job to get stock, so far the war has been beneficial to trade in many respects. Girls are earning good money and spending it. Nearly all the money, however, is during the last months, paper money. Many articles have appreciated from being scarce, thus we have cleared old gloves and brush braids. A lot of previous underclothes, woven stock and hosiery and flannels etc, became valuable. You don't have to worry about many lines because the war prevents anyone getting them and no amount of enterprise could prevail when the stuff can't be got.

By bike to dancing class at Church House, Erdington, which I enjoyed, although I was shy at first.

FRIDAY 8 OCTOBER

For the first time since I have been in business, we have been able to get a living profit on Sylkos, cottones and crochet cottons. With all prices advancing, we have a legitimate excuse for raising these, as formulated and organised by the Wholesale Central Agency, and this time retailers have fallen in line instead of idiotically cutting each others' throats in competition.

SATURDAY 9 OCTOBER

Worked for two hours on the Arnold Bennett interview. Then in the afternoon to a friendly football match between Birmingham and Footballers' Battalion. About 1500 present. It was a fair game, but either owing to war hanging over, or the league fever being absent, they have had not that race and tang and ocean force which the old games had. Recruiting speeches were made by Hall Edwardes and others and a dozen recruits were forthcoming. One or two, shambling, tattered figures, danced and flapped about like scarecrows, and dodged over imaginary obstacles and did turns and capers as they were led over the field before the crowd by the sergeant. Just like the English, I thought – merry in the darkest hour.

MONDAY 11 OCTOBER

Worked at the AB interview. I had a row with a client over a pair of gloves, and starting too hot-blooded, lost my temper – which made me feel small when I review the circumstances. I would not accept liability for the gloves (kid) and she took me up quick, and I had made my mind up and was primed to explode.

Of course it would have been better to be diplomatic. Customers heard us quarrelling – but I calmed down and compromised and she was pleasant.

TUESDAY 12 OCTOBER

Finished the AB interview then read Jones' treatise on the pronunciation of the Midlands. To bed by 10.15, but not to sleep until after eleven as was cogitating about military service.

WEDNESDAY 13 OCTOBER

Up at seven and read the Arnold Bennett manuscript ready for the lecture.

Fettled the bike, then after dinner off by lovely byways through Canwell and Weeford and Watford Gap to Lichfield. Several motorcars waiting by pretty spots while the owners' children picked cobblers and berries. A lovely scent – this autumn smell reminds me of how father used to take us out at this time of year. In Lichfield the Cathedral showed its russet ruddy front with its hundred figures. The window glittered with green-yellow light from the west.

Inside the interior was like a red forestry of stone with cavern tints and vault sounds, but what a mockery the service going on! Here is a cathedral representing established religion for a radius of fifty miles, and the congregation was at most a dozen, even in wartime. There was the priest and acolytes and choir singing away to vacancy. Undoubtedly the formal religious spirit is no longer a reality in this country. If it was, it would express itself warmly through the magic symbolism provided by such a cathedral. There is such an echoing of the voice, you can't make out what the minister is saying – yet I would not have it altered. From the point of view of art, it is perfect.

Round the Close the houses were magical. I have visited Lichfield many times before, but never before have I noticed how fine the Close is. At the end one house poised over a great gulf of scenery, then a stately stone temple of a house, hung with red creeper like exquisite lace. Then homely but pictorial smaller houses, splashed with flower and creeper, then in the corner towards the main street, a house of white painted stone or brick with black beams. Against the white and October murk in atmosphere it was beautiful. Altogether a magic and entrancing picture.

THURSDAY 14 OCTOBER

After business, through thick fog round to Maurice's. His leg was still bad as he had torn the fibres of the muscle, but he was keeping on with the OTC work and expecting to get an artillery appointment at Wolverhampton for his commission. He complained of others unmarried not volunteering to enlist. He was downhearted at the prospect of breaking up his lovely home.

FRIDAY 15 OCTOBER

Met Arthur Barker, who told me that the RNAS despatch riders had been disbanded, so he was going to join some other naval arm of the service, to the best advantage he could after a holiday. He was changed little except for being browner and taller. He thought we had the upper hand in France, but that it would be a devil's job to get them out of Belgium.

SATURDAY 16 OCTOBER

It seems that this week there was another Zep air raid on London, with the loss of many lives. It is a dastardly business. According to letter from Londoner shown me by friend, there was no panic, and this seems to be the general agreement. On the 19th inst I was told at Sanderson's that their London office had been damaged to the floors in the first big Zep raid. The general feeling with the public is that the Government are in a mess and don't like to confess it. The idiocies of the censorship go on.

SUNDAY 17 OCTOBER

Up early to meet Dowler at park gates for a spin. It was lovely in the autumn, with the leaves brown and sweet, and the sky coming out blue from milky mist. To Dunchurch where, right up against the church is a row of cottages emerging from which an old fogey came questing for his Sunday paper. He had given up Lloyd's, which he'd taken for fifteen years, because there was no war news like in the *News of the World*. He was for the press censorship, as he reckoned spies carried all news to Germany. 'We'll conquer him down if we have to fight farty 'ear!' If he was in command he would bring our fleet round to Constantinople and attack from two sides! This enjoyable talk delayed us. The fogey had a thin, yellow face, nearly toothless, with side whiskers. He was quick and eager like a bird and seemed healthy for an octogenarian.

A rapid dinner with Wilf and Eva, then away to school. Afterwards took tram with Ted to Yardley. The walk to Sheldon was exquisite, the soft films of the atmosphere being fine and the smells reminiscent of old days with father. At the church a curious effect over fields to Marston of mist drawn in a straight band across fields parallel with the river. At tea, a long talk with a very intelligent and urbane young fellow over Northcliffe, Lord Derby and press censorship. He and I agreed that the sinister feature about Northcliffe was that he was dishonest in his presentation of the truth. For instance, this fellow pointed out that he was in shell manufacturing and that it took six months to get a factory into shape for making new type of shell. Now Northcliffe, in the shell outcry, withheld this fact from the public, which he must have known, and made it appear that the delay was due to shortcomings on the part of the Government. That is the mode of Northcliffe's dishonesty. The other fact about him was his materialism, and insensibility to finer issues of the spirit. He calls a table a table, and he represents a hard-headed business class which does the same.

THURSDAY 21 OCTOBER

To business by nine – began to correct and collect manuscript in order to have all in good shape in case I should have to go away later on, if I join the OTC.

Spent some time thinking of the letter I had received from my literary friend and Bennett enthusiast, Grindle, who said he was thinking of offering himself for service. I almost decided to join then, but I have found that to be precipitate, though natural to me at times, is unwise.

SUNDAY 24 OCTOBER

To school at 3.20. I had to play, and there was no lesson, Glendon being ill with a bilious attack. Walking home with Teddy, he told me that Manse Woods, after being rejected nine times, and being once told by an army specialist that he would die in three months (that is, he should have been dead last May) had passed the army medical exam on Saturday. They wanted him to be attested then, but he wanted two weeks' leave to put affairs straight. They would give him only one week, yet urged him to attest now. 'Do you think I'm bloody green?' he asked. He would attest next Saturday and thus gain two weeks. It appeared a cousin of his had been killed at the front. 'I want to kill one or two of the buggers for that!' he said.

The tale raised by conscriptionist press that young fellows are emigrating from England to save being pressed into military service, has been scotched by the colonial authorities themselves, who state it is false.

Teddy and I went for a walk in the afternoon, I considering the great question, as Grindle, the last of all persons I should have thought would join, has decided to offer himself for service.

MONDAY 25 OCTOBER

In afternoon by tram (as rain threatened) to town. At Stork Hotel a continual *va-et-vient* in the hall. An Australian came from the dining room in rich coloured fawny khaki, and I saw glistening on his fingers diamonds and a gold watch on his wrist. 'Have ye got a match?' he asked Dowling. 'Ye'll find one in the smoke room.'

'It's this damned tooth,' said the soldier. 'Here y'are,' I said, handing him a match. He rammed same into his mouth and hands in hip pockets, went to the door. He had a brown wizened face, like a monkey's, and smelt of cigars. A chap you couldn't help admiring. These colonials – they don't care a damn for anything. They are not only not afraid of men, they are not even afraid of social etiquette. Can you imagine me having the pluck to break all rules in an hotel entrance like that?

Went to the library and obtained an estimate for duplicating the Arnold Bennett interview for the class.

TUESDAY 26 OCTOBER

I got Munsey's magazine and found Arnold Bennett's new novel, *These Twain*, completed in two parts – September and October. I was annoyed I didn't know before, as I wanted to read it early and get a review into *The News* or somewhere. Read same on bus going home. The beginning, I think, shows lack of magic, but we shall see.

WEDNESDAY 27 OCTOBER

I read *These Twain* until three, with which was somewhat disappointed. Then with Arthur went to cemetery and Sheldon and had a most enjoyable afternoon, the dun colours of landscape entrancing us. Tea by firelight and Arthur said how his cynicism had been changed by his illness, when he found out how decent everyone was to him. He said how he missed his brother, and yet all that passed between them was about four times in the week Fred would say, 'What's the time, Duck?' No-one else called him Duck – if they did, he would punch them!

THURSDAY 28 OCTOBER

In the afternoon Lee came and told us of a Dutch friend of his, Blitz, who had been arrested as a spy because he was overheard by a lady to ask the way to some works which he supplied with metal, situated on the railway at Park Royal. The lady told a soldier, who asked him what he wanted, and apparently directing him, took him to his military commander who, speaking German to Blitz, had him arrested. The soldier swore he had asked the way to Woolwich Arsenal. Blitz wired for fifteen Birmingham friends, who swore to his integrity,

Lee amongst them – no-one could doubt his being an Englishman, with his north country accent! Also he had his Amsterdam papers. The case was dismissed, but it shows how miscarriages of justice can occur through one unscrupulous witness. Blitz spent ten days in Brixton jail on remand.

Had a talk with Wilf about joining the army. He said he should do nothing until after Christmas, and I said I hadn't made up my mind, but should go as soon as I felt irresistibly that I ought. Told mother this next morning.

FRIDAY 29 OCTOBER

Worked at typing Arthur's poem 'The Enemies', and then corrected 'Saturday and Sunday'. Dinnertime I met the younger Richardson, a Canadian, who had returned on leave for four days from the trenches, where he said he had been for seven months. He said it had been interesting and all right, but they were now getting tired of it. Each section going out of the trenches made it comfortable for the relief section coming in. He said it was their hope and his that peace would be declared before Christmas and the Canadians though it likely. 'Why?!' I asked, astounded. Well, they couldn't get any further. He reckoned it would be a kind of truce with the men remaining in trenches. Kaiser Bill would declare peace and then would declare war again. He said they had no reserves – there were 4,500 Canadians and, he understood, 3,000 Australians behind, and perhaps some regulars. They wanted men badly. He said that the German trenches had three-foot concreted sides and six feet concrete top. They would take a trench and then the Germans would shell them out, and take one of their trenches. The accounts in the papers made him laugh. Under cover of gas they once took a trench, cutting the barbed wire unseen, and when they came out of the gas, the Germans were scared out of their wits. They killed every man jack, and the Germans did the same. None gave quarter. They took no notice of instructions from headquarters. Absurd for a man in a plush armchair by a big fire to issue commands. They had one foot in the grave and one out, and they took no risks. There was none to stop them. If their officers tried to, they might get shot.

Walked home to town with the Clarkes. Doug said he was intending to enlist in the Flying Corps Motorcyclists on Saturday next. I said, 'Have you ever thought of joining the OTC?' He said he thought the expense was too much, but said he'd get particulars the next day. He asked if I'd thought about doing the same, and I said the question was before my mind as before everybody's, but had wanted to think it over so I said, 'Let me know your information on Sunday, when I shall have thought it over.'

SUNDAY 31 OCTOBER

Got up and read papers, then walked to the park, thinking over the question of enlisting. Could neither feel I ought or ought not. To school on the same tack and home again. Doug Clarke was going to join the motorcyclists of the Flying Corps.

At night read *These Twain* and at 7.30 went out until nine to think over again the big question. Same result.

MONDAY 1 NOVEMBER

Train to business and walked from town to shop, thinking the big question over. Could feel no definite impulse either way, so felt that I must judge the most expedient course to adopt. If I went, should I join the OTC or the Flying Corps motorcyclists?

To bed at about 10.15, but did not sleep until 11.30 – still thinking about joining the motorcycle corps.

TUESDAY 2 NOVEMBER

Trained to town and walked from there, thinking things over. Met Arthur Barker, and I said I thought of joining the OTC or the motorcycle section of the Flying Corps. He said, 'Don't get a commission in the infantry.' He implied that the young officers, especially the infantry ones, had to go through it. I should like the motorcycling better, but should not have much time before going to put things straight.

The latest development of trade is that, owing to the scarcity of labour through so many men joining up, goods cannot be got. Scarce commodities are overalls, pinafores, aprons, woollen gloves, and kid and cotton gloves. We have had only about two fifths of our woven underclothes through and no woollen hosiery worth having. Of all the woollen gloves on order, have so far had none.

Into town to see Grindle – he is going to join the ASC. He too was disappointed with Bennett's *These Twain*.

WEDNESDAY 3 NOVEMBER

A beautiful walk to Sheldon, Arthur reading his long short story – which was fine. Had a nice tea, when we discussed enlistment, which, though natural, spoilt our joy. Arthur said he had told Manse Woods he was a bloody fool to go as it might break him straight away. He has been told by a doctor not to run for a tram. What about when he has to go at the double when he trains? He asked me not to go until I felt absolutely certain I ought, and the later the better. He said the continuous war at the back of his mind was making him miserable. Every letter you opened had reference to it. One day a friend wrote from the front saying how the birds were singing, and that he wanted a new cap – because it had been knocked off by the breath of a shell which had killed his two messmates. Now brother Fred had gone it was miserable at home. His mother, as nearly all women in this war, had been splendid. She had said nothing, but when Fred's back was turned, she had kept breaking into tears. The thought was on her mind that Arthur might go also, and he could not promise not to do so. It made him ill. Only once or twice before had he seen a woman cry and that made him ill too. He did not know what to do himself. Though on munitions work, he did not like to see men going who could be less well spared than he. If it had not been for this he had had the happiest year of his life.

I came in, sat down and thought things over quietly for half an hour in the old drawing room by the fire. It seemed best in my deepest self that I should not go at present, but wait until I felt absolutely certain that I ought. In a sense it is difficult not to go. Hard to resist the subtle, strong pressure of public opinion. To yield to this pressure is weakness – that was how I decided for the present.

THURSDAY 4 NOVEMBER

Worked at getting off manuscripts and writing out Bennett notes on *These Twain*.

At dinnertime Maurice came in. His work at the OTC was over and he was waiting for promised commission in the artillery. His firm was making him a good allowance and he did not think he would have to break up home, but he seemed downcast and scarcely cheerful.

FRIDAY 5 NOVEMBER

Busy in shop – the minnows came early to clear up rubbish from the shop as it was Bonfire Night. Their fireworks club had saved 3/8 and Wilf and I gave the minnow a few pence, but I knew they would have no bonfire or fireworks, as these are forbidden by law this year owing to the war.

TUESDAY 9 NOVEMBER

At 10.15 an elderly canvasser, of athletic build but nervous temperament, called to appeal to me to join the army. I said it was a matter for the personal conscience of each individual and that argument would be wasted, as I had thought the matter over deeply and should go immediately I felt I ought. However, I can't interpret my temperament to him and he would argue – with the result that I said some stinging things I rather regretted – but he didn't mind. He was a decent sort with an only son at the war and his wife worrying, and I felt sorry and regretful if I had said anything hurtful. But he assured me I had not hurt his feelings. But there are so many gasbags going about bleating, that I was at flash point, and I have got a quivering temper when I get warmed. We discussed the American loan, the ephemeral nature of national hatreds, the horror of bayonet practices felt by his son, the wave of passion under which men can fight, the lack of information over interpretership and the OTC, the brute ways of the army, the take-all and give-nothing way of the present conscription, the *Daily Mail*, Mr Asquith's speech, Mr Churchill's mis-statements and more.

WEDNESDAY 10 NOVEMBER

On the way to business I met Paul. He had two sets of papers down from Manchester, and we fixed up to go and see if we could get in the motorcycle section of the Flying Corps. If not we would fill in the papers. Then talked it over with Wilf.

THURSDAY 11 NOVEMBER

I felt somewhat a gloom of responsibility at having decided to enlist as Motorcyclist in Flying Corps or the RE. Paul and I went to Smethwick, discussing how we wanted at least ten days' leave to finish up our affairs, and that we wouldn't join for general service. From terminus walked to Doug Clarke's. He said he had been messed about at the recruiting office at Smethwick. On the Monday he found his friendly and educated sergeant had been sent away, as he was recruiting fellows too freely for ultra-desirable branches of the service. They couldn't pass him there for the motorcycle section of the Flying Corps, so he had gone to Butterfield's, the Levis people, and got a letter of recommendation there after spending a day in the workshop. He had asked at Curzon Hall for Lieutenant Ryland, and had to wait three-quarters of an hour with fellows whose feet couldn't be seen through dirt, for his medical examination. They had tested him thoroughly. So we decided to be medically examined at Smethwick and then send an application to the RE.

At Smethwick found the recruiting office, where posters screened the window adjuring you to obey 'The call of King and country who need you', to 'Remember Belgium', and to go 'For God and the King'. All round was the dingy bustling industrial vitality of a manufacturing town.

'And what might you gentlemen want?' asked the sergeant, as he noticed me go to the counter and fill in the application form which we had got from Manchester. We pushed past four fellows of the working class, two of whom were seated on a bench against the wall to the left. Paul handed him his papers. 'You can leave these here and we'll send them up,' he said.

I came up, 'We just want to be medically attested,' I said, handing him the papers. He glanced at them. 'Right! Go straight upstairs. Show your papers when you come down, whether you get through or not.'

We went upstairs where, at a desk in the centre sat a smallish smiling, ruddy-faced man of about forty-eight. He looked like a pleasant wholesale grocer – most unmedical. He put down his cigarette and did not answer when I said, 'We've come to be medically attested,' but took our papers and examined them. I began taking things off. 'You can strip to the waist,' he said. 'Both at once?' said Paul. 'Too cold for that,' he said. 'Better have your boots off.' He weighed me and entered on the buff form of medical history '120 lb'. Height was registered at 5 feet 6 inches. Then he tested my chest with a stethoscope. He passed me in half a minute, putting the rubber sucker below heart, above my side and by my shoulder. He gave a look at me and asked, 'No marks or varicose veins?' 'None.' I uncovered my ankles and feet. 'That's all right, isn't it?' I asked. 'Oh yes, that'll do,' he said. Then he tested Paul and gave him a little more chest-testing. We dressed. He pointed to an alphabet card and I pressed my finger on my left eye. I tried and guessed – but could not read it – nor the second line properly. The third I managed. With right eye covered I did not do so well. He did his best to help me. 'No, that isn't G. You've done it once already.' 'D, P…' I got it off. Paul's sight was excellent. He read the bottom line right off with the exception of one letter, and while the doctor smiled and winked wickedly at me, Paul kept stoutly asserting that N was O. On our sheet he put for my eyesight something like this:

R 12 L 9

We smoked cigarettes and thanked the doctor. I asked him if my heart was sound. 'Yes,' he said. 'Perfectly?' I persisted. 'It's thumping a little, but they generally do on this job,' he smiled.

Downstairs the little brown-suited fellow asked me how we'd got on. 'Clean sheet,' we said. 'Like to look?' He perused the form. It read:

'**PHYSICAL DEVELOPMENT:** Good

Physical peculiarity or defect: Nil

Fit for active service at home or abroad

Signed James Watt
Civilian doctor

Downstairs we handed the papers to the sergeant, who entered them in a book, enquiring what military area my residence was, and the postal district.

The sergeant passed us our papers. 'There you are. Go and knock everybody down in the streets with your motorcycles and run all the bloody Germans off their feet with 'em.'

We walked off chuckling. Through dingy streets we made our way to Warstone Lane, where 'the trams turn up', as a navvy shouted after us. The houses in these streets looked like private slum houses – but they were all factories, dimly alight, and many of these cottages turned over more than £50,000 to £60,000 a week. At George's it was a regular inferno of girls and fellows working in confined rooms at thumping presses and riveters. There were one or two beautiful girls with fine figures pressed against the wood counters as they stamped and cut. It seemed rich, this romance amid such grime. Four girls were having tea in one room, and one held my coat away from the fire as I passed. Another, fair and good looking, gave me a set smile as I went out.

On the ground floor in hellish gloom, in a cellarage passage of about three feet, four fellows worked at huge presses. Government inspectors came round and made them put nearly all their men on to war work. Fancy! At one end was the horror of murderous war – at the other end was this inferno where the implements were produced – young girls and boys, scarcely out of school, working like hell, bricked up in a courtyard that dripped with leaking rain and was clotted with grime. All the privileges civilisation has won seem to be waived at present to push this horrible business through.

We wandered up and down slippery ladders and in and out of doors. George showed me metal lying about, worth £100s, for which he had to pay spot cash – and not use because they must do Government work.

SUNDAY 14 NOVEMBER

I took the lesson at class, preaching on the temperance and heroism of conscience. Round the fire afterwards, I said I thought the country had been fair over keeping on with the voluntary system as long as possible. The chaps flamed out. Someone said there had been a lot of indirect pressure, which was worse than conscription. It was compulsion for some and not for others. Even in their august Rates and Taxes department they had been informed they were free to go; though an appeal for the release of a large number was under consideration by the Finance Committee. Against the tribunals you had no case unless you first enlisted. Others confirmed, saying that the MR had paraded the single fellows and given the sack. The circular had actually been seen and there was nought else to do but enlist. Arthur told me the Wolseley people had done the same to him and fellow shell-makers – told them, significantly, that they were quite free to go. Does the Government know what it wants? First it drags men back from the army for munitions work, and now munitions workers are threatened they must join!

Going home, Dowler said that he had friends, who despite having war-work badges, had been unfairly criticised by ladies and other older workers. It worried him. He said the chaps at the works in a lot of cases were ruining their health with hard work. When he went in after the night-shift, the room was stuffy enough to make you sick. He'd had one nervous breakdown, and when he positively had to have an hour's rest, the bosses called him a slacker. He told me all about the trade union tricks and dodges to make new men join the union.

The canvasser called again. He stood in the hall while I explained, vibrating, the unit I had joined on Thursday. The door to the drawing room was open and I expect those inside were agog. Rather low taste of me. I made a fool of myself when I went in, saying, 'I'll give it some of these swines when I come back with my uniform – damned impertinence to come and worry a man in his home.'

MONDAY 15 NOVEMBER

Paul called in and brought letter he had received from Manchester, returning my army form to be entered on a fresh form. This I did, concocting letter to go with same in response to straight and generous letter of Captain Wray. Called at library where the librarian informed me that Grindle, refined gent as he is, had been packed off to Aldershot on joining ASC. For a week he had not had a shave or decent wash. They were herded together like cattle. He has had almost to fight to get a place to lie down in tents! This what one gets for being a gentleman who is willing to take one's turn with the rest in the ranks, to use his own fine phrase. When people are chucking up careers right and left, why don't the authorities tell them there is no accommodation and write for them when they can put them up?

TUESDAY 16 NOVEMBER

This afternoon went down to Priestly Motor School with Paul and learnt about differential gears. Rather complex until principle grasped. In the evening read through chapter on transmission and petrol engines.

WEDNESDAY 17 NOVEMBER

Worked on the Arnold Bennett article, the end of which gave me trouble. At 11 to bike class again – on radiators. Interesting and simple. Shop closed, I went into coach-house and got off outer cover and tyre and got back wheel out. Nuts being stiff at first, this was a big job that nearly bested me, but Arthur came in and we managed it.

THURSDAY 18 NOVEMBER

I have found no pressure exerted by soldiers on the public that has not joined the colours. Not even a look of reproach. Our soldiers are splendid.

At home learned that Wilf had had to go to town on 'some rather important business', which he later said was a visit to a nerve specialist, as Eva had had a slight nervous breakdown. She was to have quiet at home for two weeks. He came to Bembridge and we were glad to have him home, but sorry for the trouble, which he took cheerfully and bravely.

FRIDAY 19 NOVEMBER

Got in train stifling with tobacco smoke and card-players. Eagerly read up section on magnetos. Contrasts with reluctance to read up Red Cross work, which I dislike, but this interests me. Down to class for lesson – lubrication. At class in the evening, none had turned up, and we just had a chat round the fire. First time in history of the class I remember a blank night. Everybody was discussing joining. Doug Clarke had passed test, which 75 per cent had failed to pass, for motorcyclist to Flying Corps. Teddy said they would not take him with his rupture, nasal catarrh and defective vision.

SUNDAY 21 NOVEMBER

Revised *These Twain* critique, then late to school. A good lesson and class. Walked to Teddy Davies' – his getting married has altered a lot of his views. He is not half so Socialist. That's now two of my pals whose radical views have been altered by marriage – and two whom I thought constant. Yet the change, of course, is growth. His wife business-like and capable – but why are young married people so demonstrative? Rather embarrassing for a squeamish chap like myself.

WEDNESDAY 24 NOVEMBER

Went to Arthur's, where he told me of heavy punishment inflicted on Fred in the Flying Corps because as cook's mate he had taken two small lumps of coal instead of one large one. Thereupon he was charged with 'stealing' – a chap who would sooner eat the pavement than rob one of a farthing. He was put in the guardroom without blankets, to sleep on the floor or bench. In the morning he was taken to an officer, but his two sentries, it was found by the sergeant, were not shaved, and as this was a more serious offence than 'stealing', the escort had to return and come to charge the accused later. Then Fred had to have a hook and eye made fast on his coat – having these loose being another serious offence. By the time these operations were over, poor Fred was getting so het up with the gravity of the charge, that when finally brought before officer, he forgot or didn't know he had to say 'sir'. Immediately he was put down for punishment. His leave was stopped, his pay was held over, and he was given double drills with a pack on. Of course, this made Fred obstinate. He has the English virtue of obstinacy. The army gets hold of a spanking chap like that, who has made big sacrifices to join – he is a splendid mechanic and all the years we have known him he has been an example of probity and unselfish service, and they straight away set to to pick on him and make life a misery, instead of showing him the way and giving an outlet for his talents. Is it a musical comedy that is being thus played in the name of discipline?

This musical comedy business is on a par with what is going on in munitions factories. At BSA and Wolseley, first the skilled workers were told they would on no account be released, then the firm, receiving circulars from Lord Derby, tells the men that recruiting sergeants are coming round, or that they are free to join, with the implication that, if they don't, they'll get sacked. Then when the fellows take lessons with the object of joining, they are told at the works that they can't and mustn't join! Apparently it is competition between Derby's and the Munitions Department. Why don't they work together?

SUNDAY 28 NOVEMBER

At home Wilf met me at the back door with, 'Eh, coming skating?' There was some ice on Longmoor! Miracle! We rooted out and fixed our skates and down to pool and the bike headlight shone over ice while we skated – the only two there, on fine black ice. It was glorious in the gloom, the ice groaning and barking while Wilf, daring devil, skated all over its fringes and centre.

MONDAY 29 NOVEMBER

After class, which was on the magneto, I biked down to Paul's. After a fine dinner we studied the frame of Lew's Humberette in the chill and desolate shed at rear garden. I learnt to understand a gear box, a beautiful, clever thing. Then I taught Paul how to drive my motor bike.

THURSDAY 2 DECEMBER

Afternoon went over to Paul's and put together many parts of Lew's Humberette. Then we discussed induction coil and then, for two hours, epicyclic gears. We could not solve these. Paul would say, 'I've got it. Now, if you lock those two wheels together, what happens? Why, this. That.' And his note of triumphant certainty would fade, as before, into doubt. I went off into roars. It was no go. It fascinated us. Even in the tram we argued it.

FRIDAY 3 DECEMBER

This morning wrote an essay on 'Cranford' for the class. Essay well received and good critiques.

TUESDAY 7 DECEMBER

I received an application addressed to Arthur asking for permission from a swell London composer to use his poem, 'Hope', for a musical setting the composer had 'instantly conceived'. It was a very nice letter and pleased me immensely. Also an offer of 3/6 from *The Novel* magazine for Arthur's poem 'Contrast'. This we accepted when Arthur came round. He was overjoyed about the request re 'Hope'. I never saw him so pleased and full of gratitude to fortune.

Went round to Skinners, where Hugh had joined the RAMC and seemed content, though he had wanted another position in the army. Five of them had been given leave by the railway, practically informing them to join. Still, I admired his pluck. There is not much honour or glory in joining now. It is just as Wilde said – you can see that soon war will become vulgar and everyone will be heartily sick of it. Then art will get a chance again. Art is certainly being run hard now.

WEDNESDAY 8 DECEMBER

Cousin Arthur came and gave his impressions of the front. Not bad in the trenches if the weather is decent. He in artillery and they made their dugouts behind the guns quite comfortable with furniture from deserted villages. Shells went by overhead like railway trains in the sky. The worst time for casualties was when they were relieving the trenches. The Germans always knew the time and shelled the communication trenches. He thought we should never get far into Belgium or Germany. Neither would the Germans get any further. He thought there was no brilliance or strategy in the leaders. Nothing to grumble of personally, but if officer in bad temper, a man was liable to be treated like muck. In hospital the grub was good, but the confinement irksome – kept under restrictions as if in prison.

THURSDAY 9 DECEMBER

This week has been some saddened by news of the retreat of the force in Mesopotamia, having to retreat 80 miles after victory, and nearly reaching Baghdad. In this direction we were congratulating ourselves we had at least won – but now we can claim that nowhere. When will the tide turn?

Arthur told me about his friend, who had his thigh splintered in bayonet practice. He had a hellish time in hospital, then came home for a year, lying helpless, attended by a doctor. Now they have discharged him as useless, and are going to give him 14/- for six months. All the time he lay out of hospital he received no pay. When he wrote up to plead his case, the hospital authorities denied that they knew him and made him look like a rogue. He can limp as far as between two lampposts – but that is all, and probably will never get back the use of one leg. Before he joined he had a comfortable life and paid £1 a week towards home maintenance. Now his mother is without this, and has to keep him in addition.

Called round at Paul's, and we discussed the epicyclic gear until I had to rush for the train, but we found that my ideas in the main were right, and for once Paul was in the main wrong. We have got the principle now, but are not quite sure of the details of its application.

FRIDAY 10 DECEMBER

Heard from my friend Gays that a sergeant from Gallipoli said the Australians took no notice of the officers, otherwise they could never have effected a landing. They asked for cover when officers wanted to line them up. He also said that what riles Canadians is that they got shot for sleeping on duty instead of being merely kicked in the ribs. Then the officer commander gets shot, FROM BEHIND for doing it. They say the failures on the British front, at Loos, for instance, are due to bad and immature officering, and that some regiments and units funked. Can one believe such tales, apparently accredited though they are?

Arthur came in late and said how the night before the chaps from his and other shops at the BDA had gone down en bloc to the Stoney Lane Barracks and there had been registered under Lord Derby's scheme. There was not time to medically examine them. At the Wolseley, Derby recruiting officers came to the factory and took down the names of the bulk of fellows, but Albert Rowley said he wouldn't do it. The factory would not let him join direct, therefore he was not going to join under Derby's scheme, which he mistrusted. All the ordinary enlistments direct to the army have been closed down these last two days, and only soldiers through Derby's scheme have been accepted. What's the idea and what's the use of enrolling munitions workers and that without medical examination? On account of such arrangements, and because also another boom has been evoked, the enlistments this weekend have come in with a great rush – so great that it could not be coped with – and this Sunday all the recruiting stations will be open all day.

THE BATTLE OF GALLIPOLI IN 1915 CLAIMED 473,000 CASUALTIES. BOTH SIDES DUG MASSIVE TRENCH NETWORKS IN AN EFFORT TO OFFER THEMSELVES SOME FORM OF PROTECTION.

SUNDAY 12 DECEMBER

I took a walk with Wilf along the Chester Road. It had snowed four inches in the night, and in the sunshine the country looked beautiful, but it was very cold. A lovely afternoon at class. I sat by the blazing fire while all the chaps sat in a circle, Percy gave the lesson and we sang the old hymns with gusto.

TUESDAY 14 DECEMBER

Read the papers before shaving. No good news – instead retirement of the Allies to the Greek frontier.

No letter from the War Office calling me to report with Paul, who came round and we wrote letter to the RE, East Lancs, about their letter and our readiness to go now.

My poem 'London' in *Country Life*. Arthur called yesterday to tell me and left me with a copy.

MONDAY 20 DECEMBER

Paul called at the shop with a letter from the RE OC asking us to go up for medical examination. We replied with a wire, referring them to the past letters.

TUESDAY 21 DECEMBER

For a week or two up to yesterday, the idea had subtly been gaining ground that Germany was fundamentally worsted and that the beginning of the end was in sight. Strange how this idea and similar stages in development of the war have germinated almost imperceptibly, and suddenly grown definite and accepted.

Now today, with the disconcerting and abysmal revelations in Lloyd George's speech on munitions, has come the perception of great disasters narrowly avoided and the fact that it is only by a series of miracles we have escaped. There almost comes the beginning of the admission that perhaps, after all, we shan't win if we just go muddling on.

Is the *Daily Mail* right after all? Could not Asquith really see until June this year that more machine-guns were wanted? It seems damnable to expose our brave fighters to be mowed down, merely because they haven't guns and munitions.

In summary, at first the impression was that once the British troops got there, all would be stemmed and well. Then the realisation of what was meant by the retreat. Break drawn at the Battle of the Marne – then stalemate and the beginning of the 'Great Drive', with Neuve Chapelle and Loos – which we thought were victories – and also the belief that Suvla Bay was a victory, afterwards learning that we had made little progress and lost heavily.

Then came the Balkans mess and the trouble with Greece, the admission of the Dardanelles failure, and the wiping out of Serbian resistance, and now we see that we are in for it getting worse before it get better.

There now comes the feeling, owing to reports of neutrals, that Germany was starving, of the desperation and bad plight of Germany.

There is a sudden knock-back in our failure to grasp, and quickly adjust ourselves to the situation. Once more the feeling that it is still in the balance whether we shall win or lose, though we believed it impossible to lose at one time. Several times during the war this vision has come upon us, and now here it is again. Shall we win? Not unless we take great care and fight boldly and pertinaciously. I don't mean we have blundered greatly or disastrously, but we lack foresight. We have meant well, but we haven't the genius to foresee and invent. Still, I believe we shall come out on top, and if we strive well and purely, we shall survive as a great nation.

Strange how our wrongdoing comes back to us. We have oppressed the workers and bred in them suspicion, with the result that Trade Unionism puts obstacles in the way of the rapid manufacture of munitions. If the Government, according to Lloyd George's speech yesterday, is so anxious for trade unions to relax their rules in every detail, why doesn't it boldly pledge itself to render back to the TUs those privileges after the war? A simple solution – but the Government doesn't offer this obvious thing, any more than it definitely offers pensions to mutilated soldiers. Lloyd George's rhetoric to me sounds empty.

Paul called round rather forlornly and showed me a letter from RE, East Lancs, which stated that they had lost our army forms B210 and Medical History sheets. They asked us to get re-examined, and to forward the same again. This delay suits me, but it irks Paul.

We trammed to the Recruiting Office in Smethwick and I pushed open the door. Three khaki sergeants writing, and one told us to go into the next room and ask for Mr 'Jefscott'. 'Jephcott' corrected another. We entered. An old man sat writing at one end of the long improvised tables on trestles, then Mr Jephcott came in.

'You can't be medically examined again free,' he said, when I explained. 'But it wasn't our fault,' argued Paul.

He read the letter again. 'I'll tell you what I might do. We could give copies. We keep these records for a hundred years, and ten years after a man's death. Mantle, isn't it? I remember the name. I remember entering these. Davis, Oswald Harcourt... though we've had many hundreds since.'

He began to make out the copies, calling out the various items, of which I made a mental note, as I hadn't got an accurate copy of the first record.

'Well,' he continued, 'we'd better send these up. Better leave this letter here to explain why we write. I'll just speak to the officer.' He went into the back room and began explaining. We could hear him say, 'Royal Engineers, Cyclist Section.' 'Cyclist section?' 'Yes, they came for medical attestation. They've been here once before. I suppose we can send...' 'Oh no, no, no. They must go to the Drill Hall, Royal Engineers. Can't be done here.'

The permanent official explained the situation. I was feeling suddenly balked and fatalistically sure of defeat at the hands of the dapper officer, but the civilian won his point, and said it would be all right. We bolted out, glad that things were settled. How different from what we had expected!

THURSDAY 23 DECEMBER

Tonight to the social at the Town Hall, through a soaking night which splashed my dress-suit trousers. I got to the Town Hall a quarter hour late, but people were only just going in. There were plenty of good-looking, well-dressed girls, a fair sprinkling of khaki, and about a third as many fellows as girls. Met Paul and went upstairs, found our party and chased Pierrot for a programme. Booked dances, then we stood wondering what to do. The Town Hall looked fine with its gloomy, golden, tawny emptiness and bare floor. The dance was very enjoyable, and all too quick the time sped by, I introducing some to Paul and he introducing me to his girl – a nice, charming person. Home by the 11.20 train, which waited ten minutes in the station while our party carolled in the high spirits of youth and glee. They made me laugh, the way they carried on, singing snatches of comic song, and doing the goat.

FRIDAY 24 DECEMBER

Mr Loach still complaining about trade because he is now short-handed for big orders. He has had to refuse a million order and do my thousands instead because all the girls are on munitions work, getting such good wages that he can't get hands. He complains because he has to close Christmas week to get his factory cleaned, and he stated how severe the inspectors are on anyone opening a new business. He instanced the necessity of having so much light and cubic space, and the fact that two WCs were required when workers of two sexes were employed. Also, that now factory inspectors would not let workers eat in the working room, but a mess-room must be provided. He complained bitterly about such regulations – yet he is a most kind-hearted and urbane man – politics apart. This shows what a struggle social reform is, yet day by day people are voting cheerfully five million pounds a day away for destruction.

Arthur Barker called at the shop – he had his uniform of temporary lieutenant in the RNAS. Manse Woods also called in and said he was having a fine time as a private in the army. This is he who was rejected nine times before getting in. He said they rose about seven and had finished duty by 4.30. They weren't giving them tons of training – just a serviceable grounding. He said they expected to go to Salonika on 13 January. He also said he could go to Worthing or Brighton Hippodrome every night. They had a weekly bath at friends' at Worthing. Funny thing, he said, to go to a friend's for baths only, but they understood.

This Christmas Eve did not quite seem to have the magic of former ones, but all Christmas Eves are like that. For one thing, it rained nearly all day – it was a soaker. Then trade was steady instead of in great rushes, and it finished at 10.45 – I suppose on account of the pubs being shut so early under the very severe drinking restrictions now in force. You can't get beer after 8.30 at an outdoor beer license, and you can get drinks only between about eleven to two mornings, and then from about six to nine in the evening. You can't treat anyone. It is drastic and seems unfair to men who are working hard and haven't fine homes. However, I haven't heard much complaint and it doesn't affect me.

SATURDAY 25 DECEMBER

Tidied up the top yard and burnt straw, and had a nice breakfast of bacon, egg and tomato. Then off with Wilf to the friendly football match, which was fair for the first half, but scrappy and careless in the second. How is the mighty game fallen, from a spectator's point of view? Off home by motorbike through the pelting rain, nearly skidding, but arrived in time for Xmas dinner. In the evening read and played cards.

SUNDAY 26 DECEMBER

Spent all the morning tidying the house, then a hurried dinner and off to Sunday school for the open reunion. As I rode home met only about five people – now the roads were swept quite dry by the great winds.

Today I am 34 – grand class!

WEDNESDAY 29 DECEMBER

Busy in shop, then after lunch, walked with Arthur to Sheldon in the rain. A lovely tea with toast and mince pies by firelight. Two kids yelled at us, 'Why aren't you at the front or wearing khaki armlets?

Arthur told me that although Fred has now joined some six weeks or so, and filled up innumerable forms, first they did not deduct his proportion from army wages and now have not yet sent the proportion – 11/- a week – which is due to their mother. Arthur has written also. If an educated man can't get his due, what chance has an uneducated one? He wants to know how their mother is going to get on if they take him from munitions work and treat his application and allotment the same way.

FRIDAY 31 DECEMBER

Fairly busy in shop. Many enquiries for dark green blinds for new lighting restrictions.

To Uncle Fred's at night. He asked me in, but with the idea of catching the 9.50 train, I declined, though afterwards I wished I had stayed and caught a later train. Uncle Fred might have thought I didn't wish to – he was so hospitable. Got home to find mother not going to Watch Night service as her foot pained her and she had a cold.

1916

Paul and I decided to go up to Manchester on Tuesday to look up the officials re our enlistment. After that, scrapped round in the shop, checking January accounts and got the bike vaselined. All the time an immense gale was raging from dinner to tea-time. It shook and rattled the house to the point of fearfulness. At home it had swayed the gable in which I was sleeping, and I feared I should not like to leave to go to 'Cinderella' at Church House in Erdington, but after testing the blinds and lights, I decided to go and arrived at 7.20, as the first waltz had finished. Had a fair time, feeling very young and gay – all the more so with the prospect of going away.

Had supper in the green room with our clique, then we danced gaily through the second half, the room thinning at 11. Not a soldier in the room, but several Derbyites[6].

MONDAY 3 JANUARY

Arrived late at business where Paul had been waiting for 20 minutes. We wrote, instead of going up to Manchester, asking the OC to fix a definite date when we should be called up, as our last letter enclosing new forms and medical history sheets had not been acknowledged.

TUESDAY 4 JANUARY

Bought goods, then to the library, and to the solicitor's where I gave instructions for a new will.

Uncle Tom called in to tea and we argued about conscription and the changed attitude of Lloyd George. He argued that George had been stoned for a pro-Boer by minute sections of the nation, when I said a really great nation would always allow free speech. He doesn't believe in the masses. 'Where would labour be without capital?' asked Uncle, with other stock arguments. He showed me a fine letter from Harold, written in the trenches. It called up a good picture of the men in the chalk dugout, with a tin biscuit-box punched as brazier, with candles stuck in crannies with pipes going with smokers with waders on, with many eatables.

WEDNESDAY 5 JANUARY

At home in evening read Marriott's *The Unpetitioned Heavens* by a lovely fire, while in a trance of delight (which I wished could have lasted hours) I heard Paul on the step, where Wilf had let him in. He was by the drawing-room door, looking darkly pleased. 'This is it.' He drew the envelope from his pocket and showed me a request to call at Manchester next Friday, 7 Jan, and to go forward to Bletchley on Saturday 8th. Vouchers for railway travel were enclosed. Overjoyed we laughed with glee. Sat and chuckled and examined the papers.

THURSDAY 6 JANUARY

After breakfast, measured for dark blinds due to lighting restrictions. Going round to Sutton Police Station on motorbike I learnt that no new blinds were necessary for the Sutton district, although at business there's a green-paper-blind craze.

FRIDAY 7 JANUARY

Got to the station and Paul and I arrived in Manchester, then rode to Seymore Grove.

The barracks, on edge of country, was a large house with square portal, converted into offices with large mess-rooms, etc behind. We were taken to gentlemanly, eye-glassed man, seated back to the light, who said, 'Good morning, gentlemen. Mr Mantle?' 'I'm Davis – this is Mantle.' 'How are you? Despatch Riders?' He introduced us to a third man of indeterminate class who produced forms. He filled up 1 Buff attestation form, 2 Yellow allotment form, 3 Travel sheet, 4 Pay sheet, 5 travel ticket (reg) for our pockets. 1 and 4 in duplicate. Thereafter inspected eye charts behind green screen curtains. Heard we were the last to be admitted as despatch riders. We heard slow heavy steps and rose. There entered a florid man, bulbous-nosed, a little greying, well and solidly built.

The corporal announced us.' Come here,' said the captain. 'Into line.' He frowned. 'Hands up. Repeat in your own name...' and he ran off the attestation. At 'bear true allegiance', not hearing properly, I was silent. The captain eyed me hard and repeated, putting down a cigar. Citation over, he turned contemptuously on his heel.

The corporal told us of great RE concert every Friday because Captain Wray well in with the theatrical stars… I should shay sho.

Away to *Manchester City News* office, but Walters out, so had fine fish tea at the Balcony restaurant. We overlooked the crowd and savoured fine feelings of the newly enlisted.

SATURDAY 8 JANUARY

Arrived at station and met Corporal Dunkley. We walked up and down the deserted quay with a Canadian who had also come to enlist, and he asked if this was a rendezvous place. At last two officers arrived at the train office, and two clerks. An SM came up with round business-like face and called two names for Gordon Highlanders, then mine. I went, hat off, to the green baize table and handed in card. Officer dismissed me. I went to walk out and the lieutenant said, 'Here, laddie, if you don't take this, I'll have it.' He handed me 5/10 – two days pay at 2/11 (two days' rations allowance at 1/9 and two days' pay at ½). Going out again when stout elder clerk said, 'Half a minute – your next of kin.'

A burly stout tall padre was handing out paper gospels and he yarned about drink – he had met a soldier propping a lamp-post up. 'Now, when you've been fighting and doing decent things like that, it's a shame to show your wrong side outside like that. You don't look nice with the paint off.' 'I can stand up – been in Flanders. I'll sprint any of ye – for 10 yards.'

Then he doled out coffee mugs from the train window. 'Come on, boys, when you've finished your coffee,' said the sergeant. A round-faced boy followed and pushed through the turnstile. He was for bugler. Train up and porters and sergeant major shouted us into the rear.

Off in the train, fine and comfy and warm through flat country, pictorially drab under blue and pallor. Out at Bletchley – sun gold against the tree-trunks – no-one waiting for us. Found our way through flat, rambling town. Asked a soldier for rest camp – my first!

At gate showed papers to sentry, who carefully explained the way – third hut from the last we entered, showed there by a fat youth.

In and showed paper to the sergeant. He got up from the stove, cracking nuts. Took out blue-paged book, entered names and initials. Said, 'Motorcyclists?' Didn't look at other papers. Then 'Follow me boys.' Into the store room opposite.

'See those planks? Take three each. Get some blankets – three out of the corner. No, you can't take five. Then two trestles each.' Led by Albert we rushed to the blankets and grabbed five each. Stumbled under them and picked up the fallen, then trestles – and bundled across mud of bare track between bare huts. In the sleeping hut put down boards on trestles and laid rugs over as best we could. 'Tea at 4, breakfast at 8, parade at 9. You can have tea in the end hut.'

Though men kindly repeated above information, we decided to tea out. Eggs and apricots in refreshment room in the village. Laughed and joked as we washed in the kitchen. Shot at the fair. To picture house – crude, tragic, packed with khaki and girls. Out to The Swan for drinks, where soldiers drank and were chummy, and never seemed to wish to pull our legs.

To hut, where after warming feet by fire, we made beds and slipped in, trousers on. Old Scottie talking until 11, when we thought he would cease. A man turned up from sick leave, seeking lost bandolier and bed. Picturesque group around glowing stove with the light of the fire above.

They began to rag the drunken Scottie. 'Have some sympathy for us,' they shouted. A chap opened the end door and switched out the light. "Lights out!' he called. 'I can't have this.'

No-one else groused – marvellous patience of men who listened to this until 1 am without grousing, though tired.

Every half hour Scottie would rise, light paper, light pipe, showing wizened red face, and stoke the stove – a Holbein picture. Then up to the switch, groping in the dark. 'Too bloody cold this end of the room.'

SUNDAY 9 JANUARY

I woke at four, not sore on boards, but cold. Put on an overcoat and slept in snatches.

Rose at 7. We warmed ourselves by the stove, then out into the dim light and mud to the far washing station and urinals. Washed in bowls under cold taps, standing on boards. Then into the other hut. On the end of the trestle table appeared a pile of plates. Other side mugs on shelves. We took mugs and suddenly there was a bath of bacon. Old hands had lain in bed, and left washing, and now appeared magically beside the bacon bath – a file of men with plates. A grey-headed veteran calmly and nonchalantly ladled the bacon out fairly. After two minutes I got good bacon and tomatoes, but no knives or forks unless brought. Dipped mug in bath of tea.

Rushed in shaving, fearing to be late for parade, which was outside our hut. The corporal called names and handed out letters – roll-call. A smart corporal spoke to each of us, as he took pass, 'Mr Davis? What are you down for? Motorcyclist? Do you belong to National Health Insurance Act? When were you sworn in? Go back to Rest Camp.'

Then we cleared and swept the hut as per standing orders, given on parade and nailed up in the hut. In the hut we wait and wait – the colonel is inspecting. It is now 10.30. Nothing happens, so we hopped off to Leighton Buzzard, giving dinner a miss. Lovely walk, soft winter aspects. At village green drank, and after talk with rustics, asked the inn if we could eat. 'Nothing except cold mutton.' 'That'll do.' 'But that's not cooked yet.' 'Look here,' said Albert, 'couldn't ye just cut off three chops and dab them in the frying pan?' 'Yes.' 'And an onion or two – just dab 'em in the pan so we can taste it.' It came beautifully braised.

Tonight men in bed by 10. At 10, corporal of the guard came round, switched light off and flashed his lamp around the room. 'Time you were in bed,' to someone who had gone outside to pass water. None snored. Amazing. A healthy group. Good discipline tonight.

MONDAY 10 JANUARY

Standing orders – reveille at 5.30, breakfast at 7.15, parade at 8. At 5.30 NCOs' voices outside. None stirs. At 7 I rise, fold blankets and run down to washing table. Lo – all the old stagers I left sleeping have vanished into the breakfast hut where we have good feed of bread and marge and sardines. Stand on parade with chilled feet. Letters flung through the air at men. Roll called, despatch riders included. Told to return at 8.55 after cleaning huts.

Cleaned boots and paraded. Marched off to Staple Hall office. Waited while groups of men passed with rifles and kept passing. Also officers, then a bugler and parson for a funeral party. Waited half an hour in line, I next to Bendle, next to the open window of the captain's office. Were marched into a passage and told to doff hats on entering and say, 'Sir!'

Stood across the room in a line. A great fire burned behind us and before us sat fine, fresh-coloured firm, kindly and aristocratic major.

'You have sworn in for general service.' 'Yes.' 'That means service abroad or anywhere in the world, I may explain.' Then all were dismissed except us six. To me, 'How long have you been a motorcyclist?' 'Eight years.' 'Then you know all about motorcycling, running repairs, etc?' 'Yes, sir.' 'Have you passed a test?' 'No, sir.' 'Just verbal – been asked questions, I suppose?' 'Yes, sir.'

He said to all, 'Now, I want to give you a few words of advice and direction. You will be made full corporals. We consider it a great privilege to be made corporals in the RE. In peacetime, men have to work many years to gain that position. You will, of course, be expected to look after your own machines. You will have no servant or orderly to work for you. Another thing – the limit of speed is the same as the civil – 20 mph. You have no right to exceed that limit. If you do, the army will not pay your fine. Moreover, it will bring you up on a criminal charge. You will be court-martialled and serve a sentence. If you receive warrant from an officer of rank above captain – a major or colonel (but not from a captain), you may then exceed the limit.'

He gathered our papers together, we filed out and upstairs, and one by one into a room where, at a desk, we had insurance cards given us.

We were beckoned in at twelve to early dinner and the door shut on us. This was stew with good meat, potatoes and beans and a second serving if wished, though with no knife or fork, I had to shovel up three beans at a time on my penknife until I sweated. Albert went off to get spoons for us from another hut, but the sergeant only said, 'You can have all the spoons you can lay your hands on,' which were nil – only one fork.

At Bletchley we scrambled into train to Birmingham, where we followed sergeant and marched up to Great Brook Street Barracks, where we wheeled in at a pair of tall wooden gates. We wondered how long before we should be privileged to get into the Corps' swagger uniform of leggings and brown boots and knickers, with leather suede sidings and short greatcoats.

A head at an open window called forth us six motorcyclists and an NCO ticked off our names. To the last of us he handed an address, saying, 'You six will be billeted at this address. You must be in by ten. All letters must be addressed to you here in barracks.' 'How are we to be addressed?' asked one. 'Motorcyclists, squad 142.' The magic word 'corporal' was understood by some to have been uttered, but we were not sure. Paul had said we should be full corporals, straight off, but it seemed too good to be true.

Our billets were found in that old-fashioned twin row of houses in Vauxhall Grove – a middle-aged woman in glasses, cheerful, welcomed us in as more 'lads'. 'Come on, just in time for a cup of tea.' We sat down to a table where four other soldiers sat. Bread and butter with fruit and cake followed a good tea. She introduces us. 'Another job of sewing on stripes,' she laughed, so it looked as if the tale were true.

After tea I took Albert with me to Small Heath, where he wrote letters in the kitchen, while I went in shop and wrote cheques and helped Wilf to serve. The green paper blinds to comply with drastic lighting restrictions had arrived that day, also green casement cloth, which had been both so difficult to procure. After putting aside half a hundred or so for orders, the customers were waiting in a file for the remainder. Then I rushed back with Albert to the billets to a supper of bread and cheese.

TUESDAY 11 JANUARY

Rose at seven to find large bowls of water standing ready downstairs, and also bacon cooked. Off to parade, arriving at 8.30. Soldiers were streaming in from all quarters. We stood uncertainly about then saw the men forming in ranks of twos. Enquiring, we found that a squad towards the end was No 141, so we fell in behind.

We were called to attention, then a fine stout captain appeared. We saw a line of NCOs form up and walk in file down the ground. After about six paces, the last one hit the next a sharp blow on the shoulder with hand or cane. He stopped dead. Then turned about, saluted and stood still. At six pace-distances this was repeated by each NCO. 'Officers, fall in,' was the captain's next command. The officers stepped up to the NCOs, acknowledged their salute, and then saluted the commanding officer.

'Parade – atten-SHUN!' called out the commander. 'Officers. Inspect our squads.'

The NCOs rapped out a command or two, and the officer allotted to each squad examined each man, back and front, from top to toe. The NCO would rap a man's water-tin with his stick, or point to a strap, or he would say, as our sergeant did to me after jerking up with forefinger the adjoining man's back hair, 'And you an' all. Hair cut for termorrer.'

The next command was, 'Call the roll.' We answered to our names with 'Sir!' and then came the command from the captain, 'Collect the reports.'

'All present, sir!' was shouted in turn, echoing by each officer down the file of officers. A very smart officer ran down this file, ran up to the captain, saluted stopping on the run, and gave the report. Meanwhile the rolls had been collected. He saluted, turned about and said, 'Carry on, instructors!'

Then our sergeant marched us off in file, and an orderly instructed us to get kits. We mounted steps like loft stairs and filed down a dark passage.

We lined up against the wall, then laconic, nonchalant, with pipe in mouth, the sergeant came out with kitbags flat under arm and gave one to each man along the line. 'Kitbag,' he said. 'Hold-all' he said next, disappearing and bringing hold-alls, which we divined were for shaving and toilet tackle, and cutlery.

Another NCO came out. 'Button-brush holder,' he ejaculated, and passed down the line, repeating the same action and words. The same happened with blacking brush, polishing brush (cheap, when used), hairbrush and comb, mending roll, braces (strong), socks (shoddy – eightpence halfpenny) and shirts. 'Not bad shirts,' I said. 'Better than you're wearing,' was the sergeant's reply.

The one striped shirt was worth 3/9 at inflated war prices, the two army grey shirts were worth 2/6 or 2/11 by the same rate.

We stuck our things in the kitbag, but were getting muddled. In another room we were asked the size of our feet. Two pairs of very good army black boots were taken from crates and thrust at us, also a navy or fawn jersey (of which the navy ran in mine) and two pairs of brown cotton pants, worth 2/6 (war rates), with zinc buttons and stiff facings. While we were fiddling with these, we were put in line again and asked height, and then felt by the army tailor, who gave us a size. After all had been felt, 'Put up your arms, size 2,' was called. None. There were some size 3s and then more 4s, of which I was one.

We went into another room and two tunics and a greatcoat were picked out for each from a pile. Paul got nicer cloth and colours than I. Then the tailor felt how they fitted and advised us to have each a size larger. I did so and found the tunics too large. Our stuff was accumulating in the dark passage and the sergeants stumbled over it.

There was no word of instruction as to what we should do. We tried on our boots in the dark, struggling with the heap of things, then we motorcyclists had leggings given us, and went to sign a list of things which a sergeant read to us. Then we were told to take the whole bundle up to the marking room, to tie the boots to the bag and lay coats on top. There they were to remain that day, each separate article and garment to be marked with regimental number. This seemed unnecessary, but we soon found, living a dozen together in billets, that it was useful.

That night Bendle, a Devon man, I had talked to at Bletchley while waiting for the colonel's examination, dressed up in our uniform – it was a thrilling time.

Bendle and I walked into town to a shop in Worcester Street, where we got stripes and spare buttons. Went to the Empire, saluting for the first time an officer as we passed over the station. We were nervous and anticipatory about this, but it went off all right, and our salutes were acknowledged. At the Empire we were the cynosure of a good many eyes, and we aired ourselves with mighty pleasure.

At rest camp there were men who had been wounded in France, one suffering from bad sight from shell shock, another from fits after his experience in the Dardanelles. They made light of it, but not anxious for more. They were mostly very fine, charitable, heroic chaps.

WEDNESDAY 12 JANUARY

This morning we had an hour's drill, forming fours in line and on the march. With so many companies being drilled on the same ground, with rifles clashing in concert and 250 men calling out in unison, 'Guard, turn out,' it was difficult to catch and execute commands. I wanted to watch it all – to watch officers and men, the other motorcycle squad, and the dogs that gambolled about the parade ground, and the passing wagons and horses. I stumbled through those drills awkwardly, starting with a mistake because someone next to me numbered wrongly. It was a gruelling time.

In the afternoon we got on very well with our own sergeant. He was helpful and not too severe – plump and well-coloured. 'When I say so and so, I want to see ye… swing them arms, strain them legs, put them heels together… swinging the lead already. It's no use looking on the ground. We've been round already and picked it all up… the farthest way round – back of the right palm of the left. I'll tie a bit of ribbon – red on one, blue on the other, then ye'll know yer right and left.'

Passes were handed out, then I went up home to Bembridge and got my stripes sewn on. Then to Church House, Erdington, where a chaffing cheer greeted me, however, I created quite a splash. A lot of nice new girls there, and had a right jolly dance until 10.50, and then back to barracks by car.

THURSDAY 13 JANUARY

This morning drill with sergeant was easy after the tension on Wednesday with the officers exercising manoeuvres on us. Tramping about in the open air makes one surprisingly thirsty and hungry, and one understands why the army drinks.

Afternoon we were told to go and get revolvers. At the armoury a man in shirtsleeves rose and rushed at us like a tiger. 'Get off that God-damned hearth! Can't ye see it's just been cleaned? he yelled. 'Help yourselves,' he cried out when we explained our errand. 'Now, how many? Eight? Each take one. Who's going to be responsible? Who's yer senior to sign for 'em?' None volunteered, so I said I would. 'Two more? That's ten.' He went to a desk in the gloom in the corner and wrote out an invoice for them in duplicate.

A sergeant met us and explained the action of the black Colt revolvers which we had fastened around our waists by thick straps. He showed us how to aim, to open the chambers and load, unload and extract, to cease fire and fire continuously with one hand and to change hands. I collected the pistols back and they gave me back the duplicate I had signed as a receipt.

This evening I went down to Coventry Road and called in at Skinner's, where I enjoyed myself, swanking. I was acutely conscious and proud of my uniform. It was a great pleasure to stroll into the shop and into Joe Hogg's, Woodgate's and Green's and the newsagent's ditto. 'Swank!' called out someone to my swagger on the pavement. Undoubtedly the army makes you swagger. The joy of khaki quite came up to expectations, only with the light restrictions the streets were so miserable and dark you could hardly see anyone. The road looked dead and listless. The shops didn't seem open. What a change! Our brisk and vivid Coventry Road had become forlorn and lustreless.

FRIDAY 14 JANUARY

Eight of us motorcyclists were chosen to act in squad at a military funeral. Now after first drill a corporal marched us out of barracks in double file. Soon we walked easy to Coventry Road. At Balsall Heath Road we found the street lined each side about two deep with populace, mostly squalid, battered-looking women and old men, but pretty children. The glories of Empire, thought I. We were the centre of the gloating throng and we solemnly enjoyed it. The hero had been through seven fights and died in hospital.

Soon the coaches came to where we stood with lounging bandsmen, and we were lined up as bearers on the pavement. The captain chaplain with black stuff on shoulders came out with the undertaker and the coffin was given to us, we carrying same on our shoulders and bracing each against each with arms under and across. We lifted and slid it on to the gun carriage, then as we had been instructed, two of us pushed the wheels of the carriage to give it a start uphill, while another manipulated the brake. The band played 'The Dead March'[7] from Saul and we stepped slowly behind. A photo was taken as we lifted the coffin, and it appeared in *The Picture World* next morning, showing our backs. Reaching Mossely Road, we went off at a quicker march without music. With great gusto and pride we marched thus to Alcester Lane's End, four of us each side of the gun carriage and the bandsmen silent in front. On nearing the cemetery, the band struck up again and we went augustly down the centre to the chapel where we unloaded the coffin on to a rest.

We smoked outside during the service, then bore the coffin on our shoulders, which hurt at times. The sexton and funeral labourers took the coffin and lowered it into the grave while we stood away. A one-armed bugler who had accompanied us played *The Last Post*. It expressed in its strong, plaintive, beautiful notes all the repose, pathos and inspiration of death, and moved me deeply. In front of me stood a mourner – a girl with most beautiful mid-brown hair in a long twist pigtail. This hair seemed more beautiful and wonderful even than death.

Back to barracks for pay parade. I found written up on the red wall, 'A to E' and walked up. While another man was receiving pay, the sergeant seated at a table next to a lieutenant, called out, 'Davis, A H'. I started to walk up to behind the man in front. 'Say "Sir"!' he called out angrily. 'Go back to your places and call out "Sir!"' I did so, walked up saluted and received a note for 10/- from the officer who handed it to me without looking, I saluted again, turned and went away.

Bendle and I walked into W and R's to see if brown boots were to be had wholesale. We created a sensation. I went up to Mr Howle and shook hands. 'How is it you're two stripes up already?' he asked, mystified. 'Ah, that's the secret,' I said. Brown boots were not to be had at Lunt's either, so back to Mansfield's, and got rather a nice pair for 22/6.

SATURDAY 15 JANUARY

'Safe for another night,' our good lady said as I came down in the morning. 'Safe?' I queried, suspecting burglars in the vicinity. 'The Zeppelins haven't come. I heard dreadful things about their going to come.' I laughed. You never hear the soldiers talk about the war. They absolutely forget it – as now did we. I haven't time or opportunity now to read papers and I find it is the papers that foster this morbid preoccupation with the war.

After drill this morning, learning to turn and salute and form fours in line, in file and on the march and wheeling and right forming etc, we were told off for an hour's revolver practice. We had to wait about some fifteen minutes before we started. The art of wasting time with gusto has to be diligently cultivated. It is, however, marvellous what the army gets through. After seeing all the complexity and detail, one sees what an immense machine is in motion.

I rushed round to Mr Nodder's and told him a few of my experiences and asked him to be my literary executor. Mr and Mrs Nodder liked my khaki very much. Then away to Arthur's where I asked him too to be a literary executor. Then went to the Repertory, soldiers having to pay only half price, as we found. *The Clandestine Marriage* by Garrick and Coleman was beautifully produced, but the technique, after modern construction, was clumsy and artificial – but the play possessed fine old world charm and flavour and wit and candour.

SUNDAY 16 JANUARY

Met Paul outside Coventry Road coach house and Woodgate came out with the car, which and drove splendidly to Stone Bridge where it was a regular motor atmosphere in the bar parlour. After some talk about motors we were ready to go. 'Put down three monies,' said the barmaid, alluding to the 'no treating' law.

To start Ford car, see that side brake is jammed in right set. Switch on. Put about three points down of petrol and mag, then crank up. Then push down the left pedal hard until the car gathers momentum. Releasing the same pedal puts the car in top gear. It is in neutral when same pedal is pushed to half way, or released to half. To go downhill, put in neutral and let car go down on gravity. To stop, push down into low gear and also ram on the right pedal, which is a brake. Then let in low gear to go slowly to stop, and ram side brake on hard so that the car can't go forward if cranked up. To steer, press lightly the steering wheel in the required direction, after each turn correcting a little with back turn.

MONDAY 17 JANUARY

Got on well with our drill, forming fours on the march. Boots and leggings now hurt but little, though Albert has badly strained his foot and one or two others complain of soreness. 'Boric acid powder,' said our sergeant, 'is the thing.'

WEDNESDAY 19 JANUARY

Someone went to fetch revolvers, then a corporal lined us up and marched us to Saltley Station. In the grey-blue cold morn it was fine tramping and whistling down the street with our revolvers at our side. From Kingsbury station we heeled left across fields, soon seeing the butts, showing white squares with black figures squatting against embankments of earth.

At back of our embankment, right, was a tin hut. From here, by couples, we took out targets four feet with a black bull painted on and inner and outer white rings marked on them. Bulls 4, inner 3, and outer 2 was the scoring. We were given cartridges in packets of a dozen, then placed about thirty yards apart, facing alternate numbers. Then we loaded and fired 24 rounds – six with the right and six with the left. I was very nervous at first, handling the firearm like a baby. There was but little kick, but the other fellows' shots going off startled me, and I was slower than anyone else at first.

At first I was nervous and didn't relish firing, but when I found I didn't do so badly, and that I had scored two bulls, two inners and two outers with six shots, I got more confidence.

After the other half of the squad had fired and the whistle had blown, we rushed out and pasted up the shot-holes with white or black paper. While the officers practised, we went off and bought tea and cakes at the house of the range-keeper. Great after the open air. We sat there while the sergeant reckoned up our scores. I made 64 – the highest being 87 out of a possible 192. Better than I thought possible for my first handling of a firearm.

THURSDAY 20 JANUARY

After drill we marched off in fours to Woodcock Street Baths. Getting tickets, we were ushered into single bath chambers with a wood seat and imitation marble bath, and a wood grid for feet. A fine hot bath and head wash, all the fellows singing and jesting and whistling in chorus or confusedly. It seemed all rife with youth and jollity.

In afternoon an hour's easy drill, then after a break I volunteered to take drill and did better than I expected, throwing my voice well but bawling somewhat. I made some foolish mistakes while I was giving 'salutings and turnings on the march'. I was nervous and yet I enjoyed it.

FRIDAY 21 JANUARY

After tea went to Aunt Lizzie's, Uncle not yet being returned from travelling. She is at high tension, acutely suspended on the thought of risks run by soldiers. It seems strange to us soldiers (I suppose I am one) to see civilians worrying about us when we are having such a good time. Praises and good wishes fall thick and fast upon me now I have joined the colours. I suppose before some people thought that fellows of my way of mind delayed joining because of fear. Strange misconception. When in business I worked much harder – yet by some I was possibly regarded as a 'slacker', though none suggested as much openly to me.

SATURDAY 22 JANUARY

After dinner went to Grindle's, but he wasn't home. The same nervous tension observable in his mother, she imagining all sorts of horrible things if one of her sons should again cross the water. She asked me if I did not fear going. I said I never thought about it until the time should come. We didn't think about these things in the army. She did, and she shuddered. Nevertheless, I could not help admiring her and all mothers for the suffering part they are playing in this war. They have the worst of it.

While waiting for Grindle I walked around St Michael's Avenue and Vicarage Road just opposite Soho Hill. The most magical avenue I have ever seen, like some place of dreams. Brooding trees and enigmatic, lonely veiled houses on the border of the tram route, yet withdrawn in secrecy and mystery and peace. I saw a bull-nosed curve of road that I had remembered since I was about five. It seemed part of my mind. The topaz sun glistened and shone. In town the people teemed like a sparkling thick cascade. War seemed far away were it not for the frequent khaki and the figures, tired, muddied and slipshod, who attended by family, had obviously just returned from the trenches or Flanders.

There was a great change observable in Grindle as soon as he opened the door. Instead of being reservedly cordial, he was jocular and hale and hearty. He had grown during the three months since he had joined – stout in the stomach and plump and pink in the face, after being pale and somewhat strained. He was like a trooper at his meal as you see them depicted in those old cavalier pictures.

For the first two weeks, he said, he would have given 500 golden sovereigns to anyone who could have procured him his discharge. This was due to the fact that they were packed four in a bed, some of his companions were dirty rogues, and that they were kept lounging about in file, hundreds of them, without anything to do, in the biting cold and wet. Never before had he known such cold. But after a fortnight of this, things turned and now his opinion was the same as mine – that life in the army in England at present for most is champion. No responsibility, no strain, easy hours. Grindle wonders, he said, if he will be able to set back to work in civvy life at the tremendous pressure he has been in the habit of working under.

I said that the loss of artistic interests in the army was a deprivation, but he said he thought this life of writers and artists was unwholesome. I disagreed, and said that though the soldiers were fine, they were largely animals, unobservant and unsavouring of the fine flavour of things. He said, 'But at a time like this you don't want the observer and student. You want the man who will give a friendly hand and do things.' I said that both sides ought to be developed, and that so far as I could see the army was impervious to art. As usual, he overbore my arguments, but whereas when he was a civvy he had a distinction and a grace of form which impressed me, now I was unimpressed with his rough-riding nonchalance and careless physical expansion. However, he is good all through.

MONDAY 24 JANUARY

While 'Sleepy' was drilling us, the major came up to us and asked him where he got his stripes. Sleepy replied 'in the YMCA' Waited to attention and he came round to each of us. I replied rather roundabout that the major at Bletchley instructed us we should be made corporals, when he broke me off, saying he only wanted to know who told us to put our stripes up.

There was much discussion in the squad about this incident. It was explained to us that at first motorcyclists in our regiment were made corporals, owing to the fact that they could not be reduced in rank, and in some instances had hesitated in complying with orders, having to be shot in France, it had been decided to make them pioneers on entry, and then corporals on reaching Dunstable after the two weeks' drill at Birmingham.

TUESDAY 25 JANUARY

In the afternoon, at turnings, our feet went with a great machine-like clack. We started well and secured a 'very good indeed' with our salutings to the front and salutings on the march. We formed fours well and formed section finely. 'That'll do,' said the captain continually. Instead of twenty minutes we were passed out in eight.

The captain said we were the smartest motorcyclist squad he had inspected on the square. When we formed up for roll-call a sergeant darted out and said, 'Very fine!' The captain said we could break off for the afternoon as we had done so well.

THURSDAY 27 JANUARY

This morning Sergeant 'Darky' Swales took us for a severe introduction to Swedish drill. At first break the captain came down and said we were to take off our stripes, as they were not due until the completion of our course of training. The stripes were to come off at the first break. Accordingly, behold us feverishly cutting off our stripes with scissors and penknife, Jock helping me and I lending scissors. The command caused acute disappointment in our squad, and up at the YMCA we were smiled at as we made the finishing strokes and plucked threads out.

Got to dance in evening, after trying on khaki suit – a splendid fit. Only about a dozen and a half gents there. A soldier is now quite a normal phenomenon. Plenty of nice girls, with whom there was not enough dances to go round that night. Walked home with Paul and had two teas and custard at midnight stall. Five customers during our presence, one a rough chap in civvies said, on our telling him to join the army if he wanted a good lazy time, said he was home from 11 months in France for a week's leave. The other said his army pay was poor. 'You can have my job for a bob,' were his words.

FRIDAY 28 JANUARY

On duty in the NCO's mess-room I wiped tables down and laid same. Jock and I fetched spuds in sack from the storeroom and peeled same. Meanwhile, Jock told me about his family, a sister and four brothers, and a father of 59 who had never had a doctor. All except the youngster were at the war. Jock would have joined with his chums in the Cameron Highlanders, but he was not old enough. That was why, as he was a motor mechanic, he joined the motorcycle corps.

A friend of his in the Camerons said that at Loos the Highlanders in dare-devilry went too far forward and were without reinforcements, or they could have chased the Germans a long way. He said the Cs went into the charge laughing – the Germans thought them mad and fled. The Germans always got away before the Cs could get up to them. His friend had nine months at the front and regarded it as great fun. We finished the spuds at great speed, talking thus, and swept up the kitchen.

My impression of the past three weeks has been one generally of robust enjoyment. The drills never grew monotonous, because of their being so frequently broken by breathers and breaks and by the variety of other duties we had to perform, such as the revolver practice, the bathing parade, the military funeral, the two mornings of light fatigue duties, the 'passing out' and the drilling of our squad by ourselves. Day by day, I and the others have enjoyed what we thought would be onerous. Especially delightful is when the day is fine, to march about the parade ground with so many other squads in the sting of the open air.

Nothing was actually irksome, though there is the rigour of the lock and key, under which you must repress your soul and individuality. The army method does not encourage initiative, but English independence thrives in spite of it. The army encourages the timid and the timeserver to prosper because they are the type which gladly becomes docile to cast iron rule. One sees how Germany has become enslaved. The soldier, I think, ought to be encouraged to keep his soul alive, not to kill it. So far, in many things – and those vital – his soul is fettered and handicapped. My direct contact with officers so far has not been discouraging, though at times disconcerting, and at other inspiring me with more confidence. Our captain is fine – the major, I believe impartial. The major at Bletchley was perhaps the finest specimen of a gentleman it has been my lot to meet. It was an inspiration to merely see and hear his dignified words and mien.

SATURDAY 29 JANUARY

Corrected poems and then to Vauxhall Grove for driving licence. Then to Mr Nodder's – who told me Bert had looked upward as he walked behind the glaring brass band that accompanied the Derby recruits. A fine, modest, sensitive youth, his soul revolted at the public display. How is it the nation doesn't understand that the bulk of our class is at heart sensitive and dislikes a parade of its qualities when they are called virtues? It was torture for him as it would have been for me when I was his age.

I told Mr Nodder how the REs, in true army style, looked down on the RAMC and that light infantry regiments were better than ordinary infantry. It has grown obvious that the first batch of groups under the Derby Scheme have been hardly dealt with. For instance, now the groups are again thrown open, one can join the Flying Corps and other regiments direct – a privilege denied to men who joined the Derby scheme under less pressure. By right those who first voluntarily joined should have greater privileges, and were promised them – but they aren't having them. It shows that while you wish to be fair and patriotic, when you are giving up all to the army, it does what it likes with you when it has your oath, and is not particularly keen on keeping its part of the compact. It shows that you must make the best bargain for yourself while you are free. If you don't push the army will push you. A nice thing for the canvassers to come and tell you you will be treated with every consideration and your wishes, where possible, will be met, and then for these early batches to be held back from good regiments, while late-comers can join regiments that are flung open from time to time after being temporarily shut.

SUNDAY 30 JANUARY

Breakfasted reading Swinnerton's *Life of George Gissing* and critical study. Typed up the lesson, shaved and bathed, then to class where fun was made of my new rig-out which I had put on with much delight, and which Arthur had somewhat decried. The cut is good and the breeches horsey, but the colour of the tunic is not so fawn as I wanted. I never seem to get the smartness I aim for in clothes.

Took a tram to Dartmouth Street and walked to Vauxhall Road. Gramophones could be heard going in the night and through chinks I saw in one yard couples dancing wild turkey trots in an orgy of delight – working classes thriving. As soon as we got in, had news that we were to move tomorrow, so went through kit with Bendle.

MONDAY 31 JANUARY

At 10.30 paraded and were paid 'billet allowance' viz, 3d for 21 days – 5/3. To billet, crowding into the kitbag two boots, two tunics, all my shirts and socks, and wearing own garments and new tunic. We sang two hymns in Bill P's room at billet – Bill on organ, Mrs Langham breaking down, and Vi and Maud kissing us. Off to the one o'clock parade, all joking. We marched joyously to New Street Station, waiting on Platform 1, the centre of curious and admiring eyes. Off at last, cheering. Singsong, jollity and mouth-organ on train.

On to Leighton Buzzard, changing for Dunstable. Walked across level plain through the gloaming in crisp air, tramping fine in fours. Antique and fair in half light, Houghton-Regis came into view.

In kind of farmyard waited at orderly room. After giving name and number and address in office, led off to hut for tea – as much bread, butter and jam as we could eat, then duff, but only three quarters of a mug of tea.

A sergeant whom we thought was bluffing, took names and numbers to appear at 6.45 the next morning. Told us, scarcely intelligibly, there was parade at 7.15, breakfast at 7.45, second parade at 8.45. Naught else. Left orders in typescript to be read by us.

In the sleeping hut, Albert bagged beds toward the stove for self, Paul and me. Made beds, visited murky canteen with oil-cloth counter and bare wood tables. Our candles only light, but a good stove and fire. In the reading room a corporal played classical music finely. Suddenly bugle, and I was back in the hut just in time.

TUESDAY 1 FEBRUARY

Rose at 6 and having cleaned boots, washed, shaved and made bed, was preparing to go on parade when orderly corporal said, 'Who'll clean up the hut?' No response, so I offered. 'You needn't go on parade,' he said.

In the hut noticed you want a place not near the door because it is always opening and the hut orderly sweeps dust past your bed to the door. Too near the stove and people sit on your bed. Swept both ends to the centre of the room, then out at the centre steps into a box. Refolded nearly all the blankets and placed towels over. Unhung kit bags and placed on floor, placed dirty boots under bed-boards, tidied the shelves. Fetched coke for which I had to sign, and noticed all old hands picked all the large pieces of coke.

At dinner, bench after bench was told to file up to cook's counter, grabbing a plate. First cook ladled out mess of stew, second as you passed, slapped on plate four jacket potatoes. Next dished out peas. No bread in basket. Noted that servers were rude if you asked for fat or for more veggies.

In afternoon Sergeant Pindar told me to get things to a written order: one tin hub-grease, two and a half gallons of gear oil. I went up with fellows who wheeled a barrow for fifteen tins of petrol. Gave the order to a tall, dark languorous giant in blue overalls, who pondered over it. He couldn't understand it. I took the order back and learnt that the pots were for the oil, and I was to bring a 56-lb drum of grease. Also fetched from the spares hut a case of Daimler spares. Gear oil dripping very slowly like black treacle from the tap or barrel plug, so I helped carry spares and came again for oil and grease. On the road fellows were testing bikes. Signallers on the green were heliographing.

A good argument for individualism – progress impeded by constant checking of stores issue in state-controlled army. In private business it is each man's interest to see he's not deceived, but here all has to be constantly regulated and barred against abuse.

WEDNESDAY 2 FEBRUARY

Afternoon we went off in fours to get new machines from the station at Dunstable. Arrived at siding, we got motorcycles in crates from three covered trucks. Knocked open the crates, cut the cords, put spares from the case in front into despatch box and wheeled the bikes off. Back in time for tea – bread, dripping, large hunk of cake and tea. Drank ginger wine with Paul in the inn in Houghton Regis.

FRIDAY 4 FEBRUARY

It rained on parade – sodden and in two inches of mire. Drilled for an hour in this mud, slipping about clumsily. Wells, our instructor, gave a lecture on map-reading, we squatting, he pinning map to blackboard. Conventional signs on a map, contours and how to read them, heights of road and how indicated.

SATURDAY 5 FEBRUARY

Breakfast of porridge with bacon and eggs stuck on top. Bought porridge milk for a halfpenny off man who came round with tomatoes, bananas and oranges.

At 11 six of us were told off to go down to the old crock bay and there to deal with ten machines – one minus wheels, silencer, piston and cylinder, gearbox and saddle. Old parts lay in boxes at one end of the bay with outer covers. We attempted to assemble old parts to old buses, but lacking tools and parts could do little.

Walked to Dunstable and took passes to Paul then to Luton with him and MacVitie. Inspected electric torches at shops and bought one for 3/3. Luton streets dark and crowded – much youth about of both sexes. Paul and I went to the Castle Hall – a rather ragtime blaring towards the end. Afraid to wait until the last train, we left at

10.30 and walked rapidly. In dark shouldn't have managed without the torch. Progressed fiercely, not wanting a late mark.

SUNDAY 6 FEBRUARY

Church of England men asked to fall out to the left. Marched to the road and waited a quarter of an hour in file, then into church on the left side. One hour's prayer and hymns. Plenty of girls, but the music tame, and the audience thin but for the soldiers.

Reviewing the events of the week, what has made it so enjoyable is its uncertainty, and the knowledge, dawning surely on us, that we shall not be overworked. I have enjoyed the week immensely. On arriving Monday, we were told by the older despatch riders it was bloody awful, and by an old campaigner that it was better out there. The discipline is supposed to be severe, but so far it has been as good as a holiday.

Fellows who've been to France, especially early joiners, think Dunstable trying and would sooner be in France. Men in stores, etc have usually been invalided back from France. The stores corporal, McQueen, said he had been shot – back wheel away and legs injured, jaw broken and teeth shattered – he took out false teeth and showed us. Wells and Leahy say we'll have good times in France.

Not one of my companions has a sense of beauty sufficient to appreciate the romantic scene outside the hut – a long mellow wall and outbuildings beyond level of field, and hoary church, and then green fields and two individual houses. It is lovely to live open to such fine rustic influences. If I mention it, fellows laugh at me or assert only luke-warmedly. To me this compensates for all other slight hardships. No conveniences in huts. Half of one shelf and two hooks for each man. Why no locker? All must be tidy on shelf or in kitbag – but I got my typewriter down and camouflaged it.

MONDAY 7 FEBRUARY

Paraded at 12.30 and were told that the General would inspect us on the road during nine-point schemes, but we were not to get frightened of a brass hat. 'For goodness' sake, don't get into a drivelling funk. Half of you will, I know, but the other half, please keep your wits about you and buck up.'

After dinner, back to electric tidying of hut for inspection. We all worked like heroes, first gathering refuse from tables in mess-pans, then sweeping tables with foul brushes. Sweep floors, meanwhile replenishing boiler outside with water. Wash and dry up and place mugs on hooks the right way. Mop the floor, clean pans and pile plates and urns. THE GENERAL WAS INSPECTING US.

TUESDAY 8 FEBRUARY

After parade carried verbal messages at intervals of ten paces.

'Hooge Cateau is beyond railhead' came out as 'Hood's shutter is beyond Fraser', and 'Germans wiring aerial reconnaissance' as 'Turn out Archibalds'.

WEDNESDAY 9 FEBRUARY

Morning drill after being joined up with new squad that had trained for a month at Leighton. New instructor, Sergeant Schofield, smart, tall and chummy.

THURSDAY 10 FEBRUARY

Outside map-reading by mill and Dunstable Downs – a fine sunny day. Afternoon roadside lecture by Wells, and a discipline lecture by Schofield. Told us to avoid the red and green lamps at Abbeville. Fellows with money who went with such had symptoms of VD – sore gums, running nose, chest and face pimples. Sent to VD field hospital, tents in field and fed on bread and marge and sops and syringed by the MO. 56 days' pay stopped and allotments. Home folks written to, and these so shocked that the Government had to modify their notification as 'detention'. Some wives and sweethearts went off with other fellows – so some other course may be adopted.

FRIDAY 11 FEBRUARY

This morning parade square being four inches deep in mud, we were taken into huts for two hours' lecture on signal office routine. Tips on riding Douglases, and also army formation and despatch riders' work.

Jock Bruce bled at the nose and fell in a faint and doctor sent for. I ran off and meeting a corporal MC asked him to take me to the doctor. Upstairs the doctor was talking to NCOs and two men. 'Man found in No 3 Hut bleeding at nose and unconscious.'

Uncertain whether to wait and show him the way, but went back to hut, where Jock on improvised bed. Soon the doctor came and asked if he had felt unwell in the morning, then told his orderly to fetch a petrol can of warm water for a foot-warmer, and gravy. I volunteered to get both ('or warm milk if you can't get that.') I did so, the chaps chaffing me as I ladled out the gravy they should have had. 'You've got that for him?' said the doctor on my return. 'Yes,' I said delightedly. Jock was better and drank the gravy, looking at me every time he took a sup. Osborne and Kirkwood had remained helping him, and I revised my opinion of rather swanky Osborne after this.

Down to the guard-room – a hut eight feet square with a corrugated tin roof. Stout orderly sergeant, a pale, full-contoured lad, and another youth were there, but they went off after explaining our duties. We drew lots 1, 2, 3 and I got 3, from 10.30 to 12.30 and 4.30 to 6.30. First I filled generators – one hour gone. Wrote diary and did odd jobs. From time to time we checked DSD men, time of entry against their time of going out, number, name, bike make. Some out for first time that day. Scarcely no fire, and all seemed chill and forbidding. It grew warmer and we got some wood burning and I felt happy. Turned in at 9.30 for an hour's sleep. The head corporal aloof – the other chummy and unconsciously pushy – got on very well with him. Rose at 10.30 and went on guard. A sense of performing important duty made the task enjoyable. At about 11.00 I saw a bike lamp coming up the drive which ran behind the hut. 'Halt,' I called, 'who goes there?' 'Hollis,' he replied. He gave number, which I shouted into the guard room to Corporal Thomas. 'What's up?' I asked. 'The tyre valve wrenched out. Like a mug I bought a brand new Dunlop, then the belt broke. I had to cut a hole with my knife – no belt punch. Pulled out again. Hunted up a farmer for a gimlet, but that didn't last. That's my history for the day.' I lighted him to a place in second motor-cycle bay, and off he went, bikeless.

At 12.30 I went in and sat on floor before fire. Could have slept, but dared not because the round can punched with holes from which the stovepipe rose – our stove – had at the top a square orifice to receive coke. To supply it we had only wood pinched at intervals from the yard. These staves being four feet long, when they were half burnt, the top half would fall to the ground, once nearly setting me afire.

SATURDAY 12 FEBRUARY

At 4.30 after a cigarette, I changed guard. As last half hour of first shift had hung so heavy, I anticipated dull, heavy, slow time, but it was not as dark as the first shift. Walking to and fro I constantly heard banging and shutting noises. Located them at last as horses' hooves knocking at the stable walls. Two or three pieces of paper flitting on the floor frightened me once. By now I had lost the sense of importance – the thing striking me was the immense casualness of it. I was nobody, yet there was I with this end of the camp wide open to the lane which ran down to the road, in charge of a hundred or so motorbikes, the headquarters of one of the most important junior branches of the service. Quite British, I thought.

At 5.30 I heard steps down the drive. A figure. 'Halt.' 'Friend… GNR' At first I didn't grasp the meaning of GNR, like a fool I forgot to flick my flashlight on him, but I could discern his uniform and wicker basket – a railway guard, I divined. 'Going to work?' I asked. 'Yes.' 'Right.' Now I saw one or two lights in the village – a bike lamp, a cart's red rear light. In various windows lights sprang out dim yet warm. In the yard I met Bostock, who was going to wake up the dayshift man. His ideas concurred with mine on the casualness of the routine. I saw a cart coming down the lorry drive. 'Halt.' 'Right-oh – lavatories,' called a cockney's cock-sure voice. 'Latrines,' prompted Bostock. But I felt I ought to have gone up with a torch and examined the cart. I had missed an off-chance – a few minutes' uneasiness followed.

After drill, a beautiful route march to Chad's End on the hill above Luton Road. Fellows groused as they walked and climbed, but I enjoyed it keenly.

Pass forms were handed out – I had got a blank one from the other orderly corporal in his hut. Why aren't you formally told how to get passes? Because they make a point in the army of telling you nothing useful, and making it awkward for you to find out.

SUNDAY 13 FEBRUARY

Parade at nine and told off into Church of England, Wesleyans and Methodists, as if we had hues. This time in the hut we had decided to be Wesleyans because last week the Nonconformists were dismissed at church parade.

'C of E, move to the right. Left turn. Forward. Right turn. Forward. Dress.'

'Wesleyans to the left. Methodists … any Methodists? Move up right, Wesleyans, Methodists to the rear. Wesleyans fall in at 9.35.'

As we ran to the hut Boyd said, 'It's Presbyterians we should have been. They were dismissed. And if you're Roman Catholic you have to get up in the dead of night.'

At 9.35 we were marched off to Dunstable and to the fine Wesleyan Chapel, clean and business-like inside and with spacious efficient schoolrooms at the back. It was a treat to get the old Nonconformist atmosphere after the chill deathly ceremonial of Houghton Regis Church. I was at home and gazed about, dreaming.

MONDAY 14 FEBRUARY

In the afternoon a lecture on Triumph gear box. Triumph bike brought up and gear-box dismantled by pale, good-looking sergeant. He asked frequently, 'Is that clear?' but was only once asked for repetition, though afterwards it transpired that few really understood. Hitt asked me kindly if I savvied. I said, 'No.' He lent me a drawing explaining the gears and this drew a small crowd. With this drawing and the Triumph booklet, I mastered the theory of the gears and wrote same with a sketch in evening in the reading hut.

TUESDAY 15 FEBRUARY

In the afternoon lecture on the magneto, then we entered a goods shed, and equipment was dished out to us. Laconic sergeant read out list of names, then razor, overalls, mess-tin, belt, ammunition-pouch, haversack, lanyard, clasp knife, water bottle, pistol case, etc. To these names we answered 'No,' if we hadn't already received same, and before we had had time to check them we had to sign for them, army way.

Doubled back to hut – officer in, so went and assembled in hut. Here as I went in I heard, 'Tell you what it is, that Davis and Mantle are too f—— clever!' from a loafer by the stove. Unpleasant!

Marked equipment, and then hair cut in the little village shop, followed by gin and peppermint in the Cock Inn.

WEDNESDAY 16 FEBRUARY

Wells as mess sergeant has slowly been reorganising the waste, but conscientious as he is, an orderly officer still suggested alterations. Today someone complained straight to the CO and Wells was hurt, as he had tried his best to get things and meals more punctual. The waste that occurs in the army is due to the fellows themselves and not to army officers, though more efficient organisation would cure it. Fellows take bread and then leave it. Take a tin of herrings and leave it half emptied, while others – a few – go short. Bully beef is only half eaten. Porridge goes well and the liquids. Potatoes get left and much meat, but all the pudding is eaten unless badly cooked – which is frequent.

FRIDAY 18 FEBRUARY

Lieutenant Burton pleasant and gently ironical to us and to himself, lectured on vertical intervals and contour-drawing in section, and how to determine visibility of interrupted slopes and 'that sort of business'. 'Blue flag with white hole business', 'pendant' or 'pennant' or whatever it's called. I'm not well up on these things.' Afterwards he was transferred to the Flying Corps.

In the afternoon more on visibility and Henderson came out and performed. His method of determining gradients seemed easier at first, but Lieutenant Burton disproved its facility. Henderson stood his ground honestly. Lieutenant Burton said, 'It's not the method that ought to be used.' The army way again. Not a high standard of intelligence expected from students. 'Set the map – or there's a long word – I forget it.' 'Orientate?" I suggested. 'Yes, orientation.' Paul commended for his paper and taken away to do drawings of magneto action.

SUNDAY 20 FEBRUARY

9.35 Wesleyan Parade. At 9.00 Baptists, Congregationalists and others were ignored, or invited to join Wesleyans. To Wesleyan Chapel again. Preacher, Cornish, elderly, florid and enthusiastic – a firm preacher but of queer voice.

Walked, rather tired, by pleasing then monotonous roads to Leighton Buzzard. Lovely and old and pictorial. Narrow winds with five old-fashioned inn signs within a hundred yards. Inns in hooks and crooks everywhere, retired in nooks and angles. One with wood frame in front like butcher's to dangle legs from and sit drinking. At Albion Hotel, grand time at tea, exquisitely served. Then sat writing and dozed in gloaming by fire with oak antiques around, church bells ringing, footsteps and muted Sunday sounds in the street, and a girl's voice and piano in the house. While such beauty reigned glamorously at one end of the scale, it seemed absurd to kill each other at the other end.

TUESDAY 22 FEBRUARY

Slept with a draught playing on me from the window – broken a week ago. There are about six broken windows in the hut today, some from football being played in the hut. No fire – hellish cold. Hut orderly assiduously sweeps hut in morning, and then vanishes for the rest of day to warm reading-room. Plenty of such sinecures in the army.

In evening wrote in YMCA, then game of footer. We were soon puffed, all four of us. Fellows don't stand a great deal of exercise. I note that some 50% in our hut take pills or medicines. All young.

WEDNESDAY 23 FEBRUARY

This morning we were told to bring haversacks and get rations at breakfast. Pieces of cheese were dished out – one and a half inches each cube – then pieces of bread. 'You're in a hurry, young man,' said the orderly corporal, as I grabbed a piece from rear rank. 'Sorry,' putting it back, 'I've only seven teeth and can't eat crust, and that's why I grabbed it,' I said. 'Start from that man,' ordered he with next plate of bread. Next man was I.

Marched from Dunstable crossroads in batches through snow and blizzard to Eaton Bray. I enjoyed robust travel and stinging open air. Failing to pick up our OC, we opened office at map location in a pleasant huckster's shop, where there was a good fire all afternoon. A pot of tea all round and bread and butter set us going merrily. Our despatch rider clerk or signal office expert, who had been a despatch rider with Indian contingent out in France, wrote messages and sent one to Fourth Army Corps. I, first on roster, took it. Then we kept sending or receiving similar messages (any bullshit) until four.

THURSDAY 24 FEBRUARY

Heavy fall of snow in night and quite a drift through the door at the top of the hut, on to blankets and beds. Brief parade in driving blizzard.

After tea, men ordered out and snowball fight arranged – G Company and A Company. We marched round the field and were told to get into trenches – a jump of nine feet. Made snowballs, then leapt out and attacked pioneers and sappers in their trenches. After eight minutes, drove them out and chased them to the end of the field. Mid-way in fight I had to cease – my bare hands in keen agony from returning circulation. Put on gloves and fought well. Then another fight in open between despatch riders and all pioneers, despatch riders winning both times. Spoilt cap and lost badge in the fray.

Afternoon walked, my heel rather trying and limbs tired, in route march to squad snowball near Luton Road. Built five snowmen and women, the phallic symbol, as ever, much in evidence among the creations of the boys and Schoey[5]. The snowmen stood out almost phosphorescent and grey against white snowy hill background. Trees hung on hilltop like draggled plumage on telegraph wires.

FRIDAY 25 FEBRUARY

For my badge, lost in snow fight, I tried at QM stores, 8.00 in the morning 'What's your company? Oh, the MC company get theirs at the clothing store yonder.' I go there – more buggering and arsing you about. 'We're not open 'til 9 to 12.30 and 2 to 5.30.' 'I'm on duty then,' I said. 'Well, ask to be excused by sergeant of squad.' Did so, and got there. 'We ain't got none.' The army way – make it as awkward as they can.

Off on weekend leave, I hurried through beating wet snow and blizzard to station and rode to Birmingham, then caught the 9.50 to Chester Road. Sat up late with mother and Ettie, both joyous.

SATURDAY 26 FEBRUARY

At shop talked with Wilf and had dinner with him. At Bardsley's couldn't get shaved because all his men had gone to the war. Got to Church House at 7.30. Enjoyable dance. Fine, candid, joyous girl in red silk dress. Walked home at midnight through streets so pitch dark I could scarcely see my way. At home I got letter from Everyman with proof of my article on Norman Gale.

SUNDAY 27 FEBRUARY

Got early to school by car and enjoyed it – all fellows there. Home to tea, then back to town in sleet, and took the 5.45 train to Leicester. Lovely warm travel in train full of soldiers and sailors. Changed at Leicester and got to Luton at 10.30. Strenuous walk to camp over snowy roads, my back aching with load of bag and typewriter.

TUESDAY 29 FEBRUARY

This morning we were added to new large squads from Birmingham. Started with lecture on Douglas bike, then fifteen of us told off to help Sergeant Wells. He laughingly led us to sack of spuds and knives. We sang sacred and profane songs and worked happily until 12.30, then we had the first table allotted us. Men on either side of me who didn't like fat always got nice juicy brown fat. I, who loved half my meat to be fat, invariably got scraggy lean.

Afternoon, wrote paper on the Douglas bike in the reading room. We don't at present hear anything further of these papers, except the commendation of Paul for his magneto papers and some such remark as 'Is this three and a half hours' work? Here's a man done six pages.'

WEDNESDAY 1 MARCH

Lecture on discipline by Sergeant Schofield, then route march to Luton Road. At officers' mess complaints had been passed on the way we motorcyclists marched, so Schoey made us swing arms and said he'd show them.

THURSDAY 2 MARCH

Walked off toward Eaton Bray, our corporal choosing me for signal office clerk as we set up in a farmhouse.

Fixed up map and roster – flags on maps with pins. We started, our corporal very keen on work, and making me copy outgoing register. As our fellow despatch riders came in and saw nothing prepared for dinner save for signalmaster, clerk and Paul, they looked blue. They ordered tea themselves. After our dinner of meat and Yorkshire pudding, a message came in from YF[9] that 'YFs despatch riders should be treated with more courtesy'.

Nice walk home to hot high tea, then wrote all night and played Beethoven on piano. This disappointing, as notes missing on piano, I nervous and not in the mood and soldiers like only popular music.

Oswald's first diary finishes here – in March 1916, and resumes at the R.E. Abbeville Depot on 18 July 1916 when, training completed, he is in Northern France, having crossed the Channel on 8 July.

TUESDAY 18 JULY

Route march because we hadn't fallen in well on parade. Walked in mac and O'alls. Afternoon lecture on Signal Office work.

SATURDAY 22 JULY

Ready for scheme[10] on second parade, when 'Kemp, Stokes, Bartrop, Davis, O H ,' called out. After waiting, stepped back to Sergeant Major – Paul and I had mutually promised to ask to go together up the line. 'Excuse me, sir, I wanted if possible to go up the line with my cousin. That is he.' 'You can't now. It's sanctioned by the OC.' 'I wanted to.' 'Well, I'll see what I can do. Mantle may come up afterwards. Give me the two names.'

Went over to bikes. Heard Pip Crompton's name called, and soon he walked away. I ran up to him 'I'm going in your place. You rejoin ranks.'

Afternoon we marked bikes and swept the parade ground. Evening made purchases and strolled by the canal. A sad goodbye to Pip Crompton, who took charge of a party of men bound for XIV Corps, to the station.

SUNDAY 23 JULY

On 9.30 parade, Pip Boyd's name called for 15th Division. Jack Lawrence, Paul and I desolated. After we were dismissed sought him out in the rain and went into the YMCA hut. Deeply moved at the thought of Pip leaving us – tears in my eyes – one of the few times in my life. A great gap it would leave – thought of naught else.

As we sang, all the pathos of life and the tragic partings of the war welled up into the music. Service was simple but attended with gusto and fullness. To the latrines, for I was still suffering – but not so badly as in England – from piles. While here, heard called out, 'Davis, H O, Mantle.' 'Here,' I cried. 'See Sergeant Moir at once.' I hastened to his hut. 'You're on draft – you're Mr Davis, aren't you?' 'Yes – I wanted to go up the line with my cousin, Mantle.' 'I know nothing about it – I Anzac Corps, by road.' Paul scouted round for Jeff and found him in the sergeant's mess. 'Who are you – Davis?' 'No, Mantle.' 'Oh, all right.' Dismissed airily. I got a move on, being told by officer that I was to get away as soon as possible. Triumph that was fairly new dished out, and spares flung at me.

It turned out Pip Boyd didn't have to go after all – and I got away after Sunday dinner.

Rode up the long straight hilltowards Amiens. Proceeding onwards met ambulance cars, lorries and troops, tin-hatted, on the march. Thought and felt

Iwas nearing war! RAMC unit on the march, sweating and dusty, up and down the great sloping roads. At Amiens, thriving and full and bright, quested for the town hall to Signal Office, where I was told to go to Querrieu. A despatch rider I met at the office said he was having the cushiest time of his life – it was great. Arrived and went down to billet where I met Wally Osborne and Bendle in a ramshackle room in cottage. Beds about like stage scenery. Bendle made me some tea and talked about shooting rabbits with beaucoup ammunition they had got dished out.

Querrieu signal office a long, dark hut in a small forest – Fourth Army HQ – which was where I met Jimmy. Wally Osborne, riding with supreme skill over the whacking holes in the road, conducted me gaily to my destination. He was fed up, he said, notwithstanding that he had got out as he wanted when he was fed up in England. 'We have such riding, especially in the recent wet weather – it makes you sweat as you ride, lest you skid under the lorry wheels.'

Contay, home of I Anzac Corps, is a nasty, dusty, unbeautiful village – a square and a long road splitting out on to the hill at the end. Sleeping quarters a dark, ugly loft over a stinking stable, where horse kicked and the electric lighting outside 'tuf-tuffed' all night. No-one welcomed me much. In response to my timid enquiries it was conveyed to me that a dirty piece of sacking nailed to a low wood frame could be loaned to me for the night. Slept with rats running all around the floor of the loft.

In the morning Lieutenant Larking came to me and turning to Bruce, the Sergeant, he said, 'They've sent this man for the pigeons, apparently. That puts us one up – another despatch rider's coming today.' 'Now, you're going to do a job of trust and responsibility. If this is too much for you, tell me, and I'll get someone else.' This from Mr Larking. Told by Bruce to get two days' rations and report to II Corps at Senlis.

The other boys put the wind up me when I tried to ascertain what kind of a job it was. Oh, Keith had stuck it as long as he could – no-one else would take it on. I cursed my luck and imagined myself specially selected by Fate for some evil stroke. Rather miserable.

Liked Senlis better than Contay. Reported to Major Day and was referred to Corporal Keeling, who would billet and train me. Met Nicholson, who got me rationed then found me a room to sleep in, musty, foul with rubbish left behind, full of crumpled packets of abandoned cigarettes and tobacco, bully-beef tins and the stale Machonochies smell that is always associated with the Somme. Sat and wrote by the window – felt half down-hearted, and half dreading the future, mingled with faint leaps of hope that all wouldn't be too bad.

In the shops you could buy chocolate – pre-war sixpenny bar – for 1 franc 50 centimes. Eggs about tuppence halfpenny each at the farm café, coffee tuppence a cup. Farm café and others full up all the time with crowds of soldiery, Anzacs and Imperials, sometimes cursing the Sommeois, sometimes good-humouredly laughing off the discomforts. Beer bad, wine and grenadine dear, and the estaminets universally foul.

MONDAY 24 JULY

In the evening turned in at 9.30, but guns and moving columns going past the door all night and two rats scampering about kept me awake until 12.30. I half nervous – knew nothing about the steadiness of the line, and I wondered to myself, 'suppose the Germans have beat us back and come on here – no-one will tell me.' Through my broken shattered window, however, could be heard the Anzacs, cheery and plain. Their hoarse voices came through plain, manly and fearless, giving me courage.

TUESDAY 25 JULY

Morning saw Keeling and discovered bike engine fouled by oil leaking from the pump, so was late – then discovered oil-tank was empty – so Keeling went alone. Cleaned the pump – conscious of my shortcomings against the masterly Keeling, who raced off with his pigeon baskets.

At first these pigeon baskets, about 28 inches square, put the wind up me. Suppose aught goes wrong with the bike – or I get hit – how to manage or fettle with that stifling, strangling load strapped round my back? But with custom I gradually forgot these drawbacks.

Talked to Corporal Searle, the loft-man at Warloy, where the loft was in a cottage farmyard. On the left was a mud-walled cabin containing a broad civvy bed and chest of drawers. Over this cabin was a small loft containing some forty birds. Searle a nice and generous chap, giving me tea as he started to grouse about the injustices of pigeon men.

Sergeant Hiscocks had now returned from Corps. Alert, high-strung, intelligent, with aquiline features and spectacles. Spoke in the Oxford manner, deliberately and inclined to be quietly supercilious. He showed me how to handle the birds and talked about the organisation of the pigeon service.

Sunday, Monday and Tuesday had felt gloomy and lack-lustre, confined in an all-khaki life. Bereft suddenly of all my friends, I pictured a drear existence ahead. I was nervous about tasks to be allotted me – the talk of going past Division to brigades. Hitherto pigeons had been delivered at Division, but now it was intended to send straight on from the lofts, which were under Corps and near Corps HQ. I was all for keeping on sending to Division – naturally – but I felt Fate would be against me. Nick never went past Division – why should I?

WEDNESDAY 26 JULY

Carted my stuff to where Hiscocks was staying. In the afternoon Hiscocks and I collared twelve birds each at Warloy and made off. A few miles out, Hiscocks observed some of my birds flying back – I hadn't securely fastenedthe pigeon basket. Returnedand repaniered and on again, past Bouzincourt, worming our way past columns of Division going in and out of Albert. It was as much as I could do at first to keep up without accident, for I hadn't yet learnt to get my gear lever bent down so that it could be operated by foot. The dust and traffic were thick and Hiscocks put a spurt on wherever we met an open stretch. To Australian Division HQ, where in a conservatory sat a number of Anzacs in careless, lounging attitudes as if having an after-dinner siesta. Large and small pigeon baskets lay on the floor – this was the signal office of the division in action. Hiscocks spoke to the superintendent who said he could spare a despatch rider to show us the way, and that it would be best to have a central meeting-point where all brigades could come for their pigeons.

The despatch rider appeared – a bright, quick, well-knit and alert man. Halted by the church, from which toppled the Virgin, which I had seen afar like a tortured skeleton going to take a plunge. No, that was nearer. Afar, the figure looked like a candle-snuffer's top melting and bending at top with heat. So this was the Church about which Blackford had said, he raced past it for another piece had been knocked off. I had imagined a desolate corner by the Church under moonlight with shells whizzing near, instead of this populous square with its come-day, go-day crowd. All around were burnt-out factories with twisted ironwork, lath and plaster roofed houses with sacking or shredded curtains instead of panes. We had a look down the Bapaume road – but stopped before a desolate stretch of mud. He said, 'That road's too hot – under observation and they're always bumping it, else the best meeting place would be along there. It means one brigade will have a long way to walk – but it can't be helped.'

After more riding past trenches going in many directions, we struck a clay hillock on which was stuck a red flag. This was the appointed meeting place and I was sick at heart at the thought of journeying up there day after day with a load of pigeons.

This first trip up was in the morning, and Hiscocks and I delivered the birds to rough and ready men who heeded not the sergeant's exhortations, but silently grabbed the birds and made off, shoving the poor mickies in anyhow. Took basket to Warloy with birds returned. Their dismay because five birds were carried in one infantry basket. The chaos of the service and this round impressed me. Can I introduce order? Thought it out as I walked up the lane by billet, and in the evening sun watched the great maggot balloon that had risen from the hollow below.

PIGEONS PLAYED A VERY IMPORTANT ROLE IN WORLD WAR I AS THEY PROVED TO BE AN EXCEPTIONALLY RELIABLE METHOD OF RELAYING MESSAGES.

THURSDAY 27 JULY

Down to Brigade HQ with Hiscocks and birds. I deliberately made it plain to the men that they shouldn't mix cocks and hens and not to keep the birds in the trenches too long, because at Corps Hiscocks had said this was urgent. Now, 'Come on Davis, we can't stay here all day,' was his admonition. Rumbled after that that he was perhaps windy. No shells fell near. You could see shrapnel burst beyond the white ridge – our guns going all the time. Just away from HQ trying to pass transport on the narrow track, I had a spill down an eight-foot trench – bike under horse's feet – handlebars bent and magneto control broken, but I not hurt.

FRIDAY 28 JULY

Fetched twelve gas-masks from company quartermaster's stores and by a miracle got them, dragging off the carrier, to Warloy, where I met Victor Turnpenny, whom I thought laconic. He had a message, just come in by pigeon, to take to Corps, but had a puncture. Lieutenant Larking said, 'Lend him your bike, and get on mending his puncture while he's away.'

'Well, Corporal Davis, how are you getting on?' 'Pretty fair, sir, but the men don't do what they're told. I think that's the trouble.' 'You must tell them off.' 'Well, I'm not the pugnacious sort myself, and those great strapping fellows are not the type to be told off.' 'Now, don't run them down. I'm an Australian myself.' 'Are you, sir? Well, I like them, but they carry independence too far – they don't take notice of what you say.' 'Oh, I think you'll find things will go on all right, Davis.' 'I hope so, sir. It seems a bit chaotic at the moment. Before we took over the pigeons have just been dumped, and they've done what they like with them.' 'That's why we're having this new arrangement of going direct to Brigades. You'll find things will go all right.'

I went into the Division yard where, under eaves, stood the sorry steeds of the Australian Division's despatch riders. There were many Douglases and some Triumphs, but a crocked-up looking lot. The heat was sweltering and I was parched – tea had just been made, and a smell of Machonochies was in the air. I asked for a drop of tea in the collapsible mug I carried, and only realised on seeing them look thoughtfully in the Dixie that they were probably short of grub. I flushed, but they gave it to me, and it was nectar.

SATURDAY 29 JULY

Took both lots of birds myself in the morning – chaos at the other end. In the despatch riders' yard by the side of the château saw Percy Boyd – he said later that the way my jaw dropped was fine. He had come up the day after me. Old Jeff might just as well have sent Paul, but wouldn't out of spite. It was good to strike a pal.

Evening, read the 'secret service' notes of Sergeant Hiscocks. I made a quick copy and handled pigeons, which at first I found awkward, and had to force myself to repeat the processes, as I did not take to it naturally. Hiscocks said, 'Larking wants you to know the service from A-Z if possible. You're to go up to the front line and see where they keep the birds.' Wind up me – spoilt half an hour's sleep. Next day he purported to make enquiries of signals officer if safe to go up with a guide. To my unutterable relief H returned with 'He's

[Jerry] knocking forward area about badly today. We can't go.' I know his relief was as great as mine. What heroes!

SUNDAY 30 JULY

In the evening talked in the kitchen with Paul – rather a fine, dark girl who walked about in white under-bodice and skirt, the old man and old lady present. Went over to my pal Percy Boyd at Contay, we faring there at a dirty café on omelette and fruit with chocolate and cake, I bought at Henencourt in a 'burst' at finding that I could buy stuff at the canteen there, while at Warloy the canteen was always full and you had to wait in a long queue.

MONDAY 31 JULY

In evening was ordered to Senlis, and riding at dusk was no breeze – potholes in the road, loose stones and where the horse lines were, tracks of engulfing mud. In a ditch of loose stones, came off a crash in the absolute dark, and thus began to acquire the knowledge that night-riding was even more agonising than the pigeon service.

The II Corps signal office was a long wooden hut, and on the open ground nearby were the despatch riders' bikes. I placed mine there and removed my kit. Back to the road and through a gap over a stile, I found myself in a small, mud-walled barn – a two-storey framework of wood covered with wire netting which constituted in all about sixteen bed-places. I chose an upper portion of the floored frame on the right. As I lay on my right side, feet towards the road, I faced Corporal Leahy – a young man of staid and sound disposition, the brother of one of our drill corporals at Dunstable. At my back was a pretty boy named Couper, of effeminate face, whom I called Lillywhite. On the top floor opposite, in the best corner, was John Wagstaffe, a Birmingham man, rotund, Falstaffian, honest and reliable, but a bit fussy on health matters. 'I hope to God I don't have another winter out here,' was his continual refrain, when it rained.

The next man was Peter the Painter[11], reputed to be swinging the lead since he had had a rather cruel smash. Instead of keeping on the roster and doing ordinary dispatch riding work, he was 'on the counter' in the signal office, rather in the role of post-office sorter. He had some colleagues, of whom the brothers Stacey, of patrician mould and accent, were chief. There was also Mason the artificer and his brother – both sound and sporty – Moir the inscrutable and pessimistic Anglo-Indian, and Hitt.

Most of these latter, with the sergeant and Keeling, slept and lived in minute shacks made of scratchwood and felt about 30 feet to the rear of our bird-cage in a field. Here there was a bigger shack where presided the cook – a man of frog-like aspect. I never saw him smile and when he spoke, merely from the lugubrious, dragging and untinted tones of him, you saw life in its sad and sinister phases. The memory of his voice recalls all the Somme hatefulness – mud or dust, Machonocies and bully, sluttish inimical peasants and the strategic dominance of the Hun.

TUESDAY 1 AUGUST

Took birds from a loft at Senlis – Corporal Jack Waddington in charge – a merry, quaint, good-hearted fellow. Unfortunately he lacked education and so was dependent on his mate, Pioneer Keen – a morose and conceited fellow – for entries into his ledger and for making report on his birds' flights. Keen took advantage of the situation and did little work.

Corporal Vic Turnpenny had fixed himself up here quite comfy with makeshift civvy bed in a room with Keen and Waddington, leaving me to shift for myself. He told me later that Lieutenant Larking had told him he was not to go up the line. During all the time he and I worked together on the Somme, until 16 September 1916, he never volunteered once to take a load of birds up for me, nor even to lift the great basket of pigeons on my back. I can not imagine myself being so unsporting and selfish. He gave me advice on my bike, but though he saw I had no mechanical gift, he did not help me – but read magazines and novels all day in the blinding heat, or slept.

THURSDAY 3 AUGUST

Unusually hot. Got birds out in one lot – I now began to know the road by heart, through Bouzincourt, then past burnt-out factories, giving a glimpse of the sandbags, boarded up rents in church and toppling virgin on the steeple. Cross the Bapaume road and you leave the heavier traffic and meet horses, troops, cyclists and light transport, until you arrive at the brow of the ridge beyond Becourt Wood. Here on the right stood the famous coffee bar of the Anzacs, and every day, coming back I used to have a drink. The bar was for Anzacs only, but as I was in the service of their corps, they let me have drinks there – always free. If I was carrying mickies back they were always interested and I explained what the birds did. They would start talking about what had happened up the line the night before. 'Hell of a do – our fellows cut to pieces. Johnny's too strong, but he don't like the cold steel.'

From there you went skedaddling down towards the battlefield – for the first old Hun trenches from which he had been driven started just outside

Albert– whichwas drear and monotone in tint. Some howitzers were always shuddering the few trees' blunt trunks thunderously. A thin trickle of traffic came over the tracks – ambulance carts with wounded, cheery or writhing in torture – transport and ration carts, carts with empty shell cases, officers and men riding, an occasional despatch rider ploughing through the dust or mud.

Many trenches now dug, alongside or across the road and the guns began to start in earnest, and you had to watch when crossing their line of fire that the shot didn't deafen you or the shock throw you. Flame and flare come out like a furnace blast. Off the track, all across the ground, were red, yellow or blue telephone wires lying loosely on the ground. You could see a few canvas screens stuck up in the waste – the latrines. Yet this wasteland was populated. In the dugouts were artillerymen, and in the trenches and dugouts were hundreds of men. On hot days they would sleep out in shade, in spite of shell risk – or take off their shirts and examine their brown naked bodies for the indestructible lice.

The guns now were visible all round, stretching roughly in triple lines behind sand-bagged emplacements without cover. When Fritz came over the guns seemed to go on shooting just the same, and there was the added 'woof-woof' of the anti-aircraft guns, which were invisible until then. At last I reached the red flag, under which was an entrance of some fifty steps to an old deep-galleried Fritz dugout. Candles guttered in the corners and bunks led off to right and left – then another flight of steps. Here was the signal office – a small oblong subterranean chamber where some four men sat at telephone or telegraph. They generally knew down here where the pigeon wallahs were to be found and would either shout them up to me or instruct me where to find them. If the men weren't there, I labelled the basket precisely with the date the pigeons left the loft and their ring numbers, and bracketed them if they were paired.

THURSDAY 4 AUGUST

Took a lot of birds to 6th Brigade HQ. Weather menaced a change, which I dreaded as my road would be impassable in wet weather and yet I had to get the birds there. The Lieutenant of Brigade – young, fair, unworried and keenly interested in the birds, asked for twelve more. The Anzac officers as a rule, as typified by him, talk to their men as men, don't ask for salutes or get them, but get equally good service. The men are more independent and not so much sucking up as with the Imperials.

Got home at 6.15 and was just drifting into billet watching the lovely pink sky when Vic caught me – and a pang of foreboding filled me. As it grew darker, the flashes would throw a faint lightning illumination in pulses over the sky and land. Word would come into the billet… 'Another stunt on tonight. They're going to have another try for Beaumont Hamel. Perhaps nothing would happen – postponed for a night.' Or at eleven the guns would break out in a thunderous roar. They would come in great rumbling waves of sound, two or three larger guns, one after the other, starting each wave. This seemed to go on all night. Usually I slept through it, but if it got extra heavy I would wake and hear the heavy roll and great muffled bursts. It seemed like an uneasy monster, turning in torture.

In the morning we would eagerly ask the despatch rider clerk or night-duty men what had happened and get various rumours in return – and sometimes the truth. 'A wash-out again,' ie, cancelled at the last minute, or 'Held up with heavy losses,' 'Taken Poziers Ridge but losses heavy.'

SATURDAY 5 AUGUST

We were having messages in about Hun concentrations at Le Moquet Farm, and 'enemy making observations from Courcelette church tower', which he used as an observation post. The messages used to come in in the clip, which the bird carried to the lofts on its leg, either at Warloy or Senlis. At Warloy, Searle with telephone, dictated the messages as they arrived – but he used to get too excited, and not being a good scholar, and the flimsies[12] being written faintly or indecipherably at times, he was in a stew reading them. Then, dictating over the phone is no bagatelle. Your instructions get mixed up with the message, and it takes quite a time to get messages through, important though they may be. The man at the other end is maddeningly cool, while at this end other pigeons may be coming in. So at last an expert telephonist who occupied his spare time in the cabin learning French was sent and all went well, the attendant pigeon man going to Corps on push-bike if message couldn't be read at Warloy.

Motor transport drivers had heard first-hand of the capture of Bapaume Ridge and Germans scooting. When I was up Sausage Valley there was an air of exhilaration, men sitting in cubby-holes scooped in the top side of trenches, showed me souvenirs captured that morning – they gave me captured German postcards to read out for their information, but the German handwriting was rather difficult. In evening sat on the green mound below the church then wandered back when Vic caught up with me on his bike.

'You've got to go up with another twelve birds. Sorry to bring bad news.'

At the sight of his questing figure, foreboding had filled me – riding up Sausage Valley at night when it got heavily shelled filled me with dread. Into the beauty of the pink sky and living dusk there crept some of that evil and horror which waits round the corner. 'Just my bloody luck. All right.'

Raced off to Warloy for the birds, bumping and crashing the bike in my eagerness, then back over the Albert road, which was dangerous with unlit traffic. Turned round into Division and in the office struck that plump, curly-haired auburn sergeant who looked anything but a soldier and radiated the cheerful insouciance that characterised the Antipodeans.

'Can we do anything for you? You're lucky – we've got an orderly just going down to the 6th Brigade on horseback. We'll fix that for you.' I dropped my basket as if the plague had slipped off me. Streaked out and in the yard I heard the clinking of horse chains in the dark as the orderly dismounted. 'I don't envy you, old boy,' I muttered, and rode off back, happy as a child going to the sea.

SUNDAY 6 AUGUST

This hot weather I used to feel strangled as I loaded up in the morning. First a haversack for extra tools and spare tube, containing also clips and perhaps message blocks – quite a weight. Then the gas helmet and the tin hat, the straps of which you fastened round your belt. The tin hat kept slipping round and chafing you and rattling – how we used to curse it, until it was needed. Now came the two strap-crossings which held your pigeon basket to your back. On top of the big square basket I used to carry two smaller ones, making 28 or more pigeons in all. You can imagine how trussed-up I felt.

Just as was retiring, heard in the street the tramp, tramp of soldiers coming up, their whistling and humming. Jokes and snatches of shout and conversation threaded up. They seemed cheery. Hopped over to the other side of the birdcage and saw below the glowing ends of their fags. The pathos of it all was almost unbearable. In the night their voices had the quality of another soul-striking world.

THURSDAY 10 AUGUST

Got the wind up about Bouzincourt being heavily shelled. Would they shell the sacred Corps? I understand that the man who yesterday had given me some jam he had scrounged at tea, has had his hand shot off while in his lorry.

Our lugubrious cook always looked at me reproachfully when I was the last in – the meat was getting cold and dried up. Always the same dinner – meat cooked up, the fat pared off to make thick gravy, new potatoes and no cabbage – sometimes bully – and rarely sweets, unless rice. We ate it in a makeshift erection of sailcloth and canvas in the old garden. In the heat of those days it was none too palatable. At supper bread and cheese were laid out – happy and enviable he who could scrounge an onion! That made the cheese delicious… or perhaps he could light on some pickles.

SATURDAY 12 AUGUST

During my first days here life had looked appalling in prospect. The months of autumn and winter stretched before me like the courts of Dartmoor Prison, and I wondered how I could manage to exist through the monotony and discomfort. Getting up and washing in six inches of slime with scarce water. Looking back, the life does not seem unpleasant, and I suppose, with familiarity and confidence and interest in pushing my work to success, the misery of it must have thinned like mist and gradually gained colour and warmth.

Prisoners frequently came past – almost uniformly they were haughty and supercilious, of fine and tall bearing and physique – but always pallid and often gaunt – caused I suppose by trench life in their perfect underground systems. They were imprisoned without brutality in the house opposite where a bayoneted sentry stood on guard.

Often these prisoners, one by one, were admitted for interrogation by an intelligence officer who sat in an arbour in the garden adjoining our birdcage. By stepping on a ledge and putting an ear to a big crevice in the plaster, one could hear fairly plainly what was said. Germans were treated by our officers with unvarying courtesy, while our own humble Tommies were treated as often as not with the most disgusting disdain and humiliating brusqueness. I think the II Corps must have had a record lot of shits, as we used to call them, for officers. I'll bet many a man would as soon have shot those appalling officers as any Fritz under the sun.

Mossel came in at 9.30 and said that he saw the military policeman at point duty at Bouzincourt blown up – and only his tunic came down – but just then some wild tales were circulating, and Mossel would have his swank. It later transpired that this actually happened.

SUNDAY 13 AUGUST

In the afternoon Lieutenant Larking showed his Military Cross which he gained for going up to the front line and laying temporary lines. One man with him was killed and one wounded. The boys at Corps said he was a daredevil, but others called him a fool, risking other men's lives needlessly. I felt he was fair, always laughing, rather weak-chinned, but he put the wind up me rather, because you never knew what he was going to do – or ask you to do. He used to get drunk and was unpopular with Major Evans and other prim officers on this account.

THURSDAY 17 AUGUST

As I was going out this morning via Millencourt, an officer at the side of a column marching towards me looked impassively in my direction and edged close to the troops. Just as I was on him, he turned his horse toward the gutter. I was doing about 18 mph with all my load of birds, but I hit his horse such a thud right on the chest with my head and shoulders… 'B— f— Hell!' I cried. 'What the bloody hell?' He said nothing – not even an apology as I gathered myself together.

FRIDAY 18 AUGUST

Sausage Valley impassable for the motor bike in the rains, so took the birds to Division on Tara Hill – quite a sinecure.

A light, battered but gentlemanly officer advanced towards me at Tara Hill. Across his chest were two rows of ribbons. 'What have you got there? he asked. 'These are the pigeons, sir. I'm taking them to Division.' 'A big load for you, corporal. Are they doing well?' 'I believe they're doing useful work, sir.'

I put my bike on the stand and walked off, leaving him gazing after me. He was General Birdwood, whom nearly every Anzac had abused to me – whom, the gushing daily papers said was so solicitous for his troops' welfare, that he used to visit them in the trenches and inspect their feet. In my presence those same soldiers gave a different version. They cursed him because they reckoned it was due to him and the papers' gushing about him that they always got pushed into hot fighting which, being human, they did not relish.

SATURDAY 19 AUGUST

Good news from the trenches – hundred of prisoners kept coming past the village with mounted guards. It's reported that Thiepval has been taken.

TUESDAY 21 AUGUST

Up with birds to Brigade, but on arriving at the bend of Sausage Valley saw a road empty of transport and vehicles and officers and men watching down it. Two brown spurts rose up, and then the shell-bursts came. An ambulance, then two general supplies wagons with Anzacs on came crashing through between bursts. My road was being shelled. Should I walk or ride? Waited, and when the intervals lengthened I dashed through, riding with such trembling and haste as I had never ridden before. Rather quiveringly put out my birds and labelled them for brigades with the tabs I carried, and attached clips. Then down in dugout to rest my nerves and wait so that lull in shelling should certify itself as genuine.

Here the sheltering Aussies, probably spotting that I was green, enlivened the atmosphere with gruesome yarns, referring to one boot less to clean when their officer's leg was shot off. It was certainly warm[13] round here. I dashed back over the damp earth thrown up by the shells, where holes, about four yards wide were still smoking and chemically odorous.

WEDNESDAY 24 AUGUST

Usual trip up – but the shelling had ceased. Afternoon, in warm sun, got a bath in an old biscuit tin behind the canvas in the garden – the first since I left base a month ago.

Going towards the office to see Lieutenant Larking, was met by a very young, debonair officer in champagne drill khaki. Altogether the picture of gilded patrician youth. 'Here's our pigeon despatch rider, isn't it?' 'Yes sir.' 'We want you to take birds from a loft at Lavieville – work it with your other lofts and you can rest them a little. Start tomorrow morning.' 'Where is the loft, sir?' 'I don't know – but you'll find it.' I saluted and turned away, feeling a fool for not asking more questions.

I went to see Searle. 'Do you know of a loft at Lavieville?' 'I do know of one – it's in a farm. Why?' 'An officer at the Corps said I was to take birds from there in the morning.' 'Ah,' said Searle, with profound gratitude. 'Warloy's going to have a rest. This loft's worked harder than any. It's against reason. At last they're coming to their senses. That'll be Captain Mudge – he came round yesterday.'

That evening I rode to Lavieville and struck the farm and got the pigeon corporal in charge of the loft, which was in a gabled roof over the farm out-buildings. He was a hard-bitten, obstinate northerner. 'You don't get birds from me,' he said at once. 'I've had no instructions to that effect, and I never do anything without an order from my boss. This isn't the only loft here, you know. There's a mobile one out in the fields – Dixon's in charge of it.' 'This pigeon game is some game,' I remarked. 'Every loft I strike I see you chaps reclining in the kitchen, drinking coffee or reading – what a life.' 'I'd exchange it for yours any time. How would you like to be in the same place always, never move, no change – daren't leave for fear of old Alec…' 'Who's old Alec?' 'Don't know Alec? How long have you been a pigeon DR?' 'A month.' 'Don't worry. You'll know him too soon for your liking.' 'So long.' I gave an envying glance into the cosy interior of the farm kitchen where the aroma of cooking viands tickled my chaste nostrils.

Out on the road from Lavieville over open tilled fields, and saw massed mobile loft, which lay in a clearing with posts and cables making a fence – an old motor bus whose top had been converted into a cote. The signals man was calm with strong profile and he listened to my yarn.

'If your corps is to take us over, that's the first I've heard. However, if you bring written instructions I should think it would be all right. We've been resting and about fifty of the birds could do with a trip. I can let you have about twenty a day if they come back well. This is my mate Harry.'

A dark-moustached Londoner came from the interior of the bus and smiled amiably. Not often a pigeon man volunteers he can spare the birds you want. 'I shall get on with this bloke,' I thought.

Went to Contay and reported. Captain Mudge told me he would fix up about the loft and I could start working it this afternoon to give the others a rest.

SATURDAY 26 AUGUST

Sausage Valley this morning was turned to the slipperiness of ice by a shower. The slopes of chalk got just wet and were unrideable – scarcely walkable. Was struggling with the bike when I noticed the ominous watching of the road by soldiers nearby and the dashing through of transport. Sodden bike began to heel over and curvet and a prancing steed got in my way. Just then shells began to fall on the ridge immediately in front and right and left. Small panic with me. Got off bike and then couldn't stand on the wet chalk with her weight to hold up. Couldn't get her up or fix her on the stand – or even get a flat place.

At last managed it and looked round for a dugout. On the left a man beckoned and I went into a dugout about six feet deep. Two tin-hatted RGA men inside – one an MP. As he went up the steps and looked out, bits of shell went swooshing through the air and struck the sides of the dugout. After twenty minutes it ceased and I walked along the light railway track to Brigade.

In the afternoon, of a sudden, heavy German firing had broken out and over Thiepval round which our men had just taken trenches, the bursting of shell and shrapnel was so thick the flashes looked like bright flying fish in shoals leaping and turning in the air. Above was a dark blue-grey, rain-threatening sky. What a plight those men were in, holding on under that bombardment. Why should they – how could they – stick it? My lot seemed a prince's to theirs.

THURSDAY 31 AUGUST

Arrived at Lavieville this morning, where Vic was now installed at the mobile, and here he was to be seen most of the day turning over magazines and sleeping.

'You've got to go up to Ypres,' shouted Vic. Again, foreboding tugged at my heartstrings. Again I was to be singled out by Fate from my fellow DRs for the sinister task. 'But you'll have a motor car to do the work in,' said a new corporal, who, it appeared from his leggings and posh black artillery boots, poncho with signal band painted on right and left sleeves was a DR.

'What's all this about?' I asked, taking off my basket. There had, however, been rumours of our moving – but there always are. 'We're taking over from you,' said the newcomer. 'Corporal Davis, Corporal Smith,' Dixon introduced us. 'You don't believe in the motor car, then.' 'Certainly not,' I said. 'There's one on the army establishment for use of corps training birds, and I always had the car from Second Army. Doesn't your sergeant let you have it?' 'I've only seen him once. A swarthy chap named Boilard. Supercilious sod, he looked. Came in at Warloy and made some clever remarks about nothing then buggered off.' 'You should scotch him. I've heard about him from the Scots Guards' HQ's pigeon sergeant. Somebody's son who had to be found a job is Boilard. Well, up there it's different.' 'I suppose it's hot there?' 'You see a bit of life, of course. What's it like here?' 'At first it was rotten, but I've got used to it. I'm not keen on changing it for Ypres.'

Meanwhile the pioneer had been eyeing my baskets. 'Are you going to carry that load?' asked Smith. 'I've done so every day for a month or more.' 'They've got you for some guy. You won't find me doing it.' Swank, I thought – and went on strapping on my cumbrous load. 'I'll come on the ride over with you,' he said. 'My boss asked me to take over.' 'I'm only going to Division today as roads are too bad in Sausage Valley – will you have a look at the Division?'

We circled and skidded off the slimy field path and ran down Division after stopping in Albert, where he said, 'You've got a nerve.' 'How?' 'Two or three times you passed lorries on mud where I wouldn't take them.' 'Well, I'm no rider, I consider, I didn't know I was doing anything.' 'You can do it once too often and I'm getting on in years. You're not a particularly good rider, but you take risks.'

I was secretly elated. What, I, who had always thought myself timid and on the edge of cowardice – did I really take risks? Risks that intrigued the veteran Smith?

FRIDAY 1 SEPTEMBER

I took Smith to Brigades. On the brow of Sausage Valley we had to leave the bikes, as Smith's – a Douglas – soon got choked up with mud under the mud-guards and round the gearbox and pulley. We tramped down the tracks, skirting the shell-holes. Light railway tracks kept veering off over the lumber-strewn wastes of chalk and clay. Bully tins, ribbed box respirator tubing and gas helmets, countless heaps of cartridges thrown away, dud shells, brass shell casings, jam and biscuit tins dotted the drear valley – the very hell of colourless untidiness.

'Christ!' yelled Smith. A 9.2 gun across whose purview we were just walking, had fired and blown his cap off. He seemed quite upset. 'Let's get out of the line of those guns,' he said, walking left. If he found it so upsetting merely to have our own guns going off on top of him, he can't be used to such dreadful things, I reflected. Perhaps it wasn't so dusty up there.

'This place is absolutely plastered with guns,' he said. 'God, look at the demons! The emplacements go back like seats in a theatre.' 'We send over eight to every one of his.' You could indeed count this proportion as his and our shells sailed overhead, slitting the air like swimmers on a summer pool.

On the way back, he shouldering an empty stock basket, was grousing and aghast. 'Be conscientious – but you've been shit on. You must have a rotten officer to let you be put upon. Not for me, though, thank you. My officer is a gentleman, and looks after me. You won't see me going past Division. I shall send in a report and soon alter all this.'

'I didn't come out to exactly pick and choose,' I said. 'War is different from civvy life.' 'Maybe,' he said, but there's reason. The system's bad. Now, how I managed it. I had depots – one at Dickebusch, one in the Ramparts. We call them refilling points. There's a big aviary at each place – a cage of wood and wire net, and a couple of men in charge at both places. They take the birds from me and hand them over to the Brigade men and make it officially the refilling place for picking up incoming and outgoing birds. Jack Hilton was at the Ramparts, and at Dickebusch I got two men. I'll give you all particulars, but I don't expect the Canadians will let you keep the men.'

'I shall start the same system down here. Report to my officer and he'll take my word. He's a decent sort. Not for me, my boy, anything past division here.'

SATURDAY 2 SEPTEMBER

At dinner Lieutenant Larking came to Lilley with orders for me to pack and report to him immediately. Both my wheels were out, but Pip helped me while I cursed at my hellish luck, as I was looking forward to moving up with Pip and the boys. Larking told me to report to Lieutenant Bingham at Abeele for instructions – nothing further. Complete wind up me. The boys of II Corps had already said, 'Abeele. Mont Noir – oh, camping out in the ground on top of a pimple. Abeele is just a village.' Sorrow. 'Ypres Ramparts touch for you, sir. Flowers will not be sent, by request.'

Got to Abeele at 9.30 and reported to Mr Bingham, but while waiting met Bill Pritchard, who said, 'Bingham is a shit. Come and sleep with us.' Bingham – small, patrician – was kindly worded, showing me on the map where to go – to Pop. I over to Bill. 'He's a shit. Do you meant to say he asks you to report there tonight, after travelling all that way. Bollocks. Take no notice. Tell him your cousin Paul's here and you want to see him.' Mr Bingham grudgingly gave me permission, as long as I was away by 6.30 next morning.

SUNDAY 3 SEPTEMBER

Rose at 5.30 and found the Canadian Corps DRs packing kit on bikes with Bill telling me I was a fool to get up. Don't-care-ness was the chief note.

Along the broad tree-lined road, with wooden huts across the ditch in places, and detached brick farms and houses here and there, past various en-campments and into Poperinghe. The road curved then into a gaunt square at the left end of which rose a vast, fire-brick coloured building – the town hall. A bit further a small placard, 'To Ypres, 11 km'.

At last found a very dingy house with a foul torn lace curtain across its windows, before which a smoky signals flag sulked. In the office, sleepy, they directed me to the hut behind, in the fields, where Seabourne, Davies and Lewis were still asleep when I called at 7.30.

A pleasant, smiling Welshman with pale face and black eyes invited me to have breakfast in their hut, and by the time I'd eaten it, Davies was up, genial and nice, and Seabourne and Lewis gruff.

'Who is the fellow – pale chap but good looking – who gave me break-fast?' 'That's Roberts. You'll have to watch him.' 'Is that the Roberts that Smith warned me against? Good Lord, he looks pleasant enough.' 'Yes, at first. He wants everybody under his thumb. He'll have a go at you. Stick to this hut. It was built by Smith and belongs to the pigeon men on duty here. Did he tell you?' 'Yes and he said Roberts would try to pinch it and boss me.'

Davies took me to Debyses Loft, an untidy cottage down a lane where the front room was occupied by a large family. Stout Mrs Debyses, young toothy daughter and kid and Belgian husband and son, and the back room was occu-pied by a shoe-maker, while the other side room housed Corporal Couper and his two mates.

Walking to the other loft met a man, like a village idiot, being led by the arm. A few shells were falling and he was suffering from shellshock – a kind of hysterical paralysis. Loft was a fine big house, unfortunately marred by a couple of shell-holes in the side. Over magnificent kitchens was a modern loft with tiled walls, perch and cage, built specially with partitions and sliding windows. We saw Cassier's Loft, but Vandevoorde's was closed, but by now I was getting mixed up as to the location of the three lofts.

To Ypres along the Vlamertinghe road, tree-arcaded, there was normal life, and fields were gold or green, though dust-laden and wearied. But at Vlamertinghe, which at first I thought was Ypres itself, desolation ruled. On the right a white mill was used as a dressing station, then some decayed houses, shrapnel-hit and gutted, and the great drear church in ruins.

As we approached Ypres, the fields were green – so different from the Somme battlefield. But now we were well in the shelled area. Farms in the fields were sunken as if shrinking in fear – like huge wicker baskets, so riddled were they with shells. By the railway crossing a château stood uninjured. 'They say that's a spy's place,' said Davies. 'It's always remained unhit.'

Across the road lay bits of branches hit down from the trees by shells. The road was now empty and inexpressibly drear. 'A dull day, so there'll be no balloon up – else on a fine day Fritz can see you in the square, and you're not supposed to cross it.' It was like a plague city. We rode over another set of rails and then I was too busy dodging bricks and shell-holes to notice much except that we halted on the edge of a vast desolate, uninhabited square with tall shattered buildings lying back from it.

'This way,' said Davies, without fear. 'He's been shelling, or it wouldn't be so empty.' We slid across the square and down a narrow road and came to a high embankment with dugouts, fractured trees and smashed buildings atop. This was the Ramparts. A gap in it, continuing the road by which we entered, was the Menin Gate.

At the Ramparts we came in at a sand-bagged gate, climbed a ladder and emerged on a low, dark chamber, arched like a railway tunnel. A big aviary of wire netting and scrounged wood largely filled this vault. Inside the aviary, cleaning it, was a small sturdy man of over fifty, with black leggings over khaki trousers and a grease-stained cap. He came out, his movements brisk and his eyes sparkling. He was introduced to me as Jack Hilton – I was introduced as the DR taking over. 'Carry on just the same, Corporal?' he asked Davies. 'Yes, but I've got no instructions yet. Suppose it'll be all right.'

'Corporal Couper at Debyses loft arranges which birds are to go up, which lot you take. You just call at Debyses with the car for them. I should take the same as we've been taking – only every other day at present. It's tomorrow they go and we've taken none today.' 'I can see our corps keeping that car on, I don't think! Too bloody mean. On the Somme everybody said the major was trying to run our corps signals as cheaply as possible. That's how they got promotion.' 'Ah, but it's an army car – nothing to do with corps. The Second Army treats you like a gentleman. If the Fifth Army is going to do the dirty on us down there, we shall kick. The corps has a right to the army car for training and other purposes. You must have had a rotten army sergeant.'

We wound out by the station, which was a rank, grass and weed-grown space, a forlorn façade with a few portions of portal and platform, and numerous twisted lines and uptorn lengths of track.

The paving before the station showed curious dents, as if a giant heel had tried with hobnail boots to strike sparks and kicked a hole.

Leaving, we came to a couple of sand-bagged dugouts at a crossroads, wound on a little farther and stopped our Triumphs by an estaminet, which looked like the last drinking-house before you entered hell. A dark, low house with a room each side of the door, with paper stuffed in the broken windows and one shutter up.

'That's Dickebusch– your bird loft,' said Davies, pointing to a building across the fields. 'And that's our second aviary and filling point at the top of that third field. It's called CYAR – there's a signals office report centre there – CYAR means 1st Canadian Report Centre.'

'But couldn't the men from the line call here for their birds just as well at this loft as at that aviary? It's only a few fields away.' 'Well, you might get the two lots of birds mixed, and Smith wanted to find a job for those two men – something cushy – so he fixed that arrangement up.'

Going over duckboards we came to the loft – an abandoned house, the gabled second storey of which had been roughly made into a large pigeon loft. Through a door and down three stone steps was a large cellar fitted with beds, equipment and a cooking stove.

'Corporal Evans – Corporal Davis, Anzac Corps pigeon DR. They're taking over.'

Corporal Evans desisted from smacking the punching ball which hung from the ceiling. 'I hope he'll get me some new clobber and we shall be friends. Look at these bloody breeches. The bloody army keeps you like a pauper. My boots aren't fit for a rat. I want a 152 book and some more clips and 418 books.' 'Smith gave me a list showing a lot of equipment at the various lofts,' I ventured mildly. 'There may be some at the aviary – they're not here. The men have left there, so I suppose you'll be bringing the birds here. 'I expect so,' said Davies, 'for the present'.

We went to the aviary over the fields and brought the 418 pigeon message books to Corporal Evans and asked him to fetch the few basket there.

There was now another man there – plump, well-groomed with the bloom of a careful toilet on his face. He wore an expensive wool cardigan, costly riding breeches and golf hose with well-cut tan boots. 'Get me a pair of breeches too.' He lounged luxuriously, smoking on the bed.

I thought of myself, toiling up and down Sausage Valley every day, loaded and wringing wet with sweat – of my meals on the ground and my bed on the lice-rotten, rat-smelling floor of the Senlis birdcage. I looked at this plump fat, manicured, wheezing beau with all the good things of army life, and as I entered in my book the details of what was required, I certainly did not put down two pairs of breeches.

Back at Poperinghe, Davies showed me how he entered, via the books at Hilton's and Evans', all the birds to each brigade that took them. If the birds didn't turn up at the allotted time, he rang the brigades to find out why. This seemed rather a bold proceeding for a corporal. 'We've a telephone here in our hut – that's one of the reasons why you've to keep in with Roberts and the signal office – they'll cut you off or ignore.' 'But how do I know where the brigades are?' 'Ring through to Division. You'll soon find which division is in the line and what their brigades are. Ask for code number of the brigade – it'll be P 20 or like that. Strafe them if the birds haven't come back and say you'll report it to OC pigeons of your Corps.

'I don't see myself shining in the role of strafing Brigade signals officers. I shall lie low a bit.' 'Well, they've only a pip or two up – it'll probably be the signal sergeant. If they find you're not looking them up they'll let things slide – it'll be napoo pigeons in the lofts.'

'They instructed us at home that only officers sent wires.' 'You'll soon be sending 'em. Just walk into the office and hand them the telegram.'

We spun down the road towards Abeele. A little footbridge by an ASC station, crossed the road ditch to a small wooden house-cum-shop with a balcony. Davies went in. 'Hello Madeleine. Bonjour Marguerite.'

Madeleine, upright, firm-fleshed, fair to auburn pigtails and colouring, smiled.'Good afternoon Sam.' Marguerite was dark, suave-featured, soft-bosomed. Both girls were flawlessly dressed, as clean as pinks, and perched as daintily as birds in the scrupulously clean hut. A stove burnished like silver glowed, and by it sat the young mother with a sturdy imp on her lap. 'Go to church, Madeleine? I did.' asked Sam. 'I don't think,' said Madeleine quaintly. 'We did. We always go at six o'clock.' 'To pray for your sins and show that new blouse, eh? How they dress up in Abeele for church. Was it the same before the war? I guess not.'

'I'm going away. Will you write me, Madeleine?' 'In French, yes.' 'French'll do if you'll put the English crosses at the end… compris?' 'Bad boy. I shall see.

You will not write – too many fiancées you shall have there – no time to write.'
'Good-bye mother. Au revoir Marguerite.' And we rode away.

MONDAY 4 SEPTEMBER

I fervently hoped Davies would stay another day to go the rounds with me carrying the birds, but he had to go down to the Somme. 'You should be all right – the car wasn't running last time, it went into the workshop for repairs. If it doesn't come you'll have two runs up the line.' 'That's done it. My luck all over – no car for me,' I muttered as I stamped up and down in front of the signals office. However, out of the cars and lorries that kept whirling by, our corps box-car emerged and pulled up.

Our DR sergeant, Bruce, was in with the sergeant major and, with ostentatious magnanimity, invited me to land the pigeons in the car instead of carrying them on my back. As we rode into Ypres, sergeant major said, 'By God, when we were here we used to get cakes, coffee and champagne there – it was a café. The civvies were here and you could get fine dinners.' Bruce and the SM strolled about the Ramparts while I delivered the birds. Then back to Pop and then another run up to Kruisstraat, where Bruce again took all the particulars I had already booked to 'report to Mr Larking', in pseudo-business-like fashion. Birds coming back to this loft had their messages transmitted from the signal office in the trench dugouts at the rear of the loft. These were just elephant dugouts (curved pieces of corrugated iron on a wooden floor).

TUESDAY 5 SEPTEMBER

Free, so visited the lofts. The third loft was Cassier's, which had contained some of the finest racing birds in Belgium. In the Boeschepe street on the wall of a tall house was a black tablet, 'M Cassier. Notaire'. Up the passage behind the church you could pass through a dismantled jeweller's workshop until you came to a beautiful garden blooming with roses. Over the workshop was a tiled loft with pigeon trap on the roof.

The other loft, Vandevoorde's, was near the square, three storeys up over a leather and fancy goods shop, which was run by the wife of the proprietor, he himself having the wind up too much to come back to Pop.

Gradually began to find Pop enjoyable, though the streets emptied when the shelling started – but this happened only about twice a week.

WEDNESDAY 6 SEPTEMBER

Woke feeling Lewis was gauging me. He was one of those deliberate and reticent personalities who make you feel small, and as he moved about in god-like, strong and silent guise, monopolising most of the room, I wished my own bearing was more impressive.

Larking came rolling over the field to the huts and drove the car round. I had all the details at my fingertips, picking up the birds at the various loft and tossing them out at spots between Pop and Ypres. Larking drove like the devil. We lurched over the rails by Ypres, then at parting I made a stuttering ass of myself. 'Suppose anything goes wrong, sir?' 'Oh, it won't go wrong,' said Larking, and sailed away.

At the hut they told me there was a DR waiting for me. Across the fields in a poncho and leggings came a tall youth, ruddy and handsome with a black moustache. 'Ma back's just broken with riding. I can't bide this pave – ma guts is hanging loose in me. Jolt, jolt – ma head's clappin' like a bell. Ma bike's sitting in the road, but she'll sit there until I've had a rest.' He handed me a note: 'Corporal Caseby is our new pigeon DR. You will instruct him in his duties and generally look after him. Ronald G Larking, RE.'

I had feared our corps were going to change the good system we had in pigeon work, and I dreaded things being made more onerous, risky and laborious for me. Caseby coming up promised well, although Larking had spoken as if the car was just a one-day favour. Only those who have humped 32 pigeons and three baskets on their back, as well as equipment and tools, can imagine what a relief it was to be able to use a car instead of a bike.

FRIDAY 8 SEPTEMBER

Rode off with Caseby, who groused tremendously at our loads. Coming back from Ypres we met Lieutenant Larking and he stopped and asked if we could manage, as there might be difficulty in getting the army car. 'We can manage, sir,' I said, my heart sinking. 'How's the other DR getting on?' 'How are you getting on, Caseby?' I called. C came up grinning all over. 'A bit heavy for ma back, sir. Only used to carry eight. Rough on the mickies.' It is a bit of a stunt,' I said. In the car were the training crates, so I said, 'What about training the birds without the car, sir?' 'They'll have to go only every four days.' 'Very good, sir.' Larking drove off. 'Why didn't you crack on what a terrible time we're having?' remonstrated Caseby. 'Why didn't you? You're the one who objects to it. I don't like it, but it might be worse, and I've no genuine complaint. You had your chance and you only joked.' 'It's not ma job, it's up to you.'

MONDAY 11 SEPTEMBER

Caseby: 'Breakfast's never ready at Dupont's and the bacon's cold. I can't bear cold bacon. Why not mess down here – we've only got to slip out of bed into the mess.' 'It's awkward for a bit I know, but we've got no orderlies up yet and no-one to cook properly. Smith told me the best plan was to run a mess on our own. If we get in with Roberts we'll be under his thumb for rations – I'll have to get our rations for our lofts through him, and we'd get all the rind and the end scrapings. I'm not going to be run by Roberts.' 'What's the matter with the man? He's always very pleasant with me. I like him.' 'Do as you like. I'm going to run a mess down there.' 'I'm going to make myself some breakfast in our hut this morning.'

Soon after, Roberts came by and looked in at our hut. 'Sleeping room and cookhouse all in one, eh? Not very healthy, that, is it?' I didn't reply. 'Who's the senior of you two?' 'Caseby is by army service.' 'Caseby, you're in charge of the hut, then. See it's clean.' Caseby blinked, and when Roberts had gone, 'Sod him. Who's he – a Taffy and a corporal, to talk to me like that? We're no soldiers, Davis, we're just despatch riders. They take no notice of our stripes – any old sweat thinks he can talk to a DR. I was in the army before him, I'll warrant, and I'll show him I'm as much a corporal RE as he is.'

We fetched birds from the mobile loft at Abeele, from Trewatha and Roberts, who was the driver of the bus loft – a flaccid-faced, broad, generous young cockney – incurably lazy and wasteful. His eyes appeared glazed and sleepy like a dove's. His invariable salutation was, 'I haven't had those socks and boots yet, Davis.' 'Look here, my boy, why can't you get your socks mended – or mend them yourself. I always mend mine and I don't see that you should mind doing what I do.' 'I never wore a pair of mended socks in my life, and I'm damned sure I'm not going to do it for the army. What have they done for me? Stuck here all day in one spot – no bloody leave, no bloody clothes. Sod them.' 'By God, Roberts, I should think you want something to grumble at. How would you like our job, up the line every day?' 'The best job in the army,' said Trewatha. 'I'd give everything for a bit of change – the monotony of being penned up with these lofts. I daren't leave it. If old Alec came up and found me away, he'd strip me.' 'I'll admit I like my job,' I said. 'Anyhow, up here Mr Larking is letting me run the job on my own and I like being relied on.'

TUESDAY 12 SEPTEMBER

Took the birds up to Ypres in the car with Galligan. He said to me, 'I'm glad you stuck out against Roberts, young man. Don't you mess with him – it's a rotten mess. He tries to run it all on his own, and if you dare to disagree with him, he puts you on a fatigue. He's got everybody under his thumb there. It's a cushy job down there at Pop, and if they cross him they're afraid he'll report them and they may get shifted up to Brigade or Battalion. I never speak to that rat.'

THURSDAY 13 SEPTEMBER

I'd mentioned to Lieutenant Larking that Smith used to take classes up here, and I thought it would be a good stunt for me and also help the service. As the car moved off he said, 'Our men don't want training. They've been trained.' So judge of my surprise when I was called out to the road by signals office and he said, 'I'm sending you thirty men for pigeon instruction on Saturday. You must arrange billets. Christie will send you 90 rations down. Ta ta.' He rode off, leaving me dumbfounded.

Behind Cassier's loft was a big empty house, and I saw the town major's sergeant and fixed up to bed the men there. I then sorted out a scheme of instruction.

FRIDAY 15 SEPTEMBER

My plan for our own mess, persevered in the face of much opposition, crowned with success. Finished arrangements for instructing men – now increased to 42.

SATURDAY 16 SEPTEMBER

The men arrived on the lorry at 10.30 for instruction. Lorry to Cassier's and showed the men their quarters. Lectured until four in the great, empty gloomy chambers of the abandoned house.

SUNDAY 17 SEPTEMBER

This morning, strange to say, Corporal Roberts, having some clothes left over from his indent for his lot, offered me a tunic and boots, which I accepted gratefully, despite the unpleasant terms on which we had hitherto existed together. Perhaps he saw it was no go with me – or wanted to spite some of his own men.

TUESDAY 19 SEPTEMBER

Questions and repetition on the course, then in the afternoon went over the written answers – the work done keenly by the men. At 4.30 Lieutenant Larking telegraphed – another thirty men coming tomorrow.

WEDNESDAY 20 SEPTEMBER

Met Lieutenant Larking at Reninghelst, where the Anzac division in the line had taken over. The loft was at a *boulangerie* by the Croix Rouge.

Going away, Mr Larking admitted, 'You've made a good fist of this pigeon business.' That was the first phrase of recognition I'd had, and it did me good. I got on smoothly with him for the first time.

FRIDAY 22 SEPTEMBER

We had now got Anzac orderly duly installed, and with us for cook I had Jim Murray, a dark, sunburnt Ozzie who always wore his sombrero and looked at you from beneath its shadow, smiling broadly when you chipped him, and made you think of the saying, 'Of these shall be the Kingdom of Heaven'.

There was a noise like sheet iron being rolled in a mill and Tom, in command of the loft, said, 'They're shellin' quite close.' He went a shade whiter and his eyes enlarged. We went outside and saw a great column of bricks shoot up from Boeschepe road at the end of our garden. 'Must have a decco at this,' said Jim, stuffing his pipe and going down towards the last burst. I didn't wait but got off on my bike back to signal office as soon as I could. People were out at doorways or rapidly putting up their shutters. Two shells hit houses just behind me after I had passed.

At the signal office I met Sergeant Edmonds, Second Army pigeon sergeant. 'He's shelling the Cassel Road – we'll pick up birds from Couper's and try the Reninghelst Road.'

We had just got down to the shell-broken cemetery wall with our load when a great brown wall shot out in front of us. The driver jammed on his brake and stopped. Simultaneously with a horrid bang, glass and metal tinkled copiously on to the road before us and the car shook. A shell had taken one of the houses on the right, twenty yards away. Brick dust and fumes hung densely in the air while we backed up and waited, and then took the debris-covered road at a rush. However, after waiting a few minutes, some of the civvies about didn't make any bones about going in and looking round. I don't think anyone was killed and the house must have been unoccupied. In the car we thought it a wonderful escape and felt rather bucked at having run some real danger.

SUNDAY 25 SEPTEMBER

By afternoon finished my fourth school group, and went to the pictures in the evening. Chaplin consummate.

MONDAY 26 SEPTEMBER

Very often it was dead of night when the men were warned to come down the line to the school. It was a holiday for them to come down the line and they enjoyed same keenly.

TUESDAY 26 SEPTEMBER

Went on the round and saw the pigeon men. The car used to call at Vlamertinghe at the château gateway and not infrequently Fritz had just finished planting a few in the field in front of the doorway. In a shack of wood and galvanised iron, furred with sandbags, dwelt Sam Booth and Woolstenholme. Sam was sturdy and straight, and of broad Yorkshire speech. Woolstey was pale, pimply, and dark-eyed with glasses, and he looked as if he had just rolled out of bed into his gumboots.

The loft was a gimcrack affair built by the trees in the château grounds – one of the nearest fixed lofts to the line. By long practice, Woolstey had perfected his system. He went up with his birds ready and labelled for brigade in small baskets. At shattered Brielen, in a house whose windows and roof had been blown in, there was a sort of signal office, where the signallers slept, read, shaved and appeared to be in a continual state of half-dress. Here Woolstey met an elderly taffy, who without a word took the fresh birds, transferring them deftly from basket to basket, a black pipe permanently rooted in his mouth. At the close, he shambled off down the Essex lines towards the canal bank, quite happy in that he had a cushier job than his fellow-infantrymen. The pigeon wallah's job at this time was reckoned to be 'cush' and there was much competition for it.

As Woolstey and I came into Ypres we used to hold our breath a little when we saw a fresh part of the road battered about, and we coaxed the car over a new shell-hole towards the Ramparts. I used to envy the nonchalance and skill with which Woolstey flung his pigeons down, took up the empty baskets, muttered a few words and was finished, while I had to arrange about various stores, returns, clips, clothes, etc. 'How is it you never have any trouble of this kind?' I asked Woolstey. 'You want it here,' he said, screwing his finger against his temple. 'I let them indent for all they want through the usual channels. It goes up by brigade transport, and then it's not my fault if they don't get it. Why should I bother my arse about it? I don't do any more for the army than I can help – they think no better of you.'

A few shells would whiz or go sleekly through the air above our heads as we stood. Sometimes they would hiss so near as to make us duck, and we'd see heads cautiously gauging the situation from the low, narrow entries to the big dugouts under the Ramparts. Old Jack Hilton disdained to duck or to carry a tin hat unless shells were actually being dropped on the road on which he stood. Ever cheery and calm, he inspired courage.

SATURDAY 29 SEPTEMBER

Had lent a blanket to an old Anzac and got it back lice-ridden. Lice on me of a ferocious kind, which put the wind up me. Soaked the blanket and every stitch of clothing I possessed in petrol until the hut stank and my flesh smarted all over, and a rash started on my elbow and armpit. Went to see the Anzac MO at the field dressing station. Very old orderly cleansed my skin with ether and gave me zinc ointment for the rash. With the horrible fears bred in one by lack of privacy in the army and fear of syphilis infection, I said, 'I suppose I'm all right, doctor?' 'Well, I don't know what's under your foreskin. When were you last with a woman?' 'I've never been with a woman…' He looked as if he didn't believe me.

TUESDAY 3 OCTOBER

In the evening went to the pictures. We used to say, after the labours of the day at tea (bread and margarine with jam and perhaps sardines), 'Well, who's coming to the pictures with me?' Tom and Jim Murray and I would go and queue patiently for half an hour.

Sim Coope had arrived, north-country, splay-footed, pale and flabby of face, going bald and with nervous mannerisms of speech as if absent-mindedly lost. When he first came he addressed me as 'Sir' when I took his particulars and installed him at Cassier's loft. He was one of the most conscientious loftmen, and like all such men in the army, got into trouble early.

The famous Alec came round and Sim happened to be standing in the passage of the school billet instead of in the garden or loft. 'Why aren't you watching your loft while it's working?' 'I am, sir. I can see the trap from here without scaring the birds – I'm still rather new to them.' 'They don't know you by this time? Now, my man, if I ever come round here and find you not in the loft or watching on the spot here while your loft's working, I'll have you court-martialled.' Collapse of Sim with wind up.

After a morning of shells, tales of the time in 1915 of Pop's day of horror, when the streets 'swam with blood' and the telephonist in Dupont's loft was blown against the wall and killed. The safe was blown open and the contents scattered – nothing was ever found officially afterwards. Other telephonist who had just risen to answer a call was saved. The slain man was due for leave.

FRIDAY 6 OCTOBER

Yells of delight in the camp because Superintendent Roberts was under open arrest. He very unpopular because he had our cook there arrested and put in the town hall for being drunk and the boy was crimed and sent away. I couldn't believe my ears that such a piece of poetical justice had overtaken a man in our army, so compact of jobbery, injustice and crookery.

It happened through him being so cocksure and swollen-headed. The captain of the Intelligence complained that he hadn't been able to get through to Pop Signal Office. Roberts said it wasn't our line, which was all right. To prove this he told the men on duty to ring every half hour for 24 hours. Naturally Captain Hall wanted to know what he meant by it. Said it was insolence and he'd report him. Now came Roberts' big mistake. Next day he rang up the Signals, perfectly in order, and said that Captain Hall's complaint that he had rung their operator up at night was untrue. 'How did you know that Captain Hall was making any such complaint?' asked the signalmaster. 'As superintendent of a signal office one gets to know.' 'You mean you were overlistening on the phone? There is no other way. Consider yourself under open arrest.'

Corporal Clift came, handsome, mild, fresh-looking, about 45 – an old regular with SA Medal – the first old sweat I have met out here who was decent.

SATURDAY 7 OCTOBER

Took birds myself and arranged with Jack Hilton to have the names of not only the brigades but also battalions to which ring numbers of birds were sent. This was in case a bird came back without message stating who had liberated him. Then we knew where he came from. Each day I handed my officer a list of the birds and where they went to, so that if a message came in, they had only to refer to his ring number on the message and to my report to find who was sending the message. As soon as I brought birds up to the Ramparts, they were let out in the aviary, and then had to be caught again when the men from brigades came for them. If Jack had to catch certain numbers for certain battalions, it would mean he would have to go through the aviary handling the birds several times, which would not do their plumage any good. So he used to issue a dozen or so birds, take their numbers and give me a copy of that allocation.

SUNDAY 8 OCTOBER

Went up again with birds to see that the new distribution was going all right. Had tea with Pip in the San Martin – Adrienne, Julie and Hélène there. In the kitchen, with a Belgian soldier – a cousin – we were quite one of the family, with the two scented, rumple-mouthed sisters, the old mother and the fine, erect, strong young girl in black from the convent school who liked to be there. The trade done in the shop at 66 was enormous, as soldiers resting back at Abeele bought silk aprons, squares, handkerchiefs and all sorts of souvenirs, cigars, books, cigarette cases – there were half a dozen other shops like this, all with a big turnover.

TUESDAY 10 OCTOBER

Received telegram: 'Evans at Kruisstraat loft ill. Caseby to go out in charge of loft'. Indecision. To be efficient wished to send Caseby at once, but didn't want to do the dirty on him, especially as he was an older corporal by service. Left it, my slumber at first invaded by speculation.

Caseby never took any responsibility and never volunteered to help. He grinned because I had to accept responsibility – and at the same time he knew that our etiquette as DRs, who were opposed to the discipline of the ordinary army, forbade my taking advantage of my seniority on this job to order him about. He sheltered behind this and just grinned lazily, throwing it all on me.

'Why should I go tonight? One man can manage there. I shall do nothing when I get there. There's a mass of stuff I'll have to shift. What does it matter? The pigeon service is a farce anyway. It's all a joke.' 'You'll have to go if it's necessary.' 'My bike's US and they've sent no car. I can't walk there. How am I going to get there?' He knew he was annoying me.

SATURDAY 14 OCTOBER

Met Lieutenant Larking as I was going to Corps to see him, and after my report he said, 'I've been very pleased with the way you've done things here. I told Captain Waley that you'd been running the service practically on your own. I've recommended you for a sergeant as soon as a vacancy occurs – and it will go forward in the papers.' 'Thank you very much, sir. It's very good of you.' 'Good? In what way good? You've deserved it, haven't you?'

MONDAY 16 OCTOBER

Went with birds and lost temper with Caseby who had arranged for men who refilled at Kruisstraat loft to stop at Ramparts and refill there, his reason being that they had to pass the Ramparts to get to Kruisstraat. I thought this would lead to mix-ups. Caseby inconsequential and blathering and he irritated me. Regretted losing my temper.

MONDAY 23 OCTOBER

In morning worked on the bike – gears and carburettor. Cotterell had asked for leave but cannot spare him – went to Corps about his request and settled that he's to stay. Then to Abeele for distribution of presents to schoolchildren by British brigadier-general and Belgian officers.

TUESDAY 24 OCTOBER

Cotterell impassive on receiving news about his leave and said he was going to 'beat it' to the Corps to see about his leave. 'Well, everything has been settled. It'll make no difference. I don't think you should leave the loft' 'What's it to do with you?' 'I'm supposed to be in charge of this service.' 'Oh, you've got charge? You want me to remain here always and you don't want me to go to Corps. I've heard from someone what you're on for.' 'I'll tell you to your face, I've never disguised the fact that I don't like you, and I don't think you're particularly keen on your duties.' 'In what instance haven't I been keen on my duties?' 'Well – your suggestion to go to Corps, leaving the loft with no GHQ man here shows that.'

Evening to cinema and saw the funniest Charlie Chaplin film. Great.

SUNDAY 29 OCTOBER

Met Mr Larking as I went over to arrange about training journeys. He in fine spirits and colour. 'Been rather tied for time lately, Davis?' He gave permission to have my pal Pip Boyd work with me as Caseby still away, and no spare loftman supplied yet by GHQ.

WEDNESDAY 1 NOVEMBER

Rose at 7, old Pip still sleeping heavily, and got off early to Abeele. In afternoon wrote reports. Titbits and cinema at 6.00. I went to the cinema on the policy that on the Somme I hadn't been able to go – and there was no knowing when we might be shoved down there or out somewhere in a Godforsaken hole where we couldn't get entertainment, so 'have it while you can', was my motto.

THURSDAY 2 NOVEMBER

Lectured in morning – good men. At dinner Caseby (back now) said, 'One pigeon man who has flown pigeons ever since he was a boy, is in a hell of a rage. He was going to report you.' Suppressed passion began to work in me. 'I don't believe you, you're such a bloody liar,' I said. 'It wants tact with the men,' said he. This annoyed me – I prided myself on getting on well with the men. 'Easy to be tactful when you've nothing to do,' I snarled. 'I fetch the mail every day, beside the classes and getting birds up. I have to settle all the difficulties, and if there's anything unpleasant to be pushed through, I've got to do it. I don't believe in being false to people in order to get on pleasantly.' 'It's that you're two-faced,' he shouted. 'You say I'm lazy, yet you said the reports I wrote at K were splendid.' 'I say so now. You're a good writer, and I'm not. But you don't take the work really in earnest. You laugh at the Pigeon Service, and I can't expect the pigeon men to do their work well if you're making fun of my instructions.'

THURSDAY 4 NOVEMBER

Down to Dupont's this morning, then to Talbot House – David Hunter there
– tall, refined, good-looking Scot, with a strong bony nose, fine eyes and a clear-
cut face. 'Bruce has sent me to replace Boyd.' 'What in the name of Fate for?
You're pulling my leg?' 'No, Pip has to return at once.' 'What's up? What have
you been doing with the mademoiselles, Pip?'

Hunter's handsome face went graver and colder. 'It's simply that brute
Bruce wants me out of the way. I'm too independent. The other fellows give
in and let him have his own way – but why should we? They're afraid of him,
and he's trying to curry favour with the signalmaster. The superintendent asks
for four DRs for the counter. I say we can't spare them and the others think
the same, but they don't say it. As it is, we don't get five on a shift. I never get a
proper relief off. One relief runs into another – so Bruce wants me out of the
way.' 'Well, David, bar Pip there's no-one I'd rather work with, but Pip's my pal
– always has been – and I'm cut up at losing him.' 'I wouldn't think of splitting
you, but I've no voice in the matter.'

I didn't fancy asking Lieutenant Larking to let Pip stop, as I was never quite
sure of my ground. Dumbfounded. 'Shite – that's what old Bruce is – a shite-
hawk.' But very philosophically he packed, leaving half his clobber behind in
my hut. In the evening Larking rang up to ask if Pip was coming.

That night particulars arrived over the phone after I had got into bed – had
to get out in underclothes to the phone – and learnt that there were over a
hundred fresh men coming for training. 'Seems to me that you and I have got
to train the whole British Army,' laughed Mr Larking.'

SUNDAY 5 NOVEMBER

In orderly room, where I used to go for mail, they said to me, 'What's this about
Cotterell being arrested?' 'Arrested?' I felt myself go white and my heart seemed to
strike and go dumb. 'I know nothing about it.' 'Well, he's under close arrest.' 'Do
you know what for" I asked weakly, hiding my agitation. 'No idea.' This news fell
on me like some knell, which had been waiting its hour to toll for me. Had my
malicious conflict with Cotterell led to this, that on my information or indirectly
through it, a man had been thrown under the harsh onset of British Military law?

All during my round with the birds, I was perturbed and preoccupied, asking
various pigeon men if they knew why Cotterell was under arrest. Someone
thought it was for insubordination to Mr Murray, the officer in charge of the
signal office. I was told he was prisoner in a camp of whose existence I had not
heard before. Walked over fields and came to quite a group of sand-bagged

shacks, before one of which a man stood on guard. 'Have you got a man called Cotterell here?'

He called inside and a man appeared and called Cottrell forward. Cotterell seemed much down and pale as if sleepless night had been passed. He stared at missive as if he absorbed elsewhere. Genuine pity stirred in me for him. I away, thinking deeply on the ill chances of the army and the lack of sympathy from upper officers once the man has fallen.

I learned the truth later. Cotterell had been playing cards and drinking too freely and the rations corporal of signals had had no rum to dish out. Cotterell went to the officer. 'I want my issue, please sir.' 'I haven't got your rum.' 'The corporal's got no issue for us?' 'Can't help it.' 'Well, it's being held up here and it's not the first time.' 'What do you mean? You're drunk, man. Get out of here.' 'I'm not budging until I get my rum.' The officer went to the door and called out for Withers. 'Put this man under arrest, then fetch a guard over from the camp to put him under close arrest for insubordination.' Cotterell's luxurious days as a loftman were finished.

When I heard this I admired him for the first time. Though usually wrong, he was quite possibly in the right this time. Officers and NCOs did pinch the men's whisky and it needed someone to have the pluck to stand up and tell them so. It was in keeping with the perverted justice of the army that it should be on this score that Cotterell was brought down. No doubt felt, 'I'll stand up to 'em and tell 'em the truth for once. It's a scandal we should be robbed of our rum.' It required a man to stand up.

THURSDAY 9 NOVEMBER

Rain so heavy that the field at rear of hut was flooded. With birds to Kruisstraat, then had left class at four prompt in the afternoon and Mr Larking was after me again, catching me up on the Cassel road. He said he was expecting to go away to II Anzac Corps. Would I like to go with him? If so, he would arrange the transfer and look after me.

Really didn't want to go, as I rather feared his bold, irresponsible spirit and what he would be leading me into. I said all my friends were here and that the Corps treated me well, and that I was satisfied so wouldn't trouble him – but thanked him. He said that was all right, as it would be a trouble to arrange the transfer.

He showed me his new 1917 model bike with flat decompressor[14] – he as pleased as Punch. Said that the Army might move any day to Pop as he knew that billets there had already been marked out. So we could expect things.

FRIDAY 10 NOVEMBER

Morning, a new lot of thirty scholars. In the afternoon over to Abeele to be photoed in group of DRs with Mr Larking in the centre. The photographer was a business-like Belgian girl, inhabiting a dark-room shed at the back of the estaminet where Bruce was said to 'run' one of the proprietresses – he was always playing in there and getting drunk during service hours.

SUNDAY 12 NOVEMBER

Had difficulty in keeping billet clean. Didn't like to force men to take turns, and none would take their share voluntarily, and the cook was too busy. This was a sore and uncertain point with me. Evening band and cinema in Pop at the Station Theatre.

WEDNESDAY 15 NOVEMBER

I addressed myself nicely to Caseby, giving him the second run, but then at dinner had a row with him as no clips had been taken up with the birds, and here I was a little unfair, as Hunter and Sim Coope also forget the clips. Still, it seemed that unless I personally supervised, mistakes generally occur.

Went to see Martha – the fat dark girl at the shop and coffee house on the corner of the lane. She sidles and gazes as if bemused.

SATURDAY 18 NOVEMBER

In morning finished off 36 scholars and in the afternoon, through the rain to Corps. Presented myself a sight in dripping cape and overall, trousers too large, dragging in mud, to be introduced to Mr Underwood, who struck me as sturdy, small, neat, capable and quiet. I bade farewell to my old OPC, who seemed moved at his leaving, as was I.

SUNDAY 19 NOVEMBER

In afternoon rang up Corps to see if brigades had been apprised of a new order relating to a daily service of pigeons from 20 November on, instead of service every other day. Major Eyles replied, 'I don't see that that concerns you. You get orders to do a certain job, and you do it. That's all.' A deadly chilling contempt was in his voice. Evidently he said to himself, 'I'll teach this corporal a lesson – he's getting far too presumptuous – imagines he's running the service, I suppose. 'Very good, sir,' I said, utterly snubbed. If I hadn't spoken and men hadn't turned up, it would have been, 'Why didn't you arrange things?'

SATURDAY 25 NOVEMBER

To the Ramparts from Cassier's loft in pouring rain. I returned soused to a late dinner, glad to have work over. Jimmy met me with twinkling eyes, rubbing his elbows, 'You wouldn't go out again, I'll bet.' 'Wouldn't I? I should have to if…' And at that moment an orderly handed me a telegram. It was from Caseby, 'Await instructions. Broken down.' Hunter said, 'I shouldn't go out again. Wire him to come back.' I cursed, went off through the dull Saturday afternoon down to Boeschepe Street and the Reninghelst road and met him coming back – magneto trouble. He'd managed to get the magneto going, so thought it best to leave the birds and come back while he could – a thing I've never done. I insisted that the birds should go up and went to the loft, got them out again and took them, just catching Taylor, who was still waiting for them.

MONDAY 27 NOVEMBER

Another GHQ man was sent down – Sergeant Christian – big, sandy and hairy. A new man, Forster, at Cavill's and he to work Couper's routine. I was not hasty in taking up his assumption of control, and it then emerged that these were GHQ instructions.

MONDAY 28 NOVEMBER

As I walked into dinner, saw a smart grey car in the passage beside Dupont's loft and mess, and had dim idea who was there. 'Captain Waley's upstairs asking for the DR in charge,' said Foster. My heart beat and my voice was disturbed, though I strove for calm. 'Poperinghe lofts are closed down under Corps approval.' 'I did not know the reinforcement would be up so soon – we've usually waited so long for them.' 'You'll open them tomorrow then,' he snapped, annoyed at this reflection on GHQ. Plenty of men to do the work.

'How many birds are up the line?' he asked. 'Forty-four up today and twenty-two of yesterday's still there.' 'What time do you get them up?' 'About eleven o'clock.' 'And the men fetch them then?' 'About then – an hour to get up the line…' 'That leaves only three hours for them to be flown back. They might as well go up later, and the trench birds be flown next morning.' I gave only one answer, though I ought to have given several reasons for going up early – viz: liability of bike or car to break down; birds returned in wet and misty weather, and that it was better for the lofts – but I told him about school to be attended to and that ever since the Somme I had always gone up early in case a second supply was wanted.

'Why a car?' he asked, 'they take them to Pop by bike.' 'Well, it's better for the birds,' I muttered, conscious that it was best for US. I ought to have mentioned taking up of stores, trainers, clothes etc for the outlying lofts. He gave no word of praise or encouragement, and I cussed him for a churl.

WEDNESDAY 29 NOVEMBER

I remember I had at first been upset at losing a bird or two, but Edmonds said that with the winter coming on it was inevitable, and I got to regard the loss of two or three a week with equanimity.

After a fine dinner, wrote reports and worked at Talbot House. Warm chips and eggs at next-door estaminet for a change – joyful men inside.

SUNDAY 3 DECEMBER

On round with the birds and in afternoon Caseby to the mobile loft. According to him it was a foul-up there with Roberts in charge.

MONDAY 4 DECEMBER

Up to Corps to see the new man installed. Was introduced to Sergeant Scarf – pale and aesthetic-looking, yet mending a motor-car puncture and changing a wheel. I told Underwood I knew enough French to ask at the Abeele château civvy loft if I could buy some cock birds. However, the girl there behind counter of adjoining shop – pale, elegant, painted and scented – said she could not sell any of her father's birds, but could lend them 'pour jouer'.

Got word that Anzac orderlies, Murray, Salmon, Bromfield and Gay, are to depart. Pathos of their departure down to the Somme to rejoin their battalion.

TUESDAY 5 DECEMBER

In afternoon was called to signal office mess hut to meet a bowed-down 40-year-old Hants man with greying light hair, of yokel utterance and dribbling lips. He had been told to report to Corporal Davis for orderly duty. Gave him tea and I sent him down to Dupont's. After some doubts, comparing him with other orderlies, decided against Caseby's advice to keep this man with us at Dupont's in Jim's place as cook. I didn't like to force the worst of the bunch on Couper, who was a decent man. However, this uncertain one began by cleaning the sink and dixies and Caseby was much astonished and started to turn round. 'Pa' said he had two certificates as an army cook – but I think he was a liar.

WEDNESDAY 6 DECEMBER

Via Abeele, Boeschepe, Berthen and the curling roads to St Jan's Cappel and Bailleul for a lost bird. I had promised Wagstaffe and others that I would call, and I did so. Jeanne, plump, well-favoured about forty, greeted me heartily, and prepared dinner of Brussels sprouts, meat and spuds with beer. While it was cooking I went round to the ICO mess room – a schoolroom in the convent behind the square. Warm and comfy there after the grey ride. Saw Moses and Gibbons – the first time since England. They were well in with Corps and made me welcome.

At dinner Jeanne showed me the BCO souvenir – the old roster with the white round checks hanging up and the names of the old boys and some photos. She would never forget them and 'Waggy'.

THURSDAY 7 DECEMBER

In papers learnt with sorrow and shame of Asquith's resignation and the baiting by the *Daily Mail*, which calls Haldane, Grey, Asquith and Balfour 'the gang of wire-pullers'. Woolstey argued at tea that the *Daily Mail* was right. Undoubtedly the *Mail* has substantial following in the army.

I find a gradual change of feeling as I got rid of the old apprehension bred on the Somme, and now began to feel at home in the Salient. At first I feared it would be the same and that fierce doings might at any moment ensue, or we might be spirited down away to some rotten front. Slowly this feeling changed to one of security – never quite sure, however. There was always the dread of what might be done to you.

FRIDAY 8 DECEMBER

Felt shame and gloom at the *Daily Mail*'s dastardly and insidious attacks on Asquith, Grey, etc. The fall of Asquith's government seems to me a catastrophe.

SATURDAY 9 DECEMBER

Our new cook, unpromising at first, cleans dixies and floors and gets good meals. He's a shameless wangler down at the Town Major's ration dump, scrounging rations and timber and coal with the innocent face of an imbecile and then tipping us the wink. 'Well, if ye darn look after yerself, nobody else ain't a-going to. Since I ben in the army I learnt to look arter myself like an ol' sweat.'

MONDAY 12 DECEMBER

A total change of public feeling at news of the fall of Bucharest. One feels again, 'Is Germany going to win after all?' One remembers the tides of feeling that have swayed us since the war started.

THURSDAY 14 DECEMBER

During a long telephone conversation with Mr Underwood, I had insisted that Skinner was the best man to relieve Archer at the Ramparts. 'Why not Buckley or Deering?' 'Not pigeon men, and not the intelligence of Skinner.' I believed in Skinner because he was such a nice scholar and the son of a past President of the London Federation of Pigeon Clubs – and he'd been so modest as never to tell me, and never to come scrounging round for a cushy job as an orderly, like some had done. So I chose him, believing in my own judgement of character.

WEDNESDAY 20 DECEMBER

Afternoon instructed two pigeon men, though dog tired. Evening wrote and fetched rum from the Town Major's. (The tame lion[15] which they have as regimental mascot was rolling about in the back room there.)

SATURDAY 24 DECEMBER

Christmas Eve, and we've received Christmas parcels. Another row with Caseby over the WC door – left open. 'I'll stop it up – ghastly smell. I'm digging myself a hole at the end of the garden. I'll board it up.' Lost temper.

Evening to cinema and concert party – civvies invited – at Pop Signal Office, with Christmas spirit in the air. The canteen decorated and peace in the air with the proposals of Germany and President Wilson.

SUNDAY 25 DECEMBER

Christmas Day. In morning waiting late for Second Army car, then Caseby to the Ramparts and I on bike to Hallebast Corner. Was mending tyre in afternoon when Martha, dressed up, passed by with her mother. To Corps in time for the 4.30 spread at Zilma's cottage shop in Abeele – decorated with Xmas trimmings. We had soup, two turkeys, cold roast, peas, sprouts and spuds then plum pudding and coffee.

I broke a plate and the food dropped on the floor. 'Give him his money back,' howled Charlie White. 'A nice ruse', said Bill Wilson, 'the first man to get two servings.' To the San Martin and drank and sang. The last thing one thought about was war. War-dance in billet – 'Macnamara's Band' and Davies pirouetting about with match-stick legs while Lee writing to wife in the corner.

TUESDAY 26 DECEMBER

My birthday. Wrote a missing bird report for the OC 23rd Division and in afternoon various business calls on bike. A beautiful day and a ride back through the sunset.

THURSDAY 28 DECEMBER

In morning to Ypres Ramparts by bike with a cargo and called at the cellar dugout of VIII Corps DRs near the Cloth Hall. You went in to an earthy-smelling passage with a shattered roof, right down the cellar steps and there was a big acetylene lamp going in the cellar, where they had built a kind of oven fireplace under the chimney. The boys had been sent up here to do navvy-work because they had appeared on parade at some high officer's inspection not particularly cleanly dressed.

Fox of Second Army had been put on a similar job. He had been invited to a Belgian soldier's leave home-coming and was stepping out of the door when he collided with a staff officer, who said Fox was drunk. A trial ensued and he was convicted and put in the San Joseph at Cassel. He simply broke down the door and walked out, but they fetched him again. Fox never was drunk – and he said he was not going to clink for what he didn't commit. So they stripped him and put him in the camp in Ypres on fatigues, but were annoyed because he was always clean and dapper and they couldn't break his spirit.

SATURDAY 30 DECEMBER

Repaired my roof with felt, old Moss at last turning out decent and advising me how to nail it over the crossbeams with slats of wood. Afternoon wrote in comfy billet and then round on work. Wrote reports, early tea, bathed and wrote comfy – but kept coughing during the night.

SUNDAY 31 DECEMBER

Was I well enough to get up? Did so and saw to business until 9.30, then in afternoon felt dizzy and bones ached, and by evening was feeling shuddery, chilled and rotten. The sergeant at the Town Major's kindly gave me rum which made me warm and bemused. At night got little sleep because I was coughing continually although I lay down so tired and drowsy.

1917

New Year's Day. Thoroughly bad with influenza and kept to my bed. At eleven Jock came in about a row he'd had with 'Dad' the cook. Dad came in at three and told me of row with Jock. Chaos in the mess as soon as I was not there. Caseby had threatened to get his own back on Dad if he ever came out as an officer. Dad told him to go and **** himself and do his own cooking. No sleep this night because of pain in hips and because in next-door hut, just as I was dropping off, the inmates began their nightly debate on Socialism in raucous voices with the new Jewish cook. The new year was ushered in by Moss and Couper walking about with drums made of biscuit tins, kettle drums of frying pans, etc. Awful din.

Pain went and I felt sleepy, so decided at 7.30 to remain in bed. Jock Campbell brought me breakfast and chatted with unexpected amiability. Foster, the lugubrious, always full of mournful prophecies of England's downfall, showed me an extract in *The Times*, and brought me dinner. Jock again brought tea. Just as I was dropping off, Galligan came in.

'You mustn't think I forgot ye,' he said. 'All the camp's thinkin' on ye – but Jock took it on to see to ye, and it's a one-man job. Now is there anything I can do?' 'I never felt until today how much I am one of the camp,' I said. 'You know I've always felt I must have appeared a bit awkward, after having to quarrel at the very first. But I felt I must stand up to Roberts from the first. I had been warned against him, and though I'd rather face shells than quarrel with a man, I felt I was right in this case.' 'So ye were. Ye did well. Now ye mustn't think we forgot ye.' He insisted on making me a splendid cup of coffee.

WEDNESDAY 3 JANUARY

No sleep over night – too hot and twisted and sore. Rose, though still queer, after a mug of tea from Galligan. Everybody nice and glad to see me back. Taught morning and afternoon, then in evening a debate at Talbot House on the *Daily Mail* – I leading supported by Stanbridge. I won a very good debate that 'Lord Northcliffe be strafed' by 33 to 31.

FRIDAY 5 JANUARY

To Reninghelst up the Hallebast Road, skidded and came a frightful cropper. Cut my hand badly and muddied it and self, bent the bars and smashed the lamp. Was picked up and led to estaminet off the road, where a soldier broke his iodine bulb over hand and dressed it. Slatternly woman in farm serving coffee – very kind. To destination with cargo, then going back belt rim of rear wheel broke. Wheeled it back to Smith's and left in the loft coal shed. Walked back through a fine day – weary but glowing.

SUNDAY 7 JANUARY

Jock to hospital re his teeth. I having no motor bike and no car, push-biked it to Hallebast Corner. Beneath the dignity of a DR, but didn't care so long as I got the goods delivered.

Evening a band and cinema with Skinner – then read *Morning Post* and *Titbits* – we argued as to whether it was legal and right for men at home to strike, also whether we ought to debase ourselves as the Hun did with gas and bombing by aeroplane. I against, but the majority for.

MONDAY 8 JANUARY

Got the new wheel and off late to the Ramparts to see Jack. The streets were deserted and shrapnel was falling to the left. The Huns had been 'bumping' heavily that morning. An hour after I left, twenty-two were laid out up against our pigeon cote – men belonging to the water carts that stood there when I arrived. Jack the only one in the group not hurt. A sentry to whom I had spoken had his arm blown off.

TUESDAY 9 JANUARY

Up to Hallebast Corner and the Ramparts, doing two runs. Not so lively, but still some of the roads barred by debris.

In the afternoon I was repairing the bike and Skinner was writing out lists of birds in the lofts when 'Whoooo – crash!' We had a look outside and saw an indeterminate black cloud above the roofs in the direction of the station. 'Bang

– whoooo – crang!' About eighteen shells, one every five minutes. It made me miserable and nervous because we were next door to the second biggest church in Pop and it was such a mark for the guns and you couldn't help thinking, 'he's bound to drop one here next'. Skinner continued his work apparently imperturbably, and earned my admiration.

SUNDAY 14 JANUARY

I to Hallebast Corner, and bringing back some returned birds, left bike outside while I saw Jack. Coming out, no bike. An MP said, 'I should try at the APM's, so I went in to the passage just above and saw my bike in the yard. Two or three red-nosed, scrounging and ear-holing MPs blocking up the passage, shuffling about. 'The APM wants to see you.' I went in. 'Yes, I had your cycle brought here. You know very well you shouldn't leave a machine unattended and unobserved. We've had a lot of trouble lately with stolen cycles.' 'Well, sir, I had to get those birds inside the loft, and I'd always left the machine there – there's nowhere else to put it.' 'Don't argue. Why didn't you ask someone to keep an eye on it?' 'I saw an MP there and thought it would be all right.' 'Did you mention it to the MP?' 'I did not, sir.' 'He might be changing over.' 'I'll be careful in future, sir.' 'I shall take your unit and report the case.' A fussy, rotten sod.

WEDNESDAY 17 JANUARY

Debate at Talbot House on 'That the war would finish this year'. The usual fatuous optimism of some, the cynical witty scepticism of others and the incredibly futile sanguineness of officers who should have known better.

A Mr Berry rose and said that we drew on the Huns to attack at Verdun, at Ypres gave way with intent in the same way, and he inferred that the Russian retreat might be due to the same kind of strategy. He had the air of assuring us that he and the brass hats were in the inner know – that we need have no fear, their mighty intellects had got the Hun weighed up, and it was only because we, the rank and file, were obtuse and of little faith and uninitiated, that we ever doubted. So convinced was he, or so anxious was he to dupe us, that he almost persuaded us against our ingrained belief in the superior cleverness of Fritz.

THURSDAY 18 JANUARY

In morning tuition and fetched rations with the men in afternoon, they being short, and finished with viva-voce exam. In evening to 55th Division cinema – the front row. Enjoyed it more than ever.

SATURDAY 20 JANUARY

Up with Caseby – cold, bracing and dry – enjoyed it. Odd jobs in afternoon – cleaning billet and shelves, mending, getting and sending washing etc. Met Fry and talked with him about debate. He had several ideas for combating submarines – phials of coloured matter, the hue of which, bulbs being broken by smash of sub prow, should disclose the whereabouts of the sub as it rises to the surface. Refined and intellectual, he was battalion runner, and when battalion in action was now a brigade runner, given him as a cushy job. Skinner said his nerve had gone. A short time later he was killed.

MONDAY 22 JANUARY

In evening I drank Muscat in the San Martin and worried about Trewatha's birds and the snow. They're young and not used to it – he was worried and the other pigeon men called him a washerwoman.

TUESDAY 23 JANUARY

While up at Ramparts asked Jack Hilton to take me round to brigades. One was in another Ramparts cave near the Lille Gate – men lying in bunks sleeping or underneath, playing cards. Fighting looked the remotest thing from their minds. The old sergeant major was in an area curtained off with a flannel blanket, and he offered me rum.

Then along the Lille Road and over the moat bridge. We were shelling all the time and Fritz occasionally replied on the left, some 200 yards away. 'He'll take up when we've finished, so we're all right,' said Jack, taking no notice and proceed in gcheerily. Once I went in to the ditch. We were under observation of glasses. Crossing the fields just after Shrapnel Corner, past the Verbranden Molen road we got down by the embankment of the railway and walked along over trenchboards past the dugouts. In the Brigade dugout signal office we found the signal sergeant and asked him to bring back the birds by hand if snow was on the ground, as same hadn't yet melted enough to show the roofs (Jack's formula). Then back, about a thousand yards from the front line – the nearest I've been.

WEDNESDAY 24 JANUARY

Very frosty weather the last four days and half an inch of snow on the ground. All in my shack frozen hard and had to melt ice with the Primus stove to shave. To Hallebast Corner with birds – intense cold cutting my face, but I enjoyed the bracing run.

TUESDAY 6 FEBRUARY

Cleaned billet and mended clothes in the morning and started work on stove at the signal office hut. Galligan kindly helped me to fit the stove-plate found at Dupont's. It burnt well after first smoking badly – then a fuel hunt. Meant to spend long evening reading by stove, but it went out. Two bombs fell nearby. Relit the stove and wrote letters until 10. Cold frost freezier than ever.

SATURDAY 10 FEBRUARY

In afternoon to Corps, trying to get coal from the house beside the station – I dodging MPs as it is supposed to be illegal for soldiers to buy coal, though they pinch it right and left.

SUNDAY 11 FEBRUARY

New sergeant, Barnes, arrived in place of Couper – a decent, fluent, affable sort – Cockney.

WEDNESDAY 14 FEBRUARY

Captain Mudge meeting Caseby at Corps arranged with him to look outside for Mobile Number 5 near the heavies at Brandhoek. He was pluming himself on this, and suspected me trivially annoyed – which I was, slightly – but still I recognised that this was one of the jobs he could do well. Caseby gave an account of the heavy officers, who knew nothing of any proposed pigeon loft installation. Nice major was mildly horrified, according to Caseby, at the first two proposed positions because of Fritz's balloon observation.

SUNDAY 18 FEBRUARY

In afternoon got the wind up at camp over threatened visit of the sanitary officer – no cover to the latrine seat or something, and the incinerator bad. Assisted in cleaning up the camp, getting tins and paper and boxes out of the hedge.

MONDAY 19 FEBRUARY

Two runs to Hallebast Corner as argued with Caseby. 'You make a certain arrangement about the Ypres runs, and now Ypres is getting warm again, you want to change it to your own advantage, so that you shall get few Ypres runs. Just like you. But I'm not having any this time.' 'You're a bloody liar,' he said. 'If anybody's a bloody liar, it's you,' I said. 'You're the biggest I've met. But that's one thing I don't do. If you call me a bloody liar again, I'll hit you one, big as you are.' 'You are one, all the same.' I hit him in the face. He sprang at me and we wrestled at risk of hitting our heads against the big kitchen stove range.

Tom Cavill separated us and I offered Caseby out. He would wait until he had washed. After washing he went on messing with his boots. 'Are you coming to have it out?' I asked, hoping he would refuse, my impulse cooling a little. 'I'm coming when I've finished my boots and cleaned my teeth.' He was quiet and bent with red face over his boots.

I took off my tunic and Tom Cavill laughed to see me in my tight navy jersey. Caseby had to come out as the others were waiting, with Tom as referee.

To my surprise the first round was mine. Caseby whirled his fists about fiercely while I practised the only thing I knew – hit straight and hard with the left and thrust to my reach, which I knew was fairly long from the one or two bouts I had had at Dunstable.

'I got it that time, Hughie,' said Caseby, turning to Wright. 'I can't see.' One of his eyes was closing where I had socked it. A slight spasm of pity crossed, lightning-like, through my mind that a man as big as he should be so humiliated and stand there with a bunged-up eye and appeal for sympathy to the onlookers. 'My fingers are all chapped,' he said, coming forward to the second round. 'That's absurd…' I had just said it, thinking he was going to argue out, when with a gleam of hate in his one eye, he rushed at me and hit me a crack on the head which made my senses spin. 'You dirty cad,' I thought. 'I wasn't ready.'

A severe blow in my eye quenched my rising rage at his lack of sportsmanship, and my exultant feeling of unsuspected power and conquest gave way to a feeling of misery, hurt and self-doubt. I wished that somehow the fight could stop. My thumbs were knocked up on his hard head and they pained me.

As we paused for the third round, I asked him to apologise for calling me a liar. He wouldn't and I rather admired him for that. He kept on refusing, so with grave misgivings I asked him 'Come on then'.

This time I hammered him terrifically on the head as he made a turn. 'I'm fed up,' he said. 'You've got the best of it.' 'Right, that's enough,' I said, as hastily as I dared, glad to be out of it so well. 'As long as you give me "best man". If I can't have it verbally that you're wrong, I've got it physically. Don't you call me a bloody liar again.'

'By Crikey you made me laugh, dancing around in that little navy jersey of yours,' said Tom. 'If you could have seen yourself – you did look a comic.' So much for the dignity of victory.

I felt sorry for Caseby's humiliation, and tried to help him with his puncture, but he was sulky. Owing to my battered eye the fact of the conflict leaked out and jokes went round as to my pugilistic leanings.

WEDNESDAY 22 FEBRUARY

Soon everybody in the service knew about the fight and came to take a peep at Caseby, and when his special Scots chum from VIII Corps came to see him, it was the climax of bitterness for him – he must have hated me. I thought to myself, if he gets his commission and comes out here, and ever gets over me, he'll have it in for me and lead me a dog's life. However, he was extraordinarily quiet. His loud laughter and joking, bluffing and boasting were now no more heard. Nothing had ever so much quelled Caseby as that fight.

MONDAY 26 FEBRUARY

Went to 'Pigeon Rapide' at the château with Pip and got two stray birds. At 10 pm met Paul coming into Corps signal office – he had left the Canadians and was at the Second Army with Billy Pritchard. 'Hello, Foster, why so quiet?' I said. 'I am quieter,' he said. 'Difficult runs and rotten bike.' He was sadder and more subdued than he used to be, while I was gayer.

THURSDAY 1 MARCH

With car to the Ramparts. Returning, we were just coming round to Rue de Boeshinge when 25 yards in front of us, on the cathedral close, a mass of grey and black stones shot forward like a wall in transit through the air. We ran on, out of harm's way. Nothing fell on us, though bits spattered near. We shot up the road, you bet, at high speed, Vickery the driver quite cool.

BRITISH CASUALTIES RECEIVING TREATMENT AT A CASUALTY CLEARING STATION NEAR YPRES.

FRIDAY 2 MARCH

To Corps workshop then in afternoon wrote at the new 66 café room, built behind the shop. Good news from Mesopotamia and the Somme.

SATURDAY 3 MARCH

In afternoon to 2nd Casualty Clearing Station about a new dental plate. Men were waiting there for attention from all parts of the line. The NCO passed you on to the doctor, who after cursory confirmation with NCO, gave the latter instructions, which he carried out. Doctor young and jaunty, hands in pockets, but capable.

SATURDAY 10 MARCH

Attended concert – Captain Mudge's farewell, he going to England to give special course of instruction there. It was held in a big hut past Eileen's es-taminet on the Watou road – a men's recreation or mess hut. We sat on benches and beer was passed round in mugs filled from buckets to all who cared for it. The same old items always heard by the Corps:

Zanazi, called Zanzig, sang 'Old Iron':

> *You look a treat,*
> *From your napper to your feet,*
> *Yer father's new brown tie on,*
> *But I don't care*
> *For the chain you wear,*
> *Old iron, old iron.*

Or

> *Down in our street lived a girl from America,*
> *She rides a bicycle day and night.*
> *One summer night she was riding her bicycle,*
> *The moon shone bright and I had a good view,*
> *View – oo – oo – oo – oo ad lib.*
> *All of a sudden she fell off her bicycle,*
> *I saw her stars and I saw her stripes too.*

Zanazi sang with blotched, red, motionless face, red, beery and clownish, with creases from his wide nose to the ends of his mouth, while his audience shrieked with laughter and applause.

There was Stan Brown with the song he used to sing in the San Martin.

> *Oh I love the dear silver that shines in your hair,*
> *And the brow that's all furrowed and wrinkled with care,*

And I love the dear hands that are toil-worn for me,
God keep you and bless you, mother Macree.

How that used to move us. Then he gave us, 'When we come to the end of a perfect day, and we sit alone with our thoughts'.

Fatty Wright sang 'Glorious Devon', half tipsy, his eyes rolling, but hand-some and florid. At last, laughing and bemused at himself and scratching his head, he did a skit with another fellow, singing,

If I were the only girl in the world, and you were the only boy,
Nothing else would matter in this world today,
We could go on living in the same old way.
A Garden of Eden just built for two, with nothing to mar our joy.
I would say such wonderful things to you,
There would be such wonderful things to do,
If you were the only girl in the world, and I were the only boy.

The two chaps miauling this at each other were fine. Then Captain Mudge made a sporty speech, keenly regretting his departure and thanking us all.

THURSDAY 15 MARCH

Met Trewatha and Sam Booth, and had tea at the San Martin. Tales of the Hun's fourteen-day stay in the area – Julie's narrative was graphic. They'd been law-abiding here and paid for goods, but in Watou several outrages – the breast cut from a woman, etc. They foraged in the farms around for food.

FRIDAY 16 MARCH

Cleaned bike and got pay, then in evening a pub-crawl. Rumours around about Russia from Sergeant Edmonds. The Czar is reported in quod and a revolution going – which I didn't believe.

SATURDAY 17 MARCH

At Brandhoek Mobile No 5, Roberts glib in possession of facts re Russia. The newspaper – only *The Express* left – confirmed this, but then *The Times*, found in a shop in Pop that evening, gave a full account. To me it's an absolute miracle. Perhaps it will quicken the war's end.

St Patrick's day and Cally, Tyson and Jones got drunk in the foul pub over the road. Cally soothing and striving to keep the others under his wing, but Tyson stumbling and vociferous, while Jones maudlin and laughing.

SUNDAY 18 MARCH

Was asleep at 10.30 when Galloway burst in with news of the Somme advance on a 45-mile front. Too excited to sleep for half an hour.

TUESDAY MARCH 27

To Ramparts with birds on the bike. While putting bike on stand, I heard Jack Hilton call, 'Run!' as he bobbed out from the Ramparts. Soft earth from shells dropping on the Ramparts fell on me and the bike. While talking with Jack shells rattled several times around, debris falling on the corrugated iron roof of dugouts and cookhouses. 'He's getting terrible lately,' said Jack. 'This shop's going to be hot, I reckon. It's been gathering force every day. I should chance going now before it gets worse. If he goes on like he has a few times recently, you'll never get through.'

I raced round the back way through slush and along the front of the barracks, which has been badly pounded – then up the sinister narrow street at the side. I shot obliquely towards the street to the station when my crankcase hit some jagged bricks submerged in a pool of water, and wrenched out the screw-plug. Compression gone and oil hissed out. I stopped – wind up and in a small panic. Didn't know what to do, but as I saw men running and heard shells falling behind me, I got her going with low compression and got out as quickly as possible. Kept on as far as the château and then, feeling safe, dismounted and plugged up the crankcase with wood.

At San Martin forgot troubles. Adrienne coquettish and said I was proud and wouldn't speak when I met her in the street. Did this refer to the time when she and Julie passed in black shawls as I was talking with Mr Underwood, so didn't like to say anything? Moved from table to join a large party as she moved to my table, and then regretted it.

Back at hut a DR came in. 'There's two specials and the waiting man's gone out. Who's next?' The dread word 'specials' – especially dread when a shop was getting warm, thrilled through us. 'I'm on,' said White. 'Where's it to?' 'Ypres.' 'Damn Ypres,' said Charles, making to go. 'Let me take it,' pleaded Algy, with the emotional keenness of a schoolgirl. 'I want to have a look round. I should love it.' 'Don't be a jay,' said Charlie. 'No, I mean it, awfully,' said Algy. 'Oh, if you're looking for trouble, take it, and I'll have your run in your shift tomorrow.' Algy left the room precipitately. 'He's the bloody limit,' chorused the room. 'Funny kid, Algy.'

WEDNESDAY 28 MARCH

Pigeon class in morning, then in evening a new review at the Pop theatre, called 'Thumbs'. At Marie's was told that Hunter had wanted me for the spares list. So like a fool ran down in the rain to Corps with the list. Going back, after handing same to Bruce, found the filler cap missing and like a fool went back to DR's billet and announced the loss, suspecting Corps. Later found filler cap wedged between exhaust and chaincase. How?

SATURDAY 31 MARCH

To Ramparts with cargo on car. In afternoon Sergeant Edmonds put the wind up me with reference to new offensive. In evening to estaminet near station – the weekend low gaiety of Pop, with the nondescript girls, the crushed dancing, concertinas playing and wailing, drunken song.

THURSDAY 5 APRIL

Did the round of the new horse-drawn mobiles that had been drawn up at Kruisstraat, taking stock baskets. I try to be modest, but am conscious of sneaking importance. Saunders was aloof and uncompanionable and indifferent. Wallace was red and more anxious to fall in with my suggestions, as was his pioneer, the great baby Bill Bailey, who had a parcel every other day. Met Andy Butler, who was working at fixing his loft on wood supports, as the wheels were sinking into the ground and the men had drawn him there and left him.

Wanted to replace my leaking petrol pipe, but the shop was closed. 'Why don't you borrow Price's?' said Hunter. 'He's on the counter.' It didn't cross my mind that Price was Bill Price, DR. I figured him as a linesman or OT on the counter with bike laid by. 'Which is the bike?' 'There you are,' pointing to the shed. I got the pipe off – or was doing so, when Bobby Brown, artificer came up. 'What you doing, Oswald?' 'I wanted a new petrol pipe for tomorrow – the tiffy[16] shop's closed and Hunter suggested borrowing Price's.' 'You better put it back, my lad,' said Bobby, grinning kindly, in his creamy voice. 'I'll get you a pipe. Wait a minute.' I fixed on the pipe that he gave me.

In the evening in the San Martin I was warned that Price was rampant. 'S'after your blood, my boy,' said White, scenting a difference. 'He's going to make you sit up. Oh my.' He threw his great head back like a dog baying, and laughed. 'I shouldn't like to be in your skin, Oswald – our good boy, who never wins anything.'

I went up to the billet and as soon as I entered Price spoke. I saw the card-players at the ramshackle tables on which were heaped piles of ration cigs as stakes. Other boys lay on beds reading, or mending tubes. The light came from a pendant incandescent lamp and candles stuck on tin sconces and in niches.

Price's voice was quivering. 'Oh, Davis, have you got my petrol pipe?' 'No.' 'Whose have you got?' 'My own.' 'Where's your broken one?' 'In the workshop.' 'Whose is on your bike, then?' 'A new one that Bobby Brown gave me. Who made you grand inquisitor?' I, like Price, was vibrating in voice, no matter how cool and self-possessed I desired to be. I hated his magisterial way, not then divining it was just the armour by which he shielded his sensitivity in what he deemed to be a just case.

Brown was bent kneeling over his bed. 'I thought you said…' began Price to Brown. 'No,' said Brown, colouring. 'I caught him taking your petrol pipe, but I got him another.

SATURDAY 7 APRIL

Caseby to Hallebast Corner and I at signal office phoned for him to 'come in' to go home for commission. Just like him to get away with stunts coming off, we commented. Pip to come back and work with me.

Got a phone call from Mr Underwood to go down to Corps at 2.30. At Corps, 'What's this about you pinching a petrol pipe?' 'Pinching one? What I did was quite open, sir.' I explained – and finished, 'It's funny that's the only time I've come near to scrounging anything off a bike, and I get pipped at once.' 'Well, the OC wants to see you. Wait here a minute.' He announced me to Captain Stevens, who had the reputation of being an absolute shit. The OC came out with absorbed face. 'Follow me.'

We went to the bike yard and he pulled out a sheet of foolscap. 'You're charged with stealing a petrol pipe from the bicycle of Corporal Price. I haven't entered it as a crime. What have you to say for yourself? I just wanted to talk it over with you.' I told him and concluded, 'If you want a witness, Corporal Hunter can corroborate what I say.' 'But you should have spoken to the sergeant. You must do these things through the regular channels. Do you have any difficulty in getting stores?' 'Well, there is a difficulty in getting spares as a rule, but I've no complaint to make. It's not the tiffy's fault.' (It wasn't – it was the sergeant's, who was always getting drunk and running after women instead of getting in spares for us.) 'There are no stocks.' 'If you can't get things, come to me,' said Captain Stevens – and the interview finished. He was a gentleman to me.

Price had reported to Sergeant Bruce, and Bruce, the dirty dog, had run me because he was annoyed that I was so free of his authority. Strange I should have got 'clocked' the only time I half pinched something.

TUESDAY 10 APRIL

Pip and I went up by car with the birds. On the Brielen road shell spurts to the left. At the Ramparts had to wait in the car, and while doing so the tower surmounting the building in which 55th Div's right-flank brigade HQ was housed, quivered under a shell and before our very gaze, waggled sleepily and lazily fell. Instead of going back that way, we went towards the Cloth Hall square and away, several hits being made left and right of us. The suspense rather hateful.

WEDNESDAY 11 APRIL

Pip to two mobiles and I in hut to write reports. In evening received instructions for special stunt next morning at eight, so Pip and I warned the loftmen.

THURSDAY 12 APRIL

Rose at 5.30 and duly got the birds up the line on a bright vivid morn. Strange that we should have warm work the instant Pip started working with me and he doesn't like it.

SUNDAY 15 APRIL

During the past week continual news in signal office of advance by Vimy Ridge and Arras – 13,000 prisoners, 126 guns and 156 machine-guns captured.

MONDAY 16 APRIL

In evening to San Martin, then a noise of a do at 66 – *chocolat*, eggs and peas round with mob in the large new room at the back. Everybody flushed, Pip creamy and laughing openly at Harold Wordley as he sang, with retreating chin and contortions o the mouth. 'Look at him – a parrot.' I was afraid Wordley would come and hit him. Then into Bruce's room – talk of champagne. Some six bottles came out – Bruce, Lilley, Vic, Glenny, Pip and I. Jimmy, the quarter's bloke, as pissed as an owl, saying in maundering style, like a man asleep, 'F--- the army, f--- my king and f--- my country.' I felt ashamed of myself joining Bruce's party because I detested him and I felt a cringer. I had looked to a bright 'fizz' party – instead here was just Jimmy, drunk like a muddy beast.

MONDAY 23 APRIL

Training birds today. Mr Underwood wished us to push on urgently with the training and was set back when I told him how long it would take before the birds were ready to train – ie the end of April.

SUNDAY 29 APRIL

Fine day and in morning trained the birds in pearly skies, then reported to the OC and made arrangements for getting the trained birds into the trenches for two dummy runs. Got his permission to go to Cassel, where I met Billy Pritchard and Paul.

Afternoon took the straight road to Wormhoudt, which I had never ridden. That way to Bergues, ancient and beautiful. Splendid tea of peaches and pasty at Jeanne's and then a walk to San Marie Capelle, I telling Billy what my job was and how I had prospered. Drank in full pub at SMC and walked back happy. Beautiful evening and soldiers gay about us, as if no such thing as war existed. Home in dusk to a chip supper.

TUESDAY 1 MAY

I to Hallebast Corner – shells for the first time on La Clytte-Hallebast road and in field where a dump was set on fire and an aeroplane brought down in smoke and flame, fluttering like a piece of paper.

SUNDAY 6 MAY

Went on round with cargo in car – all satisfactory. Something in the wind with all this training of new lofts and birds. Rumours of our army going to do something.

Went to Corps and saw Mr Larking. 'I thought you'd got wounded, sir,' I said. 'It takes a lot to kill me. By the way, why haven't they made you a sergeant?'

At night there was a terrific British bombardment after we'd been shelled in Pop two nights in succession, with the shells flying over our shack. 'That'll teach Johnny a lesson,' said my pals grimly.

TUESDAY MAY 9

Fine weather – I to Hallebast Corner. Paul in estaminet with Duggie Brown, the tanned gypsy with bare knees and arms. Duggie never, however urgent the call, went out without oiling his bike. A marvellous rider – his bike always better than anyone else's but no-one knew why – he spent no time on it. He was an expert Douglas tourist trophy rider. 'They've stitched Duggie up,' they said. The camp commandant apparently objected to Duggie's laugh and that was why he was sent to Pop. I thought this a trivial reason until I heard his laugh, two kilos away over the fields as I approached Pop.

WEDNESDAY 10 MAY

I to Ramparts with birds in car. All quiet, but in evening with our open-air Machonochies, stunt started.

THURSDAY 11 MAY

Early to Bedford House along the Lille Road from Ypres. The road was punched with big shell-holes, the way narrow and bumpy in between. Dust in bursts and bits of metal. I was waiting and outside and saw half a dozen forms on stretchers, covered with blankets, their toes up in hard boots, blood coming from under them. Dead. I wondered what their mothers or wives were now thinking about those unstirring forms which came down regularly in such bunches every morn, the nightly sacrifice in just one small sector.

Bill Harrison had joined us after recovering from a bad leg – he told us tales of Loos, of 'Daddy' Spicer, the general, grey-haired and crying over the loss of 'my bonnie lads'. He told of the rain, the mud and the confusion. 'We came up too late or they sent us in the wrong direction. I never saw such a bloody mix-up. I reckon they threw us away.'

He had other tales – of the new lady VAD who spoke to a patient, 'What's the matter my man, do tell me.' 'Oh, I can't, ma'am.' 'But you must, please. I insist, really'. 'Well, it was a bullet through the arse, ma'am.' 'Oh, RECTUM, you wish to say.' 'No, but it pretty nearly did.' Or the military policeman reports to a sergeant that there is a horse dead on the Reninghelst road in Pop. The sergeant walked with him to the square where the horse was found. 'I thought you said it was on the Runninhurst Road,' said the sergeant. 'So it was, but I couldn't spell it, so I dragged the bloody horse to the square.'

THURSDAY 24 MAY

New stunt – I to Hallebast Corner. For the first time shell-holes and debris on the La Clytte-Dickebusch road, and in the fields and hedges around. Thirteen men arrived for training. Shells dropping near – one in front of the signal office.

MONDAY 28 MAY

I to Ramparts with cargo on bike. Dread feeling after seeing dead mules in the ditch and rumours of things doing. A lot of gas shells had fallen about here the day before. At the Asylum in Ypres the pink and black of bursting shells.

Wrote reports in evening then to San Martin and saw troops pathetically marching up in the evening sun, bands playing and cross-roads traffic stopped, men red-faced and good-humoured, some sweating and cursing.

TUESDAY 29 MAY

To Observation Post office, the sand-bagged house ont he Dickebusch road where my little Northumberland Fusilier kept his pigeons in nicely sanded cage. At first thought him self-opinionated, but later found him constant and good. Then on to the Canadian casualty clearing station about my teeth.

In the evening Mr Underwood came when was reading in the greenery and white blooms of the garden – I without any teeth top and bottom – all being repaired. He briefed me to have things ready for the coming stunt – a day which he would not name, but when it came I would understand he was referring to it. All evening thought stunt over and how we could best manage.

WEDNESDAY 30 MAY

To Ramparts with birds on car, lot of stock and final trainers so as to be fully equipped. On the road limbers and general service wagons and horses napoo, all along the Dickebusch-Ypres road. Fritz was quite aware something was coming off and he was searching the road every night, shelling the transport and ammunition limbers.

FRIDAY 1 JUNE

Paul called in the morning with some stories: 'Leigh Haslam was passing a pioneer on the road and the fool hit a grenade with a pick. A grenade won't stand that. Neither man nor pick was seen again and Haslam went to Blighty.' And of the local spirits: 'These liqueurs are all right, but the stuff isn't made to drink off like Englishmen drink. You go in and try these fireworks – little fellers, they are – and you find yourself staggering.'

We are now getting shelled every day.

SUNDAY 3 JUNE

Got stores up on car and to Ramparts with birds. Ypres copping out and we could only get in one way by going round from Brielen. Dead mules lying around and ammo boxes all over the place across the roads, and limbers broken. Dickebusch and Pop exit being shelled. Sped over fields pocked with shell-holes old and new, every two yards. Jack Evans got the wind up. 'When this show starts, hope I'm not here. Fritz will level every bit of house in Dickebusch.'

Watched the bare-to-waist Anzacs firing big howitzers in stumps of houses – careless, brown, supple and negligent of Fritz circling above in planes, giving their position away by continuing to fire. Then above Hallebast Corner we watched the English firing along Fritz's front line – a long horizontal strand of brown, fawn and black dust spurts making a wall where continuous shells fell.

We couldn't approach VIII Corps Stringer's mobile lofts because the field in which lofts stood was being shelled near the Elverdinghe road. Then houses each side of the route were hit by Jerry copping the ammo dumps nearby.

In the evening I sat stewing in the sun – it had been a bright and flawless day of sun – and wondered what to do. Didn't want to spoil Vic and Pip's Sunday night, but felt we ought to get stores up to EV 1. Should I go? I worked out the quantities then told Vic and Pip, who were unenthusiastic and argued that we could go up early tomorrow – they get up early? I decided we ought to do it tonight.

Took stores from Pop to EN 11 and thence took the assault baskets, pigeon message books and infantry baskets to EV 1. We couldn't tie these assault baskets up properly and we roared, weak with laughter at seeing Pip riding unconcernedly with the baskets floating round him like seaweed. Over the fields above Hughie's loft, transport was going diagonally across, bumping over the broken planking that bridged the deep gaps in the hedge.

Shells were soaring quietly overhead like slitting silk, and fire blazed over dumps hit by Fritz's shells. It was a lovely night – the sky was clear and red in the west and the houses of Dickebusch glowed rosily red with the tattered and broken brick making them look quite genial in their ruins. A glamour steeped the village in poetry of atmosphere and warm dusk light.

TUESDAY 5 JUNE

In morning Vic asked to go to Ramparts with cargo on the car as he liked the excitement – more than I altogether relished. Tense final preparations.

In afternoon saw Mr Underwood and put stock out for the special car in the morning. Gave Sergeant Barnes all written particulars of birds wanted. Pip and Vic were to get off with two heavy loads each – two runs each during the morning. It was suggested that I took all on the car, but I thought, 'Suppose the car gets knocked out? Both depots will be without birds, while it is not likely that both the two DRs and the car will get knocked out.' So I stuck to my decision. All responsibility for getting III Corps pigeons up rested with me.

WEDNESDAY 6 JUNE

Special Corps boxcar called at nine, then at ten I was off with nine stock baskets full of pigeons and with more stores. Roads quiet – all work of preparation done. Straight to Ypres. Just past railway crossing a forest appeared on the road that I had never seen before. Green boughs, trunks and logs and not a soul to be seen. We up with the wheels bumping over the tree trunks, bashing them somewhat, fearing that shelling might start. Obviously Fritz had got wind of something and had blown a roadside forest into the path. Boxes of ammo and shells, splintered wagons and dead horses strewed the other side after we'd got through the barrier.

Streets of Ypres ominously quiet and stripped of men – shrapnel overhead. 'Lucky you've come now in this lull,' said Jack Hilton. 'By God, it's been a rough-house. Don't stay too long. I'll see it's all right. Leave your pigeons here.' Good old Jack. We retraced and called at Corps' forward dump – a cellar under a ruined building in the main street past the Cloth Hall. There on a bed lay Hooper and another, sleeping. Hooper, the fathead at whom we had all laughed at home, was there quite fearless, although he had been slightly wounded that morning with a shell that burst through the upper part of their house.

Called at Dickebusch Lake and there met a small swarm of agitated men who'd come for pigeons, but didn't know how many they wanted for battalion or brigade. I knew how many were allotted to each division and shared them out as best I could. They didn't want to take the assault baskets – they looked ominous. Vic and Pip had cleared off after dumping the pigeons. Got up and had a deco at the lakes – in daytime you were not allowed to show your form above the bank buttressing the lake.

In evening it came over stormy. 'Thought it was too good to last,' we murmured. Fear entered me. 'Suppose we have to go up with more birds this night,' I wondered. 'Shells and storms.' The general atmosphere was suppressedly tense and nervous. All knew a stunt was near and some were going to stay up and watch the shoot.

At eleven, just as was sleeping, very big shells fell near – one every five minutes seemed to whistle over the roof of the hut. Pip got up and a few minutes later he rushed in for a water-bottle and says, 'Everyone's clearing out except those who've got to stay. Fritz is sending gas over and using liquid fire, and Pop is going to be strafed all night. I'm going to Abeele.'

Vic and I looked at each other and slowly rose, rather shaken. I'd got no gas helmet – I was a fool. Couldn't find my pants. Vic put slippers on. Outside the hut we found Dougie Brown and Fox preparing to pack and ride off back to Army.

In spite of my incredulity, the panic that was astir began to affect me – but it seemed so absurd. We had always reckoned the Ypres line as absolutely fixed. It could never break and we right behind at Pop purchased absolute security by right of that stout and settled line.

I thought, 'If we are so perturbed by rumour, what about the forward stations at Vlam and Kruisstraat? What about the men out in the trenches, even at that moment facing the gas and liquid fire? Suppose they had no more guts than we – where would the Second Army be – the boasted Second? Imagine being a man on his own out there – how could he be expected to keep his nerve when his comrades so far behind in safety were losing their nerve and showing disregard of the fact that even if the line had given way, it was our duty to stick and support?'

At the cost of three weeks and drunken figures lying about after work in the fields, a dugout had been constructed in our field. Many civvies and some soldiers were now in or grouped around the entrance to this dugout.

Thinking thus, I walked around to the signal office. Inside was a busy, strained air and one or two standing about. I said in a low voice to Galloway, 'What's this bloody gag about leaving Pop?' 'That's Corporal Cliff's advice, and I advise it too, for those not obliged to stop.'

It appears that MPs in two different offices told Jock Campbell and Fox that Pop was to be strafed that night. 'They've sworn to raze it to the ground,' someone chirped.

'But is there anything official?' I probed, sceptical. There wasn't, so I felt allayed and rang up Corps, albeit my voice trembled and it was with difficulty I controlled it as I spoke. No instructions had so far been given me, so I was justified in asking. Matter-of-fact replies were received from my OC, and I took it for granted that we at Pop had been the victims of a panic.

For twenty minutes our veteran conception of a secure war for the cush had vanished. Mob panic had become real. We imagined Huns under cover of flame-throwers sweeping down, having masked their intentions for months by a quiet which had lulled us into a false feeling of security. We saw them preceded by gas shells, sweeping down the Vlam road and overcoming us. The old life of nonchalant safety had been, in reality, a life near a volcano which had abruptly become active and threatened ruin. We had lived a foolish dream, but that dream had broken and we had glimpsed war.

At first the panic had seemed absurd, but others believed it so intensely as genuine that, against my will it had the live reality of things and not a folly. I was a fool not to believe the terror. Then, at the orderly and routine remarks, I began to recover the old outlook.

Meanwhile, it had only thunder-showered slightly. At 1.30 I went to bed and slept until at last the boys came in, some from the dugout.

At 3.10 the mines on St Eloi and Wytschaete went off, but though it stated in the papers that Lloyd George heard them in England, I heard tell of no-one in Pop who heard them. I didn't hear same. Next morning, was ashamed of panic, which had seemed so specious.

THURSDAY 7 JUNE

Early this morning in fine weather, the Battle of Messines and Wytschaete had taken place.

As I rode over the track from Dickebusch road, all the soldiers that had been lying in reserve there had disappeared and the many dugouts in the embankment were empty. In their place, along the track came parties of captive Huns in straggling groups of about fifty, some wounded. Our accompanying Tommies were smiling broadly.

The Huns showed a kind of dark sardonic mirth, like men to whom further experience mattered not. They were now not haughty like the prisoners who used to come down the road on the Somme, scorning our chummy advances.

Then our men came for pigeons. They were in good trim and said our men of the 41st had simply walked over, that Fritz was offering watches for bread or a tin of bully.

FRIDAY 8 JUNE

Vic to Ramparts, seeing dead horses and human limb on the way. There was a crater where I had seen the displaced forest. I to Dickebusch and arranged for a method of reporting where birds went to, to obviate the chaos that had reigned on the 7th.

SATURDAY 9 JUNE

I to the Ramparts, passing split shell-boxes and prone dead horses galore. Ramparts quiet. Dickebush now absolutely vacant and dugouts abandoned because reserve troops all gone forward. Walked along lake banks that used to be immune from dread during the day in plain sun – like a picnic.

We brought up a prisoner in the car – a civvy, clerk-like specimen, who showed us a photo of his home and kids. When we tried to explain that we should win the war because of the Americans, he smiled incredulously and said, '*Ganz Belgien voll Deutschen Soldaten…*'

Intensely hot and sultry. To bed late and didn't sleep well. During the last four nights the guns and heat have militated against sleep.

SUNDAY 10 JUNE

To Division, where I met the Observation Officer, Mr Hogg, who had used our pigeons with great success, giving 400-word descriptions of actual ground gained and positions by pigeon.

The newspapers carried idiotic descriptions of spectacular victory, amazing feats of thrilling élan – an incomparable affair. Compare the drab, though sunny reality – a matter of carelessness. The looseness, casualness of it, was like breaking up a football match.

MONDAY 11 JUNE

To Voormezeele with Pip to arrange for new forward depot there. Already employment companies had been up and chucked great loads of loose stones at the sides of the road. Cutting our tyres, bumping cartwheels and car bonnets and horses' hooves, following the uninterrupted line of traffic and seeking a lull to dart through and gain a few yards' progress. The idea of running daily along here instead of along the good surface and fairly cushy route hitherto patronised, did not please. The slope of the hill we had captured showed up gently dun, dim and desolate and the few tree-stumps on it stood up like dark tusks.

In afternoon to Corps and saw Mr Underwood. We'd done very well. He said he'd recommended Jack Hilton for the Military Medal. I said I was glad and cracked Jack up as a brave and cheerful, conscientious veteran.

'I didn't intend saying anything, but I've recommended you too, Davis.' I was amazed and thrilled. I had not dreamt of this honour, and at a time a MM seemed much to me.

'I'm not a man who expected that kind of thing, sir. I'm not one of the fighting sort and it's very good of you. I appreciate it keenly because I never dreamt I should be worth one. It's something money can't buy. I'd sooner have it almost than anything.'

'I consider you've earned it – and Hilton. But don't say anything about it at present, and I shouldn't tell Hilton until it's put through.' 'I won't, sir.' Elated but suppressedly glad, back to camp.

TUESDAY 12 JUNE

This morn on bike with birds, shells dropped constantly at side or in front of me. I found all ways barred by debris or shells falling, except a detour round to the north side and along the canal and moat embankment. Not a soul to be seen – me with the wind up.

Bumped my belt-rim twice on the crater edges in the long stretch along the Ramparts before arriving at the Menin Gate. I got behind the church through lumpy waste ground to the barracks, expecting shells any moment. Down the Dickebusch road I turned up the road opposite the Asylum. Pink and black were shooting up from the Asylum. I rode over logs and rushed round the corner. Immediately as I got twenty yards away shells dropped again. I drove furiously. Something swished and came down an awful whack on my breastbone, nearly knocking me off my bike with a thud, in shock and fright.

'I've got it at last,' I thought, stopping and feeling with my hand for blood. I fished down and brought up a big piece of hard rubble – it must have blown up from a lorry that had been hit near the Asylum and came down hard on my breast. I laughed.

WEDNESDAY 13 JUNE

Round with plump, undemonstrative Fifth Army pigeon sergeant to see Ramparts and lofts. He was not enthusiastic about Jack – simply said the Fifth Army were going to take over the lofts – and yet I hadn't been officially informed about it.

'What's to become of Jack?' I asked 'Don't know – it's not settled yet. Meanwhile he'll just carry on. He can draw rations as usual I suppose.' 'I don't know what Division's coming in. I knew all the brigades of Second Army, but if you're bringing up a new army with fresh divisions, where shall I fare? I'm at home with the X Corps. I will say they've treated me well. Mr Underwood's a little gentleman.'

We took an inventory of the stock there and at the lofts. We had shifted our depot to Voormezeele on Saturday and taken Mac Sloan away from Jack, who was heartbroken, for Mac was a good mate.

In the afternoon to Voormezeele to pick sites for lofts 40 and 59. Sweating in sun I walked amid the fine support and reserve trenches parallel to and in front of the Kemmel-Ypres road – well traversed and built with clean dry nooks and corners and square, straight dugouts. No sign of devastation or filth – must have been fairly cushy in reserve.

At last found test-box – a low mound on the ground which was the roof of the dugout. In the dark a man was glued to telephone and switchboard. Walked and rode and waited and at last struck Mr Ward, who in lad-di-da style talked freely and we picked the one pitch for Hughie's loft 40 on the right before the dressing station in a decent field. For Whittle and 59 we chose the flat green stretch on the other side, one having to watch that there was place for the vans to cross the ditches and that water was available.

In morning I had gone with Vic to look at the old front line. Passing Voormezeele, where there were still stuck the notices saying 'Ration dump blue line' and 'Tottenham Court Road', we went up the road. Trucks and engines were loading and running on improvised light railway lines, and a wooden aqueduct had been run on a rough bridge over the small river. The trucks ran forward on the shifty embankment and troops and employment companies passed up and down. The road had been planked or corded with stout two-inch joists because it had been so badly shot away. This new wooden road forked right and there we saw our old front line, the trenches one and a half yards wide, rough, jagged and irregular. At the top of the first ridge were the old Hun front-line trenches – bashed to bits. A rat couldn't have lived in them.

THE STREETS OF VOORMEZEELE, 1916

Bits of revetment netting and concrete were mixed up with the dirt of in-fallen trenches. Concrete points had been blown in and on the right was one of the great mine-craters, as big as a pit in a brickfield. No dead Germans to be seen, but many rocket ends and grenades tumbled about – cartridges, gas-bag piping, thick German wire toggles and so on. The planked road proper ended here, but a sort of path wound up the other side of the slope. We saw what a fine position the Huns had had for looking down on us as we hunted for souvenirs.

SUNDAY 17 JUNE

My first look at Westoutre – a rural village, homely and of red brick, set a-twisty in green fields with church and a three-cornered square in the middle. It hadn't quite the genial comely look of an English village – there was a harsh trait in it and a hint of Flemish hardness and angularity, as square cheeks give a touch of forbiddingness to an otherwise hale and agreeable face. However, in the Sunday sun it was warm – even rosy.

We sought out Crampton – IX Corps DR, in an estaminet midway on the second square. We had a drink with him and he pressed us to stay on but we went to Julie's estaminet in the village, where Pip had fixed up bedroom and writing room accommodation for us for 20 francs a week.

We knocked at the estaminet. 'Come in.' shouted raucously. Julie was seated in the corner, her gendarme lover – heavy, fine, handsome, braided with red and silver, leant near in the attitude of interrupted courtship. 'You can go upstairs,' she said in a voice throaty and contralto. She was a broad, a bit fair, a Flemish woman – clean-dressed and solid but not good-looking.

At the top of the steep flight was a small landing, off which was our room. It was small, stuffy, full of two beds with a small gap between. We dropped our kit, completed our drinking with Crampton and got back to Pop.

Blinded by frequent dust clouds on the Hallebast Corner-Ouderdom road had two spills. I pinched the bulb of the horn – no sound – and I smote a sergeant crossing the road. Then in the afternoon got knocked over by a lorry as I was trying to pass in front of it then turn to the right. Pitched into ditch – Pip said it was lucky that it didn't knock me under the wheels and smash me – I was over-rash. Arrived very dusty and cut at new billet, all loaded and sweaty, and bedroom unbearably hot and stuffy.

MONDAY 18 JUNE

I had previously gone over the roads and found the best route was into Dickebusch, then to Voormezeele along the Kemmel road to Ypres. The other road from Café Belge too shell-holed and the top-heavy vans might have gone over.

At EN 11 we found the wires were in the way of moving the lofts, and men on horses had to be commandeered to lift the wires with cleft poles while the vans passed under them. Then at the site an exact position had to be found, with the trap of the loft towards the front line, from which birds could fly straight and alight, and yet so situated that the loftmen could watch the trap from within their tents. These had to be pitched on a sheltered site if the men were to enjoy any ease and warmth during the long winter months. Then to prevent the lofts sinking in the soft ground, broad planks should rest under the wheels. The planks had to be put down and the horses run over the ground so that they could pause and bring the loft to a standstill on the boards. If they overran the boards there was scarcely room between the shell-holes to turn round in an arc wide enough to run on the boards again. The drivers were cursing and it required strength of character to get them to repeat their attempts to get the wheels on the boards.

At EN 1 Andy Butler's loft had been stuck in on ground unsupported and had so sunk in that three of them were working for donkey's hours before they got it out of the rut. Faint with thirst we waited at the taps at the cisterns set up after the battle – the queue of men waiting for water shows how important a water supply is in fighting. Imagine men in that parched state having to fight.

TUESDAY 19 JUNE

Made umpteen receipt sheets for stock, which I was handing over to the Fifth Army and left each loft well and honestly furnished with clips, and small and large baskets. How different from the way stock was handed over to me. At Dupont's I left a splendid great reserve of stock, including assault baskets fitted with message book, pencil and two clips, all ready for several great stunts. Learnt it was after all another Corps, not Keeling's which was taking over the Pop lofts. How sorry I was to part with them. It cut me to the quick to leave my old home, however, everything was left in order.

At Barnes' I met one of those fed-up youths – a young DR come to take pigeons from XIX Corps. 'How many are you going to use?' 'Don't know and don't care. If it depends on me it'll be eight. Quite enough of the footling things. My officer leaves it to me – he knows bugger all about the business. I'll just carry on with what you've been taking up.' I thought 'The usual old style as it used to be. They'll soon feel the difference at the lofts if that's the way things are going on.'

WEDNESDAY 20 JUNE

Tried to get to the ramparts to see Jack Hilton with a registered letter for him, but shrapnel barred the road and spurts of shell debris were rising in the distance. Men had been walking away from it, leading horses. A group was waiting at the bend by the bridge over the canal. 'What's it like?' 'He's been shelling heavy.'

I went on, not a soul in sight. It looked menacing, like a bit of world given over to destruction and bent on compassing the ruin of any stepping therein. You felt that now the dark and vile, and death have got their chance, and they're going to have you after all the exemption you've enjoyed. Fate has favoured you by affecting not to notice you, only to draw you on to be rash, in a false feeling of security, so that you can be wiped out completely and callously. So I turned tail…

SATURDAY 23 JUNE

At No 40 heard that Jack Hilton had been wounded – couldn't make out whether it was on the day I had been prevented from getting through to him by shells, and I wondered if my taking it might by chance have diverted this. Spoilt my ride home by this reflection, and grief at Jack hurt. At first they were not sure he was not killed. Remembered how old Jack used to come down to Pop sometimes and insist on treating all and sundry to drinks.

The departure today of Archer for the Somme – I felt pity for him that he, a coward, had to leave his funkhole and brave the rigours of the line. He did not grouse, but went looking pale and hunted.

SUNDAY 24 JUNE

Jack got wind up about arrival of Joshua. Thought Joshua had been sent by GHQ to learn his job, so that Jack could be put on a mobile, which he did not appear to relish.

MONDAY 25 JUNE

Pip ill at home with bite on leg from our billet dog – a great shaggy black dog chained to a kennel. He went down to hospital to get it cauterised, looking rather pale.

We'd have 'dos' at the billet – the first when the butcher came home on one of his three-monthly leaves. They asked us to join them and we drank *vin rouge* and ate *salade* and bully. The butcher used to have our downstairs room for a shop and it was still used to sell vegetables grown in the burgomaster's land adjoining the garden at the rear. The burgomaster was a kind of rusty rural black broad-cloth farmer with a fat japes of a son about whom we used to taunt Julia.

In evening to a debate at Talbot House on reprisals – I against. We lost by 62–31.

WEDNESDAY 27 JUNE

With car to Voormezeele – heavily shelled. Brought the car up to flat ground by bridge and Vickery, because he was nervous I think, and wanted company, walked with me to the dugout. Shells were falling about 50 yards away on the RFA guns along the bank. Sales ducked nervously. 'You needn't jump yet. They're nowhere near here,' said Corporal Taylor. He was quite unmoved. Vickery and I strove to sound calm, but to me our unnatural voices spoke of our effort to control nerves.

THURSDAY 28 JUNE

I with Vic to Voormezeele to the mobiles that had been shelled. One had dropped right in the hedge making a Jack Johnson hole just ten yards from Hughie. A wonder they weren't hit. Selected a new site by the brasserie with Mr Underwood. We walked and tramped, the weight of my tools, tin hat and gas-bag causing me to tire and lag and sweat. Then we moved the lofts with the teams of horses that had arrived and I carted the birds in stock baskets – a sweating game, to and fro all day.

FRIDAY 29 JUNE

In afternoon a message to go to Westoutre signal office, where I had fixed to be called from my billet if required. It was Corporal Staples, congratulating me on the Military Medal, which had gone through. Pip piqued because I had been quiet about it – nevertheless, I was deeply glad.

SATURDAY 30 JUNE

Congratulations from Mr Underwood. In the evening to Pop and got the ribbon – had it put on, then sat in the Tivolies with coat on, but open – wanted really to have greatcoat off. Kept looking at it, yet shy about it. Looked keenly at others wearing the MM and how and where they wore it.

My feelings on getting the MM – the sales girl smilingly and scentedly (how scented the Belgian girls are) pinned it on. Looking round to see how many men had one. At Westoutre shy and self-conscious and imagined everyone was looking at my left breast. Wanted to see how it looked in the mirror. Told O'Connor and Foster at the Reninghelst signal office – and felt foolish thereon.

SUNDAY 1 JULY

An extract from Company Orders, dated 29 June 1917:
X Corps Signal Company RE AWARDS:

The Officer Commanding has much pleasure in announcing the award of the Military Medal to the undermentioned men for devotion to duty during the recent operations of June 7 1917.
148768 8.4. Corporal Davis, O H
115598 Pnr. A/Corporal Hilton, J
X Company HQ
Signal Company
Dated 19. 6. 17

OSWALD'S MILITARY MEDAL, AWARDED "FOR BRAVERY IN THE FIELD" DURING THE BATTLE OF MESSINES, 1917.

MONDAY 2 JULY

On arriving at the mobiles learned that the second pitch had been shelled. It was a field, a bit holed, with green turf and one shady corner where Tom Cavill was. As I made to go, shrapnel burst, plonk, overhead and leaves and bits of twig and branches were spattered around. Wondered if hit, and away like greased lightning with wind up. Met Graves limping back from the field ambulance, a bit of shrapnel having scarred his calf that morning.

TUESDAY 3 JULY

By car to the mobiles – which had been shelled at 3 am – must have been marked by Fritz. RE men nearby said pitch had not been shelled like this before. Five birds killed and gassed, five wounded and gassed. Two shell-holes inside the palisaded square of Wright's loft. One spoke broken and two split, glass and roof riddled. The mobiles had to be moved, so selected two sites and watched their removal by teams – one to the slope left of Vierstraat to Hallebast Corner road. Here the loftmen were quids in, being far enough away for safety, yet handy to the line, and good fellowship all round.

In evening debate at Talbot House on State Socialism – against State Socialism lost, 19-54.

WEDNESDAY 4 JULY

Held up because of crowd at square to see arrival of the King in Bailleul. Soon, on a very thin tide of cheering, he floated into the square in a car. Umpteen brass hats around to be presented to him, he shaking hands in leisurely fashion. Slight, spare legs, pronounced stoop at the shoulders – anything but kingly – rather meagre and insignificant-looking and small of stature. Rather puffy or bloated appearance at the cheeks. His chauffeur was kingly – a lance corporal, clean-shaven and supercilious, stretched languidly in Rolls Royce car, head back, eyes near closed. Car dark blue with papier mâché shield of the Royal Standard on the front of radiator and a silver figure above the bonnet and a small Royal Standard floating from the top of the car.

FRIDAY 6 JULY

On a visit to Mont Rouge we could see Lille in the distance and with glasses you could see faintly steeples and stacks in the mist. Wondered if we should ever reach it – it seemed impossible at this rate. Our progress the rate of lichen growing compared to the distance we had to cover to get 'em out of Belgium.

Changed £6 to get francs for medal celebration.

SATURDAY 7 JULY

Got ready for 'do' a little anxiously. Arrived at 5.45 – a few fellows waiting around but wouldn't come in – it apparently being a point of honour not to seem anxious to drop in for free drinks. At six Pip and I and DR Davies in – umpteen bottles of champagne – 200 francs' worth at eight francs a time. Then a few others joined and at 6.45 Paul, Wright and Cavill. Pip was going about creamy, filling up glasses and saying 'bogey, bogey,' making queer noises and forming a pistol with his fingers. Seward squirming like an eel after a few glasses and noisy and Charlie White thumping on the table and singing. Adrienne got anxious and touched me on the shoulder, asking that no more should be drunk. Jock was lying outside in the yard and refusing to be moved. Vic, who had been pouring with Pip, had his blue eyes bulging in a dull daze and was up and down stairs puking. I like a fool drank very little. Bruce spoke nicely.

Songs good and a complete success and record for the DRs. Pip was wandering up and down and I waited for him in case he couldn't ride, but he could ride better drunk than sober, like many DRs.

SUNDAY 8 JULY

A year to the day since we started for Southampton en route for the BEF. It does – and does not – seem a year.

THURSDAY 9 JULY

I went with the famous Wingham to the lofts – I'd heard a lot about him – the poshest pigeon DR there was – brown leggings and boots, the leggings laced, officer's cloth cap, officer's collar under Anzac cloth tunic, silk scarf, Burberry. First time Barnes met him mincing over Debyses he thought he was a brass hat. I wasn't much impressed by him.

TUESDAY 10 JULY

In evening had a comfy read – but frequently we had to put our lights out because in fine weather the Boche humming tops could always be heard coursing directly overhead to Bailleul. Sometimes we'd go down and watch the tracer bullets in the sky – the drop of bombs and red flash, the searchlights and the Hun machines suspended in them. The hungry insatiable noiseless search-lights were fine. We kept under the eaves when the shrapnel was dropping around and we would guess at where the bombs were falling.

WEDNESDAY 11 JULY

Morning to Bailleul to place behind the station where had been told could get hot bath. Found a bathroom in a wooden shed with rickety enclosures with plain calico hanging as curtains. Middle-aged woman talking French all the while attended to boiler and fire. A pink-bloused sylph with loose bodice and grey skirt and fine fresh, clear complexion swept into your room to ask if the water was 'bon', though you might have your tunic and shirt off. She, however, demure and nought doing, though no doubt many soldiers thought otherwise.

The estaminet in Bailleul was up steps into a long corridor. On walls were curious pictures of battle and hunt – and a billiard table. Flitting about in the background a young girl of mature curves in a cerise blouse and with black hair – nice and easy with the soldiers. In the forefront a zinc counter and dirty madame and against this background a girl of exquisite, firm and young fresh figure, clad severely in grey – fair with mists of mystery in her eyes. Gazing into space and unheeding, except with calm humour, of the soldiers' gags. 'Crossed in love,' murmured her mother. '*Fiancé parti.*'

TUESDAY 17 JULY

In evening to Bailleul picture house. Strange, as you sat there you could hear, about every ten minutes, a shell dropping somewhere at the end of the town, but same never seemed to drop near the cinema. The civvies took no notice. Round to Jeanne's and saw the old II Corps roster. On opposite side of the road was a very pretty girl in a baker's shop that sold sweets, souvenirs and *bonnes bouches*. She was pleasing and modest, and I wondered none had captured her – but probably she was booked.

THURSDAY 19 JULY

All this week big rumours of our moving. I didn't want to – didn't fit in with my OC's instructions – nevertheless we feared a move. I expect it was due to the big changes and the Corps and divisions pressing in on the left of us, getting ready for Passchendaele.

In the afternoon to Wytschaete. No sign of life. Creeping up, we lay down in the hollows of the ruin which topped the ridge at half-hedge height. With glasses we peeped over the gaps in the ruins and saw a gradually ascending ridge on whose various crests appeared steeples, and clusters of red-brick buildings like workhouses or factories. They must have been Wervicq and Comines. It seemed so pleasant – like Somerset on a sunny afternoon – and magic too, for we had lusted to set foot into that miraculous land where the Germans worked in tranquil safety and plenty ever since the line stood fast. But we had never achieved it. Should we ever? And what would it be like when we did?

Some shells began to fall behind and before us, so we decided to go back. We had just got towards our bikes when the ground shook and emitted thunder. A great din spread all round. The ground on every hand, that had seemed to us barren and lifeless, flashed fire in all its hollows – it was yellow chaos. The ground was sequined with flame and the rattle was continuous. We'd never dreamed a gun was near – but the place was infested. They had been well hid. Men standing to must have watched us go up and return. How we cursed that we had not been still on the ridge where we should have seen the effects of the fire. We saw some Fritz flashes at the beginning and behind the far rise. On the hill of Kemmel, on a little hollow plateau, were a group of brass hats, come up to see the shoot. We had a look at Kemmel – the dugouts built mysteriously in the hill, and the caverns from which, report had it, guns were pushed out to shoot on rails and then drawn back again.

SUNDAY 29 JULY

All last week we have been bombarded heavily day and night. One night Hun planes dropped bombs very near – incendiaries – and a big pink flash lit the sky. All this time we were expecting 'the stunt' any day.

MONDAY 30 JULY

At EV 37 we heard the clap of shells at the brasserie. It sounded ominous and the sky was dark and cloudy. We knew trouble was brewing. Recalled the time that I rushed shit-hot past a gun-pit on fire. As I hesitated and watched, the flames rose tree-high in the air. Should I pass it or take the turn to the right and the bad road – nearer to the shells and shelling. There was no-one about. At last I rushed it and as I passed I saw no gunners, but saw the big two-and-a-half foot shells standing amid the flames. Didn't know if they might go off as I raced past, but nothing happened. At Kruisstraathoek crossroads I told the MP, but he took notice in the usual army way. It wasn't his concern if the whole pit and the dump on the other side were blown to blazes. It was no-one's job – it never was. I never saw any time in my army career when it mattered. No-one took responsibility and it was a wonder anything was ever saved.

A VIEW OF KEMMEL HILL, BELGIUM, SHORTLY AFTER THE WAR.

TUESDAY 31 JULY

Went round the bend to the dressing station where I saw a crowd of captured Fritzes waiting, captured, exhausted. As I stopped to regard them, a shell dropped near. The Jerries ducked, nearly to a man – but the Tommies didn't. I lit a cigarette to show off, but I didn't stay an instant longer than I needed to complete my swank.

Suddenly there was no-one at the dressing station – even the MP, usually on the corner, had deserted his post and gone into dugout. Wheeling left by the old church the road was wet from shell splashes bursting in the moat alongside. 'Shall I go on?' I said to myself. But I wanted dinner and little is more vexing than to leave a job incomplete just at its point of finishing. So on, but in shadow. Debris was everywhere and a new Triumph motor-bike lay on its side.

At this I slipped off my bike in a panic and put it on its stand in the middle of the road. This seemed an unbusiness-like thing to do, so I ran back and propped it up at the side of the road.

The sky was dark. I thought, 'Fate has spread her nets and all through my own folly in persisting, she's going to cop me this time.' On the left there were the remains of a brick wall – the sole remnants of a house. Two Anzacs were crouching on the other side as protection against the splinters. 'Hello. Where are you going, digger?' 'To the dugout by the embankment.' 'Well, I should bloody well get there slick. He's been bumping hell into this joint.' I leapt away from them, my pigeon basket on my back, and over the slippy shell-holes and rubbish, going awkwardly like a frog. A shell broke near and I smelt the fumes and smarted under the brick dust.

Between me and the dugout ran a small stream, deep cut and crossed by a plank. Overhead was a rough bridge, carrying the light railway from side to side of the embankment which the river divided.

Slipping down to the bridge, I saw, crouching against the embankment, two men carrying pigeon baskets. They beckoned me to go down to them. 'Safer in the dugout, I think,' I muttered, and then stuck, jammed in the woodwork buttresses supporting the bridge. My basket had caught, so I unstrapped it. The ground shook with a dull explosion that felt rather than sounded near. I expected the bridge to fall in on me at any moment – a rotten way to be killed.

For nearly a minute turf, sand, bricks, rails, wooden logs seemed to be falling around me from some fountain in the air. I waited anxiously. Nothing happened.

I ran out, scared and white, but I had left by basket behind and I went back for it and flung it and the poor mickies into Mac's shelter. I remember scraping my way down the narrow passage to dugout. No heroism about me – I wanted to get under cover. 'Come ye,' said Mac. 'How ye've got through is a miracle. It's the closest thing I've seen.'

When I got half way down the steep steps I paused, panting. Below the entrance gunners and signalman were sheltering. Still throbbing, I told everyone my tale as if no-one had ever streaked through shells before.

At first I was absolutely out of breath, then, heatedly, 'I've just been covered with shit – wood, rails, turf. I was under the embankment – shell hit it just over me. Scared me to death.'

I went down and had a look at Mac's abode. Floors were waterlogged, and in the clay rooms where their berths were, water was half a foot deep. Deep sorrow entered my heart in the clammy chill half-light. Fancy living and sleeping here, on poor rations (they were often short of sugar, tea, bread) with shells – and often gas shells – knocking about day and night. They thumped overhead on top of the dugout now, but it was some 20 feet deep in the ground.

Mac went out and brought the birds in. After waiting ten minutes I went out quickly to my bike. I cast an envious glance at the brand-new Triumph, my fingers itching to scrounge the horn, lamp or pump – every DR well knows my feeling – but instead I went to my bike and rode away like the devil.

WEDNESDAY 1 AUGUST

As usual, because of our attack, except with Messines, the weather has definitely broken on the very day we open our fighting. Today heavy downfall of rain all day.

Pip and I to Voormezeele and back, quick. Mac said, 'Yon shell that missed you killed a friend of ours – Corporal Taylor. They found him after you'd gone. He must have been waiting to get away – he'd left me half an hour before you came.' 'That must have been him that beckoned me to go down to them – they had pigeon baskets – I'd forgotten all about them.' 'The other man was Heseltine – his arm was blown off – a nice lad. A DR and some others in the embankment dugout were wounded at the same time. I never did think much to that dugout,' observed Mac with a professional air.

'I felt sure that shell was coming for me – instead old Taylor got knocked out. I'll bet he never expected it – he's been up and down the line safely so many times. That's just how it happens, Mac.' And I went away sorely grieved, for Taylor had been a conscientious pigeon-man, modest and long-suffering. Of such were the ranks of the heroes – and Heseltine was a bonny, well-built boy, always cheerful, with proud form and aquiline nose and broad face, never grousing, never weary.

THURSDAY 2 AUGUST

Guns heavy at night. Rain all night and dawn. Poor fellows out there. We used to meet men coming back from the line absolutely muddied to the eyebrows. Through rain to Voormezeele, the railway line buckled, the aviary smashed under the improvised dugout on which a shell had landed. Birds in bad condition down in the dugout, and Mac concerned. I hauled the broken cage on to the car, Vickery keen to get away – you never knew when a shell was going to drop on us.

MONDAY 6 AUGUST

At Voormezeele searching shell-fire had just ceased, so Edmonds thought it advisable not to risk the car, and I putting on tin hat and box-respirator at the ready, crossed over fields parallel to the Oxford Circus trench. How dark-coloured and chaotic it was. Right past the RFA guns in the riverbank. These were the guns that Fritz was always feeling for, but never seemed to knock out. They hung pluckily on. Half ran to dugout – Mac and Sales came back with me, lugging the baskets.

TUESDAY 14 AUGUST

In evening met Hinde, who had been out a month and was swanking about hot times from Division to Brigade at Brielen and Elverdinge. But now we rather regarded ourselves as old hands and we resented this. 'A man who talks about shells here is a bloody fool,' said Paul. 'Trash. Like preaching oysters in Whitstable.'

THURSDAY 16 AUGUST

This evening at supper Fred Skinner shouted through the door the news of Langemarck taken. Talk of guns being rushed forward and of Ypres now being safe.

Roads very bad and traffic at loggerheads. Troops cheerful, especially the Anzacs one meets. They never seem to get depressed no matter what happens. I never remember seeing a depressed Australian.

With the Russian collapse, things lately have seemed dire again. Sergeant Edmonds goes about as sanguine as ever, predicting speedy overwhelming of the Hun. But with this sole exception, opinion of the DRs at Second Army has now switched back again to pessimism. The talk goes, 'Where are the brains? Our brass hats are no bloody good and never will be. They haven't a glimmer of a ghost of an idea how to run a war. Here we've been stuck for three years, and we shall be here another three unless Willy pushes us into the sea. As for France and Belgium, the Hun was bloody cute when he turned it over and went away. It's not worth fighting for.'

FRIDAY 17 AUGUST

In evening to Abeele for mail, and going down the road I had a spill. Two kids ran out from my side just as a lorry had passed. I knocked one, arm and chest, and thought he was badly hut. Thud – the poor little mite. He sat in the ditch, dazed, but I waited until he ran off across the fields and home. Felt very sorry.

SATURDAY 19 AUGUST

Keeling had converted the basement of EN1 loft into a buzzing signal office. There was a telephone with special operator for all the messages of the surrounding mobiles, which were handed in here. Keeling was working like a city magnate. He told me how he had come over and sized up the position for his Major Day, who trusted him implicitly, and advised on the installation of the signal office there. The room hummed with activity. They were working my old birds all out, that I had trained to perfection – and unavoidably were losing many.

Weather-bitten and case-hardened, Mason sat there: 'Never had such a cutting up in our life. The Somme was nothing to it. Heartrending to read the messages.' 'Where do you take the birds to?' 'It was Birr Crossroads,' said Keeling. 'We couldn't stand it, so I got an artillery major's report, showing how many shells fell per day on the area, and we got it moved back to Ypres. We used to be waiting half the day before we or the chaps could get up.' 'How did you get on with Evans?' 'Oh, we don't speak. I had my idea he was cooking his times. I made them all get their times marked for trapping according to the time they were handed in here. Some of his birds had been in the habit of doing the cancan or going to sleep on the trap before they came inside. His loft's been neglected. I asked him who was boss, and told him I intended to be that here. So now we don't speak.'

I heard these details tremulously because it was rumoured we were going to relieve II Corps and I wanted some wrinkles.

SUNDAY 19 AUGUST

As I approached Voormezeele, Mac slowed me down. By EW1 was a motorbike shot in the tank and guard. On the saddle was a DR's cap with a bloody slit through it where the shrapnel or splinter had entered his head and killed him. I believe he was an ASC or ammunition or artillery DR. A Jack Johnson hole in the hedge by Hughie's Wright's old pitch.

MONDAY 20 AUGUST

There was a lot of mystery about the Fourth Army, who were waiting on the coast to push on the flank when the Passchendaele drive had been a success. It was reported that divisions had been trained to land from the fleet – these divs were supposed to be barricaded in with barbed wire and not allowed to go out of camp lest information should be leaked of our plans. Sadly, owing to weather or bad staff work, we were not successful enough to justify this.

In the evening the band of 33rd Division in the square – very enjoyable. Then a walk on the scented hills around. It was very beautiful in the hillside fields, ripening for autumn with the yeomen working as if war was a country away instead of eight miles.

TUESDAY 21 AUGUST

Visited Pip Compton, who's with Prince of Wales Corps. Pip says the Prince is a sport. If they meet him on the road, 'Good morning, Corporal. Bad weather for your work.' 'Just shows the difference between a gentleman and an outsider. We've got some howling nip of a APM in our Corps – a guardsman – wears those horrible golfing breeches when he's on the spree – and he looks you up and down like horse-muck when he takes your salute. Bloody fool – if he only knew how he looked. And we've several others who absolutely ignore your salute – you might as well be a cabbage stump. That's your brass hat all over – the manners of a railway porter and the brains of a toy dog.'

'Pip, some of the brass hats haven't even human decency. I once heard a talk on the telephone between two big guns. "I want 200 blankets for my men," says the OC. "Sorry, but it's imposs," answers the quartermaster. "But why not?" "They're not entitled to them." "But we must have them – my men are suffering." 'Sorry, but I cannot break the rule." "Very well, if you can't let me have them on grounds of humanity, I demand them on the grounds of expediency. My men are dying from exposure. We cannot afford to lose men from this reason and I shall report it." "Oh, if that's the case." By God, Pip, and all this time quartermasters and sergeants are flogging blankets all over the shop.'

He went on, 'The Prince is very decent – goes buggering about up the line with a pushbike. He doesn't like swank and if any of the big nibs come bussing round, he makes himself scarce and bees up the line on his bike. He wouldn't have the guards rushed into long marches and pushed straight into the fighting. No – he let us have some charabancs. He stuck out for them. But he's cute. He doesn't sign receipts for DRs or orderlies. He throws the chit away, because everyone pinches 'em for his autograph and says he's lost it. So he says, "Are you waiting for the receipt?" "Yes." "That's all right – I've got them, you see." As I was riding back I met him, a Staff Captain, on a bucking horse over the railway. He saluted in return to my DR salute. Takes salutes but doesn't look for 'em.'

WEDNESDAY 22 AUGUST

Read *Married Life* by May Edington – planes overhead. Searchlights wonderfully defined and bright as Pip and Jamo came back late, creamy. Jamo left his headlight on despite the planes and sat drinking the beer they had brought with them, talking of the WAACs and VAD drivers they had seen and the girls in the red-lamps in flimsy attire.

SUNDAY 26 AUGUST

We had drinks in a forlorn estaminet on top of the spur of Mont Rouge. Full of soldiers and civvies of both sexes, but none of the latter young. This used to be a great holiday ground before the war. Now you could get nothing but flat beer at about 1 franc 25 per bottle – and they were not too easily forthcoming at that. People used to come up here to gaze out over the battle-plain which showed well from under the mill. Mac, cheerful, stowing his pipe full, departed stoically towards Voormezeele and the drab existence of dugout and shells and gas. I felt sorry.

FRIDAY 31 AUGUST

I was awakened at midnight with two telegrams about classes and locating new point.

Over at Corps outside the yard, Mr Underwood said 'we want to get a bit farther up. They're complaining we're a bit too far back. After the push that's coming off, I want to have our aviary ready and hike it up to the old front line – that'll be somewhere near Verbranden Molen.'

SATURDAY 1 SEPTEMBER

To X Box at Voormezeele and waited till noon, then to Verbranden Molen with Mr Underwood, and he rushed on in front of me, crash and bang over the shell-holes, but I took it more carefully. If anything went wrong with my bike I'd got to pay the piper – he merely had to chuck it to the tiffy. Shells were falling 150 yards to the left, but we rode on. Soon the road was barren and black with burnt-out lorries and cars, ditched and desolate.

Left our bikes at the roadside and walked over hillocks and holes to a line of trenches before some dugouts and humps of land called Strong Points numbers 8 and 9. Mr Underwood met an officer and asked if it could be arranged to install our aviary there, and house our two pigeon men.

Just then Fritz lengthened his range and swept leftward. The shells crept over the ground 100 yards away. We saw men in groups running for cover and the RFA guns kept on shooting, despite the nearness of the bursts. In our trench, men sat lazily puffing pipes and looked on as if it were a friendly football match. 'Now men, get inside,' called out the major. 'I don't want any more casualties because you're all too lazy to move.' The men, with grumbling looks, chewed their pipes or removed them and slouched reluctant into the dugouts.

Bending, I entered a dugout. The shells came nearer. 'If one hits this roof, I shall be crushed under the beam,' I thought. The cook kept dodging outside to his fire and relaying news.

'He's searching – if he shortens the range, he's got us. Oh, damn him, we must have summat to eat.' Whooooooooo-phit.' 'Not quite, yer bloody Kamerads. Go and cook your own spuds and leave me to mine. Joe Pett was working his gun there only yesterday, and his two mates got buried in the dugout. Poor Arthur – both legs…'

One man sat writing field postcards, careless of the shells thudding near. Another man was routing out knives, forks and spoons for their dinner while one man slept – and another looked as pale and nervous as I felt.

After two hours' shelling ceased, we hurried back over the lumpy ground. An RFA man with bare chest was still working unconcernedly at his gun.

Mr Underwood's bike, a new one, had been knocked over by an explosion, and his tank dented and the pump gone. Both bikes were covered with earth – but my old crock was otherwise unscratched.

'Not good enough,' said Mr Underwood, and I could see the idea of establishing a dump there had had a nasty jar. I said, 'Looks a bit hot if the men have got to be there all the time and no hope of relief,' but I was really thinking of myself, and hoped against hope that we shouldn't have to take pigeons up there daily. Probably that two-hour bombardment saved my skin – for if we had gone at a quiet time, our depot would have been fixed at Verbranden Molen.

Heard there was a stunt to come.

TUESDAY 4 SEPTEMBER

Pip early to Voormezeele to advise removal and I met Sergeant Edmonds and helped to fix Mobile 41. E turned up wiping a moist brow, 'Who would have thought you could have such trouble just moving a mobile? I've been scouting about for hours. First they didn't turn up, then took the wrong road and had to go on to find a place for the team to turn in. Then the traffic held us up. I've been circusing round 'em like Harlequin all morning, then I had puncture trouble.'

We fixed the loft on a nice green near to a mound and EW 2 signal office, highly pleased with ourselves. Out came a corporal. 'The SM says you'll have to move that contraption.' 'We had army instructions to place it here,' said Eddy. 'We've ridden all over the ground and on the other fields guns were snuggled up to the hedges and would frighten the birds with the howitzer roaring – and you can't have a loft where there's continual traffic in front.' 'Well, you can't have it here.' 'Will you ask the SM to speak to me?' He was like all artillery SMs – well-built, handsome, bronzed, moustached, with the exception that his grammar was bad. He was quite decent, 'But we can't have no lofts here – that's the major's orders. And if you don't move it out inside an hour I've got instruction to pull it out. So hitch your horses in.' 'But they've gone half an hour ago.' 'Well, pull it out. I'll lend you a team of men.'

Eddy and I conferred while the SM retired to his den. I didn't know what to do. 'It's always best to see the highest in authority,' said Eddy – who kept cool and suave and tactful where I should have been ruffled and lost my hair.

We asked for the major at a sand-bagged parapet and a young sub came forward. 'The Major's put that in my hands,' he said, with a nice, rather lofty drawl. He was supple, brown and young, with coal-black eyes and moustache. 'You see, this battery position is the prize one of the Brigade. The Hun has no idea of us being here. We've issued strict instructions to the men not to make a path over the grass – they have to use a different route every time they walk over. A Fritz plane sees the tracks and rumbles a position – no-one is allowed outside that barbed wire at certain hours.' 'Good heavens, man, you're dead under observation there. The balloons are right on you. Tomorrow they'll shoot you away!' 'The balloons are down now – the sun's direct in their eyes in the afternoon. Tomorrow first thing they're right on to this target.'

We had overlooked this fact. 'Now, what about that hedge there? You'd be free from observation there?' 'It's not so nice for the loftmen – it's salvage ground and decay in the ditch and refuse. They like a decent pitch as they'll probably be spending the winter here.' 'I see nothing wrong there. They must make a dugout.'

So it was settled, and the mighty team of men came forward with legs and ropes and hauled the loft to its new pitch. It was 4.30 before we'd finished.

WEDNESDAY 5 SEPTEMBER

I to Shrapnel Corner and railway dugouts where we had established our new depot. Pip had moved the aviary with the car while I was fixing the pitch for the loft. Previously I had searched for a depot up and down the Lille Road. The château was in ruins and the only available place was a foul-smelling coalhole with a corrugated sheet over it. We decided it wouldn't do – some bloody brass hat choked us off. 'You can't come here. Who told you to? X Corps HQ? Well, tell X Corps HQ we've appropriated the whole of this building. How extremely insanitary,' he broke off to his pompous friend. 'These men are disgusting.' We damned him and cleared out.

Had a look at the dugouts in the canal locks, but all were occupied. Every available tenantable spot was taken over by the army. Anzac batteries lined the Lille Road, yet Mr Underwood managed to fix up a dugout in the railway embankments, and Mac put our old sign up, 'Reserved for III Corps Pigeons' 'We're really out of our boundary,' said Mr Underwood, 'but say nothing and see there's always one of you here, and we'll have that dugout for good with luck. If anyone asks you who you are, say the X Corps HQ fixed you up there. Divs and brigade generally fight shy of offending the Corps unnecessarily.'

At fist Mac had a fight to keep his dugout, but later on the troops moved up the line and he luxuriously appropriated the dugout – a fine place, fit for a king. The shelling at night was heavy here, and Mac's rations at first were bad – so we used to take him tea, sugar and bread.

THURSDAY 6 SEPTEMBER

Pip and I had reconnoitred the old 41st Division quarters behind their signal office, which was now an advanced Corps signal office and exchange. There were many huts here – some first class Armstrong huts.

'You'll be better in one of the huts at the back,' said Vincent O'Connor, who was superintendent. 'We've a good crib here, and we don't want to foul the nest if the brass hats turn up and if they see us in the staff huts. Besides, the area commander at Westoutre – he runs Reninghelst too – is a decent stick. He's given us permission to come here without going into details – so we'll play the game.'

Behind the SO was a fine garden, then a field which ran to the switch road constructed to relieve the main road while so many troops were passing. We chose a hut near this road with a dugout handy – but this latter was so fouled and insanitary that I never put more than a nose in.

In the staff huts were nice canvas beds and chairs and tables. A number of these had already found their way into huts occupied by the REs, and at our establishment other shortages were noticeable. This afternoon we packed the car with our multitudinous belongings. It was like a house-moving. Gear and souvenirs had been slowly adhering to us in the course of our year's stay in the Salient. Blankets and canvas buckets galore, petrol cans, wash basins, overalls, black boxes, spares, tools… If all the army carried junk like us…

In the sweltering heat we carried these over duckboards, tripping on wires to our hut – a convenient and dry, high-standing shack with a handy latrine and a pump outside the signal office. These conveniences to hand mean a lot.

THURSDAY 14 SEPTEMBER

A fine day, but news on the Russian revolution very disconcerting. Something akin to despair hovered in the air.

SATURDAY 15 SEPTEMBER

On my way to Shrapnel Corner, ten Gothas steered white and stately, like pieces of pale Gothic masonry loosed from some cathedral roof, each floated, scorning earth against the silver blue of the sky. Men ran to dugouts, expecting great bombs. I bolted down the road in half panic – a lot of transport came galloping up the road. As the Gothas were overhead I passed alongside an ammunition dump. 'If he lets fly now…' I couldn't understand why he didn't. Naught happened.

At EV 37 West Indian troops, thick-lipped, loquacious, brawny and black, were now encamped around the lofts. They had an unpopular SM and several nights in succession had thrown hand grenades into his tent – of which many lay about in the field. I saw one of the offenders being punished. In a barbed-wire enclosure he was stood against a cruciform piece of wood and bound loosely to it, his arms out. Civilisation! Is not the aristocratic caste which rules our army damned for ever by this fact? And likewise the aristocracy behind it? What about field punishment No 1, when a man is strapped to a wheel and exposed to the gaze of all? Can the aristocracy be justified when this is the method it has to adopt in extremes to buttress and display its power? Just fancy, we hadn't one democratic leader strong enough in Parliament to protest against this, or to try to see that rough justice was meted out for our men. I cannot acquit Lloyd George and the other rulers of blame for not taking steps to see that the common soldier had justice.

WEDNESDAY 19 SEPTEMBER

To the railway dugouts, where the scene represented an oriental bazaar. Piles of pigeon infantry baskets, brown cumbrous gasmasks, stock baskets, were stacked against the embankment and under Mac's shelter. Men were streaming down from various parts of the line for birds, and some stood waiting. The car came up loaded with birds – six stock baskets – which we carted across the fields, sweating.

Mac was yelling and forceful. 'Who's the boss of this show? Ye'll wait yer turn, mon, and thankful to get the birds. This mon's been waiting first.'

'Corporal, this mon had two new baskets yesterday, and they're already due us four. I say he's to go back and bring 'em before he gets birds.' 'Well, as there's a stunt on, we'll forgive him this time – but it's a bit thick the way some of you fellows come down every time there's a show on without a bloody basket. You come down with empty hands like a child at a Christmas party. You know you can't take pigeons back without a basket.' 'Wish to God we'd got our old divs,' muttered Mac. 'Never no trouble with the 23rd.' He glared ferociously at the offender, thrust a book under his nose and said, 'Sign!' The men did as they were bidden and departed laughing.

'Gasmasks. God forgive ye for a lie, for I won't. Ye had two forbye but a week ago.' 'I don't want two new ones, I want two to replace these old ones,' or, 'the sergeant says...' 'Your sergeant knows more about rum than gasmasks. However, we don't want to let ye down. Pass two new gasmasks, Corporal.'

I laughed assent. We had to put up a front against too many demands, for gasmasks, as my OC said, were 'flung across the face of Flanders' by our brigades, merely because it was known we could always supply them. There was a plentiful supply because I made a business of badgering our quarter for them. I got insulted and abused by both quarter and SM in the process, but I got them and I man-handled them to our lofts and took them up the line by bike or car. Had it been left to the brigades to indent for masks and baskets, as most pigeon DRs left it, stock would have been wanting at the critical minute. The only time it was tried, the brigades would have been without stock, had I not known the 'wonderful organisation' of the army, and provided against it by carrying forward my stocks as usual from a reserve.

Mac would take the pigeons out of the stock baskets in pairs and thrust them into the infantrymen's baskets, cursing if the baskets were not clean. Sales, his henchman, would enter the ring number of the birds in the book, and to whom issued. We got a signature and sent the men off with birds, books, baskets and masks. From this book they made out a list, which I took next day to the OC. Hence, should a bird be liberated without its being stated where it came from, we could tell by referring to my report.

When I first did pigeon work this used to occur frequently, but by this time I had trained such numbers of men in correct writing of messages that the default was rare.

THURSDAY 20 SEPTEMBER

At night I lay thinking of the operations to follow, and I prayed for good weather – but fatalistically felt it would be bound to break for the 'do'. As I pondered thus, raindrops began to patter on the felt roof. We had to move our beds to avoid the drips. 'The very devil's in the weather,' I groaned, feeling for our men out there. I cussed and agonised. An explosion – went out – no rain but mushy. At five it was dark, at six very dull, damp and thick. Bright by seven. I heard two officers speaking as they passed to latrine at back of our hut. I wondered how the attack had gone: 'Have they started?' 'Yes, and doing fairly well.' 'Oh.' No excitement apparent – both talked casually as if it was the result of a football match. 'They've taken the red line and going for the green,' and the two walked away.

This was the first big battle after the readjustment, in which the Second Army had been side-slipped to the left and we with it, so that at the railway dugouts we were now in our area. It was now V Corps at Pop who had relieved XIX Corps.

At Shrapnel Corner saw many wounded prisoners in a cage of barbed wire, and our wounded walking down line. A few shells left and right, leaving a peculiar metallic quiver and resonance afterwards, like the clash of cymbals. New as far as I was concerned. I was slightly nervy at first, but remained dishing the birds out as coolly as I could.

Since 31 August the remaining half of Bedford House had been smashed to the ground, and in the grounds trees lay at all angles and shell-holes gaped. A more eloquent scene of destruction it would be hard to imagine. However, I was beginning to enjoy the excitement.

Going back, prisoners passed up the Pop Road and old Madame Patou – a sullen, irascible old dame – came to the door and, seeing the Germans, she smiled for the first time in her life.

FRIDAY 21 SEPTEMBER

Badly head-wounded Fritzes seen being brought down. The stunt a general success. I believe this was the day I saw the two, not one, West Indians tied to two trees in barbed wire cages, humiliated if not tortured. The happy 'Chinks' about singing and gay at their work. Their coming into shop at corner of Ren-Abeele road, where also Anzacs talking of the terrible times had lately. 'I don't want no more of this Ypres joint. It was bad enough in 16 but by --- now, pitch dark, the mud, and corpses thick as sheep in a storm.'

WEDNESDAY 26 SEPTEMBER

This morning heard at the signal office dugout where we used to hand in loft messages from Bradford and Olding, that all objectives had been gained in our big attack. No news up the lines, but later and on Thursday and Friday learnt in office and from papers that Zonnebeke and Polygon Wood were taken. Luckily the weather is cloudless and gives us a chance, as supremacy in the air, which keeps changing sway between us and the Huns about every six months, is now with us.

One offensive every five days now. We felt no elation, but a sense of steady, slow triumph.

THURSDAY 27 SEPTEMBER

We are to be turned out of our hut, out of the spite of one officer – who never did use it for his men. Off to stay with Jamieson in his hut.

SUNDAY 30 SEPTEMBER

At last, bundled out to occupy our desired hut, which had just become vacant. Plumped our kit and boxes down and formally took over. In afternoon set out to find Wilf. Knew from Pip Crompton that the Guards were in their Corps and signal office had information where Wilf was – Happy Valley camp. Got there and struck the first camp I saw. Enquiring at the canteen was led to field where new arrivals were ensconced in wigwams. Found Wilf asleep, plump and hale. 'Hey! Wake up!' Rubbing his eyes and staring like a child bewildered. 'Blimey, fancy meeting you!' We talked and talked as we ate in Division canteen. Wilf's experiences to date: polishing buttons and cleaning and creasing greatly over-done. Taught to look down on line regiments. Sergeant's reprimands to him for standing with hands in pockets on football field. 'Hi, you there.' Wilf walked over. 'When I speak to yer, yer gotta double. I don't want no George Formby tricks, see?' 'All right.' 'You "all right" me – by God I'll strike you down if ye talk to me like that.' Wilf said to me, 'If he'd struck me, I should have hit him, court martial or no court martial.' 'Yes, and your army career would have been ruined – it might easily have ended in you getting shot. You've got a devil of a temper underneath.' 'It's a rotten system. In our crush[17] the sergeant's evidence carries all before it. I'm not going to try for stripes. It's beneath you. It's all done by back-handing.'

'My dear sir, you're a heretic. Don't you know the NCO is the backbone of the British Army, full of initiative and resource, and it goes without saying – a hero.' 'Oh, and not public school men – that wouldn't do – the officer might think he was the same flesh and blood, so to prevent mistakes, education is barred.' 'Wonderful isn't it? The wealthiest nation in the globe sets out to fight the cleverest, and the wealthiest hasn't the humility or generosity or sense to appreciate education. We shall lose the next war for that very reason.' 'If a man won't oil the palm, education is no good in our army, and he goes to the wall. Officers are frightened of a well-educated man, because often they've learnt manners but nothing else.' 'War today is essentially a matter of brains and education. Complex instruments have to be handled by all men all the time, yet they expect us to win easily by using men who can't read or spell – can't do it because the aristocracy who rule us has been too stingy to see that the children who worked for it got educated.'

MONDAY 1 OCTOBER

Little sleep last night due to ceaseless progression of Fritz planes across the sky. Does this bombing pay? I shouldn't think it paid Fritz. He never did much damage, but it was laughable to see the working of our machine-gun in the garden at the back of our huts.

There was a little officer bobbing in and out of his tent, an NCO and two men, and the hooded machine-gun. The hood would be thrown off when the officer had been sent for and he would squint up a telescope, make out he saw the Hun, and yell, "Fire!' Dutifully the men potted, the cartridges slipped out and the new trays of ammo came forward.

After tonight's do he went into the signal office and got on to his senior OC, excited. 'We gave him such a bally doing,' he giggled, 'he got awfully wobbly and finally turned tail.' I went out and said to the NCO, 'Your boss thinks he scored one last night.' 'He knows nowt about it,' the other smiled. 'Only we have to do something to keep him his job and keep him quiet. He wasn't on to Fritz at all – Fritz was a mile the other side – but what's the use of arguing? He don't understand. Our job is just to fire along the route of this line, so he can't come down close on this section. That's what we do and that's all I'm going to do.' As I said to O'Connor, 'I wonder we ever won anything in this war.'

THURSDAY 4 OCTOBER

Our divisions are now 33rd and 39th – or had been for the 26 September battle, but now they were 7th, 21st and 5th.

The traffic nowadays is awful and if you chanced to strike unlucky it might take the car an hour or so to get from Shrapnel Corner to Vierstraat. Troops, cars, lorries, guns galore and prisoners came down in batches of 500.

FRIDAY 5 OCTOBER

I cleaning up in hut when rang for by OC Signals, Captain Mudge at X Corps.

'I wonder if you could scrape together twenty more birds for the 21st Division – they're asking for them urgently.' 'Let me think a minute.' I reckoned. 'Yes, I can manage that, sir.' 'Good man. That's splendid.'

I thought of the difference from the days on the Somme, when day by day I had to go to Captain or Colonel for permission to supply a dozen more birds, and this day, when it was left for me to decide in an important battle if we could manage the extra birds wanted.

Leave promised in four weeks – I don't think. Have got so accustomed to the idea of leave not being granted to NCOs without lies and influence, that I don't believe this miraculous thing will ever happen. Rumours at signal office of first 5,000, then 10,000, then 15,000 prisoners taken. The correct number is 5,000. I saw one this afternoon with bowed, grief-stricken head in cloak. Perhaps his brother or son had been killed.

SATURDAY 6 OCTOBER

Rose to cold, raw rain. Dread rides twice through slush ankle-deep and mire-like in ponds. Shrapnel Corner desolate. Going back passed troops marching patiently up with bent head, waterproof sheets slung flapping around them. The hail pelted down, blinding. The mud was fouling them more and more. I would get wedged behind a wagon, car or lorry, or sink into mire with my crankcase foundering on the protruding boulders, nearly rupturing myself with the jarring. All the time the belt slipping, so wet with water, the engine getting hot and running out of oil. Shells fell near and horses leapt and pawed – the sodden misery of the men going to get shot at and endangered until hurt, gassed or killed, just because, despite all the many times they've been flung in before, they haven't yet got killed. I wonder they stick it. They get no medals or praise, but they are the winners of the war – the men whom I honour and bow to in admiration. Bronzed, magnanimous, defiant, and ready to go to death without a whine, without a prayer – and treated like dogs, for they are the nobodies.

SATURDAY 13 OCTOBER

I in car through mud and storm and argued with loftmen who were saying that we couldn't have the birds we wanted. The birds would be no good – it was killing them. Made arrangements for the morrow.

SUNDAY 14 OCTOBER

Rose at 6.30 and got up the line early, but was delayed and didn't get to Westoutre until twelve. Lecture until 12.30 – no rations arrived. Rang Corps then back to Ren and found the rations dumped there in a sack. Fumed and cursed, heartbroken, and phoned quartermaster angrily. Vickery kindly took the rations to Westoutre for me. Class until 4.15, then gave a chit to the men to get baths.

MONDAY 15 OCTOBER

In all the pressure, we have had battles on 2 and 26 September and 4, 9 and 12 October.

THURSDAY 18 OCTOBER

Rained heavily. At night woke and heard the sinister and ominous dripping on the roof. Pitied the poor fellows out on the front. The roads all deep in paste and could scarcely ride in the filth. Pip with Mr Underwood up the Essex cord road about Shrapnel Corner to find site for the new mobile lofts.

FRIDAY 19 OCTOBER

At Shrapnel Corner, sky bronzed and streamers of grey and storm – Fritz shelling wildly. Fumes, fires and shrapnel on the ridge before me. As I left dugout, cataract of rain and bitter hail – traffic blocks the road absolutely. Wet, wound in and out of horses and shell-hole puddles with lumps sticking up, banging crankcase and nearly rupturing as bike canted over.

SATURDAY 20 OCTOBER

Visited Ypres. It was not so knocked about as I had imagined from rumours. Came in at Lille gate end – Anzacs sunning themselves in the open. Quite a bustling place now – an ordinary divisional distance behind the line and scarcely none wearing tin hats. Old Jack's depot still intact, but the roof above damaged each side and the base sand-bagged. I climbed up. Life has flowed up into the desolate city, desolate no longer, but gay for war.

Paul and Bill Pritchard to al fresco tea at the hut – tinned apricots and Ideal Milk galore, and bread, marge and jam. Their company livened me up.

MONDAY 22 OCTOBER

Heartbreaking day – deluge night before had made thick paste on roads – just drying. Clutch wire and saddle-spring broken – every quarter hour stopped to clean the doughy mud from the front and back mudguards with a screwdriver, otherwise the bike skidding and jerking unrideably. Roads awful with shell-holes. Anxious about Pip who did not arrive until 5.30, but he came home – so happy.

WEDNESDAY 24 OCTOBER

To Corps, and at Company Office and OC's office instructions given by Mr Underwood – he pointing out on the map while Captain Stevens scowled. In the middle, Captain Robinson came up – a bit of a dandy with pleasant chubby face, brown eyes and MC. He introduced as new temporary OC pigeons, and told me of a special class for two days while Mr U was giving me figures.

'That'll be 50 for each division.' 'Two divisions, sir?' 'Yes, 5th and 7th.'

FRIDAY 26 OCTOBER

At five heard, as often before on like occasions, the dreaded apprehended thud and patter of rain on our roof. Again the very devil was in it. Rose to mist and downpour – the usual fatal weather for our righteous cause.

Delays at Scherperberg, the lofts there having been handed over to us. Pip had called the day before and asked them to have birds ready. When I arrived thought they would have them down at Trow's loft – Trow whom I had met once before, seemed independent and almost on the edge of surliness. 'No birds been brought to me. I know nothing about them.'

When I got there, the two Pictons looked amazed at my wanting birds. Started to get flustered. 'Now sit ye down. We shan't be but a few minutes.' Sat down in their very comfortable wooden hut with stove, beds and all appointments. I explained I was taking over.

Eventually I staggered off, slipping on the uneven ground, round the ploughed field with farm a field away and past the big YMCA hut. Disheartening wet weather and news – officer tells of nasty smack in the eye for Italy – loss of 10,000 prisoners.

SATURDAY 27 OCTOBER

Rose at 6.45 and tried new dodge of sending Pip forward as courier to get birds assigned and ready, and warn loftmen. By speeding up, got there with car before noon, but found that all along the side of the embankment water had risen owing to rain and our depot was in two feet of water and the baskets, gasmasks and troughs were floating on a pool of water some sixteen feet square.

'Robinson's been down,' said Fred. 'He's quite the toff. He fixed his eyeglass up and looked at the water and said, "Oh this is impossible. Impossible. We must find a new depot. Ah – gumboots – don't you think you'd find gumboots useful? I'll see the quarter and see what I can do at the Corps for you. Now, what do you want to draw for pay?"'

I liked Fred. He himself was a gentleman of purest dye, but on this occasion I was wrath. 'Yes, but a new depot next week won't dry our stock today,' I said. 'This stock needn't be left soaking in the wet as it is. Couldn't one of you get it out?'

But I couldn't speak harshly to Freddy – I hated to wound him. I took off my things, walked gum-booted into the water and angrily chucked out the big gasmasks for them to spread to dry on top of the embankment. This took an hour. I rooted all the stock up from the submerged lower portion of the shelter and put it out.

SUNDAY 28 OCTOBER

Grave news from Italy depressed us.

TUESDAY 30 OCTOBER

Hun bombs galore at night, then awakened at 11.30 and 12.30 by two wires. Had to decide and write a wire in answer. So many birds had to be at depot by 5.30 or 6.00 am because the stock basket of one of the division brigades had been blown to bits, pigeons as well. To make sure, rose at 3.45 – it was Pip's turn for the night run, but when I turned the light on his pink, smooth face with the silken eyelashes and youthful, almost childish submersion in profound slumber, my heart was again touched, and I left him and rode to Railway Dugouts, arriving at 5.15.

In darkness went along the Reninghelst-Ouderdom Road, but the moon shone and above me Fritz was droning, searchlights following him as he dropped bombs. Rode up the Hallebast Corner road with curious feeling of being naked and unprotected against a bomb, I saw not a soul. It was the dawn of another and final battle for Passchendaele Ridge, but there was not a soldier or moving sign of the army anywhere in sight. At Dickebusch I met horses and men moving, but not traffic. On the open field around me and in front across the skyline, the barrage flashed like sun after sun being chucked up over the horizon and on the left, through a coloured haze, the splashes of light came up in balls. Went into dugout, woke them, and talked, and when I came out it was misted light. Observation sausage ascending on the Kruisstraathoek Road in the pink, filmy, misty light. The howitzers trumpeted from the hedges and the long navals quivered and slid like dogs' fine snouts.

WEDNESDAY 31 OCTOBER

The final battle had taken place on the 30th, bringing the Canadians to the underlip of the ridge. This day and part of yesterday, fierce counterattacks were delivered by the Germans.

I rode back and entered the wooden shack opposite the railway crossing, where a miserable old girl dispensed coffee and biscuits – but how I enjoyed it in the conscientiousness of unpleasant duty done!

SATURDAY 3 NOVEMBER

At Voormezeele heard a racket and saw running and was told a Hun aeroplane was over, machine-gunning all he saw. Sure enough, as I got past the big railway siding, he came swooping up from the ridge, not above 200 feet up. Archies were clattering at him from every side, but he ignored them, unhit. The field and road were suddenly empty. Like the hero in an HG Wells story I found myself alone on the field without weapon, chased by the plane. I started to run towards Curry's loft, seeking company, for there was no soul in sight. The plane seemed to intercept me and I wavered – wondered why he didn't machine-gun me. I suppose I wasn't worth his while and he was dodging shrapnel. I darted to a bivouac-shaped dugout in a ditch nearby and lay down, expecting a bomb. With phoo and phit, shrapnel bits fell around but nought else.

In evening to 'Whizzbangs' – 5th Division concert party, to which my cousin Harold used to belong. Anzac crush – rushed the stairs, breaking banister and doors, then swarmed into the hall, we with much jamming and struggling, borne with them. Laughed delightedly, but an officer came on to the stage and very politely said, after we had waited for half an hour, that the evening had been reserved for 39th Divisional gunners and would we be sporting enough to vacate the hall? We did so after demur.

MONDAY 5 NOVEMBER

Captain Robinson at Forward Depot and EW 1 said that the Corps was going on rest. 'You can do with one, Corporal?' 'I can, sir, only with the usual irony of things – I'm due leave soon and have been out sixteen months without it – I'd sooner have leave when we're working.' I suppose he thought this hypocritical.

With mixed feelings heard news about the Corps and rest – when all is said and done, I liked my job.

TUESDAY 6 NOVEMBER

Fine until 9 am then changed to drizzle which made mud like suet pudding. Didn't get home until 5.15, and Pip had two bad spills and wasn't back until six. Maurice Hirst was waiting for me and cried, 'Oswald H Davis!' but though recognising him I was too disgusted with the day's sliding and skidding and struggling to answer until I got my bike in the stand. He told me of his experiences of mustard gas and observation and RFA work on the shell-and corpse-sodden ground before Ypres, and it made me feel small. For a year or more he had been working in the same sector as I. I must have often passed his dugout daily, yet I had never met him, and owing to not writing, neither knew our units.

THURSDAY 7 NOVEMBER

Detached front mudguards, and then it rained – but kept guards off and the wet mire swished in my face, blinding me.

THURSDAY 8 NOVEMBER

My eyes watered and pained from mud flung up into face from riding without the front mudguard – impossible to ride when not seeing except through a haze. Rode on – returning called at Brasserie dressing station but the prospect of waiting there endlessly and being handled like a log repelled me, so back to Reninghelst. Here in the Anzac dressing station next to Patou's loft and shop, a casual red-haired orderly came strolling up, cursing indolently, seated himself, turned my eyelid up with a matchstick and had the bit of dirt out, thus relieving all my fears.

SUNDAY 11 NOVEMBER

Sergeant Edmonds says he is going to Italy and the Fourth Army will be taking over – this, of course a secret – army moves always are, I don't think. He introduces his successor, bluff and plump and unruffled – Sergeant Graham – who asked us if the whiskey bottle's any good, as he's got a brother in the ASC and can get it easy. He's carrying one about with him in his greatcoat. A very decent sort with whom I knew I should fare well.

WEDNESDAY 14 NOVEMBER

Instructions by phone re closing down. Got permit to come after and not 'come in' to the Corps. Learnt that I was to go in person and see stock put on lorry and close down. Via Vierstraat and bid lofts good-bye. Already had seen IX Corps and II Anzac Corps officers prospecting their new possessions. Neither of them, however, wanted our depot or our stock. For some time past, Mr Underwood had told the pigeon-men that our Corps had finished with the fight, and they used to round on me and ask what I wanted all the pigeons for. I was between the devil and the deep blue sea.

Mac had got all his stock ready and borrowed a bogey from the railway workers. We got the stock on it and pushed it down to Shrapnel Corner, where we dumped it and handed it over to the sergeant. Mac and Harrison rode off on the back of the lorry, and thus came to an end our famous Railway Dugouts forward depot.

Riding down Ouderdom road I thought, 'Damn it, let's get home,' and put on speed, swerved from a pave projection thinking, 'That's a bit risky, mate,' and the next instant was in the gutter with the bike on top. Footrest snapped off, handlebars bent, etc. I cursed and moaned over this – it just spoilt the virgin delight of getting away in good trim. Pip fixed it temporarily for me.

THURSDAY 15 NOVEMBER

Rose at 6.45 and worked hard packing kit. All turned out to wish us good luck – there were a few remaining as rear party for a bit. When you get kit up after riding without, the machine wobbles and you have to learn to ride again. We went to Westoutre, shook hands with Skinner and had a drink, then took the fork to Godewaersvelde. There was the inn with the warm reputation, and the gabled shop selling souvenirs and *bonnes bouches* on the corner.

Steady traffic was on the broad road to Hazebrouck – how refreshing it was as we glided, sliding and skidding through the town, to see again numerous young women and girls. Radiant, gaily dressed, vivacious – life seemed sweet and colourful as they passed before our eyes. It was over twelve months since I had passed through a town larger than Cassel, where all the girls seemed immured as in a convent, and the other sex had been represented by ferocious and painted types of Pop, or the rare violets glimpsed here and there in Abeele – but these were all appropriated by the Corps boys or the Flying Corps men.

'Wonder what this Fruges is like,' I queried to Pip. 'Some bloody hole, just like the Corps would get pitched into. They're too windy to stick out for a good place. I've been told it's a dirty good-for-nothing lost-in-the-bog stunt.' 'Never heard of it until someone said the other day it was about the size of Halesowen.' 'Halesowen? That's in the Black Country – a horrible place. They might as well send us to prison. However, I've never found a man outside an author who could describe a town he'd seen so that you could see it, so it's bound to be different from all expectations.'

At Fruges we stuck our bikes against the church, walked to a teashop and saw our revered OC inside. 'Hello Percy, where's this billet of ours?' 'Ride straight up the hill until you see a light to the left and bikes outside. The billet's quite close. Anyone will tell you. That's our mess, where the bikes are.'

Arriving, we went up a flight of steps to a shop, and on the left a brightly lit room. Our tiffy walked out rubbing his stomach. 'We're quids in,' he said, 'this place is full of estaminets. Liqueurs, triple sec, Benedictine, cherry brandy, *café rhum*.' Then, 'More camerades, Madame!' He waved us in. 'She'll get you a chop and chips if you want.'

A thin, cheery, dark good-looking woman smiled at us and said, 'Steak, *pommes de terre?*' I could scarcely believe my ears. Dirty as we were, we sat down to it, then moved over to the sleeping billet – a dirty barn up a foul lane. Here we planted our kit on the ground and mooched off to look at the pubs.

Loud were the complaints over the billet. Lilley was up in the house in a fine room over the SM. 'He's far too thick with Sam Brown,' said Tubby. 'All he cares about is keeping his own nest warm. Why doesn't he speak up like a man? This barn's not fit to sleep in. Let's go and get it medically condemned.'

'Shut up, you fools,' said Jimmy Sinclair. 'Lilley's all right. He's quite sporty – he's got a difficult job to please everybody. I know he's a bit windy of the SM, but who isn't?' 'Well, I'm not,' said Tubby. 'For two pins I'd shove the bastard down the well. A fat lot the bloody rat cares as long as he's got his own bum between clean sheets.'

'The truth is,' said Bunce, 'the staff on this Corps do what they like with the signals. They think anything's good enough for signals. They pick the château and the hotels for themselves and their bloody batman and map-painters, and signals can go hang. We haven't got anybody who's got the guts to stick up for us.' 'Never mind boys, there's plenty of pubs and drinks and nothing to do.'

FRIDAY 16 NOVEMBER

Sure enough, next day we were paraded at nine, then at twelve. After, my OC met me and I asked for early leave for Mac, Pip and myself.

Café rums – my first day off duty for sixteen months – also the first parade since I had arrived in France.

In the market close by were to be had veggies, meat and spuds were plentiful and we always had afters of custard and fruit, rice pudding or bread pudding.

After dinner we used to go to one of many cafés. Today it was the spacious, clean one like a huge farmer's kitchen above the square where in deep contentment we sipped *café rhums* or liqueurs. All our sorrows and toil were forgotten, and life amid young bloods and little work was indeed bliss.

In the evening I had my first active service DR run. It was to Arques and St Omer. The night was pitch dark, the lamp blew out in the wind and my bike crashed into a tree as the sudden dark after light blinded my rather weak eyes. I thought, 'Not so easy as it looks, this night-riding. Yet the fellows make no bones about it.' I felt timid, foreboding failure to arrive on a late return, which would stir my comrades' scorn. The wind buffeted as I breasted the high hill. The road was rutted and slimy, and every now and then you felt the wheels roll and swerve in a skid.

Found signal office in St Omer at the back of a square, then I was off to Arques. In the square at the side were lorries, cars and guns. No glimmer of light could be seen, save for an occasional opened door. An officer said, 'X Corps Heavy Artillery – over the canal bridge, Cassel Road, there's an office of some sort. I believe they've got a blue and white flag out.' In the dark, no signal flag could be seen, but waiting about I saw a door opened and went in. The office was in a shuttered room – one of the nerve centres of the Army.

SATURDAY 17 NOVEMBER

A special for Division came over the phone. 'Send it down with the night man when he comes off duty,' said Micky, and turned over to sleep again. The night man comes in, throws the 'special' at Micky's sleeping form and gets down to sleep himself for an hour. At 8.30, 'What about that special?' 'Right. I'll have some breakfast,' says Micky – and spends an hour consuming bacon. 'You not off yet?' asks the sergeant. 'Tyre's punctured,' says Micky shortly. 'Why the devil didn't you see to it when you came off your run?' 'They've both gone,' says Micky, 'and the worst is I've got no bloody spare that's not punctured. Oh, sod it, I'll ride it on the rim.' And off he goes. That attitude is typical of DRs both in rest and in action. I should be frightened to take such risks, but they take them light-heartedly, often leaving their bikes unoiled or unrepaired after a ride and not seeing to punctures until just before a ride. A DR who was worth his salt always carried on somehow.

I envisaged a night out in the cold and wet. However, at 5.30 the man on our relief held the fort. What a blissful moment it was as six o'clock struck, and we knew we were free until 6 o'clock next night.

SUNDAY 25 NOVEMBER

We heard we were going on leave. The night before we went to the orderly room and said we'd draw as many francs as we were entitled to – some 200. Wordley, dark-eyed, cool, seriously humorous, gave us a medical certificate (though no MO had examined us), a type-written pass for circulation in Blighty, railway voucher for travelling half price, and our green leave warrant, with money in franc notes, along with instructions.

MONDAY 26 NOVEMBER

It was a bright morn and we slung ourselves with pack and revolver into the quarter's ration lorry, and with others sang our way up and down the hills of the Hesdin-St Omer road until we came to the white bluffs of Wizernes. At the station to the RTO for information.

'What time does the leave train start? We wanted to get a posh dinner to celebrate if possible. 'Can't help that,' barked the soldier. 'Parade in the waiting-hall at 1 o'clock.' There was no train from there until evening, so we jumped on a lorry and off to St Omer.

We walked off to the famous Lines of Communication DRs' billet and climbed up the tortuous stairs to the mess-room. Here round the top of the wall ran a series of caricatures of L Sigs DRs – Tiny beaming, tiffies wielding tools, the thin, the fat, the drunk, the dandy, the artistic, with characteristic phrases issuing from their mouths. At one end of the room was a bar and every kind of drink was to hand. The place looked dull, but livened by carousing DRs and a fire, one could picture a place of geniality.

'It's no capture, this stunt,' said Pip's friend Wood. 'Certainly we're away from the line, but our rides run to hundreds of kilos and mostly at night. Often we have to go in pairs – you imagine. After continuous runs like that you can spend the whole of the next day seeing to your bike. As for the spares we carry – we have almost to carry a spare engine, and the rotten bikes we get dished out to us… bloody awful. What an army. I wonder we've not lost long ago. But of course, if the pace gets hot we have a breakdown. We know every estaminet between here and Calais and every town and every road. Every man's got a pub and a girl somewhere, and we got our compensations with a timely breakdown.'

Later in the train, we were happy in a slow way, yet not thrilled. We were waiting – longing for our leave to start. As thralls of the brass hats, who had leave themselves every three months, being servants of a wonderfully wealthy and grateful country, we were liable to be hauled back any minute by wire, and our pitiful fourteen days reft from us after our wait of sixteen and a half months.

All the way we talked of evading the ranks and rest camps at the other end by slipping away on the dockside and sneaking into a private hotel. All the corps men had advocated this and had given us precise directions and hotel addresses. The train came to Boulogne at five, in the dusk. 'Form up in the yard,' was shouted from the front. The multitude of soldiers shuffled into fours and we were marshalled right by an MP on horseback. We struggled along the roads – but in fact anyone who wished could escape. Half suggestions were made, but none of our party slipped up the side streets. Why not? Despite lack of confidence in its leaders and their present handling of the war, the instinct of obedience was strong. The British are a law-abiding race. In the mass, soldiers are gregarious and do not easily break routine. Besides, there was always the threat of being sent back if we broke rules.

As we trudged to the notorious Boulogne rest camp, the road mounted and mounted. 'My God,' I thought, 'it's enough to make these men slit the throat of a brass hat when they meet him. After a man's been humiliated like a cur, and flung into the mud and the battle-line again and again until it's a sheer miracle he's still alive – when at last he's granted by grace (leave is an act of grace, not a right in the army) – when he's got thus far and thinks to enter into a brief bliss, they bugger up his leave like this and poison it at the start.'

'I suppose the swine who had the brainwave to plant this camp up here got a row of ribbons for it,' groaned Pip.

At last we emerged on a broad space where at a gate stood a sentry. Before us we saw dim hut shapes, unlit. Passing between them we came on some electric standards and under the pallor of these we were lined up.

A group came forward with hurricane lamps and papers. A grizzled sergeant in slacks came forward with a megaphone. 'Fall out warrant officers, staff sergeants and sergeants,' a mocking artilleryman said. Sure enough, the sergeant called out those words.

The swaying yellow spots came towards us. 'You ten men,' bawled a voice, 'the last tent, D line. Draw blankets from the hut over there.'

We moved off uncertainly and scrambled up to a tent and found it occupied. Walked to another and, each seeking a place farthest from the door, flung our traps down with sighs of relief. One good Samaritan produced a candle – an indispensable gift. Another disappeared and bore a roll of blankets back.

We moved off to the big huts and found two lit. In the first we got slips of paper which, for 1/3, entitled us to a hot meal with custard and fruit from the BEF canteen. It was warm, but not enough for a schoolboy. In the other hut was the wet canteen – a bar from which, when you'd borrowed a second-hand condensed milk tin, you could get decent beer and sit on barrels and drink it.

Then to the tent, which we found was very dirty. On that windswept plateau the cold was intense and the two blankets gave little warmth – they were dirty and rumoured lousy. By this time snores resounded and I had a brief doze in the cold.

TUESDAY 27 NOVEMBER

It was freezing cold when we arose to wash and shave. We were ordered to parade at 9.30 – nothing happened and no-one appeared. 'They're down on you like a ton of bricks if ye pinch half a day's extra leave,' said Houghton, 'yet as soon as they've got ye here, they forget us for weeks.'

At noon an officer shambled up, called out 'Fall in', and we ambled off in loose fours. 'Is this the boat touch?' we queried of each other, gaily. Our hearts rose at last – but no official deigned an explanation.

We left behind us the horrible monotony of the army camp, the squat huts and pointed tents. We veered towards the hills and no sea came in sight. At last along the straight road some tents appeared. We saw the head of the column wheel right and fall in, line behind line between the huts and tents of another camp.

Again the megaphone chant – this time enriched with many a double negative.

'Fall out all men of the 5th Division. Fall out all men of the 5th Divisional Artillery, and all men attached. On yer direct front is the Bee Hee Heff Canteen. Rear, the Salvation Army Yut. 'Alf left is the latrines and ablution shed. Cookhouse and mess 'ut, right front. No smoking and no stoves is on no account allowed in the tents. In the event of a tent fire, the hoccupants will be detained, all the lot on year, a court of hinquiry 'eld, and the cost of the tent deducted from yer pay, and the time docked from yer leave time. In the event of fire, parade 'ere and wait instructions. Should 'ostile aircraft come over, on the blowin' of the whistle, seek cover. At a time that will be told ye, report here. All men confined to camp.'

There was absolutely nothing to do but parade round and round in the huge enclosure where we were trapped behind barbed wire like animals. 'How proud of us England is,' said Vic. 'Why not put us in jail and have done with it?'

We heard rumours of delays – they were sweeping away a lot of mines – the recent storm had loosened them – and the water was too rough. At last I knew the misery of being a prisoner. We were jailed and there was nothing to do except long for time to pass. If free we could now be in Blighty, enjoying the precious hours.

As we sat at tea, a burly man pushed through shouting, 'Reveille at 3 am – breakfast 3.30, passes stamped at five.' Our veins tingled at the promise of departure on the morrow.

WEDNESDAY 28 NOVEMBER

At three was heard a whistle – the breakfast queue was hopeless, but this time Pip observed another queue, nosing and edging its way in a different direction. We followed round the tents and at last a light in the rain and mud. Slowly we came to the door of a hut. 'Pass through quickly,' said one of two sergeants at a table. 'Hurry up. We only want your leave warrants,' called one, dabbing a stamp on it.

We paraded in the blue streaming murk of dawn, soaking, and waited like oxen by a pond. At last we were out and away to the centre of the town, sweating and slipping. At last we knew it was true – we should take ship. We were on the quay and wound along up its narrow side into the docks, and at last to a ship, camouflaged with white and blue zig-zag stripes. How we prayed for good weather and feared a gale would postpone our trip. But at last we were for it.

At Folkestone things were rather dingy, but the countryside seemed in a swoon of peace and indolence. As White said, the aristocrats – who tried not to appear aristocrats – now fed the tame animals who had done their dirty work. Dry sandwiches of paste, cheap cake and cocoa.

At Victoria Station outside the rails, hungry faces, starving for the sight of son or sweetheart. Wonderful as we stepped out from the station, and girls flashed up a gaze at us and a little crowd watched the brave men home from battle. They feasted on the sight of our revolvers, our blue and white signal bands and our short British warms, black leggings and breeches.

I took Pip to St Pancras, then back to Union Jack club where for 1/- a night one got a nice clean cubicle, and for 1/3 a splendid breakfast in large fine hall.

Out to ABC restaurant at corner of Waterloo Road – there was magic in going into an English restaurant after so long an absence. One sat between the well-dressed clean people, the pretty tidy waitresses and the clean tables. However, I found there was but a small portion of sugar and a shortage of many eatables.

On to the Soldier's Club in Ecclestone Square. Here two silver-haired dames strove, with the aid of visiting girls from office or factory, to make enjoyable the lot of soldiers billeted near – mostly RFC men. One was nice to me and asked what my medal was – what was my blue and white for – a wound? Wasn't it a shame that wounded soldiers in London area should be ordered to get up and salute an officer? General Lloyd had come to see her personally, and she had persuaded him of the rightness of their view.

THURSDAY 29 NOVEMBER

To Paddington, where in the train felt lonely – passengers slightly selfish and callous – so different to khaki. Got to Small Heath about 1.30 and caught the Sparkbrook car. Walked up from Palmerston Road and mother hugged me and led me into front room, where was fire and fish dinner. Back to Small Heath and trotted about in growing dusk. The air had magic – it was wonderful to stumble over people one had half forgotten and to see people looking at one, half remembering.

FRIDAY 30 NOVEMBER

To town with Paul and green chartreuse in the Great Western Hotel, then an afternoon of visits.

SATURDAY 1 DECEMBER

Morning to business and afternoon with Mr Nodder to football match. Crowd struck me as selfish and callous and scornful of us for being soldiers instead of munitioners. To Sparkhill Institute and found same very enjoyable – fair and floating light forms in filmy dresses.

SUNDAY 2 DECEMBER

Morning to chapel, a little late – the only place that hadn't changed. Enjoyed it fully as all friends crowded to shake hands. Dinner then class, where I found Phil Elliott, Harold Dowler, Arthur and Percy Glendon, Percy Newman and wife – like old times. Tea, then home to our place for a fine evening at home with Mr and Mrs Nodder visiting.

MONDAY 3 DECEMBER

Morning to business, and in afternoon to Uncle Fred's. Evening to Acock's Green dance class with Ettie – a frost with only about ten there.

TUESDAY 4 DECEMBER

Leave leaping by and nothing done. Paul had had to return last Saturday. He was upset because the Second Army had gone to Italy and by some mischance his name had been left off the list. What would he do? Wangle a return to Italy instead of to Cassel?

Morning to town with Ettie – all the warehouses delighted to see me, and kept me talking. Dinner at Great Western with Ettie then afternoon back to warehouses.

THURSDAY 6 DECEMBER

To Camp Hill School and saw the roll of honour – saw my name among the men who had gained distinctions, and some other chaps I remembered.

Met Ettie, mother and Eva to go to the theatre, where *The Better 'Ole* was given – the Bairnsfather convention of the British soldier, seen through the medium of musical comedy – silly yet honest.

FRIDAY 7 DECEMBER

Morning to business. Walked with Ettie and Jess to Villa Road, where caught the car and saw Grindle's father – a coincidence that Grindle was also home on leave. Went to the Tretham Road Institute and it was a munitioners' night out – many good-looking girls in fancy dress.

SATURDAY 8 DECEMBER

To the bank and business until 2.30. Later saw many old friends, and felt the mellow romance of the day. Atmosphere of the Saturday afternoon at home on Coventry Road – perfect as it was.

Met Ettie at the Sparkhill Institute where, joining Dowler, we had a happy time before heading home.

SUNDAY 9 DECEMBER

In evening wrote to Arnold Bennett, giving some lights on army life and methods. Prepared for the morrow's departure.

MONDAY 10 DECEMBER

Rose at seven, breakfasted by mother's fire and departed with Ettie, leaving mother looking bravely after us as we lengthened our distance and turned the corner into Grantham Road. Left Brum at 9.30 and met Arthur in town and had funereal dinner at Golden Cross Hotel in the Strand, where, to my vexation an English-looking hotel was run by a foreign boss and servile yet cheeky waiter. Nothing good to drink, no decent sweets. Bought stuff at Selfridges, and sent parcels to Wilfred.

Row with ticket-puncher at Euston Station because he wouldn't let me accompany Ettie to the train. I went past him, but instead of dallying, kissed Ettie and went back. He got my dander up. 'Do you mean to say a fellow can't go and take his sister to the train when he's not seen her for a year and a half, and may not see her again?' 'If I let one on, I've got to let others on.' 'Don't be absurd.' 'There's those about that maybe'll get ye into trouble young man.' 'I walked back to him. 'Do you know what they do with those out there?' I said. 'Shoot 'em.'

To the Hippodrome and saw George Robey and Shirley Kellogg in *Zig-zag*. Rotten – both of them. Some pretty children on the stage, but Arthur pitied them for the fact that their lives were being spoiled.

TUESDAY 11 DECEMBER

Victoria station was like a vast chamber of doom with the nation going to its death, unmoved. We got to the platforms where womenfolk were gathered to see the last of us. The tales recurred to me that we had heard of the brass hats, hissed by women who were bitter because of the long time their men were denied leave. No wailing on the platform – the occasion was too great and tense – we really touched the great and sublime things of time.

'And that's that', said a big artilleryman as we steamed out. 'Rest camps and the partings are as bad as a firing party. Hope to God we get no rest camp touch going back.'

At Folkestone we were led in batches into various large boarding houses, emptied of furniture, and were allowed to run in and choose nice airy rooms with sea or street views, and dump our packs. At 2.30 we marched off through the dull and army-blighted and blackened town to the wharf where we kicked our heels in desolation, and then got aboard amid the excited to and fro of blue, black and white hats. Slept in the passage jammed together down on the lower deck, sated with misery and discomfort.

At 5.30 moved off to the Hill Rest Camp again – that hated resort. Here we were arranged in lines again and waited for half an hour, being arsed about.

'Parade here again in an hour and a half. Go to the messroom, have supper, and take with you your haversack rations.' This, we presumed, meant away that night.

In the camp they had told me KCO had moved – of this I had not had the slightest inkling when I went away – so was in perplexity. Got into a luggage van, all the dark trains being already full – and inserted myself into sleeping sack I'd made, and tried to sleep on the floor. At about two the train started to jumble and jolt and screech on its long slow journey. Dawn was breaking – punctuated by men stepping over me to piss outside the carriage – when I next awoke.

WEDNESDAY 12 DECEMBER

The train stopped at Hazebrouck and I thought it time to get information. I went to the RTO's office where a pale clerk assured me our Corps was at Esquelbecq. I couldn't believe it.

At Esquelbecq I left the train and came in by the château to a big cobbled square, over which towered a big church of decaying spinsterish appearance. In the square lorries were drawn up and there were half a dozen army huts. Following the flat road along a curving line of ordinary shops and houses, I came to the last estaminet where a knot of DR gathered round the stove.

'It's the pigeon-wallah!' Cooings and billings resounded through the room, with subtle whistlings, supposed to represent the loftmen calling the birds – and me in particular.

Our billet was in two rooms over the public estaminet. Percy and Bobby Brown had got a little room over the kitchen of the baker / grocery store a few doors away.

In the evening wrote at the long dining table next to the sheeted billiard table, with the gramophone going, while the boys played cards. It felt comfy with the drinks of café and red wine, heated and sugared.

FRIDAY 14 DECEMBER

'What's the idea of coming back here?' I asked Lilley. 'They've got the wind up since the Cambrai stunt. We're GHQ reserve. They're building trenches hotshit all behind Ypres now and between here and Pop.' I did not like the sound of that.

SUNDAY 16 DECEMBER

Went and saw the old members of 142 squad, whom I had not seen since I rode down to the Somme in 1916, when they were at Querrieu. They were genuinely pleased to see me. Tea at Jeanne's with music, then supper in the Casino restaurant. Here at a long table Tommies sat to a hot supper of steak or cutlet, with beer or wine, while the civvy habitués in the next room drank or sat at the piano and sang.

WEDNESDAY 19 DECEMBER

Bunny came to the door of the estaminet and said there was a special to the 29th Division at Hucquliers. My heart sank. Right on the edge of night, this was a big ride into gloom and possible bad roads and weather. I thought, 'I'm struck out for this rotten special, of course – the worst we've had since we came here. Why me?'

Went down to Signal office. Bunny was talking seriously. 'I'm afraid there's another – rough luck, Oz. It's to Division Artillery.' 'Where's Div Artillery?' I asked. 'One DR shouldn't have to take two specials, should he? Isn't it against the rule?' 'Well, it's scarcely worthwhile sending two men down if you'll take it. We don't know where the artillery is – coming up from the Somme, I believe – and you may have a rotten run finding them. But we'll get through to the Division and see if we can't arrange for them to send on the special to the Artillery by their own DR. We'll do our best'.

I could see Bunny didn't want anything to do with the run. I was thus learning, now I was on the ordinary roster, that there are many men who talk big about riding, who when it comes to a nasty ride at night, betray no anxiety to take on more than they can help.

'Give me the stuff,' I said, fearing my none-too-good luck, but not such a rotten poltroon that I wouldn't take my chances or would show any fear.

As the dark came down, I put on my overalls and prepared to have some tea. I sat down but was too excited to eat well. Away at 5.15 with unsatisfactory generator and light. At Cassel bought glycerine to put in generator to stop water freezing. Pushed on into the gloom at 6.45, through patches of mist and in and out of frozen ruts into Fruges. It was like riding between high walls of a prison with a slit of sky above, the monotonous swish through trees and the village.

At 29th Division a DR came in and said the roads were almost impassable with snow and mist. It had been snowing since I started and gradually got worse. The DR – a cheerful irresponsible soul – said he'd take the stuff, but as they were specials I thought I ought to take them myself.

I yearned to let the damned stuff go and sleep the night at Fruges, but decided otherwise. Misty now and road shod with ice and deep-tracked snow. All well until I came to the first turn at a stone column. Wasn't quite sure whether to go straight or left. Saw red lights in front and came to a ditched lorry. Got past it to the second ditched lorry. The drivers did not know the route and couldn't move until morning, but my loneliness was cured by meeting them there. With difficulty, turned on my tracks and, not knowing the way, went up to a cottage which showed a glimmer of light.

'Pour arriver à Hucquliers?' I bawled. There was an old woman dimly seen within and an old man reaching for a coat. 'Tournez à gauche,' he cried, as if it was quite usual to be knocked up by 'les sots Anglais' at midnight. I turned left and was soon jumping off and pushing as the belt was so wet with snow it slipped instead of gripping. Met another DR who had done three kilos through drifts. 'This is as bad as you'll find it,' he said. 'Turn right two kilos along and after a kilo you can get along good roads.'

My bike was going in low gear, but as the oil was frozen and I couldn't pump any in, I feared all the time the engine would seize. At last the tracks came to an end. Before me was a trackless tableland of snow. Trees stuck up in slim but lonely and dehumanised beauty. There being no road visible and no hedges here, it just looked one wide waste of white. 'Well, this is about the finish,' I thought. There was a farm near and I manhandled my bike into the yard and stuck it on the stand and started to walk. I saw a light ahead and shouted. There was a dim shape blocking the way. A long-moustached ASC wallah peered up from beneath his lorry wheel at me, not a whit surprised. 'I can't get the dratted girl to budge. If I could just get her gripping once.' 'Could you give me a lift if you get going?'

He got chains and bound them round the wheels, he dug the road out with a spade and hammered wedges underneath, never despairing but patient and cheerful. After an hour of it I said, 'Look here. I'm a DR with two specials, and instead of sleeping in an estaminet with good company, I'm trudging this road in order to keep the flag flying. What would England do without us? In the circs, and you seem rooted, I fear,' and I strode off, he still muttering under his wheel. Tramped it on vague, wild deserted icy road, which now got more passable as it dropped into the quiet, sleepy, old-fashioned village lying in the trough of a vale.

I went over to the house where the signal office used to be. Now it was another unit. 'Go along to the church and turn left. It's on the hill there.'

Up the steep hill I found a little house emitting a glow of light behind a blanketed door. Inside were three men at desks with instruments and on the floor a relief of three others, sleeping.

'KCO,' I said. 'Two specials.' The clerk looked at me pleasantly and humorously. 'You've arrived at last. We're sending out a special man at daybreak with the artillery stuff.' My suspense and anxiety were at an end. 'I had to chuck my bus inside a farmyard and flog it the last ten kilos. As they were specials I thought I'd try and get 'em here.'

I strolled about the village and saw a fire burning in a big room – but no space there. Eventually I slept in the school on the cold brick floor, exhausted and chilled to the bone. The room was full of men seeking a place themselves. They made me welcome and gave me some tea, which was being brewed over a blaze in the yard. They were in flea-bags, helmets – any old thing – a most incongruous, gritty and robust lot with a fine reputation – the 29th Division.

THURSDAY 20 DECEMBER

It was beautiful in the snow-garbed village, which in the blue of dawn was like a pantomime picture. I called at the signal office for return stuff for Fruges and struck an old estaminet where the old man and woman made me an omelette and got me a piece of bread from a soldier's mess in the next room. 'Rations are short, matey, but we can spare you a piece of crust.'

Walked back up the hill. The weight of the snow had borne down the telegraph wires and they hung dejected and trailing for miles. Often the poles were brought down too. The sun shone, the bright white of the snow scalded the gaze, but my heavy clothes impeded and delayed me. Old men caught up and passed me with ease. A young man walked with me and said, 'A *boire, la-bas – estaminet.*' '*Oui, oui,*' I said. '*Cognac?*' said he. 'By gum, yes,' I shouted. '*Ah, beaucoup soif, eh?*' He laughed.

At the end of the next village was a quiet estaminet. It was like the lodge of Father Christmas. '*Gentil, eh?*' said my friend. An old man with a sealskin cap and checked scarf swathed round his head, sat in the ornate ingle-nook, which was tiled with white and blue and had many curious fire utensils, scrupulously polished. A huge fire was in the hearth and pears were roasting and butter warming to go on bread for the old man's breakfast. A comely dark girl walked in and tended to the man's food.

After a drink I got to the bike and after an hour managed to start it. The French took me for granted as one of the mad English and I simply worked on it then rode off to Cassel and Paul's.

FRIDAY 21 DECEMBER

At ten, I to signal office on night duty. The portly spectacled Bill Adams says to me huskily, in the tones of a man who has endeared the rum bottle to him that night, 'You can take it from me, Davis, I shall not call on you unless absolutely obliged. But of course there's no accounting for those freaks at the château.'

SATURDAY 22 DECEMBER

Watched the Wormhoudt Road turn blue from the grey of dawn. It was one of those moments when the quiet beauty inherent in anything that merely exists in an atmosphere made itself felt anew to the senses. The mellow weathered wall, the cottage of white and green, the bosk of still trees – all spellbound amid the universal confession of beauty which arose like the unspoken, yet felt, prayer of a circle of priests. The magic of earth, rotating into day.

MONDAY 24 DECEMBER

Breakfasted at our new billet after a nice sharp walk through the village. An old man and woman ran the estaminet *Adieu au soif,* but the principle figure was Hélène, a young mother with a bright child – somewhat spoilt. She had a soft, bright complexion, brown eyes, a cheery and bustling manner and was daughter-in-law to the old people, her husband being a prisoner with the 'Alleymands'. She never complained and worked hard with us, taking all our rough chaff in good grace, never overstepping the mark despite temptation– and never allowing us to.

News came by Lilley that there was to be a break-up of the old firm. Three were to go back to Fruges, which was to be retained as a rear office. I was to go to Boeschepe and five would remain. This was a bolt from the blue, midway in our festive preparations.

TUESDAY 25 DECEMBER

Christmas Day. After an early special, down to the shop in Wormhoudt, full of delicate cakes and chocolates, which I bought and gave to the chaps for 'afters'. At about four, White got a special to Fruges for the 29th Division and left, un-complaining in the snow. He must have ridden all out, as he was back at 6.15 for our fine dinner, with two servings of turkey, goose, plum pudding, fruit and custard, followed by liqueurs.

While we were drinking and playing cards, Mr Underwood came in and asked if Glenny, Allcock and myself (I had a reputation because of having beaten Caseby) would take part in a boxing tournament. Weakly I agreed.

WEDNESDAY 26 DECEMBER

Boxing Day. Went on duty from eight to one to free me for evening boxing, the prospect of which agitated me. Glenny had backed out, saying he knew what those army boxing stunts were. He'd had some before.

Evening I went into our cinema hall. In the middle, in a flat area, a ring had been roped out and sanded with sawdust. At the side sat Captain Mudge, enrolling candidates. 'Any more competitors?' he called. I waited, cowed and aghast at the terrible efficiency and substance of the preparations. Mr Underwood came and I pressed through the crowd to see him. 'I'd better back out of this, sir,' I said. 'This looks like a slaughter. I've only got nine teeth, and I should like to keep them.'

'They're all right – only men just like yourself.' 'They look to me a tough crew. I shouldn't stand an earthly.' He looked at me with eyes half amused, half scornful. He spoke to Captain Mudge. 'Are you going to or are you not?' 'I'd sooner be excused, sir.' Captain Mudge despised me. I retired and hid my contempted head amid the crowd.

Two men came out with leonine heads and chests like horses'. They paced and shook and sparred. Their fists shot out like pistons and you heard the sickening thud and thump like the blows of a hydraulic press. Glory boxing always turns me up. I now understood why Glenny and Allcock had skived it. Looking at our bosses, their eyes aglow, gloating on the debasing exhibition, I understood why boxing is encouraged in the army. It affords gladiatorial sport for our lords and masters, who are enabled to drink in the pleasure of the dainty dish of their serfs' blood, while at the same time watching these serfs brutalise themselves.

Down in signal office at 11.00 and at 1.20 Sergeant Jefferies woke me and said, 'These four specials will have to go off at 6.30. I'm putting them off until then, but that's the latest they can go.' Renescure, Thiembronne, Hucqueliers and Buraine. I aghast and excited. Awake for an hour mentally arranging my course.

In the dark, knocked up Lilley and got permission to have two men. Jamo reared up when I suggested he was next on and he should go, but he lent me a map. He wouldn't go unless absolutely obliged. I wanted a companion because of the tales of how Fruges man and JQ were using cars instead of bikes, which were unrideable. Woke Pip and he said he'd come, but he took some getting out. We got some brekker and away at 8.50.

It was very icy and slippy and cold as death as we rode to Cassel. Nice but careful to Renescure. At Faucomburg the road had been made quite rideable in second gear by a snowplough – which I now appreciated for the first time. It had swept the worst of the soft rough off and left a surface hard enough to ride on with fair comfort.

Met the boys going down to the Fruges office – they were half canned, but I had Bendictines with them in the square. Charlie Lilley flushed and convivial, but grousing about the town. 'Why don't you like it? I asked. 'In this snow the great highway from St Omer to the coast, with this townlet, pinching it in a knot and making it twist as a finger on a wind-pipe? The sorrowful square, the decent, decorously garbed church, like a person in broadcloth, and the proud little family shops that have posed proudly beneath its shadow for a century. The mournful and romantic houses thinning out on either hand, the great hills beyond…' 'Oh shut up, for God's sake. You spoil my liqueur. You always see something no-one else can spot.' 'I live, my boys – and you don't,' said the poet.

Back by dusk to a big tea and drinks with the boys in three estaminets.

SATURDAY 29 DECEMBER

Got away at 9.15 for Boeschepe and arrived with ears bitten at 11.00, having to push up the narrow mill lane, past a fallen log across the route. At Boeschepe in the orderly room, Bill Adams led me to a hut where they said I could have a bed as a man was going to hospital that day.

In evening to Abeele and saw Adrienne and Eileen, who told me all about her adventures at Langemarck when British soldiers and French came up there before the Germans advanced. How they provided soup, stew and bread for the men. Her father was a stationmaster and when the British went back, they had a day of agonising whether to leave or not. Finally the dad packed them with belongings on to the train and after a long delay they got to Ypres, full of refugees at the station, and from there to Abeele. Their father came later and the train he got was the last that went to Ypres until after the war – and it was shot at and half left behind.

SUNDAY 30 DECEMBER

No instructions, so I kept fire going and read *A Young Man's Year* by Anthony Hope. In evening to Eileen's and found Jamo there. On returning to the hut I got my instructions – to return tomorrow to Esquelbecq, as I'd come the wrong weekend.

I reviewed my pigeon acquaintances... Jack Hilton who had been carried into hospital from Ypres, scored with shrapnel, and the odd couple at Voormezeele – Curry and his pioneer; the dark-haired and cheery-faced Frogley, always willing, and his mate who was always getting diarrhoea, being ill and complaining of sickness (who got evacuated, thank God). Then Hughie and Graves – another sufferer from bad health and a reed – but a trier. Tom's partner, Edgar North, handsome and a decent sport. Whittle, a steady corporal and honest, and his rather flash pioneer, Roberts – a man of wrist-watches and inflated talk of home. They were on the right by a small pool and clump of trees at he crest of the wide slope which dropped through mud to the Vierstraat road. To all these I bade farewell.

Went with Bill Pritchard to a lecture on Verdun and the strategy of the war at Talbot House, given by a captain in the Royal Welch Fusiliers – a dandy, self-complacent buck who, with all the assurance in the world, unfolded the British plan of two sides of a square which were to be pushed together at extreme ends and thus crush the Huns left in the angle in the middle. According to him, Huns foolish in strategy. They were doing what we wanted them to do. They had given battle at Ypres when we wanted. It suited us and unwittingly they had accepted our invitations to fight at Ypres and on the Somme, as one accepts a sacrifice at chess. All our apparent reverses were only preliminary and intended moves to the great masterpiece of advance and victorious plan that was to follow. Don't worry – trust our commanders. We didn't know the inside policy – he did. Fritz had done just what we wanted – eg, the French in giving him the St Mihiel Salient had done so purposely to entice him to a disadvantageous hold. French super strategy miraculous. They had about 27 new divisions, quite fresh and untouched. We should have an early decision but for the Russian revolution, etc.

Faugh! He sickened me – the fatuous optimist. But it went down. I asked two cynical questions – the suspicion dawned on me he was lying officially – handing out dope to encourage the troops. I will say the optimistic credulity of the troops justified him – he went down quite well.

MONDAY 31 DECEMBER

So stiff with cold this morning that it took me an hour to start the bike… Took it into the workshop in afternoon. No piss-up this night?

1918

WEDNESDAY 2 JANUARY

On Continental on bad roads to camp by big scrambling village. Round slush and slipperiness and home by 3.30. How fine it was to cycle round to the mess and slip off my overalls, then sit in the corner where Tubby put out my dinner, which he'd kept in the stove. Then I read and drank coffee while the boys played pontoon. 'Going out again?' said Tubby. 'I've forgotten to leave my receipts at the signal office.' 'Bugger 'em. What does that matter?' said Percy. 'Eat your dinner, lad. I'll let you into a secret, Oz. Look here.' He went to his valise and took out three small OHMS buff letters. 'See those? They're despatches I had on my continental[18] this morning. I forgot 'em, so I'm taking them tomorrow.' 'But what about your receipts?' 'I signed the docket myself.' They're only some pass or other for a town major to go and see his wimp at Dunkirk – or a situation report. They'll do tomorrow.'

MONDAY 7 JANUARY

Demonstrations rather chaotic with only six birds. Captain Macdonald interrupts, 'Carprrrl, tall them about not releasing the pigeons in the same place every day lest the Boche should note and shell it. Shouldn't they hold the birrrrrd with the left hand, Carprrrl.' However, he worked hard, but wanted to pose as knowing everything.

WEDNESDAY 9 JANUARY

Tried the snow – rideable though crunching loudly underfoot. To Esquelbecq through a snowstorm to a meeting with the colonel. The snow blinded one and pierced everywhere.

Cleaned and dried kit and drank farewell to Jamo and Tug Wilson, who had been admitted as cadets to the Flying Corps.

FRIDAY 11 JANUARY

Rode to Westoutre and talked in canteen with depressed but honest man –
'We've had no stuff the last week. We're expecting to move, but we've always
been expecting. They've got the wind up round these parts. They're that
nervous about the Boche since Cambrai.'

I landed the Boeschepe special – bike wouldn't start. Got it going then
lamp went out at San Martin, then decompressor wouldn't work, leaving
compression weak, then going down the hill from Cassel I skidded and fell,
spraining my thumb. Then couldn't start again – skidded. Cussed. Walked and
pushed and kicked and ran…

MONDAY 14 JANUARY

Three specials called at midnight. Whitey had arranged things – Garry first,
he second, I third. We had only been saying that we hoped there was nothing
tonight. 'I'll bet there's one for that bloody artillery brigade,' said Garry.
'They're really nothing to do with us and it's the Fourth Army area, but they
keep bunging them on to us because we're at rest. And our Corps is so windy
they'll take anything from the army. What the bloody hell are artillery brigades
at Clarmarais to do with us? It should be the Army or L Sigs.'

Up the steps came heavy footfall. 'Special DR wanted.' 'Where's it for?'
'Something like Creamery,' said cyclist orderly. 'That blasted brigade,' groaned
Garry as he dressed. 'That puts me on,' said Charley. 'I hope there's nothing
more in this gale.' The wind howled and the rain flailed the windows and roof.

'I bet Charley's out and me too,' I said, and tossed, strung and expectant
until 1.30, when I was awakened from forgetfulness by an orderly shaking me
and saying, 'Special to the 17th Brigade RGA.' 'That's the Clarmarais stunt, isn't
it? Is White out?' He nodded. 'I'll be down in ten minutes.'

I could scarcely keep the road. The wind bore me from side to side, and
my cap blew off. I tied my cap comforter around it. My lamp went out. I got to
Cassel and wound down the St Omer road. The blizzard blinded me. Over the
road at the level crossing the barrier was up and I just pulled up in time to miss
the wood. The road was dark and lonely – not a soul about. This ride had been a
bugbear to all who'd had it. A tortuous lane led through haystacks of sand in ruts
some four or five inches deep. Every twenty yards the bike would skid on the sand
and throw you. On the left was a rhomboid shape that looked like the hangars of
the aerodrome which the boys spoke of as the indication, and I spotted a sentry.

'Is this the aerodrome?' 'Yes.' 'Is there an artillery mob round about here?'
'First turn right after the fork and you'll strike their lorries.' I kept on and saw

swaying lights ahead. Lorries were cranking up and warming up engines. Into the circle of light I dashed dramatically and held out my buff envelope special. Just in time.

An officer turned toward me. 'What's that? Orders again? Move cancelled?' 'I expect so, sir.' 'Let's have a look.' He glanced at it with his torch. 'That's nothing to do with me – take it to the OC. Here, Rider, show him to the orderly room.'

He led me silently up a line of duckboards. The wind was so violent that the door crashed back out of our hands and the light inside went out. 'Out,' he said, looking down at the empty blankets on the floor. 'We've been arsed about tonight. We were just getting a couple of winks when in came the first DR. I think you're the third we've had today. They don't seem to know what to do with us. Wait here.' And he got me my receipt.

I'd stopped their moving, and it was easy to wheedle some carbide out of one of the drivers because I'd procured them a reprieve. Back in very slow dawn, it starting to turn blue at 6.30. I now overtook figures in the lessening rain going in groups to working places, and also French civvies. At Wormhoudt the huts by the river were under two feet of water, at Esquelbecq our river was a wild torrent, and the estaminet was under a foot of water. Tried to get brekker in the corner café, but no go. Extraordinary how unpleasant it is to have to go without breakfast after looking forward to it from a bad night ride.

MONDAY 21 JANUARY

In the evening to teashop. Since the old days a ban had been put on the teashop when first DAR came there, and it was not allowed under civil police supervision to serve coffee in hours other than when the pubs opened. They had once tried this at Abeele. At any rate, they stopped the boys having coffees in an estaminet house – and thus in the San Martin. Jeanne said it was because many of their neighbours were jealous of the trade done by the *mavauts*.[19] Jeanne appeared to be glad to see me again. She has wonderful dark, languishing eyes, her figure is rather plump, but she was one of the belles of Cassel and the favourite of the DRs.

TUESDAY 22 JANUARY

Up to Paul at the château and there I wrote my first army article 'Army Pigeons'.

The two sergeants, Hastings and another, managed things very well at DAR. They had everything under their thumb and everything in a groove. Each morning they cast a look at the roster, knowing the runs by heart and how the roster stood, and the speed of the various riders, they could calculate with certainty what they'd have to do.

The Fourth Army didn't encourage specials. They had an astute practice of farming them out on to their corps or divisions. Everything was beautifully stage-managed. Nevertheless, there was some wonderful wangling. There was a nucleus of half a dozen original Fourth Armyites, and you could often hear the two sergeants conferring in smooth undertones with the result that a long midnight special would get plonked on to some unsuspecting youngster, while the old hand pulled the downy blankets over his head and slept the deep sleep of the old sweat.

That night Hastings came into our room where slept one such venerable wangler. 'I'm afraid there's no help for it,' said Hastings. He held a candle which lit the dun bed, the mantelpiece over the stove where reposed tins, generators and tools. On the wall were a couple of wood shelves – books, small biscuit tins, sugar, tea and cocoa tins, and a Primus. 'But what about Calder?' asked he of the red face, disconcerted at the idea of him, an old soldier, being routed from his slumber to do such a ghastly thing as a night special.

'You see, there's football tomorrow. He won't be back in time.' The red-faced one recognised in football a power even greater than wangling. 'Shove that new chap on it – Curly.' 'Well, that's not quite playing the game – to put a new man on to a night special the first day he's got here. Besides, his bike's out of order.' 'Well, so's mine for that matter – or I can soon make it so. It only wants a clout on the gearbox. I'm really not feeling up to the mark tonight.'

Hastings says, scratching his nose, 'You know I'm willing to oblige where possible, but you see, Flood's next on and he'd raise Cain rather than go. I'm afraid you'll have to, old man. Sorry.'

The only man they never got the better of was Jerry, whom squad 142 made a butt of. Jerry always kept a midday run and when finished he got straight into bed and slept round the clock until his next run.

On runs in the moonlight and dawn I came to fully appreciate the moon for the first time. With moonlight the night run is easy and you can spin along. If dark and your lamp is bad – and nearly every lamp issued to us was old or bad – you fear all the time some obstacle on the road, the grease, or the loose stones which rip the cover – and it's so hard to get a new one. In the early morn I used to long for dawn and spin out as long as possible the time of departure in order to get light down the Cassel hill spiral. It was as treacherous as a hillside of ice. As soon as I got down on to the straight by the Wormhoudt road, I could let her rip.

On into Esquelbecq. I had to wake the DR clerk up and sleep was still in his eyes when I handed the packet across the counter. Going back I'd meet Bendle or Craven, off from the run to Bergues or Dunkirk, shifting at great pace.

Then in the morning I would clean up and do the bike, then write at Paul's château, when I could resist the temptation to read in our snug billet, where they'd somehow got coal. Then in the evening to the cinema or a concert party, seeing the pallid and lame Madeleine and perhaps Jeanne – but all the girls had a chaperone or were accompanied, and it was not the thing for civvy girls to speak to British soldiers.

MONDAY 28 JANUARY

This morning on return found handlebars loose. To tiffy shop and gruff sergeant, 'What do you want?' 'My handlebars are breaking. Have you a new pair?' 'Let's look. Can't ye get them from Corps?' 'They've none. I'm riding for the army and I can't ride without bars.' He said nought, but went to a corner and flung me a pair.

While Bonnet was changing them for me he broke the exhaust toggle, and said, 'Your frame's broken.' 'No wonder I've had some skids,' I said. 'I never tumbled to it. I'll ride over to Corps and see if I can get a new bike. I never had a new or decent bike since I came out. We can't get a new bike with our Corps unless the frame is broken. Same here, of course?' 'Hey, bring those handlebars back here,' yelled the sergeant tiffy. 'I'll have to keep 'em to ride over.' 'Bring 'em back when you've got yer new bike. I'm not going to have my new handlebars sent into the supply column or pinched by your tiffy while he sends some broken ones in.' His wail followed me down the road.

Afternoon had to clean up my old bike – a new order from OC of supply column, owing to dirty bikes being returned and no bike was to be sent to the column unless clean. Hoped I shouldn't get a 'jute'[20] bus which were 1915 Triumphs done up again and were regarded with great disfavour.

WEDNESDAY 30 JANUARY

Met Glenny and fixed bike, then he wanted to slip up straight to Abeele, and we arranged a joint tale to cover the excursion – mag trouble[21], of course. Going uphill, looked back at the fine Flanders plain, stretching out under blue sky and mild January sun like a calm and misty sea. Very tranquil and beautiful. Half a dozen German prisoners, slouching, with patched suits and red-braided caps passed with one Tommy in charge. How easy for the group to surround and overwhelm him.

FRIDAY 1 FEBRUARY

Jackstaff's article in the *Daily Mail* on DRing. I'm forestalled! Great talk in the mess about it, 'I'm sure it's a DR,' says one. 'How else could he write like he does? He couldn't without knowing a machine.' 'He doesn't talk like a DR...'

TUESDAY 5 FEBRUARY

Had supper with Paul and heard of Albert Hirst's bad luck. He was with a division up on the coast and up against a sergeant who didn't like him. Various ads ran – that Albert was out of luck, that he was fed up with his crush and said before he started out that he was going to have an accident. And he did, but not what he thought. Either skidded or side-slipped on the sand or hit something and came down. Concussion, and now lying paralysed on one side, numerous X-ray experiments. He wrote to Bendle from hospital in England and said he would like any of the boys to write.

WEDNESDAY 6 FEBRUARY

Afternoon was handed buff letter, OHMS. Dreaded opening it. It was from General Staff Intelligence, and signed Camp Commandant, regretting that by Army Order so and so, neither officers nor men could send manuscripts direct for publication to the press, but must apply, with duplicate MS sent and accompanied by signed permission of OC, to 'official press bureau, Whitehall'. They said, however, there was nothing in my article they could object to.

TUESDAY 12 FEBRUARY

In the afternoon Peter burst into the room saying, 'There's a DR come to replace you – a great clumsy brute of a fellow – came bursting into Caton's room, knocking petrol tins over and leaving a trail of tubes and generators. He'll have to stop chucking his weight about. Who is he?'

'No idea – didn't know I was wanted at Corps.' Aghast. All our arrangements upset. At tea met Gillam – 'the brute'. 'They want you to return for pigeoneering, I think.' 'At once?' 'Didn't say so.' So decided to stop for the evening.

WEDNESDAY 13 FEBRUARY

Walked up the main street in Cassel to the mess for the last time – what happy hours I'd had there – peace in war. Too moved at parting to complete writing the 'Gates of Leave'[22] well, but did so.

I'd been sweating, footling and foozling in my best style (I hated packing and moving), and eventually got off at 11.30, just as it started to rain. Posted off 'Gates of Leave' at the Army post office.

Once gone it was nice to be back in the atmosphere of the men I knew, with all their faults. After dinner was peeping over Palmer's shoulder at his London *Daily Mail*, and saw 'There is an establishment of DRs' – the sentence rang with a dreamy familiarity and it came to me like light that it was my article. At Cassel in our studio I had said, 'Miracles don't happen,' as Paul packed up his drawings for *The Bystander* – but they do and here was proof. Out of defeat I had brought victory. I was overjoyed and sat in the cosy inn, the boys playing cards, and success was sweet.

In the evening went to pictures and singing contest. There was one – a batman – who sang sentimental song with awful accents, and the cook – a little man with a piping voice, who was a great favourite, and they cheered him on.

THURSDAY 14 FEBRUARY

Got permission from Lilley to go to see Paul and old Pip who was in hospital in Wisques, just outside Arques. He'd fallen twice, the last time having caught on frozen ruts and lain in the road, just missing being crushed by a lorry after lying there some half an hour. Pip's nerves appear to have been suffering after successive smashes. As was setting off, was told to 'stand by'.

In the canteen saw the *Daily Mail* on the counter and saw the title, as I turned it up, 'Army Pigeons – how they work'.[23] So my first two articles, straight in! I asked Stan Brown, 'Can I borrow this? There's an article of mine in it. I just want to read it and I'll bring it back in half an hour.'

To the mess, to tea and then brûlant to Wormhoudt to the shop where the scented and pale exuberant girl always smiled at you invitingly, and ogled officers. I got about eight copies of the *Mail*, but couldn't get more than one copy of the pigeon article. Evening sent off copies of DR article to friends and mother.

SATURDAY 16 FEBRUARY

Was told that I must get timetable charts, find where pigeons were put down on this, and arrange with the sergeant running the squad to fix up for lectures. Walked to San Martin and paused at a little house I had often looked at when out riding. Walked in – benches two sides of a mud-floored room. On the left, facing me was a huge mechanical organ-piano, about which climbed a girl as pennies were stuck in and it was churned into music. One girl looked as if at a fancy dress ball – gypsy, powdered, and another younger, all bosom.

THURSDAY 21 FEBRUARY

Lectured and then wrote for two hours. In evening read E M Forster's *A Room with a View* – a delightful book that was a new read to me. A find – but it was mentioned to me by Arnold Bennett.

SATURDAY 23 FEBRUARY

In evening bathed in the large round zinc basin – which we had to keep hidden under the table, and when finished with, had to throw the water out at the back end of the hut so as not to be seen by the OC, as it as against regulations to wash anywhere but in the appointed place… which I never found. There was no washing water laid on in camp and the men used to wash in a fouled pool in one of the fields, iced and snowy.

I noted that the lame, the halt and the blind employment company people and category men on the camp used to be drilled outside. Some of them were deaf and some crippled and they looked like stuck scarecrows when orders they couldn't hear were shouted at them.

THURSDAY 28 FEBRUARY

In evening to the estaminet where a plump crippled man sat by the polished gramophone, carefully dusting each record and handling the instrument like a cherished child. We could see on the sky-line the intense pink flashes and dim stars floating aimlessly before going out. 'There's going to be trouble round here,' said the boys. 'Hope to God it's over before I get back.'

SATURDAY 2 MARCH

Freezing cold wind – too cold almost to write.

Our sentiments in the hut are that perhaps some incredible miracle might happen which could shorten the war, but it looked like going on for ever. No use worrying – just put it off as long as possible and trust for the best.

In evening, despite temptations to go out with Bill Adams, stayed in and wrote at my next article. NCOs kept darting into my office, surprised to see me. In the morning the orderly corporals kept coming in and accosting me as one in authority because I sat thumping a typewriter in the office. Never felt so important in the army before!

TUESDAY 5 MARCH

Rose in the dark and typed the signals article which the *Daily Mail* was going to publish. Very cold and high gale – bitter weather. Finished 'Khaki Religion'[24] article.

THURSDAY 7 MARCH

Fine today. Rose at six and typed 'Getting Knocked'[25]. Out in the Corps motor lorry with the quartermaster, who was too big to talk to me now that he was among his sergeant-major pals. I was in doubt as to whether I was going to Corps for good, but took gumboots and cleaning materials only. Got back to Esquelbecq and Lilley told me I could go over to Corps the next day.

FRIDAY 8 MARCH

Tuned my new bike until eleven – Mr Underwood's old one, as he fancied the new one that had come in that was destined properly for me.

SUNDAY 10 MARCH

With Lilley's remit went to DAR to sit for a portrait being painted by Paul in pastels.

MONDAY 11 MARCH

In morning got my articles censored by taking them to Mr Underwood and Captain Mudge.

TUESDAY 12 MARCH

Our photo taken in the garden of the haircutter's by precocious youth with dark hair who spoke 'leetle English'.

WEDNESDAY 13 MARCH

As it became evident that Pip would be evacuated to England, Doug Seabourne approached me with a request to ask for him to be put on pigeon service. 'But we have to work, Doug.' 'I'll work.' He went red. I was caught napping, and not quite honestly said that it had been an understood thing that Vic Turnpenny should have first refusal. I felt a humbug.

THURSDAY 14 MARCH

At dinner got censored manuscripts back and sent them off from the post office.

FRIDAY 15 MARCH

Over to Boeschepe for a megaphone. Rode new bike down the winding lanes, curving and interesting, with motor lorries at the bridge bends and little units camped on the wayside – a few Anzacs and Americans knocking around. Bill Adams produced the megaphone and Wally came out. 'What the hell's the megaphone for?' 'The sports we're going to have.'

SUNDAY 17 MARCH

Today the sports field was fixed up by the sergeant-major and workers. Sam Brown seemed to know his way about and the ground fixed up well. Civvies came – Hélène with her boy, girls with their younger kin. We sat and watched – tug of war won by Signals, however, the cyclists did best in everything. Maxwell fought with pillow on the plank over water and won hands down.

Walking back to tea, two new DRs accosted me. One, a hard case with a shock of black hair and slightly twisted mouth from lack of fangs, said, 'Can ye tell me where the DRs' mess is? We're for you – reinforcements. Perhaps I'd better announce our arrival at the signal office.' He popped over the narrow road, leaving me with his companion, a little figure with a Charles Dickens head. He had the DR blue and white band painted on his poncho and issue leggings, but when he took his poncho off, he had no stripes. He was one of the new Pioneer DRs that there was so much talk about.

'Sinclair's my name,' said the other, as we went down over the little bridge. 'I've always been with the artillery and I'm cut up at leaving my old crush. Always been with the same mob, but I had a smash and got into hospital. It wouldn't have happened, but just as I was going on leave, the other DR fell ill. There was no reinforcement handy, so I had to stay on and tried arguing with a water cart in the dark. Our mob got put on the way to Kingdom Come with some of Fritz's heavy stuff – so perhaps it was as well. All my kit's gone west – service boots, Primus, revolver. They had to pump up a new outfit for me. I wanted to get back to my unit, but after leave, I'd been away so long they'd got fixed up – and if I couldn't get back with them, I didn't care the toss of a clod where I am. I met this chap, Skoney, coming up, and we travelled up here without knowing we were on the same trip until we started asking at Hazebrouck where XXX Corps was. What sort of crush are you?' 'Not so bad. We've got a decent mess and the billet isn't bad. One or two wrong 'uns, but the rest are bricks.'

SUNDAY 17 MARCH

A fine day and light enough for me to type in the orderly room, windy of the SM and OC coming and asking all the time what I was doing.

A great dinner in the estaminet – sirloin of sumptuous tender beef, spring cabbage, spuds and carrots, then pudding. Replete, felt like a lazy read, but decided to go to the football match between Army Signals and a picked Belgian team.

In the pleasant village of Rexpurge the great wide main street had the mellow stir of a Saturday afternoon in an English country town. Saw lorries and cars parked up and men on top watching the game, shouting and wailing – a pleasant field with huts around and the noises of football. Officers strolled about, speaking to men who did not withdraw their hands from pockets. The Belgian team outplayed and outclassed us and when they had a penalty their captain refused to do other than kick the ball into touch. They made me ashamed of the rough tricks of my own countrymen. I believe it was the Corps who played, not Army.

WEDNESDAY 20 MARCH

In morning prepared for special parade for the decoration of Mr Bevan with the Military Cross by some general. We poshed up shocking, but our clothes were not clean – grease and oil showing. Our armbands weren't clean enough and Captain Mudge said the DRs weren't good enough for the parade.

THURSDAY 21 MARCH

Morning to Pip's old crib at Musketry and Reinforcement Camp, via the St Mommelin Road, over roads greasy with mud tracks and bits of dark *pave*. Turned and twisted on to the main Calais road, which switched up and down in fine, broad shady sequence with villages and wide inns at the side.

There was a small notice outside the camp and plots of gardens tended by Hun prisoners, among the wood huts. Davies was there and he showed me Pip's old bed. I took some of Pip's belongings, made a parcel and got it censored and sent off to him. Enjoyed the ride back via Omer, the WAACs with blue and white bands up looked very provocative and it was with keen regret I left Omer. I had never done much joy-riding and thought I should have done.

FRIDAY 22 MARCH

Scottie in our billet from the signal office counter gave us the latest news of the offensive, which started on the 21st. Ground given way and bad news. However, Alf Allcock says news not so bad.

SATURDAY 23 MARCH

As walking to parade the quartermaster said to me, 'What's this rumour about moving?' 'I've not heard.' 'Haven't ye?' 'Don't say anything, then. It's going about, though.'

Back to sleeping billet when Lilley comes upstairs and says we're to pack. He knows no more. 'Get ready to move.' The shadow fell across me. I packed, foozling about and not knowing what to do with all my gear and some left over of Pip's.

From dull acceptance we had grown to like Esquelbecq. We had friends everywhere. Up in the billet at night, how dear to lie and listen to the talk. On the walls hung ponchos, haversacks, tubes. Under the bed were spare tunics, overalls and boots with black boxes, lamps and belts. There was Mac and Billy Harrison, always in early – Jones curled up like a hedgehog inside a linen sack, hanging about and dodging and never even coming on parade – never waking until we pulled him out after we'd had our brekker. Glenny and Garry and their Primuses, tea and biscuits.

All this idyll was to disappear. Only Friday afternoon I had lain in the sun reading in a green field and the OC had gone riding up that delightful road on his horse. Now it was all over – Hélène and the estaminets, and Madame, our hostess. So thinking I wandered about, trying to get rid of surplus tin hats and throwing them down at last in an adjacent garret. I had pinched a Very light pistol when we first took over the Railway dugouts and it was too bulky and risky to take, so I stuck it on the top of a rafter. It's probably there to this day.

MONDAY 25 MARCH

Much excitement with the lorries and box-cars and people moving about. The DRs were unflurried and got their stuff together at the last moment. I had to stay behind with Geordie and Skoney to show them the way and to wait for any last continentals, and I was 'stood by' for a special that the Corps General was half expecting.

Alarmist news comes through on the wires as we wait to close down the signal office at noon, the boys stand leisurely about, smoking and winding up the few things to be sent up. A parcel arrives to be handed in to the army as I pass through Cassel.

Violent rumours begin to float about. We are surrounded at a certain place and forced to give big ground.

To Cassel, beautiful in the sun, her white and grey stone suspended over the green plain and puncturing the sensuous blue of the sky, like a Spanish city of romance. As I came down to the Villa Marie Ange I recognised a laugh. Good old Doug, 'Glad to see you back. What kind of time did you have?' 'Not so bad, worked like heroes, fed on bully, slept on stone floors and rode about 150 kilos at a stretch – roads altogether different from ours – steeply banked. What's your trouble? You're loaded up… of course, your Corps is moving.' 'Yes, I just came to say goodbye to Paul. Do you know where he is?' 'At Jeanne's, I expect.' 'Well, in case I miss him, wish him good luck.' 'Chin, chin, best of luck.'

At the end of the alley I met Bill Pritchard and Paul. 'Off so soon, Oz? Can't you have a cup of cocoa with us?' 'We've got to get to Frevent tonight, and I'm not keen on leaving it too late. It's between Doullens and St Pol.' 'What's on?' 'Don't know. Into the thick of it, I bet. Just my luck. For a Corps DR I've been fairly into the shit, and I really have worked. Now, just as we were shaking down to a rest, it's up the bloody Somme again. I shouldn't have minded if we'd stayed here – I like Belgium. If Fritz is pushing us back I suppose I shall have it warm. I've got regular lazy and selfish.' 'That's the worst of having it cushy, Oz. The more cushy you are, the cushier you want it.'

We strode through the square – perhaps it was the last time I should see it unhurt. Presentiments of disaster and loss darkened my mind. I looked at my army pals – Bill, hands in pockets, dark brown eyes gleaming through glasses. It was in early '16 I had met him and thought him aloof – his supercilious air when arguing with the poet about the *Daily Mail* had misled me. The intervening two years had shown Bill to be true steel and blue loyal. None now scoffed at his teetotalism. There was not a man, bar the officers whose legs he had pulled, who did not respect Bill. There was my cousin – flamboyant, ruddy-faced, handsome – a big talker and a reckless rider, always smashing into people at crossroads.

'It cuts me to the quick to leave you,' I said. 'I wonder when I'll see you again. I bet I'm going to have a rotten time. I wish I was staying.' 'Buck up, Oswald. There's a glad time coming when you're dead.'

We came to the bandstand round which I had cavorted so many times on the bike, making twirls and rushes to impress the civvies. Cassel was a haunt of quiet beauty and musical stir with its khaki and French blue, the red spots of brass hats, the white, black, grey and brown of Sunday civilian attire flecked the cobbled square, the steps and balconies, and the pavement with its mild colour.

We shook and we rode off down the Omer road. We crashed over the bumps at the side of the *pavé*,[26] overtaking lorries all the time which left behind them clouds of dust – you had no sooner wiped some of the muck out of your eyes from one lorry than you were on another. The convoy lasted miles.

A week ago a Fourth Army DR had seen another DR slip under one of these when passing, push out his hand to save himself and catch it in the exposed driving chain. Some such thought as this must have circled in Skoney's brain and we had to keep pulling up for him. Soon we got on the Fruges road – it was a glorious ride until we pulled up at Madame's – our old mess. She made us welcome with all she had – eggs, marge, bread, butter, jam, tea – and would scarcely let us pay.

It was a lovely evening ride to Frevent, curling in and out of shadowy, cool villages. Then down a muddy lane, in a huge walled parade ground, stood a vast square building like a warehouse. Here were the Corps lorries and box-carts lined up. The boys' bikes were in a partition by the wall, but no DRs to be seen except Royle and Palmer.

Lilley approached. 'Where are they all?' No answer. 'This isn't playing the game, damned if it is. The situation at the front's critical and we may be wanted any minute, and here all the DRs have pissed off for a wet evening, not to mention the tiffy getting canned coming down, and falling off, putting his hand out. If they can't do the decent thing, I'm going to turn awkward. You two stand by while I get a roster.'

I crept out of this. 'This is no place for us. Go canny,' said Geordie. 'All right-minded DRs should get blotto the first night of a new pitch. Let's find out where we kip, drop our luggage and get out.'

Up six flights of stairs we came to a roomy rotten chamber where DRs' gear was hanging. Dumped kit, then off like schoolboys, leaving the verdant and timid Skoney to his fate.

The estaminets of Frevent had forbidding outsides and those sinister interiors which are peculiarly Belgian. It was as if everybody was trying to bear up and be as bright as if nothing had happened after a corps has just been pushed out of the way. But our DRs were not troubled by atmosphere. Here they were, laughing, drinking and leg pulling like a party.

'Lilley's got the breeze up because there's no-one for a roster,' I said, coming to the table at the side of the stove.' 'If he's aerated, he should put some gas into this beer,' said Glenny. 'It's good knife-wash – one franc fifty a bottle – highway robbery.'

Then, a voice from the doorway, 'Special DR wanted. Where the hell…? Is this a messroom?' 'I'll toss ye, Geordie, who goes,' said White sportingly. Geordie lost and went with good grace.

TUESDAY 26 MARCH

Saw Captain Mudge and Colonel Iles walking up the St Pol Road, and the SM told me not to go too far away as we might move any minute. Mighty rumours all day of us going everywhere and splitting into a divisional unit.

That evening I was 'on' for night duty. Slept in my togs to be ready, and had wind up fearing a dash to the firing line amid gas and mud. At midnight, Ward came up looking lugubrious and saying, 'We shall split up, I suppose and part go to one division and part to another. I know some of our DRs will take over. We've got to send 'em tomorrow.'

I hoped to heaven I don't have to go, lose my pigeon job and have to make good again amidst strange boys. Did I seek adventure and glory? No – I only fervently desired no dangerous special would fetch me out.

WEDNESDAY 27 MARCH

This morning, sure enough, word came to stand to, packed and we were soon ready and off. Up the St Pol road and parked our bikes on the wet green before the Herlincourt church. 'Now for a messroom and billet,' we cried. 'We shall have to be quick off the mark – I've already seen several of the operators on the mooch.'

In jealous competition we tried nearly every house in the village. However, at the *Mairie* we found there were some wood-frame beds, dark and rotten in the barn. The mayor said the artillerymen had had them before. Then I said, 'What about that building at the corner of the green? It's a school, but they might have room.'

Madame, of the thin, cheerful, bright-eyed type, smiled all over her face. We could have the schoolroom. Champion. And use her outhouse and her oven. 'We've clicked,' we shouted to the OTs who were returning crestfallen from their fruitless quest.

THURSDAY 28 MARCH

Rotten tales about retreat and losses of Allies' armies. Local tales of St Pol being shelled.

Evening wrote 'Special to Ascheux' article. On the board Seward wrote a roster in decorative letters and Gillam drew pictures of Percy and me. The boys played cards until Tubby got leftovers from dinner for supper and they came back creamy from the estaminets.

FRIDAY 29 MARCH

Special to the Corps at Duisans. While waiting for reply, great wind up in the camp as a result of my special. Orderlies fled about. 'All to the parade with gasmasks and revolvers,' I heard. On return I badly wanted to see Arras, but as a result of the alarming nature of my special, I was timid and also had to get back with my message.

So it was back on the Arras-Frevent road, and in the side-roads was the unmistakeable dust and track of war. The roads rutted with dust and stones, wagons and horses staggering in the winding hills and guns waiting at villages, new trenches starting to zig-zag.

Back on the cross-country road recommended by Gillam. I was just starting to curse him when I saw a figure bending over a motorbike on its stand.

'Hello! I was just cursing you. I've been poring over contradictory signboards at every corner for the last hour. Some bloody route.' 'It's right enough, Oz. But look here – got a spare tube? I came out with a special for the 3rd Canadians and have had a burst. Found no spare in my haversack.' 'What the hell are you doing, then?' 'Stuffing the cover with grass.' 'Aren't you one of the men that calls us a Christmas tree because I've always got lots of equipment slung around?' He laughed. 'Well, Santa Claus is going to be kind to you. Stick that tube in while I take your special.' Gillam showed me the twisting and beautiful road and we were back by two.

SATURDAY 30 MARCH

There were some rotten runs just now, such as to Fosseux – there and back some 60 miles – no pleasing run over bad, greasy roads in the dark, with no light in the forward end and the chance that you might take the wrong road and land amid the Hun. This chance was slight, but it dwelt in our minds.

Our position was not comfortable. Though nominally in reserve, we ran to fighting divisions and were handing on divs to the firing line, and personally I was dreading all the time we should ourselves go into line on the rotten Somme.

SUNDAY 31 MARCH

News alternately depressing and better. Situation felt tense. Hoping and hoping keenly for good news.

MONDAY 1 APRIL

Received cheque from the *Daily Mail* for 'Khaki Religion', which I didn't know had been accepted. It appeared in the 21 March edition – the first day of the Hun offensive, which stopped my next article on 'Signals' from going in. 'Getting Knocked' was returned. What of 'Signals' and 'Gates of Leave'?

TUESDAY 2 APRIL

On continental in morning held up by a plug at Houvigneul, where stopped for a Muscat (a franc a glass) at a clean corner pub where, as I was sipping, and a younger sister swept, the elder sister of about twenty came down, pallid and languorous and floated around the room, inviting admiration. 'Where the hell does she come from, and who keeps her?' I wondered, for she evidently did no work, and was talking about being tired and having slept until after noon.

MONDAY 8 APRIL

The quarter agreed to take my 30 francs' worth of coupons and fetch the coal if he could have a sack of it for nothing. So accepted this arrangement gladly and the coal was useful to us.

Madame at the school was interested in the movement of the armies, so we traced it for her on the map. We strove to comfort her, but we kept retreating and somehow it seemed that our assurances were false and that we should never repel the Hun. I for one couldn't see how we could. How were we to do now, in our exhausted and depleted condition, what we had been trying three and a half years to do without success?

WEDNESDAY 10 APRIL

Laughed this morning as we washed – we could see the brass hats turning up their noses at us and looking as if we were some strange beings, cast up from the sea. At eleven we got orders to shift into the barn of a nearby farm. Great were the lamentations at first. 'I suppose they can't stand the sight of seeing men who work,' said Walter – who so far hadn't been out. 'It's Davis saying, "Oh I'm fed up" that's got on their nerves. They can't stand too much of it any more than we.' 'It's more likely Oz singing…' 'If they can put the screw on us, our bloody staff always will,' says Walter. 'And not a soul among the signals has got the pluck of a louse to speak up for us. All afraid of losing their jobs.' 'Like us,' said Whitey, who never groused.

We gradually settled down, every man kept bagging a bed someone else laid claim to. The place held eleven beds. After much dispirited groping, clean-ing and messing about, we shook down to make the best of it. Tom made a bed up on the rafters with corrugated sheets laid on loose rafter logs, which bent and shook with their weight. Glenny kept his hut in the corner of the big garage shed where we now kept our bikes under cover, formerly in the open by our billet. The barn looked different with our equipment hanging up and candles going.

SATURDAY 13 APRIL

Rumours about our retreat north are incredible. Madame upset about the fresh bad news.

When they had to open the school they allowed us to eat and sit in their sitting room. Very good of them. Dinner cleared, we used to play cards by the window by the green.

At night in the barn Sergeant Lilley came in about nine, when he had got the news from the signal office, as he often did. 'What do you think? They've got Merville.' 'The Huns? Good God – where we used to get the caps made. And old Seabourne's girl at Bois Grenier – wonder what's happened to her,' mused Percy. 'But how have they done it?' I asked astonished. 'God knows. They've walked right through. The line now is Neuf Berquin, Estaires…' 'Hope we don't have to pack up in the middle of the night,' said Geordie. 'As long as I have my sleep first, don't care if they take Hazebrouck. It's a rotten country anyhow. Best thing is if they take the place off our hands.' 'By gosh,' said Percy, 'the Hun knew something when he walloped out of this damned landscape. He couldn't have done us a dirtier turn. Let 'im have it, I say. It's not worth fighting over.'

They spoke unconcernedly and with grousing facetiousness, but inwardly I was perturbed. When I first came out I was scared and always dreading being put to a worse job than the harrowing one I was doing. This gave way gradually to self-confidence and trust in the kindliness of the Fates as we moved up to the Salient from the Somme, and I found the much-dreaded Ypres front quiet. A long stay up there had confirmed me in the idea of comfortable routine in modern battle, and this had continued until the shock on 23 March of this year. But this upset again had gradually lost force as we saw the Hun stemmed and baulked and we were breathing freely again, when in came this horrible, incredible news of the advance north, where he had broken through at a greater rate than ever before. I thought to myself, is war after all going to be for me a dreadful and bloody affair? And is it possible the Hun is going to win after all? What's to stop him? And if he wins, the world won't be worth living in.

MONDAY 15 APRIL

It was now dangerous and sporty riding. All along the great roads were French reserve troops riding to succour the north. They came in lorries driven by swarthy foreign colonial troops with Asiatic faces. These men, half Mongol, drove with ferocity. They observed no rule of the road and swung from side to side, nearly sending you into the ditch. Once a lorry full of men went by and a soldier shat over the back of the lorry, nearly into my face. A Frenchman. But the finest sight of all was the guns running up. The French heavies – many of them were split in two and carried on lorries. By this means they were rushed along roads in a day up to the north, while it took our crawling tractors and limbers days, clattering slowly over the *pavé* of village and town, slow as oxen.

MONDAY 22 APRIL

Arriving home at 12.00, found 'There's something for you to read in the *Mail,*' said Charley. My 'Special DR' article in. I thought it would be my 'Signals' article – but the boys glad anyway.

WEDNESDAY APRIL 24

Going to parade, Higgins told me my 'Estaminet' article was in the Mail. Delighted. They all looked at my paper, slipping it out of wrapper before I got it. Lilley greeted me with, 'Hello, Estaminet King, now.' Delighted.

MONDAY 29 APRIL

Spoke to Mr Underwood re articles, arranging to slip them on his table. He said he didn't mind putting them through for me.

MONDAY 6 MAY

No rumours except about moving. This night First Army took us from Third, and it transpired gradually that we had been definitely put on reserve and would work a reserve area.

WEDNESDAY 8 MAY

At 12.00 called into TOPO section, where two officers kept me standing a while without regarding me, muttering over the maps in patrician language like two golfers discussing clubs. Then one borrowed my bike thus: 'Wanted down at signal office, Davis. Must take your bike.' Signalmaster, a brute I didn't know, too windy to refuse himself, said, 'This officer would like to borrow your bike. Can you lend it to him?'

An intelligence officer, thin and handsome, stepped forward and said, 'Do you mind?' 'We do mind, sir, because if anything goes wrong, I'm responsible, and we have difficulty in getting stuff. But if you'll take care – do you ride a motor-cycle?' 'I have done.' 'I'll give you one or two hints, sir, if you don't mind. This is the first decent bike I've had since I've been out here, so naturally…' I showed him the ins and outs. He started and soon stopped dead at changing up into top. 'You want to get a good speed up on second before you change up into third,' I said, showing him. And off he went. I waited, going in the estaminet on one side of which was the signal officers' mess. A nice clean estaminet fragrant with bread baked there. Here I drank red wine, sat by knots of soldiers drinking, and watched through the window the pleasant, clean life of our corps. He came back with the engine not overheated.

FRIDAY 10 MAY

We used to dress in a rush, time ourselves and get on parade in no time. Fred Royle could rise, shave, dress, clean boots, borrow someone's pistol and appear spruce on parade enough to just scrape through in twenty minutes, sleeping to the last second, and never once late, taking his breakfast after. 'I can only do it, Oz, by putting all my shaving tackle absolutely ready to hand the night before and all my clothes in order so that they lie ready to hand, and I just conjure with 'em.'

SATURDAY 11 MAY

Woke at five and rode hard in cold mist to First Army signal office at Houdain.

A man lifted up a slide like a booking clerk just before a train due, and took the stuff. 'Be ready in about an hour,' he yawned and slapped the door to. I had caught a glimpse of men sleeping on beds and one getting up. Instead of an army HQ in the midst of a great crisis, it looked like the steerage of a liner just waking.

Other DRs came popping up the street. There was a small hut to wait in, cold, with some copies of *Punch* to read. In the fine park-like grounds of the château, with noble trees, beautiful in the mist, some fine dogs, caged in a natural open-air pen.

At last found estaminet where thin, old, grey and pottering, a slippered and mean-dressed man got me coffee for 30 cents. Half asleep, felt influenza-ish. Waited two hours for my stuff, then bent on getting back quick.

SUNDAY 12 MAY

Arrived back from First Army feeling unwell. There was an influenza epidemic and half the Corps was isolated with all our DRs going down in turn except Vic and myself. A few of us were doing all the work.

MONDAY 13 MAY

At last, as I was feeling so washed out and achy, I reported sick, was excused duty and wrote, 'Flemish Village'. 'DRing in Ypres' was returned, as was too long for the *Daily Mail*.

WEDNESDAY 15 MAY

The morning continentals were vast things, calls being made round here, en route, and round Pernes and Lillers, we seeming to do XIII Corps work. Grumbles accordingly. If fine you could go at a great bat – if wet, riding was tricky. The features of these rides were taking it easy and dusty in glorious sunny May landscapes and rolling country. Might get back too late for cinema or to a cold dinner, but it was fun to fall to and then follow your leisure, but a bit desolate if all the boys had gone out.

SUNDAY 19 MAY

Decided to go to look for Wilf at Himbercamp. Should I catch him? It seemed too miraculous. He might be at any of these villages. On along the Frevent-Arras road to Avesnes Le Comte, passing Sunday groups of civil beauties in gala dress. Through dust up steep hill to where château stood. On the gates amid trees were the stars of the 1st Division.

Dusty and rotten road to Himbercamp. The HQ of the famous Guards Division, the sign of the eye floating above it, was long, like a village school-room. Here at a counter was a polite, sandy-haired DR clerk who told me where my brother's battalion was.

On to Pommière where, at orderly room, above which floated a royal standard, I met a pal of Wilf's. 'I believe he's down at the barn.' I got directions and there was Wilf.

He told me that the first time he went up the line he didn't like to complain that his feet were gibed because it would look like shirking. So he endured pain and discomfort and saw the MO on his return. Instead of recognising his motive, he got, 'Do you not know it's a crime not to show bad feet?' 'He was quite nasty and threatened to "run" me. I saw I had better eat humble pie, so answered in tune and just escaped.'

We split two bottles of champagne at 15 francs each in the estaminet on the square.

MONDAY 20 MAY

Was paid three guineas for 'War Roads'. Late for parade one morning and instead of running on late, went to latrines. Told to go round to Lilley's tent. Wind slightly up me. I had been to WC twice that morn. 'The SM's got the breeze up,' said Lilley, when I told him my reasons. 'He wanted to know who it was. Either come early or keep off parade, because if I say all present, sir, and a man comes running in, it gives the show away.'

We try to reassure Madame as to the ultimate defeat of the Huns. '*Ils sont trop fort,*' she said. '*Je desire la paix, n'importe quelle prix. Nous sommes abimés, epuisés. Ca ne peut pas continuer. Je ne peux pas quitter la village – c'est tout que je possède.*' She was convinced France would lose, but she stuck to her home four kilos from the invading line of the Huns.

SUNDAY 26 MAY

To Crecy to take our Corps General's letter. He had taken up the appointment with the newly reorganising Fifth Army which had been crippled and disgraced in the retreat. We had our new colonel – tall, dark, slim, eager and rather classy-looking in coffee-brown breeches.

MONDAY 27 MAY

Special to schools at Merckeghem, near our old huts. Saw pigeon lofts in fields as rode up, and saw Yanks in their curious service caps, like a twisted folding canoe, their light gaiters or brown boot-leggings.

I wanted to get petrol and an orderly conducted me to the QM stores. As I stepped in saw a short, stout officer. Saluted and then said, 'I've just had a special from KCO and ran short of juice.' The man said nothing and looked at me as if surprised at my request.

'If you're short I can get some at St Omer,' I volunteered. 'If you can get it there, why come here?' 'It's more convenient, and saves time as my run was here.' 'Do you ever say "sir" when you address an officer?'

I looked at him amazed. In the half light of the hut I could distinguish no pips on his shoulder. His collar was that of a rank-and-filer. I stopped myself saying, 'I couldn't see your rank, sir,' because I thought he'd be more offended still at my not discovering his rank from his bearing – but the tone in which he spoke stung. 'Yes, but I don't creep,' I said. 'Creep? Who said anything about creeping. If you're not careful you'll get into trouble. Salute me now.'

'I saluted as I came in, sir.' 'Salute again,' he ordered, with Prussian venom in his tone. I did so, and as I went out he said, 'Fix him up, sergeant.'

I writhed and swore under my breath. I hated him worse than I had ever hated a German and would have sooner shot him than any Hun. Fancy a free-born Englishman being compelled in the name of war to take insults from a swine like that.

SATURDAY 1 JUNE

Received 30/- from *The Daily News* for article 'DRing in Ypres'. A day or two after Jonah received the cutting of it sent by his sister, who knew that he'd be interested, but not knowing it was by a pal of his.

That night the specials were to the 14th Light Division at St Quentin, just outside Aire, and to XI Corps at Roquetoire. Polker suggested the first DR take both specials – this was twice I had clicked for two specials when only one is supposed to be taken by one DR. I asked if two DRs weren't meant to take two specials, and Polker said, 'Oh well, if you want to make trouble,' in the airy manner of one who's got only the easy part to take.

'We don't want to fetch another man out,' said Tubby, taking up a stance which showed he was going to keep out of it if possible. Until then I had always admired Tubby as a fine sport – now I doubted… Off I rode and St Quentin delivery done, it was now midnight. With joy off along the highroad to Mametz from Aire.

WEDNESDAY 5 JUNE

Drank with Duff and Scholfield – truthful men. Schofield said, 'You've seen the maimed, halt, deaf and blind we used to drill on the square – category men. Would you believe it, those men held the front line against the Huns for ten days? One day I was going round with the officer and some of the men were asleep. "What the hell!" "Softly, sir," I said, "these men have been here ten days without relief. They're category men – there's not enough to go round – they can't do the impossible." It's a marvel we weren't swept away, but at last the French relieved us. I've seen disgraceful sights I never thought I'd live to see. For several days I was roping in officers and men who were walking down the Pop road from Ypres, deserting. I had a revolver and was told to shoot them if they didn't go back. Can you see me doing it? But by God I felt snotty. There were men in twos and threes bringing men down from the line who had only got their wrist hurt – walking wounded. The women jeered and spat at them. It was absolute panic. If Jerry had only known, he could have walked through.'

SATURDAY 8 JUNE

Today I heard of Larking's death – my old OC on the Somme. A bold and dashing man who took all manner of risks in the front – who was at last run over by a traction engine.

MONDAY 17 JUNE

Promotions were announced on orders. Skoney and Lumb were promoted to Lance-jack. Lumb was a good rider, but Bradley was the best all-round of the bunch, yet he was not promoted. That's how merit, real and technical, are rewarded in the Army.

With great regret from us all, our OC left us for GHQ. I have not a bad word for the old OC of our unit – young, handsome, a regular, a dandy, with a mincing and deliberately drawling tone of voice, he was always a gentleman, spoke to us warmly and humorously as if we were human beings. He remembered good work and was charitable towards bad, but he did not allow liberties to be taken, nor slackness of dress on parade. He could put the wind up the whole corps if he chose, but he rarely chose. And now he's gone and also our colonel – we felt a sense of real loss. This was the first step towards the disintegration of our corps.

At first I thought Merchant was going to be all right, but on a small-kit parade, I was jawed off for having the buckle of my mess-tin strap pointing up instead of down. 'Like a lot of babies on parade,' said Sam Brown, with scorn. 'Don't know how you earned money in civilian life – you certainly haven't got the brains enough for the Army.' 'Didn't get it blowing a taxi whistle in Russell Square,' said Percy.

SUNDAY 16 JUNE

I was on night duty and Captain Macdonald was the officer in charge. We got our Primus going in the office and were brewing a fine cup of coffee, while the SO office conversed and attained that relaxation that comes when the day's chief stress is over. He must have been surprised at the liberties we were taking, however, he had been decent to me, saying, 'How do you like this after the pigeons, Carparl? What are you doing now?' 'Just ordinary DR work, sir. We have no pigeons while we're in reserve. It was busy at first, but we've slacked off now and are having a decent time. Of course, I was my own boss on the other job – here I'm one of a crush, which isn't so nice – though there's no responsibility.'

WEDNESDAY 19 JUNE

On a special to St Just, called at Wilf's, dropping off Ettie's letter of 13th inst. Neither of us could understand how we came to be overdrawn to the tune of £700, as the business had been left in good condition. It was a knock-back, and threw Wilf off his imperturbable balance. I rode back thinking it through, and as I got in, the boys said I looked sad, and I told them what had happened – bad business news from home… overdraft… and for some days or two after I was deflated. It seemed hard lines that our business should suffer. Wrote home in equable terms, for we knew Ettie had done her best. Had bankbook sent out, and Wilf, when on leave, found that Bannerman had been paid twice.

THURSDAY 20 JUNE

Four new DRs arrived on Douglases – two old hands. Glenny cursed the Douglases and said the sooner they ran 'em into a brick wall and got Triumphs the better. We had no Douglas spares. Shortly after, immense thuds were heard issuing from the shed where a group of DRs advanced in turn and tried their skill. One after another they took one of the Douglases and banged it on the floor, turned it over and thumped again, trying to break the frame so we could get a new bike from the column in exchange.

At parade today the new DRs were gently taken aside by our new OC and choked off for variously, wearing field boots, wearing hat-strap in oval loop below and above badge, wearing a Charlie Chaplin moustache, and wearing tunic light in hue –although army issue.

TUESDAY 25 JUNE

Afternoon to Wilf, as we began to apprehend a move. Found that he is also preparing to move. A last drink of Malaga in the pub at the corner.

On from six to nine, and I was second man on. I let the other man go to supper and took his place, when at about 8.40 a special came in. 'You've got to find Zanazi. Tell him we can't get the 25th Division and he must send out linesmen at once and get the lines through. He'll probably be between Rollincourt and Hesdin, feeling the lines. You must find him.' This looked like a long run and it was the other man's, but I thought it only sporty to take it. The night was calm, a blue mist was creeping up, scents wafted across and I ran along speedily to the St Pol-Hesdin road.

As I dropped down to the river I met some X Corps men by the estaminet. When I spoke to Zenazi, he cursed. 'The line's right enough. It's the 25th Division's funeral. What is it to do with us? Our corps always doing some other unit's job.'

'Well, that's what Ladd told me to say. He said they were the ADS's instructions. My luck's in now I've found you, and I can piss off.' 'What the hell's it to do with Ladd? What do they know about it, squatting on their bloody arses in a cushy hut with tea brewing at the back?' His features writhed with disgust. 'Tell him to stick his instructions up his *** and work them up him.'

Quite recently Z had received the DCM for constant meritorious service, and now flaunted on his breast the blue and red ribbon. 'Come on you swipes,' he said viciously. 'Turn out – I've got an all-night job for you.' As for me, I turned around, chortling and rode off in bravado and swung my way merrily up the hill, through the chilly dusk.

SUNDAY 30 JUNE

In morning wrote in the little estaminet near our mess, where I drank frugal Malagas to have in return the privilege of writing in peace in the empty room above the road, into which only after church a few villagers in Sunday best came, genial and chattering.

In evening rode over to Wilf, and we had the bank passbook for the business out and discussed it. I found him packing, with kit out, ready to move on the morrow. Had I not ridden over I should have missed him – we had our last drink.

MONDAY 1 JULY

Put my stuff straight and half-packed as rumours were going round that we were going to Watou, which, Glenny said, was now a hot shop. Fritz was knocking hell out of it. We couldn't go to a worse place, shelled every day.

TUESDAY 2 JULY

Finished packing and over to Esquières, where I saw Trewatha. He said the man in charge of the station there was a beast – some man I'd heard of before with expressions of disgust. In the field where his loft stood was a long wooden, felt-thatched hut where there were some GHQ reserve birds, which I brought back. It was charming to have this pigeon run and Vic and I thought to ourselves how nice if we remained in reserve, where we were, and trained birds up to a certain point near Arras, our lofts being in reserve in case of another retreat by the British Army.

As I went to the cinema that night I saw Elise going for a walk with a pal, and was much tempted to ask her to let me accompany them. The vision of delights I perchance had lost interrupted the cinema – then when I came out, met her again. She had been to see the great holes made near St Pol by the bombs Fritz dropped every clear night.

WEDNESDAY 3 JULY

Goodbyes to Marie in our farm, a daring little damsel, cryptic, who invited liberties – sometimes allowed them and sometimes petulantly repulsed them. Goodbye to the old girl with the twisted mouth. We kissed Marie, who had seen many such partings, as had all the French.

We rode off at nine. At Cassel saw Bill Pritchard and Jeanne – like coming home – then on to Esquelbec, which was packed with French troops the reserve of the French Corps we were relieving.

THURSDAY 4 JULY

In the field on the old sports ground I saw Wright and Cavill. 'What are things like up here?' I asked. 'We've been working for the II Corps. Keeling says he goes up the Ypres road as far as Vlamertinghe, but he won't go further – daren't. Been in some hot corners. The front line is Ypres now. Shells each side of the Pop road are common.' 'Just my luck,' I said with misgivings making my heart wilt. But I smiled, putting the best face on it I could, not letting them see I dreaded going up the line again.

SATURDAY 6 JULY

Called to go to see OC Pigeons, find out where the lofts of the area of the French XVI Corps were, and to make reports. I found them and talked with the interpreter of the Corps at Terdeghem. Back to Cassel and found two French civvy lofts there. Spoke to Sergeant Colombophile, who gave me particulars about lodging in house opposite the brewer's where the loft was. Back at 3.30, gratified at being on pigeons again – my own boss and using my French.

SUNDAY 7 JULY

We moved to Zuytpeene. 'Always the same – châteaux and recreation rooms for the bloody OTs and the Corps staff, but the DRs can sleep on their arses in a drain.' Glenny and Bob Browne collared a shed, and the other boys had to put boards and iron together and sleep on the ground. Vic and I, as I arranged earlier when I visited the Zuytpeene lofts, were allowed to use the shack in the corner of the field.

Trow and three new DRs explained how finely the French had worked things, using special rainproofed baskets containing only eight birds, sending them up in a car only halfway to the line. 'X Corps will soon alter all that,' I said bitterly, 'and they'll work your birds for you.'

Was told to see OC of 35th Division and arrange a meeting point where his brigades could fetch birds from. One of our boys said that when he went, the gas alarm sounded and men carried their gasmasks at the alert. This put the wind up me. I took my tin hat and gasmask, and felt a pious hope that I should emerge safe. Abeele somewhat shattered with filled-up shell-holes in the street. Boeschepe badly battered, with barbed wire entanglements at the side of the roads ready to be pushed into place.

Left bike and pushed through a gap in the hedge and men pointed out a tall, fine-looking man to me as the OC. He took me in and we studied the map, and he called his DR, who talked familiarly and with confidence to him.

He said I could get up through Westoutre to Mont Vidaigne, which was the meeting place suggested by the OC, but I couldn't get round via the top of Mont Noir, as that was under observation. 'So suppose we say Mont Vidaigne – that appears to be the most central point for the brigades?' On the map were red, blue and green lines, giving the battalion and brigade areas and the Fritz lines – which looked astonishingly near.

I said I'd report to my OC, but as I rode away I thought what a weak fool I'd been in agreeing to go so far up the line, just because his Div DR had said the road was rideable, and that they did it every day.

In evening saw my OC and he gave me instructions in the old friendly style and I fixed up about stock.

MONDAY 8 JULY

Ran well to Abeele but got a puncture. Then down into Berthen – smashed up and deserted – going as quick as I could, expecting any time to hear a shell fall. Vic waiting for me at Pibrouck – then to Westoutre. Our old billet here shattered and our old fireplace was napoo, Julia's sewing machine out on the road. A scene of wreckage. It had been just here that Sam Mayo had got killed.

TUESDAY 9 JULY

To Smith's loft at Terdeghem. How pleasant the loft in the field by the mill and cornfield, the little toy belfries and roofs, the knee-deep corn, the winding hillocky lane. A beautiful picture.

WEDNESDAY 10 JULY

To Godaerswolde – the town very badly knocked about and rather desolate – every day a new shell-hole visible. Up at the crossroads much camouflage at the side of the road, strung across like streaming banners – the work of the French. I knew the German line was not far away, and I was nervous lest I should take one of the numerous small turnings and run into the Huns. Fritz was just the other side of the hill on the plain – a matter of two or three kilos away...

Evening music at Mavaut's, and there sat with us hearty and genial Americans – not sidey, but evidently proud of their part in the coming operations.

FRIDAY 12 JULY

Had to leave my bike at Hexten Corner as the mud was so slimy and thick that the wet made my belt slip and couldn't get along. I walked with some trepidation through the village – all desolation and no soul, save occasionally a French soldier. I said to myself, 'Suppose a shell drops and wounds me? Where's any help? No dressing station – no-one about, and Fritz's balloons only in the sky looking down on you.'

The same at Reninghelst, and at every crossroads a tin-hatted sentry. I thought, 'When there is anything doing, Fritz will shell this road to blazes, as he must have it absolutely taped. I must find a path over the fields so that we can come via the Berthen road, leave our bikes there and cross by foot over the fields.' So I walked into the field – shell-holed at about every six yards or so. It put the wind up me.

MONDAY 15 JULY

Vic and I arranged to go alternately to Mont Vidaigne and Pibrouck. Each place had to be visited once every other day, so we went to Mont Vidaigne, which was regarded as the bugbear run, once each in four days, barring specials.

At Reninghelst no sign of life, already showing that weed-grown look which so soon creeps on an abandoned village. Our first habitat had been razed either by fire or shell. Our second had vanished and about a foot above our roof was a shell-hole in the wall. I thought of the drama that the street had seen – the first shells, the puzzled inhabitants, the packers-up and the stayers. Wounded soldiers coming down the street and Jack Johnson holes all over the grounds of the old signal office.

Came into Pop through avenues of fragrant trees – the Ren-Pop road punctured here and there with shell-holes. Saw Crossley and Barnes at Dupont's. 'What a time we've had since you went away – I wish to God those days were back! More than half my birds dead, and at Sim's the same. It's been hell.' Barnes came in 'Well, if it isn't Davis. We've had a life, what? When whiz-bangs started dropping in Madame Debysses pigsty it was time to hop it. The old gal stuck it well there, but went at last. But they've cleaned the civvies out of Pop. There's been no-one in Pop since April except us three lofts. The Town Major has shifted to the brewery and the old signal office. What would have happened if we'd got hit, the Lord knows. We've had shells in the garden, shells next to our bedroom, shrapnel on old Sim's roof – but old Sim seems to thrive on it.' 'He must have changed. I remember him when he came.' 'He's the boldest of the lot now.' 'I must go to see him – and I shall see you from time to time.' 'Not so many come now as in the old days – it's not healthy – wonderful what a difference it makes. None of the DRs have been anywhere near. They leave everything to me. Keeling comes once in three weeks if at all.'

I went down the lane to Sim's, not wishing to stay too long. Sim was in the door, a hoary smile spread over his face. 'I'm glad you've come to see your old pals. My word, what changes.' 'I hear you're the boldest of the lot now.' 'Tell you what it is, corporal. You get used to it. It used to shake me up. Now he's no sooner shifted the tiles on my roof, than I'm putting them up again. This is about the first week we've had nothing. Before that you never knew from one hour to another. We all sleep down at Cassier's now. It's the best cellar. We had a DR here – and he slept with us for a time. Cowen, his name was. One morning when we woke he said, "Did you hear that shell in the night? Such a rumpus – it woke me. Must have been in the garden." Would you believe me, we found it had gone right through the wall of the next room? We never knew and slept on. I don't seem to care a damn. There's no-one looks after us, and you get into that state where you simply think that if I'm for it, then I am.'

'Doesn't anybody look you up?' 'Not a limb. I wish we'd got your corps. My birds are ruined. We're pleased for them to do the work, but nobody takes any interest in us.' I bade him good-bye, not loth to go, for I didn't yet know what Fritz's 1918 temperament was.

Up Boeschepe Street and Abeele road – for the first time perhaps in its history, Pop was beautiful. The rains had washed the streets clean, white and bare. Overhead shone blue skies. Green trees grew and foliage and flowers wafted odours. Only a few khaki figures here and there.

Visited the Town Major's office – a sand-bagged fortress in the brewery – and found my old friend the Scots sergeant of the Cornwalls. It was like home again, but strange to see the familiar streets empty of life and so clean, traffic-less and unmuddied. The seething life had ebbed from it since Fritz got Kemmel.

Saw the old signal office – went round to the back and saw my old shack, unclean and empty and another shack built at the side, now knocked into one. I was drearily touched by this desecration of the hut in which I'd spent such times of comradeship. I thought of Moss and his merry men, dancing round with petrol tins for drums, of Warr lying drunk in the field at the back, of our drinks together at Marie's and the suppers of chips, the debates in the messroom, and the concerts. All vanished into limbo, and only this dirty hut remaining.

Met up with White: 'Ay, a nice time we had – a wonder we're alive to tell the tale. Those RAMC men – a nice lot. We stuck there until half the birds were lost or killed, and the rest they took away. But would you believe it, the wounded came down that road and no-one to see to them? Poor fellows, arms off, backs shattered. Almost the first day the shelling started, those RAMC fellows from the dressing station ran away and left civvies and us to look after the wounded.'

Later I heard from Joe Aindow how Sam Mayo died. 'Hardacre had had cold feet and got removed away out of Westoutre back to GHQ. They wanted someone to take over. We'd had a rotten time at Dranoutre – daren't stir out of the cellar, and I was to take over in place of Hardacre. Soon after I got in, he had been shelling on and off, the French were here and said they weren't going to use the lofts. Fritz was too near, and it wasn't safe. I thought they'd let us go, but I got no instructions. I reckon we ought to have been told to clear out. It was sheer folly to stay on. Then Fritz started sending gas over. For two days and two nights we were in the cellar with gasmasks on and daren't shift. Then I said, "Look here, Sam, we shall have no rations soon. We can't see what's going on. We can't use the pigeons in this state. Let's make a dash for it with our bikes." We got our bikes out. There was a bit of a lull it seemed – not a soul about. By God, it looked like a town smitten with a curse. We turned to the right by the church – WOOOF – one goes in the field beyond the churchyard. "Come on," says Sam, and he sprints on. We went down, turned left to go to the hospital dressing station to see what we could do – a rotten feeling there, like a rat in a trap, the road's so twisty and narrow. Then my pedal drops off. I jumped off and started to push, when I fell flop into the ditch as if I'd been hit with a bat. When I got out I saw Sam on the ground, his arm blown off, a great hole in his neck.'

Joe went away, his eyes full of tears, and I bowed my head. Sam was a good sort.

THURSDAY 18 JULY

Jonah stated loudly that it was officially given today that London newspapers state 'German offensive a fiasco', and 'Austria sues for peace'.

FRIDAY 19 JULY

I scanned the papers of the day before and find no such thing. Before this Jonah had said that Rheims had been taken, so I took no notice. Nevertheless, spirits went up, as similar rumours began to creep persistently about.

Meanwhile, all around the Chinks were constructing fine trenches. How Madame and the Frenchies cussed about the trenches that had been cut through their tall corn.

Vic says 'French victory – 16,000 prisoners and over 100 guns – 10 kilos advance by the French'. I sceptical, but Whitey corroborates. I offered drinks to the value of five francs if the news is official. I couldn't believe it after so many false rumours. Then David Hunter corroborates it as GHQ official.

Talked to my 30th Div boys returned from Palestine. They say Johnny Turk a good fighter but his ranks ravaged by typhus. He don't like the bayonet. He kills prisoners, but often more chivalrous than the Hun in other ways. They say we retreated after each victory because of lack of supplies and German divs were hurried up. Tales of crossing the Jordan and feats of real heroes.

Today got a letter from Arnold Bennett with addresses of literary agents. Rather a curt letter saying he was very busy, so wrote and thanked him and didn't continue the correspondence further, as I'd no wish to sponge the time of a great author.

SATURDAY 20 JULY

Vic had said early on he'd been potted at by German field guns, and I'd let out several hints to Mr Wetham that our run through Westoutre was dangerous, so could we meet at Hexten Corner instead of Mont Vidaigne? He said he'd look into it. Indeed I went so far as to hunt on the Berthen road for a dugout for Bill Harrison to have a depot and stock as before, but it did not materialise. He must have thought I was windy – and indeed, in these days I was. I had no wish for glory and thought we were bound to get potted on that road, or have to run up by night some time when the road through Westoutre was being shelled. I felt caddish at the time, for it meant making the infantrymen walk farther, and for them it would be more dangerous than for us, except that on foot you could get anywhere, and on a bike we had to keep to road and always had a heavier load.

However, this morn I had the wind up on arriving at the crossroads above Ren switch road, because there was a line of Fritz sausages calmly looking down on the road I had to go on. However, I was not touched. Over fields to thatched cottage, bike getting stuck in shell-hole. In this house one side of wall down, but cellar sound. In it old blue suits and old clothes. There were also trenches and field dugouts constructed by the French, full of dirty stuff, old hats and uniforms – foul and evil. What a life it must have been.

SUNDAY 21 JULY

I to heavy artillery brigade off Abeele-Godewaersvelde Road, to give lessons to officers. Arrived at big farm and courtyard. Heavy stuff – shells – fell half a dozen fields away with a new kind of tremendous bang. 'I hear Fritz has advanced on a two-kilo front this morning up here,' said one. 'The dirty dog,' answered the other. 'How deep? Ten yards?' 'No,' came the laugh, 'about half a kilo.'

FRIDAY 26 JULY

At Brigade HQ they told me every other time, they had had the wire 'Fritz coming over tonight,' and had had to stand to, packed or ready to pack and quit at a moment's notice. They said the line was very thinly held and they were under strength, and if Fritz pushed hard in force…

All this time we were very uncertain and I often wondered with Vic if some morn he or I alone might run slap bang into Germans who had taken Westoutre, Berthen or Pibrouck overnight, because we started on our run before anyone was up in the orderly room or anywhere where we could get news. The roads were absolutely bare of soldiery. The soldiers were in farm cellars or hedge-burrows and dugouts – rarely visible – so none would warn us. Gradually as nought happened, these fears died.

SATURDAY 27 JULY

Afternoon to Bunny – had no tin hat, and just before Boeschepe saw shrapnel falling over the ridge I was to traverse. Waited a bit and decided to risk it. In Boeschepe an orderly asked me if I was 35th Div DR. I said I wasn't, but offered to take his stuff – he must have missed him as he was going up. Waddled and slid about in the gluey mud of the lane, nearly skidding over into dugout. Men came rushing with a red flag. 'Hurry on. We're going to fire.' The howitzers which lay embedded under the lane with their snouts pointing just across, were going to fire over the lane, the hill, and into the German lines. Perhaps the delay due to my passage saved or marred Hun lives.

Left bike in the empty house by turn and left pigeons there. Coming back, found a derelict cat trying to get them. Waded in and out of sand-bagged grottoes in the sandpits. 'If you hurry you'll get past the guns in time,' said the flagman again. Me skidding and pushing and nearly rupturing myself trying to get past howitzer mouths before the guns fired.

Towards Abeele realised I'd forgotten the orderly's package and had to return. Old civvy replacing tiles the shrapnel had knocked off.

MONDAY 28 JULY

Micky says: 'Just heard good news! Four hundred thousand Germans surrounded in the Rheims salient.' I sceptical. 'What authority?' I asked. 'Is it GHQ official?' 'No, a clerk in the DRLS,' said Micky, going quiet as if offended.

In the mess, suppertime, Vic enlarged on the theme to the boys, '400,000 Germans cut off and made prisoner,' he stated.

Atkinson used to come and talk with me in the dusk. He had been a Guardsman, tall, bluff, florid, upright, with ginger moustache and martial air. Reputed to have mistresses in the village. When I started had to handle him carefully – he was all braggadocio.

'They're not going to ruin my birds. If I'm wanted to supply more than my turn, I'll see Alec about it. These butty sods of officers, full of old buck, who know naught of the business, ordering what we shall do. The wrong way to get anything out of me,' he shrugged, as if his patience were immense, but even the tolerance of a great man had its limits.

'Nonsense,' said Trow, his eyes gleaming. 'We've got to obey orders, and you know it.' 'I'll not obey no orders I don't approve,' said the Guardsman. 'In the South African war I was told to stay in a block hut for three weeks without stirring. Very fine – but in two days our rations were napoo. I simply walked down the line and pinched a crateful from the ration train. Could I obey orders? The bloody fools who run this army want miracles to happen twice nightly.'

WEDNESDAY 30 JULY

We hear the truth – 'Four-mile retreat of Germans on a 20-mile front, out of the Fismes pocket. Guns abandoned.' I confess I was surprised. I thought, 'They've made a small error at last!'

Car for training arrived while we were waiting for Cnudde. He was a character. He had a loft like a Punch-and-Judy show, a home-made affair which Sergeant Edmonds used to use for experiments with birds and for teaching purposes when the Second Army Signal School was here. I liked him – he always tried to do his best and his birds did all right. Ramsden, who received his messages always made things unpleasant. Cnudde hated Ramsden, who was a swine, as I soon found out. At first he went out of his way to be pleasant and found breakfast for me in his tent. His pioneer was Bob Mattock, one of the cleverest breeders of pigeons in England. Ramsden knew nothing compared with what Mattock knew, and had to seek Mattock's advice while pretending not to.

Bob was a decent sort, but lazy. Ramsden was lazy too, and I often went and found them still in bed when they had pigeons out. I ought to have reported, but while there were no battles on, I didn't trouble.

You can't make yourself a nuisance to other people all the time. Between these two, Cnudde had a rough time. The other pigeoneers also looked down on him, but I stood up for him.

It was 9.45 before we got away, which just threw us late all day. We had done training near the houses where the ack-ack battery stayed, and shells dropped regularly into the field between there and Westoutre. Any moment our driver felt his car might get hit. Today at the first bend, we saw a car waiting and the driver was edging forward and peering round the corner. The bang of shells. 'Has he been shelling along there?' I asked. 'All morning. We're waiting to get through.' As we were only training, I judged it better to stay and release the birds there. I doubted the road was being shelled, but it was well we halted. Shells got nearer and nearer while I stooped and with fingers slightly trembling in the rank grass, adjusted the clips, gradually letting the birds off in fours instead of twos to get them away.

TUESDAY 30 JULY

This morning to Pibrouck. We had been warned by MP once or twice not to use Berthen-Pibrouck road as the dust raised by our bikes was drawing shell-fire to the road, and we had to have special passes allowing us to traverse it. Until we got these we were obliged to leave the bikes at Rossignol dressing station and walk the remainder, so near were we to Fritz.

Afternoon we were training birds on this road when big stuff started falling about 100 yards in front, on artillery positions and farmhouse which the battery HQ used. Men running. My heart went tight and I had wind up – probably went white. 'We'd better move, I think,' I said. 'If he lifts, he's right on us here.' We moved further up the road to the few broken-down houses and dump near the crossroads, and there finished releasing. It's a wonder the battery people stood us tossing birds there.

WEDNESDAY 31 JULY

Today Joshua White, in his mournful key, told me of the Field Ambulance unit at Reninghelst which, while he and Smith were hanging on to the lofts at Ren, ran out into the fields during shelling, and left men wounded in the streets to the mercies of the ASC – yet these field ambulance people had four medals dished out to 'em for sticking to their duty.

FRIDAY 2 AUGUST

To Terdeghem, where Mr Wetham referred to a load of fifty pigeons we were to take up to Mont Vidaigne that teatime. There was a small stunt coming off next day early – we were trying to capture round beyond the Dranoutre hospice. It pelted down and we were off, mac-clad in the pouring rain, loaded with birds covered with sacking, at 3.15. We got up the hill all right and found it deserted. Put our baskets out under shelter of tumbled roof on the corner-spot of broken foundations of house. At last the men came – quite cool. They knew about the do. As soon as we got away, I started worrying. Had we dropped any of the clips as we bumped our way over the shell-holed and muddy route? They should have some spare clips – but it spoilt my evening, especially after we'd got through the job so nicely.

Great discussion re the new orders about army corps and divisional establishment of DRs. Orders said the army is henceforth to have, instead of a general staff of DRs covering for three corps, only nine and four attached to each corps. Corps, instead of having about twenty-two DRs, to have an establishment of nine or eleven, plus four from each division in it, and to contribute, by loan, four to its army. Divisions were to have about twenty-two, and to send four to the corps they were in.

This may have been good in theory, but in practice it was rotten. If we had three divs we never got more than three DRs from each – sometimes only two instead of the four due to us. The army always saw it had its pound of flesh from the corps, hence the corps ran short. Moreover, esprit de corps was spoilt, for we had twelve strangers with us and four of our men went to the army – White, Davies, Tubby Masters and Harlow. This was the beginning of dissension and loss for the Corps. We were asked to supply a man for an army artillery brigade, and our OC ordered Garry to be sent, when we were going to send Field, a rotter sent up to us from the base.

Today I heard that Manty, my cousin, was transferred to us, 'for re-posting under this new order'. Manty had often said he'd like to work with me, but I couldn't very well get rid of Vic, and as I had to a certain extent to insist on so much work being done, I thought it might be awkward to see, with a relative, that this was done. So Manty was reposted to 29th Division. Lilley said he asked for him to remain, to be posted here from one of our divisions. The OC said, 'What's that got to do with it, that he's got a cousin on the strength?' Vacillated all afternoon, and couldn't work properly. Should I prefer a request to the OC asking for Paul to stay? Decided not to. At tea Paul arrived in tattered overalls, in leg of which a hole revealed his bare calf. His gas-bag and haversack and gear hung all round him, his controls hung loose round his bike as ever. Half his tackle missing…

When I saw him thus, my heart was stirred and moved to pity. Soon he was to go forth to a division – to leave behind our pleasant faces and all his pals, and be cast to the outer wildernesses of a strange division. I had to break the news.

'I feel a bit of a cad, Paul – you came so cheery – I expect you think you're staying and that we'll keep you here.' 'Aren't I, cuz?' 'No,' I gulped, my heart going down. 'You're reposted to 29th Div.' I hurried on. 'Lilley asked for you to be kept as you were my cousin, but the OC won't stand any of this asking for people. He's already sent Garry right away without a word, and I feel it was useless. If I'd thought there was a chance…' Nevertheless, deep down I felt I ought to have asked.

Lilley said, 'Wordley had asked, knowing that you were Oz's cousin, and that's what got him on such a line – it looked like a put-up thing. "Everybody wants to stay here," he said, "and I won't have it. They must obey orders."'

Paul took the blow well. Keen-profiled and undaunted, I thought highly of him when he made the best of it instead of grousing. Though he masked his anxiety, it seemed to me he wanted to get transferred from his destined div to XV South African Corps.

We were all much cut up by this treatment and we resented it. In evening I was sad and brooding while I mused on this ill chance.

SUNDAY 4 AUGUST

Commemoration service and parade in Terdeghem delayed getting away. The whole business of war was held up in this quarter – perhaps lives lost owing to delayed supplies so that this service could be held. MPs on horses forbade any to pass through to Terdeghem. Troops marched up the road, battery after battery, with fine officers with sticks and gloves, walking or riding in front.

So we had Machonochies lunch at the loft and departed at 11.45 in the hot sun and golden growth of August. We tossed the pigeons behind the ack-ack hut while Fritz strafed Westoutre unmercifully. 'He's after the RFA brigade batteries,' Pink dust rose from Westoutre every time a shell burst. Fritz certainly pasted it.

TUESDAY 6 AUGUST

News has gradually changed the atmosphere and morale of troops. A new and genuine sanguineness is starting to pervade us after these weary years of hopeless waiting.

THURSDAY 8 AUGUST

Before lunch in the yard, 'Haven't you heard? Success on the Somme! Ten-mile advance, guns taken, etc.' I didn't believe the news, taking it that now we had had one or two slight victories, the air would be full of wild rumours, and I believed that Fritz was only biding his time to deal us another blow. Vic repeated the tale on returning from Cassel that night.

I saw a fellow with pack up and blankets behind, riding up the drive, straight as a rock, with a very classy appearance of chin, brown eyes and skin. This was Alan Marr. 'What's the new DR like?' I asked Lilley. 'He seems a decent sort.

Not too much to say for himself.' 'I hear he knows the ADS?' 'Yes, the colonel was with the 25th Div – Marr's old outfit. He likes these 25th Div men and is getting them round him.'

FRIDAY 9 AUGUST

Going up to Terdeghem, Smith, White and Aindow. 'What do you think of the news? Two aerodromes captured, and a general in his car,' said Aindow. 'Armoured cars operating freely,' said Smith lusciously. 'Hundreds of guns and munitions lorries as they stood…' 'Oh, chuck it. Where did you get all this?' 'From the signal office, over the phone early this morning.' Up the line at Brigade the same tale, with variations. The joy of the men, however, was very grim and restrained, as they had heard tales of our advancing so often, which ended in stalemate.

Back at Terdeghem the tales were re-asserted. Then at Cassel saw the advance marked on the huge map hung outside the 35th Div office, the various advances being marked in blue, red or green. I then believed it gladly.

Madeleine went by with her pretty country cousin, and I thought of the tennis parties I might have had, Jeanne having assured me that Madeleine would have liked games with us. However, moving about in colour and scent, they seemed in a world above me, me with my grotesque pigeon basket and dirty, mud-and-grease stained overalls.

SATURDAY 10 AUGUST

A beautiful day. In evening, over our little rat-ridden river the fields were being cut by women and the corn placed in stooks, and above them at night the sky glowed blue and gold, then settled down into the humid silver spinsterhood of evening.

At dinner, renewed victory rumours. Lilley ran in pink and breathless, 'XIII Corps HQ and 2 Div HQ captured!' Quite an exhilarating sequence of victory tales. We were getting quite used to it. Isn't it too good to be stable?

MONDAY 12 AUGUST

I to reserve brigades on Cassel-Bailleul road, and dallied half an hour at Jeanne's shop. Was tempted to have a morning off instead of going round enquiring of the brigades if they really needed the birds for practice or some scheme.

Vic said he'd seen Mr Underwood and had got bad news. 'You won't like it. The 35th Div have asked if we can go up at nights instead of mornings.' I at first incredulous – then a cold-feet spasm and wind-up, then said, 'Well, we'll see. If he wants us to get up there at nine, we'll try to get leave to go up at seven.'

I didn't mind so much going up at morn, but in the evening, when it was reputed the roads got shelled, I didn't like the prospect, especially the chance of gas.

WEDNESDAY 14 AUGUST

My first day off since here. Early in evening in beautiful sun to Jack Hilton at Tenescure. Jack told me the DRs here handled his birds rather roughly, and that he got harder worked than the other lofts – why he couldn't tell. Though he was old enough to be their father, after the great retreat, he was early chosen to go up the line again, as he had been after his hospital bout. He was not on good terms with his mates in the field, who tried to thrust all the work on him, just because he had got his birds trained first. They used some thirty of his birds a day. Said he couldn't get on with Mr Ogden, who was pigeon OC for XV (SA) Corps.

I learned how Jack got copped. Jack was showing some men the way to the water tanks. 'But I warn you, it'd be wise to wait. He's been shelling hard, but must give over.' However, they got the wind up on the way, and we sheltered in some tent. I was putting hand on tent, and the next think I knew I was with Major Wilkinson. I felt blood and my side going blank. No pain at first, then uneasy at the neck, whatever way I was sitting or lying. My neck bandaged. But I overlooked this at first. My left foot was giving me most pain. "Let's take his boot off," they said. "Was your boot too big?" they asked, "because the shell's sliced your toe-cap right off – gone through the instep of the boot and jammed the toes up. A wonderful escape. What hurts you is the toes jammed together. Here, give him a cup of tea." They were just like one of my own to me. Even as I lay there I was worrying about the pigeons!'

As he was going away in ambulance car – which did not come until three hours after he was wounded – the car twenty yards behind him was blown up. To the hospital – pain in his head increases and nurse complains harshly of his groaning. 'Do you think I wouldn't sleep if I could?' said Jack. 'I'll complain to the MO.' He got X-rayed – a piece of shrapnel was lodged between his spine and neck and he was between the devil and the deep blue sea. Might die if operated on, so it was left, and he gradually got better at No 89 Dublin Hospital.

Confab on his evacuation. 'What am I for, sir? Am I going up the line again?' 'Yes, but you're advised not to drink.' 'If I'm well enough to go up the line, I'm well enough to sup beer,' answered Jack, without fear or favour. 'If I'd been a Roman Catholic, I should have been marked for Blighty.'

At the aviary, as the intensity of shelling grew, Mac and Jack were trying to stop up the smoke leakage in the flue stove-pipe which ran through the arched chamber of the aviary accommodation.

Mac: 'Come ye down below, Jack. If I'm to die, I like it best among the many.' Jack: 'I'm staying 'til this job's finished. Might as well get shot as get suffocated. I'll go bind this sacking round the pipe – feel more like heaving a brick down on the bloody sods as smoke poor innocent pigeons out o' their loft.'

Jack was evacuated to GHQ where he had several passages with Major Waley. At one time he was showing Jack off to another major. 'This man, at his age, won the MM. Where is it? Haven't you got it up?' 'Haven't got a ribbon.' 'You can buy one. It's worth the money, isn't it?' 'Yes, but I'm bankrupt. I've been in hospital.' 'How much do you want?' 'I could do with a few francs, sir.' He went on, 'He lent me 50 francs – I will say that. He was a decent old cock – but he hadn't go my pay through yet, all the same, and I was still down for pay as a pioneer RE.'

TUESDAY 20 AUGUST

Called early to see Mr Wetham re stunt and prepared, excited. Twice to Westoutre – as we were at top of the hill, under lee of bank dishing out, gas shells came just over our heads and burst in field over the hedge. Phit. We ducked again and again – it seemed as if they scraped our caps. I white and quivering, and tried in vain to make my quavering voice appear natural. Vic went pale too.

THURSDAY 22 AUGUST

Heard that our objectives were gained early. Afternoon it was so lovely that I started off on a spin and came to Jack Hilton's – he would be moving tomorrow. Told me he was 53 – wounded on 21 June 1917, came to Ypres January 1916. His yarn of the doctor at Boulogne, who'd seen him at the Ramparts. 'I thought you'd get it,' said he. 'If you go up there again, you'll get killed. Have you got a Blighty?' 'Blighty?! I'm for the convalescent camp.'

TUESDAY 27 AUGUST

The great Allied offensive has heartened us and filled us with hope and happiness and leave starts quicker at once. I recalled the times without number that leave was opened, then just as suddenly closed, then opened again.

Good news every day – almost incredibly so.

WEDNESDAY 28 AUGUST

Morning I to Pibrouck and hung about due to changing over. The maps outside Brigade HQ made fine reading.

FRIDAY 30 AUGUST

Afternoon in beautiful weather to lecture by 'Old Nick' on elocution as complaints had been received about the men's speaking on the phone. We assembled – Cole, Aindow, Cnudde, Atkinson, Parker and I – near the office. We looked a slipshod lot as we sat down in the grass in the beautiful fragrant afternoon.

Old Nick got Atkinson and Parker to read. Atkinson read in stilted 'policeman' style. Parker well. Aindow said he couldn't read. 'Can't read?' asked Nick. 'No sir, I ain't much of a scholar.' 'What were you in civil life?' 'Electrician's fitter, sir.' Nick's face was expressionless, but scorn dripped from his voice. So Cole read, and to my surprise read fairly well, despite his atrocious Tyneside accent. 'Now, if you didn't know the words beforehand, could you gather the exact text from his exact words? Do you see how he misses out "to" "ing", "and". All these ought to be carefully pronounced. Pitch and intensity of voice common – it is TIMBRE which tells, and is individual and distinguishes one. On phone, use proper names for all letters if in doubt – E for Edward, etc.'

SATURDAY 31 AUGUST

Vic to Pibrouck and arriving back late, explained that, to his amazement, when he got there, brigades had vanished and he found people walking about without tin hats on. He left his birds with some new people in the dugout signal office.

That evening I to Westoutre, where I noticed traffic moving forward. Not a great deal more until, when I got into Westoutre, I found lorries parked up and some howitzers and groups of men and cyclists. Laughed to see DRs and crowd in the place where before none ever were to be seen except in ones and twos. How strange and magic to be able to move freely there again.

Everybody was hilarious – it was a significant day. The first real tangible evidence that Fritz was going back … unless after all it was only a trick…

SUNDAY 1 SEPTEMBER

Today Vic and I forward to Bailleul via St Jan Cappel. Most of the houses now were shattered. Beyond St Jan, where the battle line had run, the fields were badly pitted, and some trenches, but no trenches on the road. Bad shell-holes only partly filled up and guns and cars were sticking. We got past with difficulty, and the road was alive with a thin continuous stream of traffic. As we approached Bailleul shells dropped slowly on it and as we rode to our meeting place, men of the labour companies were leisurely filling in the holes.

Piles of stinking, mouldy rank rubbish all around. Eerie soiled uniforms lay in the smoking humidity – blue French, khaki and Hun. Deathly devastation – worse than Wipers. To make out where we were when we got to the square we had to shut our eyes and conjure up the picture from memory. On our right had been the town hall where guns had been stacked after Messines, and the brass hats and aldermen had congregated to see the King. Straight along on the right were the pubs where I used to go. The square itself was a desolate mass of earth, bricks and rubbish, which men were sweeping. Horse carcasses of skin like brown umbrellas still lay here and there.

I said to Vic, 'Suppose he pushes now – we're done. I can't help thinking it's only a ruse to draw us on in disorder, then thrust back again, and roll us up. Look at the bloody disorder.' A man came up, sleepy, dirty, his clothes anyhow. 'Are you wanting pigeons?' 'I am.' 'Are you 89th Brigade?' 'Ay.' 'Where's the HQ? We've been trying to find you.' He pointed to a pile of ammo boxes and a few DRs. 'That's us. Where the rest are, God knows.' We left the birds and buggered off.

MONDAY 2 SEPTEMBER

War news still continues vague, but good every day.

We had no fresh instructions and knowing the brigades had moved forward, we anticipated difficulty. I to 30th Div HQ, which was now fixed in a small dugout on top of Mont Noir. There I saw the major in charge of Div signals, who was a little, fair man with a worried, sleepy air and lined brow, looking as if a thundering headache had him. He sat with a stick and back against the wall.

'They should be at Ulster Camp,' he said. 'Know where that is?' He produced a map and gave a reference. 'I've no idea how many pigeons they'll want. Use your own judgement if you've no instructions.'

So in the gathering dusk Vic and I took the Bailleul road to Dranoutre, packed and jammed with traffic. Rupturing ourselves and crashing on shell-holes, we arrived at a house where, in a battered cellar, we found a few signallers and I met one of the pigeon men. While Vic waited, I went on with the rest of the pigeons with the chap who guided me to the camp. I had the wind up, but he took things rather calmly and nonchalant.

'Is he doing much shelling?' I asked, in a voice I strove to keep cool. 'Not a great deal. He just pumps over gas shells about this time, that's all.'

As gas was my pet aversion, owing to difficulty of using mask with my false teeth, I was not reassured. We were stumbling over wires, holes and hillocks and gratings, until we came to a little hut where signallers were working and my pigeon wallahs were waiting, sleepy. Handed birds over and got away, leaving a good pair of gloves behind that I was too frightened to go back for.

It was a painful crawl home – midnight arrival and while ravenously eating bread and cheese, heard I was wanted by OC. 'I bet that's another run,' I said, my heart sinking. With foreboding got on to OC.

'Oh, Davis, there's another eight birds wanted by Artillery, 36ᵗʰ Divisional, at St Jan's Cappell.' 'We've only just got back from our run tonight. Had a job to find the brigades, sir.' 'Mmm, I'm sorry, but I'm afraid they'll have to go.' 'Very good, sir.'

'Why the bloody hell can't they go in the morning,' said Atkinson, showing sympathy. 'They'll have to go and I shall have to take 'em. You can't go with that hand, Vic.' 'I'll take your morning run,' said Vic. 'I should bloody well think so,' I replied with vehement indignation. 'If you hadn't been well we'd have tossed up for it.'

Why should I always have to take the night runs? Any night run there'd been while I was on pigeons, I'd always taken it – first because Caseby was un-trustworthy; secondly when I had Pip, because he had the wind up, and I had pity on him; and now I'd got a pal who was not windy, but his hand was injured. Although I was first hand and ought to be able to take the easy now and then, I had not only the responsibility but also the rottenest jobs. I felt annoyed and in bad temper.

Parker and Trow were kind and got me the birds in two small baskets, and off I went, already tired to death, hating the prospect of the journey and fearing what the Cappell road would be like at night.

Just past Cassel I thought it best to turn my light out and rode in the dark. I lit again into Abeele and turned light out again at the top of Berthen hill. From here to St Jan's rode lightless, coming some smacks. Had been relieved on hearing it was only St Jan's I had to go to, and of course Div HQ were all right. I found the signal office higher up the street on the left. No-one seemed to know anything about it, but I left the birds as instructed and rode away relieved that I hadn't to go any farther to any arty unit.

TUESDAY 3 SEPTEMBER

Slept to see Vic rise early and out.

Next thing was I heard from OC that Vic was hurt. No exact news, but he was in a field ambulance station somewhere. In hospital at Wiruge, south of Steenvoord. I struck sick and couldn't eat. Ought I to have let Vic ride with his bad hand – even though out myself until 3.30 before? Regretted my angry way with him last night. No news all day, though Trow asking me to phone. The other DRs were moving this day to Terdeghem, but I was staying on for the present with the lofts. At midday Marr arrived, as almost the only DR available.

WEDNESDAY 4 SEPTEMBER

At 7 am Machen with message as to arrangements for refilling depot. Told us Vic only hurt and bandaged on head and hand, and shaken up. I much relieved and glad.

Afternoon on new round via Ren and up fork road to Canada Corner. The road desolate and plastered with drying mud. Rusty, desolate and battered huts and houses, and at CC the trees snapped off. On the left the famed Kemmel Hill, abandoned by Fritz or taken by us – no-one seemed to know which – lay bare, bluey grey and desolate, in shape like a vast sagging marquee. When I'd last seen it, Kemmel was thick with green trees – now bare as a vulture's head, the country round about the nadir of lifeless desolation. Locre razed to the ground and unrecognisable. Dranoutre also razed. Between Locre and Dranoutre we met our men – they cheerful. Tales of tank mines all over the place – harmless-looking pieces of timber, etc. A bogey to us for a bit until we struck naught.

Dranoutre now just a maze of rubble heaps and dust and dirt. It was very windy, which sent up dust, stinks and flies. The road was boarded over with planks in several places, covering craters. No sign of shells now, or Fritz. Occasional bursts far away – booby traps blowing up?

Evening to Red Cross station and found Vic moved. Wetham, fond of Vic, had fetched him in the box-car, and Vic glad as he was getting no food. His face had a yellow patch and was bandaged up in white. He doesn't remember anything happening. He was cornering sharply and the next thing found himself in the field ambulance, coming to.

THURSDAY 5 SEPTEMBER

Rumours of still further advances near Cambrai and Douai. Lens taken – exciting. Men talking already offhand of Cambrai and Douai falling, and of Lille being evacuated.

At Crucifix Corner met the men and dished out the birds. No foe to be seen. Leaving our bikes, Marr and I went into house after house on the St Jan's road. The lofty and dignified houses were desecrated. Books from libraries were slung across the floors, the pictures fallen and slashed. German ammo and grenade boxes strewed the rooms. In many kitchens the crockery lay in perfect order except for dust on it – salt-cellars and pepper and coffeepots – as if never touched from the day the inhabitants fled. Beautiful gardens were glimpsed beyond the wreckage or broken windows, their green and colour still intact and fearing ravage, like a girl turned into a garden.

In some houses, pushing open the great swinging decorated doors to the courtyard, we would hear within crashes and know that other solders were scrounging. There was none to say you nay. You wandered at your sweet will among the still and part-destroyed houses. Few were in the streets – all had gone forward. Far from being organised, all seemed a scene of disorder.

FRIDAY 6 SEPTEMBER

Went to see Mr Underwood in Nissen hut, almost bare with a table and two chairs and maps. He said, 'They want us to take the birds to Neuve Eglise. Can you do that?' 'We can, sir. I suppose it's all right. We can try, and if we find it too hot, we can come back to the present refilling point.' 'I'd like to deliver at Neuve Eglise if poss. They ask us to, and it'll help them.' 'If it gets too hot, we can but give it up. I'll go tomorrow.'

He made no answer as if he would have preferred that I make no objection. But as with Westoutre, all wish to distinguish myself had vanished, and the army had almost converted me into a shirker. I felt this and was rather ashamed.

To St Jan's with the birds for which no-one had called. Going down I called at the San Martin for the doors and windows were open. 'Anyone in?' I called. Marie came forward and then noiselessly, Adrienne appeared, covered with dust and grimed, with an old overall on. I was touched by her beauty and this strange meeting after so long a parting.

SATURDAY 7 SEPTEMBER

This morning to Neuve Eglise. Was passing a dugout at the side of road near a ruined cottage, when the fat-armed 36 Div cook came out and said that Robinson, the man who dealt so faithfully with my pigeons at Pop, had got gassed through coming out from dugout before the gas shells had got properly dispersed. I said, 'I hope to hell I don't have a night ride along here when they're gassing.' That was my dread henceforth. Yet in the morn everybody moved about and there was nothing doing. In Neuve Eglise scarce a soul to be seen.

To reach the signal office in a cellar you had to leap up over a pile of tumbled masonry, in full view of Fritz, get off your basket, chuck it down the hole without tearing the wire, then jump down yourself, leave the birds and collar the old birds and basket.

Though I brought the birds every day, the RFA arty men never came for them and I had to telephone for them to send men for them. I believe they wanted them farther forward to be of any use. This day I got back to the road and bike wouldn't start. Was examining the plug when shell fell about 200 yards in front of me. Trying not to be in a flurry, yet getting flustered, I fettled with my plug, getting hot and my hands boggling. Two or three other shells fell before I got away up the Danoutre road.

WEDNESDAY 11 SEPTEMBER

At night the rats woke me several times, scuttling about and making a noise like one hitting pans with a stick and squeaking loudly. I lit a candle and one old fellow stuck there with his head out of the hole in the shack canvas, gazing at me as cheeky and cool as you please, never budging but fixing me with un-winking stare.

SATURDAY 14 SEPTEMBER

Had to spend all the time 'jointing out' wires round Zuytpeene château that some fool had cut when the corps left, not thinking these were our wires from the lofts. A shirty, shitty little officer who was very short – Trow told him his job was pigeons not wires.

To heavy artillery and then to Adrienne's, where the estaminet was crowded with West Indians, who were pouring bottle after bottle of white wine and champagne, tipping it out over the glasses on the table, despite protests of their leader, who appeared to be a half-caste. They had plenty of money.

MONDAY 16 SEPTEMBER

American victory rumoured – 23,000 prisoners, according to Mr Wetham.

TUESDAY 17 SEPTEMBER

To Neuve Eglise. Arty adjutant wanted birds at 9 am if to be of any use. Said I'd try.

Afternoon visited new lofts, 130 and 154 near Bailleul and Croix de Poperinghe. Then to Lascelles' tent. Saw dark-eyed, soft-spoken man with square shoulders – gaunt, boyish. 'I'm the DR who looks after pigeons for KCO.' 'Oh, come in.' 'Do you mind giving me particulars in case of post, wages, etc?' 'Not at all. Will ye stay and have some dinner?' 'Thanks, I never refuse a cup of tea.'

'Jim, put an extra spoonful in – we've only got bully and cheese. Will that do ye?' I sat while Lancaster cooked. The tent was in a field that had been shelled heavily months ago, but it was now growing over with green. The grass was rank with paths through it and the shell-holes full of water. Around the field were half dismantled shacks built of purloined wood. The troops had gone forward but when this field was so near to the line, it must have been hot here.

THURSDAY 19 SEPTEMBER

Information that we are losing two of our lofts at Zuytpeene, as they too far back, so preps for departure. 'I don't care where you go, so long as I can get into telephonic communication with you,' in response to my request to be able to get a billet in Cassel.

SUNDAY 22 SEPTEMBER

We sought in vain for a billet. As usual the main work devolved on me. Same in afternoon at Cole's loft, and just too late at Mavaut's, where the day before they had let to someone else.

Meet Sergeant E, and had a drink or two of red wine with him on the quiet. He showed me the wireless billet above where the DRs used to be, but now they had got shifted to a passage up the road. 'You just be a wireless man and I can manage it for you. Let's go and see no-one is using these rooms.' A languid man at desk with maps said that no-one was, so Sergeant Edmonds said he'd tell Captain Harris that we were attached to wireless – 'if asked say the same, and all will be well'. But I funked at telling these half-lies and that night's piss-up was spoilt by my considering this question.

MONDAY 23 SEPTEMBER

As packing, Sergeant Edmonds said Captain Harris had granted billet.

Put kit on motor car, then cycling away, hesitated by shed. Should I wait there until the rain tempest over? Went on. Under the bridge on the S bend in the road, struck an RAF DR cutting the corner, full on. He turned to his right to avoid, and I doing the same. Lucky I was going careful. My head crashed on him and I hurled to the ground, dazed. Arm nearly useless – strained muscle, and I upset and shaken. 'You might have kept your own side,' I muttered, dejected by this, just as I was fixing up for a new billet and loaded with all my equipment and gear.

Stuck bike in shed and rode to Cole's loft in pigeon car, I saying to Edmonds, 'I do feel rotten. Arm useless. But just got that billet.'

Later Vic came to mess hut and said that thirty birds were wanted for a new location, which he couldn't quite trace on the map, but it looked off the Ren-Canada Corner road. 'I must go,' I said, feeling a fool for volunteering, my shoulder being stiff, sore, painful and useless. Borrowed Lilley's bike and went. The new bus went like the wind with a steady thud-thump of engine stroke that was new and delicious to me. We found the new place and awaiting us was a GS wagon on which the birds were being taken up in a very business-like way by a man who checked all that went into his carts – poles, leads, pigeons and baskets, etc from a list.

TUESDAY 24 SEPTEMBER

Every night, just after I'd got into bed, Underwood would send an orderly. 'Corporal Davis wanted please, by Mr Underwood.' I'd slip on my trousers and coat and he would nicely give me instructions for the morrow.

WEDNESDAY 25 SEPTEMBER

Palestine and Salonica victories are now announced.

Was urged by Mr U to train mobiles 130 and 154 as soon as possible, but couldn't get going with Lawrenson – he wouldn't take risks, and when he did, about half the birds never turned up again – he must have lost about eight. I wouldn't send them out again like that for Mr U or the General of the whole British Army. I tossed some away rather late at Crucifix Corner and they didn't come back – I'd felt at the time it was rather too late.

FRIDAY 27 SEPTEMBER

In evening saw the French defiling down Cassel hill, their wagons and stores and ambulance cars, the cavalry in blue cloaks preceding them. They appeared swiftly and calmly like phantoms and went on neighing quietly all night, and in the morning had got out to the left of Menin and achieved victory in the early morn.

SATURDAY 28 SEPTEMBER

Heard the inevitable and insistent rattle of rain and felt that sinister feeling – we had an offensive on so it was bound to be unlucky.

Depressed, saw Mr U at nine, then away with twenty to 34th Division, where news was not certain, but seemed of good tendency. To cinema – then called out of bed again to see Mr U. 'We've done damned well. They don't want the birds really, but they've got the gust up. But Foch has got something up his sleeve and he won't tell 'em what it is.'

SUNDAY 29 SEPTEMBER

Everybody whistling and gay because of bright nip in the air and good news afloat. I asked Mr U about it and he pointed to a map and showed me that, though they hadn't taken Comines and Wervicq, they were working round them and they were due to fall. The programme included taking Menin that day or thereabouts. All helped by account of Bulgarian request for an armistice.

At 4 pm rain set in and made us miserable, the ground round our huts being a mild quagmire. Riding on those roads – dark, greasy, pitted with shell-holes and often no light – the DR's life.

MONDAY 30 SEPTEMBER

Feared Vic might be hiked away to Houthem or Zandvoorde, as Mr U said to me that we might be chasing after units that far away.

News came of peace signed by Bulgaria. Everybody gay and sanguine in consequence. Things going all one way pleases us.

TUESDAY 1 OCTOBER

An eventful day. Told to find 30th Div somewhere near Hollebeke. At Po caught on sticking-up tramlines and fell flying. Smash – bike on top. Frenchmen ran out from their ambulance station and an RAF man helped me under the shoulders for I could scarcely walk. First to the château and then to dressing station. Undressed – nothing except abrasions and bruises, which the Frenchmen kindly dressed. BCO officer asked if he could send a message, but I said I'd carry on.

After bandages were on, got out with only my trousers on and set bike going – scarcely fit to ride on, but I considered that all were working hard and it would upset arrangements to get anyone else to take my place. Besides, I had never yet failed to deliver my goods and didn't like being beaten.

To Vormezeele, then a rotten crawl to St Eloi. The road was deep mud, gradually getting worse and more sunken and chewed up. By the time I got to St Eloi I was pushing my bike, loaded with pigeons, and other DRs were doing the same.

I came past the canal, to the end where Hollebeke should be – but there was nothing except green and grey desolation with the slime of sin on it. Saw an officer and asked, 'Is it all right along there, sir?' 'Well, it's risky on that corner, but you're all right when you get past there.' I pushed on into Kortewilde.

I left bike and walked about, heated, until I found where signallers were. It meant a big walk over fields, but they said I could ride there, so off on bike. Screwing past traffic saw two soldiers come down bleeding, and a Red Cross wagon with soldiers in agony twisting on the back. No pity – just wanted to be out of it as quick as possible. Rumours of the road being shelled beyond by Zandvoorde.

Now I was pushing past horses, getting kicks, tumbling over with bike and twisting my ankle and bruising my leg, calling out, 'For God's sake, give us a hand, can't you. I can't get up!' Hoped to God they didn't start shelling while I was in this relentless moving wedge of traffic. At last got through gap into field and enquired at the reinforced houses – staff officers were on the veranda outside as if they'd just had a conference. 'I don't know. I should assemble here – but we're another division – we can't both be here.' I stumbled on an officer who said it would be all right if I left the birds there and that 30th Div was coming in when they went out. Left them in basket with clips and away, damned glad to be finished.

On the way I met Vic's bike, perched on a bit of flat ground. He'd given up the attempt and left it, so I pinned a note on. Then I met Marr, who'd also given up. Awful trek back through grey dough of mud and split piers of wood. After what seemed miles of struggling, my bike wouldn't go. Dusk came on while I was fiddling with it. Cursed and blasphemed, but at last got away – then it stopped, going uphill. Bike over me – pain in leg, shoulder, knee and elbows. Shoved and pulled and some infantrymen helped me – good sports. Prayed I might reach Voormezeele – no food and I was done up, and crazy with thirst having sweated all the moisture out of me. Bike stopped again and some Hindu soldiers passed me, impassive.

I saw lights at the Café Belge, dim in a field on the right, but I pushed my way into a ramshackle hut of corrugated iron, wood and sandbags. Five men were in there. 'For God's sake give me something to drink.' They gave me water then tea, which was the very nectar of life – like drinking diamonds, so precious was it to my thirst. To recline and merely rest my bruised bones and aching, torn, strained body was heavenly delight.

I suggested they should let me kip there in the heat of the fire, but this was not well received. They were looking after the salvage on the fields around and waiting for lorries to fetch same. So after a drugged doze while the rain pattered down, I dragged myself wearily out and tried to start bike. Wouldn't start and couldn't budge my generator screw, so got a lorryman to shift it for me. At side of road it nearly tumbled in ditch. Took the plug out and observed beads of moisture on it, which I took to be rain. Took out carb and found water therein. Like a fool lit a match to see what I had in my tank – of course the petrol flared up and scorched my face and brows. But it was petrol only on the top, and below was water, which had been given me for petrol. With petrol tank full of water it was hopeless, so at 11.45, after an hour and a half trying, gave up the ghost and sought out a tent with a bench. I lit the little bit of candle I carried and got out my *Daily News*. While rats kept scurrying in and out, putting the wind up me, ate the chocolate and read, but couldn't sleep as I was stone cold, with only my wet overalls about me.

WEDNESDAY 2 OCTOBER

Miserable time until it dawned at six. Started at eight, cheery, the lorryman having given me some breakfast. Well away to Pop when just outside the belt broke, suddenly the lower part of the frame sheared clean off and the engine almost dropped on the floor – the result of all the pounding and knocks I'd given her. Pushed the bloody thing to tree at the side of road where an MP could guard it and half-heartedly tried to stop a number of lorries, but none would take the bike.

Hoofed it and got lifts on RAF car to Terdeghem where I went to Smith's. What a spectacle, shirt sticking out of my breeches, dirty handkerchief round split breeches, face burnt and scorched, unshaven and unwashed. The boys roared when they saw me. Lilley said he would see if Underwood could get my bike lifted on a lorry, but as the corps was moving that day to Mont Noir, this was awkward. Went off to have a bath.

There was a hope that, if we were lucky, we might be billeted beyond Ypres. Was it possible that a miracle would happen and we should have, after such long years of waiting, an advance so real and big that we could move right over the old battle zone and push into that longed-for realm of undestroyed country beyond Comines, Wervicq and Menin?

THURSDAY 3 OCTOBER

Called at Dupont's and learned that I was reported missing for two days. Mr Underwood told me calmly that he thought I'd got 'biffed' as they didn't hear from me, so when I got back I found Davies from the army helping Vic. I was inclined to pose as martyr with my burnt face and limp – I couldn't walk without limping for a day or two. There was no doubt I'd had a rotten ride that day and stuck it well.

FRIDAY 4 OCTOBER

At Wulverghem a rumour that the Turks had asked for an armistice, but I couldn't confirm. Followed a lane so deep in mud I had to ride on six inches of path at the side. Kept skidding into the mud and progress slow and painful past gun pits galore with guns stuck. Came to beginning of a cord road and mounted until the land grew absolutely barren as if a path to abandoned hell. Not a soul in sight, and I soon understood why. Practically impassable for traffic – great tractors, holed and rusting, stood discarded like mastodons. Here a tank ripped to red ribbons, then a gun all twisted at the muzzle and rusting into decay. Water flowed under the broken planks of the cord road as if it were the bed of a stream. Got off the bike and went on foot to investigate.

The top of the hill seemed a long way off, but thought I'd got so far, so I'd try it. Now rain came drizzling down and quite buggered things up. The bike skidded and slid so had to get off and push over beams, mounds and stones. At last got to the Wytschaete ridge, from which I could see the view I'd seen in 1917 – it was now all soiled and muddy, dark, drear and colourless. Carried on towards St Eloi where there is a bridge track over a shell-hole, and the German names of the roads painted up on big boards – 'Preussen Allee', 'Hohenzollern Allee'. Into Houthem, where many people wandering lost, notably our cyclists trying to find their officers.

SATURDAY 5 OCTOBER

In evening, cinema – and midnight got instructions to move which we expect-ed every day.

SUNDAY 6 OCTOBER

Rose early, anxious. Went to see OC to make arrangements. Got to Voormezeele just in time to meet the 34th Div wagon, which Mr Underwood had arranged to take our birds.

Came down the road from Vierstraat and saw Hughie's and Tom Cavill's old pitches – all rusty and waste. The ambulance station and dugouts were all banged in. Skeletons of lorries and cars dotted the side of the road, which was all torn and desolate and hellish.

In Ren saw AD signals driver who said, 'Heard the news?' 'What news?' 'Germany asks for an armistice to discuss terms of peace on basis of President

Wilson's fourteen points.' 'I haven't heard it, and I'm sorry to say I don't believe it. I should like to – but I've heard so many yarns like that.' 'I give it you for what it's worth, but this is true, I think. My boss has never yet told me anything that's not come true. He told me about Bulgaria and Turkey some days before, and both came right.' I rode home exhilarated and told them at the San Martin. And this time it chanced to be true. The French and American advance is fine and we are all excited by news of Lille and Armentières being evacuated. Adrienne and the French soldiers quite cool – reckoned they knew about it before us.

Stiff and aching with hard work, leg, knee and shoulder all pained me.

TUESDAY 8 OCTOBER

Yesterday's paper confirms the account of Germany's request for armistice – I sceptic all along receive this news with feelings of wonder, doubt and relief. I spread the news up the line – men anxious to believe, but they've been thwarted so many times that it's pitiful to watch the play of desire fighting with fear of disappointment.

ARMENTIÈRES, NÔTRE-DAME CHURCH, WHICH THE GERMANS BLEW UP SHORTLY BEFORE BEING DRIVEN OUT OF THE TOWN.

WEDNESDAY 9 OCTOBER

Via Ostaverne and Preussen Allee to Kortwilde. Approaching, noticed shells falling on the left and soldier leading horse away. Dead horse toward the crossroads at Houthem end, so backed a bit, and decided not to risk it yet. Just off the road was a pill-box, and a soldier sat philosophically on the step. 'Been bumping on and off all morning,' he said. 'He'll give it a rest soon.' After half an hour, shelling ceased and I carried on. Turned left at crossroad, the road was littered with upthrown earth, logs of timber, baulks and bricks. 'Glad I wasn't passing at the time,' I muttered.

Back late and on arriving home, learnt Vic gone on leave!

SUNDAY 13 OCTOBER

Sergeant Cole emphatic that President Wilson's terms had been agreed to by Germany – ie to evacuate Belgium and France – and another said his officer had told him it was official. The *Daily Mail* stated the same and that semi-officially Turkey sues for peace, while Austria threatens a separate peace.

TUESDAY 15 OCTOBER

Read in *Daily Express* official statement that the German government will accede to Wilson's terms, including evacuation. Also that Douai captured and the French are seventeen miles past Rheims.

THURSDAY 17 OCTOBER

Saw OC and AD Sigs who said that brigades had gone away into 'the blue', but if possible would like birds delivered to 'em if I could find.

To Zandvoorde, the roads barren with sterile grey and green, and about every half a mile a horse or two, covered with black-grey powder of dust and death, lying there stinking. Little traffic – a most sterile and God-forsaken spot. At crossroads an MP directed us on to a churned-up road, black, ashy, grating mud, some feet deep. Had to lift the bike over the ruts and holes.

There were numerous units encamped in the fields – but not ours. At Geluwe, Cowen left behind with a puncture. Met 102 Brigade man who wanted to take the birds. He led me to pill-boxes over fields where he said he was to meet Sigs of Brigade, but I declined to leave the birds with him. On into Artoishoek – worrying – a deserted village where 30th Div was in a school building, and OC Sigs was glad I had brought birds. A DR called Evans wanted us to wait for him, but daylight drawing to a close and all these horrible roads to be ridden, did the cad on him and didn't wait to show him back to the Corps.

From the HQs on the fields, lorries were trying to get off in the mud, slipping and skidding, then trying to turn in the road, holding up lines of blocked traffic. In the dark men were cursing and gears were crashing and grinding – a dark, swaying, hopeless confusion. How could anyone get anywhere in this dark, with no light to follow roads, all the villages smashed and only map locations to go by?

Still, having got so far, to a spot from which we knew the way, felt content, lighting up and chewing a bit of bread and chocolate that we'd brought with us. Back over the cord road, Cowen in front, skidded and hit a plank across the road and fell over, nearly precipitated into the foul, ghastly and putrid shell-holes and floating morass each side of the road. In the light of our lamp could see rats running across the road in front of us, startled by the light. Sometimes we hit them. Met Alan Marr, jogging along at fair speed. He stopped – imperturbable, jocular, best class of Englishman, not grousing over vile night ride in mud and over holes. How glad I felt that we were going back to warm beds.

FRIDAY 18 OCTOBER

The night before, in the hut the OC had been phoning for me. 'Meet me at 8.45 am with tin hat and box-respirator. I'll tell you then what I want.' I received this news with a groan and sinking heart. I was picked on to go and do some risky job because I'd shirked naught. Worried, it had spoilt my sleep – sinister imaginings. In the morning I was fifteen minutes late, but met the OC in the mess. I was to get birds them meet him at the power-station in Geluwe.

After mending puncture, to 30th Division, who were on the rise before Wytschaete ridge, with the signal office in sand-bagged affair. Went via Wervicq, where had another puncture. Paused by a workman's cottage that had billeted Fritzes – who couldn't have been gone more than a few days. On the wall a fat woman drawn in charcoal, her private parts rudely sketched. Not many soldiers about and I wondered if there would be any shelling or gas? But fine sun out and I enjoyed myself. Underwood heavily jocose about my tardiness. Rode off with him at a bat down the road to Menin. 'I think it's all right. We may have a bit of trouble with Fritz potting.' At Menin some roofs off and holes by railway crossing, shit on the roads – bricks and dust – but stately, vital green fields behind.

It kept fine and now we saw civvies – healthy, but timid, happy, saluting rather slavishly, and uncertain of us – and children carrying Belgian flags.

Mr Underwood said our billets were going to be taken up in the château along the road – but 'don't say anything.'

In the estaminets the glasses were still on the shelves and the doors open. Very tempting to go in and loot things, and took a book from the shelf of one shop – but problem with how to carry it. 'Come on, Davis,' called Mr U. 'Yes sir, just wanted a souvenir.'

Trying to keep up with Mr U, I came down a cropper, which shook me up and bent the handlebars. At Wulverghem junction asked MP if officer had gone that way and he said 'yes', but feeling a bit caddish I went the other way. Next day heard that Mr U got caught with a puncture and he had no outfit to get the tyre off, so he had to patch it. I did feel a cad after he's stuck to me so well.

SATURDAY 19 OCTOBER

Decided, after vacillation, that Cowen could take the birds, and I went for new bike. Re-entering Pop heard strident piano and entered estaminet, leaving new bike outside in the rain. Dancing going on to the tune of piano, into which one kept slipping pennies for it to play. Danced with the best mamselle in white blouse, who when putting pennies in the piano, leant her hand on my shoulder.

There were Courtrai refugees who had come to Pop for relief. They talked German and I talked German with them. They said they'd had a bad time with things so near.

SUNDAY 20 OCTOBER

Morning for instructions at the signal office on Mont Noir. Asked signalmaster to wire 30th Div if he wanted birds. To Terdeghem and got birds off grousing Smith, and back with heavy load. No answer to wire, so dinner and read paper.

Out with pigeon men – Atkinson, Cavill and Evans – on pub-crawl, starting with the antique and porched venerable estaminet on the Dunkirk road, where in a room on one side couples were dancing, but mostly Belgian soldiers fixed up with girls and I didn't like to butt in. Girls dressed half-smart and one or two powdered in Sunday best. On to my first pub where there was dancing, and back to the main road pubs. Rather fruitless, but the chaps were glad to see me.

MONDAY 21 OCTOBER

With birds via Menin road from Ypres, and got off on the road to see front-line trenches – filled with water, old and dirty, but well built and preserved.

After Hooge, the road churned up and being relaid by navvies, but as soon as relaid, being soft, were churned up again by continual lorry and car traction and gun traffic. Right and left, the grey and fawn mottled and sodden earth was studded with stumps of forlorn timber and invisible dugouts, and now there were the huts and dumps of the advancing working parties. In Lauwe fine, well-favoured girls about, seeming happy. Flags flying from the houses and civvy band parading in large open square, and a crowd at church. Everyone alive.

34th Div was in the school. Pulled up at the bridge which had been blown by Fritz, but the town was intact. Joyous at reaching place with birds.

TUESDAY 23 OCTOBER

This day at 9.30 found that our Corps had pissed off. We all upset for an hour and a half as linesmen tried odd pairs of lines to try and get us through – army taking over lines and ought not to have been left in disorder. No communications on what was happening. Kaput, so I had to go with Cowen – I always having to do work if the end is uncertain. Over the bridge and via Roncq, where met Captain Harrison of Second Army, i/c pigeons who, pleased to see me chasing after the corps with birds, said I should find them at the crossroads at Neuville. Here found château address and Mr Underwood. 'You'll find 34th Div at Belleghem – I should take the birds there.'

Saw many pretty civvy girls of eighteen or so in and out of house as turned corner. Piqued by the sight after barren experiences. At Belleghem many flags, large and fresh, and a great procession – the burgomaster and laced and uniformed beadles.

At Wevelghem bike wouldn't start, even though new. Cussed and groaned and it grew dark. At last pushed bus back to a farm shed where troops were camped and examined it at leisure. Took the plug out and changed it, took the carb down – no result. At last found that the new valves and exhaust were stuck up because oil had burned on to them. Freed it with petrol. What a ride bumping back over the lumps, ruts, stones and kerbs of the Menin road.

Cursed and went slow – light was bad. There were lorries, worn-out tanks, and shrouded guns waiting to move. Traffic quieter now and how welcome was the red light of a fire in a dugout. Dog-tired, home at 11 pm.

THURSDAY 24 OCTOBER

Morning twice to training and afternoon to the San Martin – a pretty picture of Adrienne at table by the stove, dressmaking. October, mellow sun and blue sky and tawny scented leaves outside. One or two French soldiers were within, one handsome with an eye on Adrienne.

Met Paul who told of going through Hazebrouck and seeing DR's bike outside the estaminet. He went in for a drink and a fine girl asks him if he'd like to go into another room. 'Don't mind if I do.' All jake-a-loo – and now understood why, when asked at the Signal Office, they replied that DRs generally took an hour's rest at Hazebrouck – they were visiting this estaminet.

FRIDAY 25 OCTOBER

Too dull for training, so fixed up vexing subject of rations, arranging to draw at Westoutre. In canteen they wouldn't serve Chinks, saying they must go to their own canteen and being a bit rude about it.

Wrote while the men played cards. The life here – tea made from water in shell-holes in which dead rats sunk.

SATURDAY 26 OCTOBER

Fine mellow weather. On arrival back in evening, OC here – he going to recommend Vic for Military Medal. Good news. Wrote well all evening – first beginning of 'Over the old battle-zone', while men played cards.

SUNDAY 27 OCTOBER

Seabourne said you couldn't get back via Lille without a permit, and Vic and I – he back from leave – decided to go via Menin road and Pop. From Ypres to Pop let my new bus out, and it thundered along like Lilley's and swayed and rocked, frightening with speed. Saw my Zuytpeen pals, who cheered us and swore we were the only ones ever looked after 'em. I'd brought pay – that's what made 'em so glad. All delight in the room and we ate cheese, pickles and bully, and all talked together, going over our doings. We had some drinks and back to hut at 8.30. Cowen groused he to return because I'd taken him as due to go on leave, and now, just as having cush, he to go to Div and work hard.

TUESDAY 29 OCTOBER

Afternoon to Abeele and asked Adrienne where I could get hair cut. She told me of hut at end of village – but the barber out and the main barber not yet back at Abeele, so to Steenvoorde, and had hair cut by little middle-aged pale woman. Back to the San Martin and played draughts with Adrienne, who was smart. Sing-songs and music, just like the old vanished times. I left the place saying naught, and getting ready to go, Adrienne came out to see me off as I was parting. If I'd said to her I was going, she would have come out. Fool.

WEDNESDAY 30 OCTOBER

To Cassel, seeking some vanished clobber and junk of Paul's from his studio. At Mavaut's, Julienne, the plump girl with beautiful suave face and fine breast was smiling and caused me vacillation. Should I stay? At San Martin I recall Adrienne writing, her face a little smutty and her brow wrinkling as she wrote for some goods and I to see at station if that had come for her. Struck me as being pleasant to get us to do her a service. I was coming away when Julienne came out. 'Popski, would you like to stay to tea?' I should very much, but said, 'No – another time,' Julienne smiled kindly and I felt immediately I'd hurt her, because doing favour for Adrienne. Also I refused because we'd promised to get rations and didn't like to leave it to Vic. Half didn't like to confess to him I wanted to stay. Thought also of Adrienne's lack of disinterestedness, and finally cursed the perversity which makes me deny doing what I want to do. Went away sad and got the rations, and when I told Vic I should have liked to go to San Martin, he said he wouldn't have minded if I had. My sacrifice in vain.

FRIDAY 1 NOVEMBER

Fine – to Boeschepe. Entered a house with a roofed porchway, where a dark-eyed girl (whereat mouth watered), a plump, clumsy younger girl, and a couple of youths on bench by fire. A large gloomy room, furnished with rough board table and a piano, a few chairs and a bench.

'Can I get anything to drink here?' 'Yes,' she said brightly, 'stoot?' I had stout and sat there. This was the plump, bright-cheeked girl always being cranked up by Lancaster. I thought she couldn't be much cop, but she was a refined girl in manner, her blouse was good and she was delicately scented.

The two boys went and left me alone. I said, 'What about some champagne?' She charged me 15 francs a bottle and I offered the girls a little, which they took as a matter of course. They ate by the fire, turning the log with their feet. Another boy turned up from the yard – probably a farmer and or brother, so I went to piano and played, and they hummed. I wanted to suggest a dance, but hadn't the pluck. Soon the father came in and sat by the fire, silent and smiling, small-faced and domestic-looking, about forty-eight. Girl said mother was near Belleghem – had gone there just at start of war and had to remain there. The elder girl was very nice and very superior – why was she not run by any officer – or was she?

MONDAY 4 NOVEMBER

Every day sensational news re Turkey, and Italian victory over Austria, which reached utter rout of latter, and they suing for armistice – which was granted. Some 300,000 prisoners taken and 5,000 guns.

TUESDAY 5 NOVEMBER

In afternoon I to Bevelghem in fine weather – enjoyed the going. On road met refugees coming back home with barrows and carts piled with belongings, and sometimes a goat or children aboard. They pushed with indefatigable patience and fair cheeriness. The autumn sun glowed redly above the dry road and I thought what a lovely life this is, riding through this country with a prospect of leave, the war incredibly coming to a successful conclusion and me with a new bus.

Wanted to ask Mr Underwood about prospective move and found him with ADS in office on the first floor in the château. He said he wanted me to pick up Atkinson and Trow and plant them somewhere by Knockke – 'Any good site, but remember, it's not far from the line and Fritz has got it under observation, so ye want to get under the lee of a hill or similar.' We suggested somewhere by the mill – and he pointed on the map. 'Yes sir. Very well, sir.' The ADS silent, but approving. He had been up with ADS in car and thought there were several good sites.

WEDNESDAY 6 NOVEMBER

Morn I saw OC then rations to Bevelghem, after argument with Quarter, trying to fix rations with Div. He said he couldn't accept responsibility – 'we're moving on any time. Get someone else.' He was 'narsty'. Tried at various offices to get 'em fixed up.

The billet I'd arranged, we couldn't take over – my romantic dream of Belgian beauty to be met in the demure mysterious house all futile. I had worried all night over this billeting, trying to decide what to do.

Today Austrian armistice confirmed!

THURSDAY 7 NOVEMBER

Out to Knokke. Rode up the hill and over fields, past the bridge down to hummocky ground. Drawbacks – difficulty of getting vans over the ditches, and also the pitches were very visible. Had also to consider that water and rations would be required. Rode up to crest of hill, wondering where the Huns were – what a fool not to have ridden on and had a look.

Traffic thick and continuous on main road, but I prospected up lanes, narrow and twisty and full of mud, but found what I thought suitable, and at farm the officer told me their unit was clearing off and as far as he concerned, we could have the field site. Still not quite satisfied, worrying about observation of Fritz.

In evening Lilley said that the armistices has been signed. We hoped and fervently believed it would be signed, but could scarcely credit the good news – that it was really possible. Rumours everywhere that Fritz delegates away to sign armistice at Guise.

FRIDAY 8 NOVEMBER

Went to Courtrai – fine city centre – and read the bills up on the Town Hall. It was fine to see the road directions, to Menin, etc, and think, 'we're now the other side of all that trouble.' There was to be some ceremony, but it is said that they don't care for Allies in Courtrai and that they got on well there with the Huns. All pubs in this town are out of bounds to troops.

SUNDAY 10 NOVEMBER

Overnight rumours of peace signed, bombing stopped, delegates imprisoned for insulting Foch, Italian army 36 miles from Berlin. Saw an alarmist article in Saturday's news re revolution the world over. Atmosphere rather tense of expectation and happiness.

This evening at 8.15, phone rings in mess. I nearest, but Geordie goes as he thinks he's out for a special. 'Boys! Armistice signed is the message – but there's an uproar the other end. I can't hear.' 'It's signed,' says Geordie. 'Get out!' 'Oui, boys, Armistice signed. Listen, wait, he's telling the staff.' He excited and we tense and quiet – rather an anti-climax. I felt personally as if some spring of life had broken and instead of gladness, a flat purposelessness all of a sudden. He gets beer in a dixie and we all get some – where from I don't know. Will someone go for some wine? Curley and I volunteer.

I could scarcely believe the news was true. Curley excited and as he rode on at a good bat he shouts out, 'War's over! Armistice signed' and then in French, '*Paix signé*! At the doors of estaminet, cheers followed us from expectant soldiers who stood by lorries. Estaminet doors opened, showing light within and women and civvies inside. All were only too willing to believe – and cheers sounded behind us. In Mouscorn soldiers asked, 'Is it true?' as we yelled the news at them. Great sport.

We went into the wine merchant's where the wife told us of the Huns' starving horses, of their predicaments, carts all made of wood and cars all had to be pushed to start. No copper, no rubber, but iron wheels. Told me of things the Belgians hid under floors – spuds and so on – and men sought who didn't declare themselves, such as her husband. The courage of civvies in hiding, though they were threatened with being shot.

Rode back with rockets going up each side of the sky. Fire outside lorries and people dancing around them and in estaminets. Got back to piss-up. Geordie got up on the chair, squiffy, and made a speech – then fell like a log and slept, and had to be carried out.

MONDAY 11 NOVEMBER

Going to Belleghem, a fine lovely sunset, and thought how fine this life. Didn't notice anything particularly joyful in the faces of the people after the declaration of the Armistice, but flags in all manner of vehicles.

At Au Paradis there was a fire in the yard behind the sergeants' mess and rockets going off and shouting. I was invited to supper in the mess, and then into the garden. Geordie, Lilley, Daniels and others unfastened rocket after rocket, taking them out of cases like canvas cricket bags. Was appropriating canvas for my beds, when in rushes Quarter. Miraculously all men disappear except Wordley. He cries, 'Take those stores back. Those rockets! What do you mean by it. I'll have your names...' I was smiling saturninely to myself, yet wind up. We doing wrong, and wondered what would come of it. Quarter dancing about like mad, then 'Throw the fucking bastard into the fire!' came a voice – then laughter from the house. 'Shoot him!' The Quarter departed.

TUESDAY 12 NOVEMBER

People appeared now somewhat more joyous.

With Glenny to estaminet in Tourcoing. Dark girl with sister, one pretty and well-dressed and making eyes at Glenny. None in estaminet save us – musical box and I half suggest a waltz – but not taken up. Walked on up deserted streets and came to main road where Glenny had been told that dancing goes on. Visited several estaminets – one full of soldiers and civilians, and a man with a concertina wailing in the corner. At the counter fight for drink, giving and receiving the vile bits of card and notes that are current money. Had one or two dances, and wanted to stay longer, but Glenny impatient to go.

WEDNESDAY 13 NOVEMBER

Met Pritchard, who says, 'If this is peace, give me bloody war. Working harder than I ever worked in my life. In war we got a system – this we're new to, and haven't settled a routine.'

To Lille – populous, busy and fine but holed here and there by the ramparts. Various notices to troops about bounds and theatres. One or two, poverty-stricken, asked me for bread or money, but most people looked well-to-do.

Leaving the other side of Lille for Armentières, the houses were darker and more sinister, and smashed about a bit –but not much, as we have spared the city.

Went to look at the old front line – in trenches, fairly tidy and zig-zag, were old English tins and wood boxes, soap boxes and cans.

Back to Cassel, a chill reception at Mavaut's, but the square bright as I sat over coffee after dinner. How strange, now deserted by troops. Open clean spaces and rifts of sky. A sadness at the close of our life there.

FRIDAY 15 NOVEMBER

In Abeele Adrienne in brown blouse, and silent. She rapidly laid a fire and swept the room. 'I'll be back in two minutes.' Her mother came in and talked genially and affectionately with me. In five minutes Adrienne back, as if pleased to make herself nice for me – radiant, frilled, waved hair and a white lace collar, her face smooth and shining.

A crowd came in and cards are played, but I not joining in. I shake hands – that being the first time in such meetings I had intimated going by shaking hands, as I think if I'd done it some other time before she would have come out as now, to bid me a lover's goodbye. As I lit up and prepared the bike in the garden she ran out to speak to me – ostensibly to speak about a barrel lent to the sergeants' mess – but why? I kissed her on the cheek and saw that she would have liked to be kissed earlier. Adrienne's face, as I rode off, mocked me with joys I had missed.

SATURDAY 16 NOVEMBER

In Courtrai Leahey told me that they had rumours of an order to trek to Germany. Prospect not liked – always on the move and they feared the bitter attitude of the Huns – could be shot in the back or have to wander about in pairs in hostile country.

TUESDAY 19 NOVEMBER

Reported at 9.15 to orderly room for leave, and to MO. 'Let's look at your chest, lad' He signed me free from scabies and vermin. Packed lengthily and to Quarter with same. Then rode in the sergeant's and warrant officers' van on the train, which had a stove. How happy – I sank back near enough to the stove, dozing and tired. Two miles outside Calais, detrained and started wet walk. Turned into an estaminet where there was a crowd of leave-goers and other ranks, drinking, and we had beer and champagne. We left a bit top-heavy and primed and got instructions to look out for factory chimney flares – the only way to find the camp.

WEDNESDAY 20 NOVEMBER

Hung around for an hour in queue to get away first boat, then gave up at nine. Wandered round the barren camp with cinema room and recreation room, etc.

After lunch I away – pleasant voyage, then Dover beautiful in creamy swathes of cliff in greeny mist with castle above. Fleet anchored there gave us a siren welcome of mixed but prolonged calls. Rush into train and Redcaps strive to guide us, but chaps cry, 'Hey up! Here's some soldiers coming!' The same old spirit of lark. Everyone joyous, gay and cracking jokes. At stations for a few minutes the children cheer as we pass. At Victoria a good free feed, then changed money. Went to the Union Jack Club, dined at the Press Restaurant and late to bed.

THURSDAY 21 NOVEMBER

GWR to Brum – khaki almost ignored. Met Morris in High Street, but no-one else about. Stayed indoors in evening as Ettie was unwell upstairs.

FRIDAY 22 NOVEMBER

Odd jobs in morning, then by train to Dudley. Girls about are bright, but in the electric train cars the males – miners and others – are sad and preoccupied-looking – very strange after the gay and rough irresponsibility of war.

SATURDAY 23 NOVEMBER

Aunt Mary called, her mouth twitching with nervousness re Paul, of whom she'd heard no word for some time, but she fancied that he might be on the way home on leave.

Gloom of convention still in house. Away about seven to Sparkhill Institute. A good ride there, and met Dowler.

THURSDAY 5 DECEMBER

Said goodbye to Arthur, then to the train and away. In London to Union Jack – but no letters.

To Dover – tons of WAACs around in khaki giving the dinner, cooking and serving – rough, jovial, lower-class. Marched down through the dull, black lifeless town, thinking how many had gone that road – never to return. Got a seat on board for the passage. Very sad leaving London and Blighty for cheerless journeying.

FRIDAY 6 DECEMBER

In the camp in Calais breakfast parade at 5.30 – queue trailing blankets in the mud to return them. Train by seven, and long ride via Bailleul, Armentières, Tourcoing, Courtrai and Menin. Got out at Courtrai and made enquiries as to what was going on, but was sleepy and lacked the courage and initiative to do other than what the flock were doing. Went on to Menin with regret, but informed by RTO officials that X Corps Camp – or rest camp – was at Menin, and we would naturally go to where we left from – although I understood from Tokeley that we had moved to Messines.

At Menin men with lamps called out, 'X Corps this way,' and we were led to the brewery – drear, draughty and full of beds with men wrapping up to sleep – no fire.

SATURDAY 7 DECEMBER

A morning of uncertainty. What to do? Went to ask Scots officer I saw bundling in and out of orderly room, but got no satisfaction. Corps had moved and he didn't know where to. That afternoon news came that all X Corps men to stay at camp until further instructions.

TUESDAY 10 DECEMBER

Unpleasant surprise after rising happy, being well installed now in an upstairs room with a fire in the stove. Rose and shaved in the brewery furnace room, dark and cold, getting water from the well over the way in capsizing biscuit tins. No sooner was the rumour current that we were shifting, than someone had found out where, and we were bolting along the street with beds on our backs – which we were told in fact to leave – and up into the new house abutting the square. A rush to collar the best rooms and corners. Ended up upstairs with the cyclist boys.

All said it would be past Christmas before we moved. I began bitterly to regret that I'd stayed and began to have sad inklings that I might be cooped up here for months and lose my unit and my chums. The Corps had moved, and 'They don't want us – they don't care about us!' ran the cry. In Corps I was a person of consequence, with niche and settled job, authority and routine. Here I was a nondescript, without standing or calling, or sense of fulfilling any useful role.

WEDNESDAY 11 DECEMBER

After keen disappointment things improved. I saw a captain and he said I should return to my unit in four days – he hoped.

In afternoon and evening wrote at the estaminet – I had to force myself to concentrate, finding it uninteresting to write hour after hour – indeed, finding it monotonous.

MONDAY 16 DECEMBER

The OC took my first manuscript without default, 'So you're a budding author, are you?'

Went to pigeon camp for boots – and got a pair too small. Bought lots of goods at YMCA en route. Got back and found that Paul had called for me several times at digs.

TUESDAY 17 DECEMBER

Morning Paul called again – delight of meeting, and he sat on the bank of the canal in the cold, sketching the exploded bridge, while I wrote. Then walked to Veuville, but my boots hurt as too small. Quids in with a nice, soft-fleshed, pale, dark-eyed girl who spoke German with me for an hour while we discussed the tinned sausages we'd bought at the canteen in Roncq, and which we got Madame to heat up for our tea.

She said that mostly Köln boys had been in Roncq, and they were usually decent. One, about 45, was alone in the house with her sister and he asked her to sleep with him. She refused and he threatened, so she hit him with a glass. Pals entered – what's up? Wounded? He told them and they said 'serve him right'. Her mother had tended a Hun soldier who was ill who couldn't stand the hospital, and he eventually got his ticket. Back in Germany he visited her son who was a prisoner – and put him right. She talked on – so interested in me that she gave me the change due to a soldier on my right. More soldiers came in and danced to flat piano, playing a dragging tune, but as if shy, she went back behind the counter.

THURSDAY 19 DECEMBER

Met Paul in afternoon, he telling me of a strike by 29th Div men. Their corporal speaks for the machine-gun company to the SM. 'We're not coming on parade. Send an officer and we'll speak.' A second lieutenant comes out and complaints are made to him – he says he can do nothing – but if they'll parade, he'll get the OC to see them. They parade and RE steps forward. He states no personal grievance, but speaks on behalf of the men, complaints: '1) staple food: hard-tack biscuits and margarine; 2) No baths or clean shift after a month's wait; 3) No green envelopes or pay except ten francs; 4) Poshing up and parades unnecessary; 5) 9th Div Jocks had gone up the line because they made themselves a nuisance and a danger to Menin. Now, we've behaved ourselves, and not got drunk and though we arrived earlier, don't get sent up the line as we want to our unit – instead we're hanging about here. Do you think our complaints are a just grievance? I do.'

Paul enthusiastically praised the man's efficient representation of the case compared to the officer's behaviour. Anyway, baths at least were arranged *toute suite* – and better rations. Later the men said they wouldn't move unless they got paid. The SM was appealed to, but he didn't appear and instead sent sergeant to phone the adjutant. A tobacco issue was arranged on the spot, but pay only promised at ASO depot. 'If this is a blind, we don't entrain,' said the men. But they were paid.

There were ugly rumours of riots at Le Havre. First of all they wouldn't go up the line at Xmas time, wishing to have Xmas comforts in Havre and not en route. Young officer asked them – begged them for his sake to leave the camp with him – after that do what they like. Then en route they stopped, debated and returned.

SATURDAY 21 DECEMBER

Paul called to say they were moving, so I went to the square to see him off, but couldn't track him. The units coalesced and formed in Menin Square and walked off in fours, a lump forming in my throat as I thus lost Paul again – although here at Menin we have not seen much of each other.

Copied 'Poshing Up' and finished at 2 pm. Good meals now. After tobacco issue walked to Roncq in search of romance. Then with hesitation to the estaminet where Paul and I had had tea. There, robed in black and pathetic, was Gretchen, with RFC man and a drunken 'Skin' from the Royal Inniskillings.

After the RFC man had gone the Skin kept molesting her, seeking to catch her by her arm or seat her on his knee. Old dame and sire smiled in the kitchen, fearful yet trying to be pleasant. Gretchen, agonised, looks desperately at me as if for protection. He argues drunkenly 'Ya know, she wants shagging – that's all she wants.' 'Do you think so? I don't thing she's one of that sort.' I sarcastic.

'What do you mean? They all are.' 'I reckon a girl's not so until she's proved otherwise,' I said, feeling afraid of him. 'Will you fight me for her?' he said suddenly. I certainly didn't stomach fighting for her – he'd certainly knock me out. I sat tense and silent, feeling a weakling. 'Fight?' I said at last. 'What's the need to fight? You asked me a civil question and I gave you a civil answer.' He stupidly repeated, 'Come on now, fight for her.' I saw myself embroiled in a drunken brawl in low-down estaminet and wished I could escape. Of course none entered, whereas ordinarily when not wanted, many would have come in. After drinking two free coffees I departed, feeling a coward, leaving the Skin in possession, but some people came in first.

SUNDAY 22 DECEMBER

Feeling of being neglected here – should perhaps finish the war as odd man attached to odd unit – but this feeling vanished now Paul had moved up. Resigned to Xmas here – regretted I'd stayed. I ought to have ridden or walked off.

Alan Marr joined us today and I got him a place next to me on the floor. We went out and met Bobby Brown and Jonah in the square said they were scouring around for things for Xmas dinner, and going to Abeele. They'd got one or two, not sporty, who wouldn't chip in with the crush – not like the old crowd, only too glad if you arranged things, but carping at the cost. There passed over us like a shadow the thought of the old days at Abeele and Esquelbecq now things of the past, and never again would we have the old frank and generous enjoyments. A different type of man had come out with some of the youngsters – swanky and selfish and finicky.

TUESDAY 24 DECEMBER

Wrote and corrected 'Cant about Khaki'[27] and 'Poshing Up' and gave same to officer.

WEDNESDAY 25 DECEMBER

Christmas Day. Dinner at X Corps Reception Camp – tough boiled beef, spuds and beans (tough), then plum duff – greasy, cold and tacky. Later to supper at about six in large room at the side of the theatre. A concert in the cold, draughty room – Jack Hilton singing the roundelay 'And in this tree there was a burrrrd', and then he encored vociferously.

THURSDAY 26 DECEMBER

Three lorries arrived – for us? Yes. Of course X Corps had made 'em travel on Christmas Day because it took two days to get back. I was sorry to leave Alan, but fear I mainly considered getting away as soon as possible.

SATURDAY 28 DECEMBER

In Tournai we were tipped into yard of a deserted brewery. We all ran up winding stairs, like that of a belfry, and found empty, none-too-clean rooms which we lit by candle. We threw down our bundles in best positions we could choose. Ate bread, marge and jam for our rations, all adjuring the others to leave some for tomorrow. I went out, my romantic nature urging me to quest a private civvy billet, my timidity and indolence of initiative urging me to be content.

In one estaminet sat dark, stout, placid madame whose son was killed in the war – but great gratification over the defeat of the Boche shone in her eyes and courage was revealed by the anecdotes she told of her attitude to Huns. All cafés under some order or other – hers reserved for officers. One had entered, arrogant. 'What have you to drink?' 'I have water.' Ordered to get coffee and got it – but never unless ordered. She not afraid of them.

She said that at big house over the road there was a lady who was well in with the Boche, but she'd have to go away now and never dare come back again as inhabitants incensed and reckon her either a spy or mistress. She herself gave me the impression of being fearless towards the Boche. She said German gendarmes were always wanting your *carte d'identité*, and making themselves a nuisance with childish enquiries. She said that at Charleroi a solder cut a girl's hands off who clapped at rumours of the 'Anglais' coming.

SUNDAY 29 DECEMBER

Rose early, glad to be going back to unit. Out on the road met many lorryloads of civvies coming back from conquered regions, with their bundles and little protection.

Got to Namur in the dark and now a very black ride along riverside road to Andenne. Absolutely pitch dark with a few pinpoints of light across the water. The villages we went through seemed castellated and darkly mysterious like little ports on Scottish lakes.

At Andenne asked for Corps office and met two DRs – asked if they knew the billet. 'Oh yes, we're X Corps DRs.' I didn't know them and it seemed things had changed in the way human things have of forgetting the absent. I felt a bit as if I was out of the current. I told them I was returning from leave, but they showed no interest.

I got directions to the mess where X Corps were billeted. I knocked at the door and went in – Albert was undressing and the supper-table was still littered. 'Bill Pritchard told me he's got a billet for you over the road.' He had a snuffling way of talking, lifting his head a little, closing down his vowels and looking brightly at you. You can go through the room behind. Into the lane and cross over – number eight.

A little elderly lady with dark hair asked me in. 'Is Mr Pritchard here?' She asked me into the back room to warm by the stove. 'Come on up, Oz,' shouted Bill. In front bedroom Bill reposed on ample bed. 'It's nice of you to have made arrangements to receive me,' I said, not knowing until Albert told me that Bill was with X Corps. I told him of the two new DRs. 'The college chums? Oh, they belong to 66th Div – a new div just out. By gosh they think they're lords of creation. Can't ride for nuts. One of them left his bike and walked back and expected Glenny to fetch it because it wouldn't go. Something stuck between the outer casing and saddle-bag.' At this my expectation confirmed of the college chums being all swank.

MONDAY DECEMBER 30

In morning welcomed very much in mess, then got bike and gear. In afternoon to 'Reconstruction' lecture in the cinema – a well-meaning civvy about ideas that should occupy our minds. Cynical interjections by soldiers, and one or two rose and contrasted the realities of class warfare with the idyllic amiable hypotheses of the lecturer. He was an architect with good ideas of house planning to save labour and give room, but the soldier argued what was the good of planning these things when first of all the worker hadn't liberty, cash or opportunity? Red tab only considered feelings of lecturer who'd come quite kindly and without swank, to ameliorate the monotony of soldiers' life. He didn't consider the feelings of the soldier. The officers, tabs and authorities fail to understand the mentality of the men in the army. No imagination.

I burning to say something eloquent and sarcastic and upbraided myself for not doing so. Had gone because Lilley wanted a good audience for the SM. (Lilley learning German at classes held by the Intelligence Officer. I too ikey to go, but used to help Lilley, who with the confidence of the ignorant, kept giving me bits of German as if he were nigh perfect. Still, he was ladlike and nice in many ways.

1919

For some time big talk of dance to which civvies invited. Asked two prominent women of Andenne to ask all the nice girls. Wanted to go but tickets five francs. Lilley asked me to go, so I poshed up, but when the time came, Lilley nowhere to be seen, although he'd asked me to wait for him. Went to our café where I started drinking.

Met Miles coming away, who said all the girls had got partners. 'It's all right, but each couple's fixed up.' Into the front door of the big hall at the end of the square, and passed in without giving ticket – and none remarked on it. If I hadn't been such a fool as to come back and tender ticket, needn't have given it up or paid for same, because I left soon after. I'd asked Wordley if it was a posh dance – meaning were we expected with 'creased' slacks and no leggings, and fearing so, he answered in off-hand way, as if I was a worrier.

All round the walls sat elderly people waiting to take the invitees home. Hung on until 9.30, when Sergeant Ladd shouted cheerily, 'How's it going?' and I like a fool answered, 'No partners,' as if it was his fault, and at once I felt what a mug to grouse and not be successful. Many of our lads couldn't dance properly and the Belgian girls had a different style of dancing, so those fellows who could dance were teaching them. Lilley came in and soon found friends and a way to secure partners. I, so easy and used to the ropes at home, felt stranded here and in the way. Hoofed it to the old café and found Glenny there and a few others.

MONDAY 6 JANUARY

One of the estaminets – the Barcelona – all said had been in sympathy with the Huns when they were there. There were tales of what was done to the girls who'd been mistresses of the Huns after they'd gone – disrobed in the square and publicly humiliated. Belgians very bitter against the Huns. Lilley's landlord said to be a favourite with the Huns, and there was talk that after the retirement of the British, they'd wreck his place. When the Huns cleared out the civvies were up against civvy traitors and had to be restrained by handfuls of our troops. Critical situation for our men and the colonel asked for a thousand – about forty were sent.

TUESDAY 7 JANUARY

Returning from MO's met Lilley, who said, 'Would you like a trip to Brussels?' 'I'm not particular – my bus…' 'You needn't – but someone's got to go, and I thought you might like.' 'I'll go.' But nevertheless, I was annoyed. I'd settled down to routine and wanted to do some humdrum jobs, and starting off at midday like that meant riding back in the dark and throwing over my day's plans. The adventure of the ride, strange to say, appealed to me only little. That lure, today was not great enough to overcome the laziness of a gentle time, though I felt if I went on like that I should let die out the desire for change and adventure that one ought to have.

Took some time to find correct way up out of Namur, but when got going a wonderful ride up the hill, zig-zagging sublimely between wooded slopes.

In Brussels took letter to a French officer at a strange hotel in the Avenue Marnix. At press of button, door swings open. Pale dwarf takes note – harem interior. While I wait outside, tall pale servitors regard from lofty window. Talk with concierge. In the square some twenty gather around my motorbike, for since rubber and metal became scarce with the Huns, not many bikes have been seen.

At a posh café, *thé dansant* advertised. Wished to stop, but timorous of offending authority. Boche prisoners pass, but only the children shout at them. At 4.30, after hunting, struck the correct route out. The fine inn which I saw about five miles out of Brussels at the foot of pleasant hills was like a spa – here a cognac very dear. Then resumed joy-ride. First call, as it was darkling, at tall roomy gaunt inn where natives foregathered in kitchen and I drank coffee and saw to lamp. Next stay at an outside railway crossing, after passing through Wavre, which was bustling, bright and hilarious with British troops, at Gemblous. At another estaminet had a *potage* and then two and a half francs for a wineglass of cognac.

SATURDAY 11 JANUARY

Today Alan Marr got his demob papers. His comments on his OC's remarks on his character. "Efficient motor-cyclist!" By *** I can ride a motor-bike. That should get me a job!' He the first demob.

SUNDAY 12 JANUARY

Morning wrote 'Lectures to Khaki'. Afternoon walked to Gives along the river with Lee, he telling me how his prospects have been ruined by giving them up for war. Walked on and I romantically perused the houses backing on the river. One was broad and wide with many windows, farm-like and very attractive, and wondered what life therein. Not infrequently a couple of lithe figures of girls came intriguingly along the riverbank.

TUESDAY 14 JANUARY

In evening warned unexpectedly for a train trip to Cologne. It was my roster turn, though we shuffled the programme a bit to get it in turn to Cologne – I the first to go. I again, didn't want to, and feared it a little, being vexed at losing pleasant routine and finding perhaps that the boys had moved when returned. But made up mind to take as came, and packed my necessaries.

WEDNESDAY 15 JANUARY

At 1.00, 'DR for Cologne wanted.' Bolted the remainder of my dinner and arrived at the signal office. As I waited, read book – uneasy. Suddenly message that the Cologne train was in, and they'd keep the train if I hurried down. Picked up post – a letter from Adrienne. Got my stuff and humped it, the strain of trying to keep running almost bursting my chest. Bolted through the station and knocked open the door. RTO: 'Are you the DR from Sigs?' 'Yes.'

Somehow got in fine Pullman – it was a RAMC train with folding beds arranged up the sides of the carriage. I found one vacant and I into it. It was exquisite lying in bed and slashing through the moonlit scenery. We cut right through the Ardennes and the twisting hills and river villages with their stee-ples, where I saw khaki moving about, at home as if in England. Strange to see this friendliness and affability and normality. At Durren English, French and Germans all mingling normally.

At Cologne everything normal, as if existed so for years. Civvies ignore you – how surprised as I stepped off train and saw business-ladies with little des-patch bags, intently walking through the station and no eyes for anything save the pavement. At the ticket office were German clerks with English to answer questions. Strange to think these people a few months ago were foaming at the mouth with rage, but were now friendly. At RTO the Hun clerk spoke English politely and with breeding.

To the Hotel Excelsior, guards outside, and went to find signal office up-stairs. Then to DR's billet, where met Micky Turner and Doug Brown, who surprised me by saying what a posh time they were having.

Was directed politely by Huns to the bridge and station, etc. On hoardings very urgent placards – political – representing all shades of opinion – social, democratic, central – all asking civvies to rally to the aid of the falling state by supporting them or the Reds '*Unser grosse Ungluck.*'

Dinner in the pub then down the Durren Road to Wilf's billet – a dark, shadowed room or old cinema theatre behind an inn. Was told he'd gone to the city but caught him outside at a stationer's, talking English with them. I tried to talk German, but found myself rusty. We went to Bonn by tramcar and as I alighted saw a Tommy in altercation with Hun civvy lift hand and hit the civvy a heavy crack on the head. Civvy hopped it – spectators passive. Tommies grin. Why the blow unless the soldier drunk?

Quick walk round the narrow streeted city, we having a job to find our way back to the cars in time. Returned in crowded car but not asked to pay. When the conductress came smiling, and asked for the fare I said, '*Englische Soldaten – nichts bezahlen.*'

In evening to the gorgeous room that housed the YMCA and then to the pantomime in the *Deutsches Theater*. Back to mess and met with Paul – he demobbing. At eleven to office and the GHQ man called me to say he was going, so I hopped it too.

THURSDAY 16 JANUARY

Back at Andenne, got to the signal office at 1.30, where the ADS wanted to know how I got on. I was breathing high and hard and nervous to be called to interview by him, and couldn't do myself justice. Wanted to be smart in my description of Cologne, yet also to curb myself and show mellow and restrained cynicism thereat.

Got pay and told yarns to the boys as I ate my hugely enjoyed dinner. It was fine to be back among them.

THURSDAY 23 JANUARY

To Profondeville – full of troops and a division was stationed there with staff in a small château and the signals in a house. The village old fashioned and dreamy and chill. The boys welcomed me and gave me a fine dinner – it was so nice to drop in on a crush of DRs – always a good meal and plenty of jokes.

Afternoon rumours of our going to Germany, and our ADS flying to Cologne. Hear we are to go, so in evening wrote and packed and like a fool gave up the maps I had of the stricken battle zone between Ypres and Menin. Two things influenced me – timidity of contravening authority and not wanting to carry too much.

We quite wished to stay at Andenne. However, our fears that we should have to march about the street in pairs and not go out after nightfall, or might be shot in the back were dissipated when we heard of the fraternising between the British and Germans, and by my experiences in Cologne, so we now didn't so much mind going.

FRIDAY 24 JANUARY

Now we had to clear up our belongings again and leave our nice billet, and Madame was disconsolate.

SATURDAY 25 JANUARY

I foozling, so Bill helped me to get my things sorted, with Lilley cursing me for being delayed. We shook hands with Madame, leaving five francs each for the boy. We ought to have bought Madame something, but her husband might have been jealous and we were short of cash. She broke into tears and I was much moved. I was shaking hands with Mr Moreau when he suddenly grabbed me hard, hugged me to him, burst into a howl of pain and kissed me, his unshaven cheek prickling me.

As we approached the border at Henri-Chapelle, some villages in ruins from Hun transit in 1914, burnt down in spite on 5 August because of resistance in Liege.

In a little café we chafed our frozen hands and threw off packs that grooved, pained and cramped our shoulders, and removed the lumps of dirt from skin and eye. We sat there drinking coffee, wishing to remain. Towards the border, land very drear and fairly flat. No definite mark of border, save Belgian sentries knocking about.

Over the border, all more practical and solid and English in style – and cleaner. Then the environs of Aachen with woods, deep and fine with lodges, restaurants and holiday resorts. Dropped in at dusk, round to *Kaserne*, where we were shown up to our rooms by German civvy guide hanging round the barracks. I went and begged coffee from the French, who were very nice and willing.

Our room was upstairs, with high iron beds and dim electric light, a bit grim with umber shadow, but there was a stove. The boys got me to enquire of two restaurants if we could get beds there, but the hotel-keeper glib, and told us that all rooms, and indeed hotels in Aachen were '*besetzt*' by French officers. They said to try the *Stadt*.

In town we stood uncertain at first, watching pedestrians in the thick crowd. We were unsure – should we engage a hotel? Majority, fearless of experiences or offending anyone's feelings, wanted to. At last at *Vier Jahrzeiten Hotel* we drank. The toffs here looked at us scornfully.

We went to *Bierhalle*. Round this large room were painted and built up of wood or card, Gothic scenery – castles, and mills, like paper models we used to make as schoolboys. We drank here, there being fierce-looking official Huns with bristly hair and many painted women drinking with Frenchies. After to cinema – without paying – then back to the hotel where we asked the girl for a number of rooms. The liftman wanted half of us to walk, but the manager told him to '*zweimal fahren*'. Lovely clean rooms with lights, beds and lavs. Charlie wanted to have supper but I was timid of asking and said I didn't want any, and persuaded Bill not to. In reality I didn't wish to create unpleasantness with the manager.

SUNDAY 26 JANUARY

In the morning into the *Frühstuckszimmer* where the waiter brought coffee – ersatz. '*Haben sie Brot?*' I summoned up courage to ask. He brought brown bread and ersatz jam that tasted like mashed rhubarb – tolerable only. This breakfast was three marks for seven of us – beds 28 marks for eight, supper 55 marks for five.

In the morning found way to Knickertsberg and the old shop I'd visited before. We kerbed up our bikes and kids gathered round, blowing the horns and pinching the tyres when we went in. As I entered the shop the old mother came in – I'd forgotten her with her drawn drum-skin face, shiny cheekbones and plaintive but kindly air. She the same, but a stoop of fifteen years gathered to her. '*Sie erinnern sich an mich?*' I asked. '*Nicht?*' '*Nein.*' Finchen enters. 'Mr Mann?' said the old lady. '*Nein.*' 'Ah, Mr Davis,' said Finchen, smiling. Then Marie entered, grown into a fine girl. The old man came stalking out of the kitchen in the old way – wiry, hale and cheery. Then Johann. I had feared we should be unwelcome owing to the war – didn't know if we would be received with scowls – but all made heartily welcome and crowded into front room, drinking wine and eating *Zwieback*, while the old man gave us a cigar each. Very generous as they had practically no resources or reserves of food.

Then over the road to Johann's house – he house-proud with two kids and a nice dark missus. Joseph came, silent and inscrutable as ever, with Iron Cross. '*Im Kriege, vom Anfang bis Schluss*'. We talked together, Johann throwing in bits of English and I talking French when I tried to talk German and mixing the two – in fact speaking three tongues. A joyous assembly, the boys grinning and the village kids outside, blowing our horns. The burden of their remarks was it was not their fault, not ours – couldn't be helped – nothing against us or we against them, but fatalistic. Fritz, the next youngest to Joseph, had been killed, as had Marie's fiancé, and Joseph had been wounded and put on reserve or garrison work. I was full of gladness that we were all reconciled again.

At Bonn civvies were very courteous and obliging when we asked the way. We rode round and round – it seemed a maze and Charlie didn't know where the signal office was. At last, outside the station, we parked up the buses and waited as it started to snow. We knew we had to go to a barracks, and while Charlie enquired at the big red building, now housing some division, Harding and I went into a large restaurant – cosy inside. *Bohnenkaffee* in thick white cups and saucers, with saccharine tablets for sugar.

Outside I asked a kid where '*die Kasernen*' were and he told me the barracks were at the end of the street. We parked bikes up outside the main entrance and up the stairs. There old Albert had got some hot tea and we fell on to bully and bread like wolves. One of the most enjoyable meals I've ever had. Jonah and Vic, who had preceded us by a day or two were going out in the snow, Jonah grousing and giving me an idea of trying to work in snow and dark, and hostile Huns if I had to go out quick. Our pleasure soon over and back to business quickly.

Harding out, so Bill and I tossed for who should take night duty. I felt a bit of a cad letting him take it because he lost. Slept well, we having two-tier iron-frame beds with mattresses and a fine big stove.

MONDAY 28 JANUARY

In evening to *Operetten Theater* – good music, but rotten acting. I booked good seats and we enjoyed it though I could understand little. A piece of Schubert and it seemed silly rot to me.

With rebellion in the air we discussed the hardship of the orders that had come out, calling us to parade at six. 'Trying to give it us in the neck as soon as we get here – the barrack stunt. If we put up with this they'll always have a down on us,' grumbled Lee. 'Let's shoot the bloody SM.' 'I vote we don't go on, that's all,' said Glenny. 'We're mugs if we start it,' said Bill. 'I'll stick out with anyone,' volunteered Jonah. 'I've no grievance,' I said. I couldn't honestly object to rising early as we weren't working hard.

TUESDAY 29 JANUARY

At six Bill Pritchard said, 'Why go on?' Harding acquiesced – which surprised me as he a family man. Glenny and Bobby said they'd stay, then Harding asked

Jonah and Vic – and they said they were game to refuse, but I feared they wouldn't stick it.

Lilley came. 'Now then, show a leg. Don't play the fool.' 'We're not coming on parade,' said Bill – the only one to answer. 'We're not thinking of coming on.' 'Why not?' 'We're not thinking of coming on, that's all.' 'Look here, it's no use you chaps playing that mug's game. You'll come a mucker.' He out and back again. 'I tell you, you'll get properly in the shit.' He went out.

We heard the parade. He came in. 'All who did not parade will appear at the 9 o'clock parade.' I had the wind up as I thought matters over. This was mutiny in the British Army, for which we could be shot, and my conviction wasn't behind the do. Should we all stick together and come out successfully? I afraid, and wished we hadn't changed the pleasure of our routine by this silly act.

Each was to give a different excuse – for if we all gave the same, that would be concerted action, liable for punishment as rebellion. We spruced up and at parade much tension, the SM keeping us after all the others had gone and apparently not knowing what to do. He dismissed us, then called us back. 'As you were.' The OC was on parade, but nothing said. How we chuckled triumphant to ourselves. Lilley came down and said 'Why didn't we lodge a formal complaint?' We said we'd groused enough about it and he ought to have presented our case. He now asked us to lodge a formal complaint, so we did so. He took this to the OC, and later it transpired the OC's judgement was that the order to parade at 6.30 wasn't meant for DRs, and was an error. Victory for us.

We were congratulated by the office telegraphers on our strike. They and some cable men tried the same dodge next day, and all absent were fined several days' pay and given CB. How we laughed there-over, and thought ourselves favoured.

No need for us to parade at all, said Lilley. All a mistake… But would we do fatigues in clearing the shed to use as tiff's room? Glenny grousing – why couldn't the SM let us have a nice shed already and waiting with electric light fixed? But we were willing to play the game over these fatigues, and we did them, clearing the sheds of refuse – bombs and gun fittings, machinery and scrap.

FRIDAY 31 JANUARY

Off duty so away to Wilf's and had dinner in the dim, low lit room. After dinner Wilf showed me Ettie's letter. I was surprised he hadn't shown it me before. It put the wind up me as she seemed bad and on the edge of breakdown. I reproached myself with not trying harder to get away. On the spot, after reaching decision, we concocted a letter to Ettie and decided that Wilf should see his PC. If he couldn't get away, I should try.

SATURDAY 1 FEBRUARY

Wilf went to the orderly room to see if he could get away. He soon came out again. No luck. His OC said that although his case was good, there were other worse cases, and he had to consider men who had enlisted earlier than Wilf. Suggested I tried for demob.

To the pictures – fair – then to International Café where pretty girls were sitting and drinking, subtly bold and looking to me as if waiting for prey. Noticed their teeth poor.

In the evening to chamber music concert in the *Burgerhalle*. Only a few soldiers, and classy Germans in front of us, who looked at us as if we were English philistines who had no right to take an interest in music.

TUESDAY 4 FEBRUARY

To see OC at 9.45 and told him my case. He said there were many cases – some harder.

Bill and I went and bought skates in a big shop by the tram square, then scoured round for a pond to skate on. We tried one pool in the gardens on the outskirts of the city, but it appeared to be private grounds, as a man came and remonstrated and said we'd get him the sack. So we shifted and went to Poppelsdorf. Here the ice was not yet used, and Bill, daring, went on and walked to and fro. Although it cracked if we were together, we both went on. Good – much enjoyed.

In evening in the tram translated notices which urged Germans not to use any more British or French terms. Went to the *Storch* – a brilliantly lit restaurant with an orchestra on a platform. Youngsters of eighteen to twenty-three sat drinking by us and said, 'Discipline used to be very severe in the German Army. Only as an officer does one begin to be a human being. The soldiers – animals.' Also, 'Before the war, Rhinewine 80 pfennigs a bottle – now seven marks or more.'

THURSDAY 6 FEBRUARY

Good skate in morning, in spite of thaw, outside edging being painfully acquired and taught to Bill. Now as we came back day after day with glowing faces, the other boys began to get into it, and Harding and Lee besought me to buy the skates so they could join us.

SUNDAY 9 FEBRUARY

A big battalion had come to lodge in our barracks, and this morning they were drilling finely in the square. As I watched with my skates in my hand, Wally called out, 'Oz, you're wanted in the orderly room for demob.' Refused to believe that such a message had been phoned through – but true. So to orderly room, not sad and not glad, but the lilt of change in my movements. However, after dinner sad.

Later sat at the table and wrote home. I felt as I wrote that I engaged on a tack that was splitting my life and leading me from adventure and romance to emptiness – and I had caused it. It was in my power to stop it. Yet here I was, mechanically, as if driven by some power, pushing my own doom. I seemed to watch myself doing it and to wish ardently to stop myself, knowing that all the while I was completing the disaster and making any reprieve impossible.

I hadn't the right, however, to follow what I desired. It was my duty to get home, so I pressed aside all the bewitching enchantments of army life as now led, and pressed on to duty.

I admit as well, that underneath this was the feeling that there might be trouble in Germany, and perhaps I was as well out of it. I remembered Wally showing me a prophecy in a magazine about a Bible reading, that in spring 1919 there would begin a more terrible war than had ever been…

Packed, almost in tears.

As finished, Glenny offered me whatever I liked to take – spare tubes, plugs, etc, bar a magneto. I took a spare tube and a plug, thinking I'd supplied the army with a lot. But that tube, though I hung on to it, was a bugbear all through my trip home.

Left at 6.20 and when wished goodbye by the fellows, and one or two hand-shakes, could scarcely speak and I turned my back – which was eloquent of grief.

Got to the *Kaserne* in Cologne at 8.30. In the chill barrack-room, compared this with the cheerful quarters in Bonn, but though I was miserable, I took it stoically. My name not called, so saw SM and he said, 'Do as you wish. Make yourself scarce – don't get pissed – and return the 12th.'

Met up with Wilf and we got a lift to Cologne and down to the park, where we skated. Ice hockey played in British style, but as far as outside edge and figure skating went, the Germans beat us. Even young girls were outside-edging, as easy as you like. The girls and most of the Germans were stylishly dressed with garb moulding their figures.

WEDNESDAY 12 FEBRUARY

Back to camp. OC: 'Show me your papers.' I produced them. 'Don't throw them down,' he snarled. 'Open them out. You're free until nine. If not back until after that hour, you go back to your unit.' How I hated the swine and his nasty carping manner. After being of some importance and helping in a minor revolution in the army, this manner shocked my new-found *amour propre* and spoilt the first part of the morning.

In the evening rushed round choosing presents and buying nothing decent – then to Palant Restaurant and split some bottles of wine on my going with one or two others.

THURSDAY 13 FEBRUARY

Next day parade at 7.30 – was put into the Dover group, and we were marched to the station. Our sturdy SM thrust civvy men and women back firmly who tried to break our rank. 'We're not civvies like you blighters yet.' He held up the traffic for us, 'Do 'em good,' as we whistled down the *Strasse*.

At 12.30 hot Machonochies, very welcome as we lay in the cold trucks like cattle. At Verviers in afternoon sunlight and into files for cheese and tea, but we were tired with the long wait. At Huy slipped out of warming truck as sleeping and raced along the street to tables in the rest camp, where served tea and cheese. None seemed to know exactly where and what we were after but we followed our leader solidly, trekking through the night.

FRIDAY 14 FEBRUARY

Called out for breakfast and waited in a weary queue at the Halte and Repas station. At 5 pm second H and R station – a long queue alongside huge factory with canvas roofing to keep rain off waiters. Got down to sleep at seven, then called out at 11.50, fatigued and sleepy, into the raw cold air to a third H and R station. Ran along and over rails, slipping in puddles and fearing I was too late to get back to train.

SATURDAY 15 FEBRUARY

Awakened at six to detrain. Relieved nature at the side of embankment.

Walked to Dunkirk to No 1 A Camp. Tired out. First they led us round to tents, then the eternal queue for brekker of cold beef – not much – with tea and bread and marge. Tales of pockets and kits being searched and some of the men quite windy, producing brooches, etc in boxes, evidently looted. 'They can't do anything with yer for this can they?' 'They can do anything in the army with yer, bar put you in the family way.' I began to wonder if I could shove my inner tube under the tent floor and wished I hadn't brought it.

Proceeded to square – all mud – where much gear opened out and getting dirty. Opened my valise and officer glanced at it. Would have done better to stay outside all together and take no notice.

Then we were marched round lugubrious camps and tents to large sheds. File in – no instructions. Then a casual soldier shouts, 'Take off khaki and underclothing. Keep only cap, belt, puttees and boots. Put your valuables in your cap. Crammed my cap full of things. Hung coat, tunic, trousers, cardigan and overcoat (with tube in pocket) on coathanger 74. Left own socks and own wool combs, and as did so, saw that all the wear was being dumped in sacks held by Jerry. These grinning Jerries looked on at us, we were thus humiliated by nudity before them. If only someone had told us what was to happen, could have saved my all-wool garment that cost 12/6.

Stripped naked we queued to doctor, dumb like animals. Doctor tells us to stretch out arms. In front of Jerries we walked thus, round into another room where our khaki came back to us, fumigated. New shirt, pants, fine old lamb's wool vest washed, vile old socks, were on bench awaiting us. Who responsible for this method of treating victors of the campaign? Might have had Englishmen instead of Jerries. Formed up again and marched off to boat.

Lined up, called into drafts as per dispersal centre, as 'A Draft, B Draft, No 4 Wing, 2 Camp.' Original dispersal certificate taken by the sergeant in charge.

Shown to tents again and issued tickets for dinner. What to happen – stay or move? No word. Then on blackboard erected in front of messroom was announced in white chalk, 'Draft B Chisledon. Tea at 4 pm, roll call at 4.45'. This altered to tea at 3 pm, tea at 4.45, roll call at 5. Probably away on Sunday 16th.

SUNDAY 16 FEBRUARY

A 5.45 I rise and arrange my gear. Out to a huge queue – men patient but shouting, 'Put a jerk into it,' and telling off men going out of turn. Spent half an hour in dim chill morn with blankets weighing on arms and muddying in chill drizzle of rain. At last some tea and bread, then out and parade – off in 29 minutes.

Away – five kilos trudge through ugly Dunkirk, seeming as if it would never end. Even when we arrived at sight of water and ships the quays seemed interminable. At last formed up – I cursed again the vile army system of rest camps as I sweated. Into single file and on board – AT LAST.

Arrive dully at Dover – no reception, but given a bun and cup of tea in a hall reception, flagged and cheerful with ladies about.

On train to Clapham Junction, switch to Basingstoke, then Andover. At Chiseldon by 10.30 pm and 20 minutes' walk to the camp – good, clean and well-lit. In tent one soldier says, 'Next time I lay down they'll have to lead me by the hand. How much do they give you? £2 – can ye get blindo on that?'

MONDAY 17 FEBRUARY

Rose at six. Men coughing awful. Handed in blankets and queued in drizzle while staff lounge about.

Dispersal procedure:
1. Roll call.
2. Dark shed. Roll call of tens – rudely shouted at, 'Don't talk to yourself. Speak up.'
3. Room with tables – spread out kit and told to hand in valise, and a cheap hessian sack was given to us. (Told to give up belt, which I'd taken off, but I kept it – slipped it under tunic.)
4. Ordnance room – gave up equipment – mess-tin, etc and valise. (We could have shoved it in the sack with private belongings.) Also handed in pistol and pouch.
5. Rifle room. Here men handed in rifle and bayonets. I passed through giving nothing.
6. Suit room. Three sample cloths shown on dummies – or go to table and have voucher checked if not being measured for suit.
7. Various tables – unemployment insurance, suit voucher checked. Paid for suit voucher – £2 15 shillings. Paybook taken.
8. A parson to welcome you – urging you to tell your experiences so that war sacrifices may turn into life sacrifices – those people may perceive what you've done and be willing to do their turn too in the times to come. By your experiences, help to arrest rotten wave of unrest and Bolshevism. These blithering idiots – I don't know what to call them – he incoherent. I thought his remarks in extreme bad taste and fatuous.
9. Heated waiting room. No word that we were discharged. As we walked about cheese and bread and marge were given us.
10. Received envelope with ration book, Protection and Identity certificate and unemployment book.

11. Party to train. At 10.30 away from pretty station where we saw WAACs walking about. During the war this village must have been a good billet. Waited half an hour then to Swindon.

Here a cup of tea then on to Cheltenham where I parted from Freddy and two other pals. Got to New Street by three and had coffee and cake with Fred in the Station Street café. Walked home – Ettie at the door.

TUESDAY 18 FEBRUARY

Down at 8.45 and lit fire and got in coal. Did odd jobs and read. Stayed in after tea. Thaw and then frost.

SATURDAY 22 FEBRUARY

In shop all day – felt better today, but cold or chill in head. Viewed future with rather grey doubts. Felt the loss of the boys – not the thrill of leave holidays in enjoyment now. That miracle removed for ever. Strange, the taking up of civvy life again, using heavy coins instead of notes – all round loss of prestige.

SUNDAY 23 FEBRUARY

Morning rush and to chapel. After dinner, a pull at the bell – Harding's manageress – chimney down – can I arrange. I annoyed and spoke rather crustily. As soon as I'm back, this damned property. Why me?

MONDAY 24 FEBRUARY

Worked in shop. In evening to Arcadians' dance with Ettie – very enjoyable.

WEDNESDAY 26 FEBRUARY

Morning in stockroom going over the heaps of stock with amazement and feelings of insurrection to find that stock so high when inflated prices bound to fall so. Thought of all the money we've worked so hard for, turned into stock that will fall in price instead of in bank. Tried to bottle up wrath and say nothing to Ettie, but couldn't help snarling and being dryly bitter.

FRIDAY 28 FEBRUARY

Looking at stock, in reality must have been £450 upstairs alone, and £600 in the cellar. Wept inwardly at sight of stock, so soon to fall headlong in value.

THURSDAY 6 MARCH

This day and all others, much time given to concerns of business. Several dances, which I enjoyed.

SUNDAY 9 MARCH

Wilf arrived unexpectedly and I discussed business with him, and the fact that I'd sacked Miss Oakley, saying to her, 'No doubt with your husband about to be demobbed, you'll welcome release. I'm going to get a man in, which will suit me better.'

MONDAY 10 MARCH

Mr Shuffrey arrived – I anxious how he'd shape, he dressing door with stands backwards. Should I point out the error? No. And it proved not a bad idea, but at first I thought he was unaware how to dress outside displays.

TUESDAY 18 MARCH

Today started Miss Aston as apprentice. Good. Went to All Saints' private dance and enjoyed it – in uniform still, meeting Miss Flavell and her pal. She bustling, plump and friendly, and beautiful of eye. They had no partners and I danced freely with them.

SATURDAY 29 MARCH

Busy in shop with sale. Marking laces – sold some pink voile.

SUNDAY 30 MARCH

This morning snow – but it melted quickly. Found by church bells and the milkman that the clocks moved on today. Housework – mother in bed, resting. Revised book of poems. Afternoon read and cogitated. Heard from Vic Turnpenny that he'd been recommended by Wetham for sergeant in charge of pigeons in the Second Army. This made me feel bitter and perturbed, seeing how, after working so hard, I'd missed the fruits of my work by leaving army at this time. The job I coveted would have been mine, had I remained as I had wished in Germany. Galling this, and it upset me when I read the news.

OTHER WORKS OF OSWALD HARCOURT DAVIS

VERSE

Poems – 1900
The Phoenix Lyre – 1903
Town Moods – 1907
Home Heroics – 1908
The Nite Ride – 1913
London Pastels – 1920

PROSE

The 'Ardencester' Novels of Birmingham life:
Soft Goods – 1923
Smite The Rock! – 1924
Home Brewed – 1932

The Master: A Study of Arnold Bennett –1965
George Gissing: A Study in Literary Leanings – 1965
This Great City – 1966

Here are a few of the contemporary criticisms and original publisher's notes on some of his works:

Home Heroics: "… a young man of genius" – *Manchester City News.*
Soft Goods: "… sincere, humorous and sensitively observant" – *Times Literary Supplement.*

The Master
"Although this book was written by Oswald Davis shortly before the end of World War II, it is published now posthumously because it is believed to be of interest to scholars and admirers of Arnold Bennett."

"Mr. Davis and Bennett met in 1915 and from this meeting came a correspondence between them lasting ten years. Mr. Davis was thoroughly familiar with the Five Towns, Birmingham and the potteries as they were then and during the times in which the novels are set. More than a mere scholar of Bennett, Mr. Davis was an enthusiastic admirer of the master and read and re-read many times the more than eighty works of this pre-eminently English and homely author."

George Gissing

"In this monograph, Oswald Davis sets out to trace what divides Gissing's public into two camps : those who, like Davis, find unfailing pleasure in this eminently readable Victorian : and those who find him thoroughly depressing!"

"In Gissing's own words, he set out to deal 'in a romantic spirit with the gloomier facts of life'. Mr. Davis' appreciation goes beyond the mere academic appraisal of 'the way Gissing does things' – the rhythm and precision of his prose, his immense erudition, his psychological insight, and the originality and pithiness of his dialogue – so that he concludes that Gissing's appeal, when it occurs, must be personal, immediate and almost intuitive…"

This Great City

"This last of Oswald H. Davis's posthumous works is the closing chapter of his 'Ardencester' (Birmingham) series of novels. It portrays the life of a Birmingham citizen during 1900-1930 and, to those who remember 'old Brum' breathes into being those vanished days."

"The hero breaks from the bars of his employer's office to realise his ambition to be an artist. But while himself struggling for recognition, he sees surpassing him, and from the same art school, 'D.J.', a most sought-after painter of more popular appeal.

"The author's acute observation of character holds firm throughout the changing fortunes of his hero. During his period of painting in France, and later in his war-time work, the theme recurs that brilliance of exultancy in art or music can exist inexplicably and independently of the performer's real regard for his own field.

"When, at Ypres, our unregarded hero has toiled to portray the saddest truths in paint, who should appear but 'D.J' resplendent from his London triumphs, and now a specially-commissioned War artist?

"The final blow falls after the war, when cataract affects the hero's sight and he turns to music, 'the greatest of the arts', owning his debt to this great city."

APPENDIX

ARMY PIGEONS – HOW THEY WORK

Reproduced from an article in the *Daily Mail*, Wednesday, 13 February 1918, page 2, Issue 6821.

EVEN ARMY SIGNALLERS ARE OFTEN IN THE DARK AS TO HOW pigeons work. The public may be excused, therefore, for finding their curiosity aroused rather than satisfied by casual pictures and paragraphs in the Press on the carrier-pigeon service.

What actually happens, as far as it may be politic to disclose, is this: From Army lofts in backward areas numbers of trained pigeons are conveyed to points in the line. Pairs of these birds are afterwards released from the trenches with duplicate tissue messages carried in a light metal clip fix to the leg. The liberated birds "home" from the line back to their own loft and drop quickly through the slats of a trap device with which the loft roof is furnished. The clip cylinder and the written "flimsy" packed neatly within it are at once removed and the message is despatched thence by other means to its exact address.

Behind this simple arrangement is the varied organisation of a service that has trebled itself within my knowledge. The supply of birds to the line is now as regular as a postal service. On the Somme film can be seen of a despatch-rider taking up the "parrots" in a large square basket. That is one method employed. To make good the losses incurred during bad weather or operations, lofts have to be replenished; or young birds may be bred from their own stock.

* * *

Once they are "settled", new pigeons are "tossed" at increasing distances from the loft to the battle sector from which they are required to make a line of flight. By observation plus instinct, most of the birds learn rapidly their route from the trenches. Shy at first, the pigeons get "wise" to shell-fire, and old birds make away from the dug-outs with knowing swiftness.

Besides fixed lofts there exist many mobile pigeon cotes – lofts that can be moved forward on wheels, like caravans, to follow up an army's advance. When such a loft is moved to a fresh area the birds tend to return to their old pitch. They have to be "broken"; they are worried off the old ground, re-settled by the wiles of the loft man, and trained again from the new location as soon as they are used to it. British Army lofts, in charge of soldiers of expert pigeon experience, are under strict supervision. The birds are checked in and out, their flights charted, and their time portioned out like the hours of a contract. Men from the ranks are periodically taken through a course of instruction which comprises handling pigeons and clip-fixing, care of birds in the trenches, writing messages, and judging good conditions for flight.

To ensure quick trapping, birds should be kept hungry but not thirsty, released in pairs of the same sex, and tossed in clear, suitable weather. "Pigeoneers" differ: men from the pigeon racing counties put great faith in the "mickies"; they are serious as priests and full of punctilio in a branch of signals which has to put up with a lot of banter.

The service is taken in grim earnest by the Boche, who paints his pigeons, issues a good clip, and ingeniously protects his birds against gas. Pigeons are in good odour with us, as they appeal to our sporting instinct. It is exciting to get a speedy flight with a good message through storm and fire. In good daylight weather the birds will get their messages through quickly with great regularity.

Pigeons are rarely shot dead while flying. A bird with shrapnel in the breast or a broken beak will gamely try to carry its missive home. In bad weather pigeons will beat up to the loft exhausted, rather than give in. They are hardy, will recover from exposure to gas, and will mend and carry on after a wound.

Altogether, the King has few more devoted and loyal, though unwitting, workers than pigeons.

D.

EXAMPLES OF OSWALD'S ORIGINAL SUBMISSIONS TO THE PRESS BUREAU

WAR ZONE ESTAMINETS.

GIVE AND TAKE WITH TOMMY.

SHORT ARTICLE, length 670 words, By Oswald H. Davis
(Contributor to Daily Mail, Daily News, Punch,
Country Life, Academy, Poetry Review, Everyman,&c.).

ADDRESS: Cpl. O. H. Davis, 148768, Despatch Rider,
X Corps H. Q. Signal Coy., B. E. F., France.

"Bon soir, Jack. Comment allez vous?"

"Très beans, Julie, but plenty fatigué and beco soif."

"Better the war finish, eh m'sieurs? When you think?"

"Finish to-morrow---peut-être!" grins Jack.

For bringing a beer Julie receives a "Merci cocoa"
and 2½d. The evening usually starts with some such libret-
to of the French-English comic opera that holds sway
nightly in the numerous estaminets up and down the front.

The floor is stone-flagged and provides standing
for tables covered with gaily painted leatherette,
chairs, a pram-shaped stove which juts out into the
room at the end of a huge pipe, and a tiny buffet in
one corner.

1

WAR TIME ESTAMINETS – GIVE AND TAKE WITH TOMMY (UNDATED)

From this doll's counter and a case of shelves behind,
reinforced by a pocket cellar, issue the staple drinks
here---red and white wine, Porto, light stout and beer.
The estaminet, correspoding to English tavern, has
always an immense coffee-pot on the stove, can supply an
omelette, and is the national house of call in Belgium
and Northern France.

Two men under full pack enter.   The elder, glancing
humorously over his glass, says:

"Bonne santé, m'selle!. Promenade with you ce soir
très bon, eh?"

"I no promenade with you," promptly retorts Julie,
picking up the gage thrown down.   "You married.   Plenty
picaninnies!"

("Six!" murmurs his pal slyly)

"Soldiers never married---jamais!,"   Julie is
gravely assured.

"Me promenade with you after the war!"   says Julie.

2

And with that clinching phrase---"après la guerre"---
always effective, the bout of chaffing is closed.

Suddenly the comrade rises. "Silence for a good
song and a good singer," calls the married one.

The "cobber" hangs his head and bays forth,
perspiring, in a mournful key, a keenly sentimental
lay. A lean man then launches solemnly into falsetto---
great applause. The fat comic contributes a song
to which the accompaniment is vamped with muscular
monotony, and a dark Irishman follows with a long
tricky chorus to his ditty.

Such is a typical estaminet evening.

     :   :   :   :   :

Some estaminets are more boisterous. Here the
sturdy waitress, chaff-hardened, almost commits
assault and battery on the unfortunate soldier who
tenders a five-franc note.

"You no change?" she bawls. (You feel her voice

3

WAR TIME ESTAMINETS – PAGE 3

like a bludgeon.) "Hota!   I'm give all my change
away.   You no change, no glass beer!"

But if this threat be unproductive, she contrives to
ferret out the required sous and various current franc-
notes, soiled and frayed, issued by towns of the
province.

"'Tis eight o'clock!" is her next slogan.   "Time
to close.   Hurry up, if you please.   Police come
tout-de-suite.   'Tis eight o'clock.   Allez!"

And she sweeps glasses away and propels her clients
doorward, while the canary family, which every
estaminet sacredly maintains, flutter their fine cage
over the clamour of the departing guests.

Estaminet hours for the British army are 12 to 2
and 6 to 8; and during these four crowded hours the
two-storey red-tiled buildings often extract from
a generous and passive soldiery the profits of a small
gold-mine.

4

Our favourite resort last year had its ebony piano, walnut-wood gramaphone, stove polished like a dynamo, and dainty casement curtains. The painted motto, "Hier vloekt men niet" (Flemish, "No bad language, please!") sounded from its cosy corner the keynote of the room. Scrupulously conducted by two comely girls (worthy parents in the background), it was the home of good song and good champagne, where troops coming to and fro the line could shed the coarse and the crude, and feel for an hour and English refinement.

From this to the fantastic wooden shacks built by refugees at the roadside, the contrast is extreme. Their walls are built of staves purloined from army stores boxes, their roofs of felt, with flashings and spouts turned from army biscuit tins. On the door is the legend, "Coffee, eggs, chips, beer/. Washing done for soldiers." But though within the floor be earthen and the benches hard, the welcome is warm, and Tommy is soon "quids in", generously foregoing unfair comparison with his native inns, so easeful and prodigal of habit in Blighty's days of peace.

5

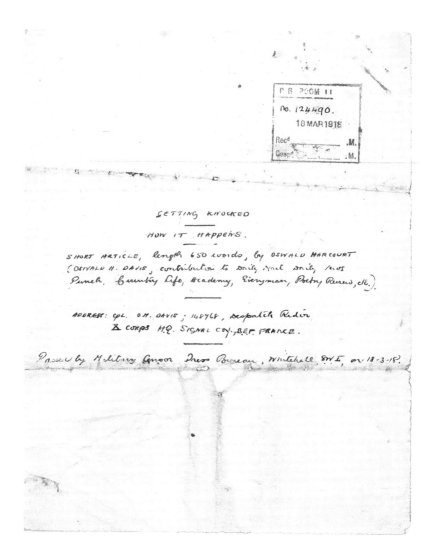

GETTING KNOCKED – HOW IT HAPPENS (MARCH 1918)

GETTING 'KNOCKED.'

HOW IT HAPPENS.

By OSWALD HARCOURT.

SHORT ARTICLE, length 650 words, By Oswald H. Davis
(Contributor to Daily Mail, Daily News, Punch,
Country Life, Academy, Poetry Review, Everyman, etc.).

Address: Cpl. O. H. Davis, 148768, Despatch Rider,
X Corps H.Q. Signal Coy., B. E. F., France.

I ought to have 'rumbled' it as soon as I saw that the
M. P. had deserted the crossroads for his handy dug-out.
The road, between house-blocks which, long ago, had been
razed like teeth snapped short at the gums, was sprinkled
with earth strewn by bursts. Round the bend, the way
was still glistening from water-spurts of shells dropping
in the moat alongside. There was not a soul to be seen:
obviously the lull in fire was only temporary. But I wanted t
get through with my job and not keep dinner waiting. I
was bringing up the line by motor-cycle another load of
carrier pigeons for reserve.

1

With the usual crashes, following on abrupt uprisings of
grey-brown spouts of earth, Jerry started 'bumping' again.
I saw, blocking my route, a fallen tree, débris, and a
motor-cycle on its side. I braked my own machine down,
pulled her on the stand, and ran, scared.

ital.

"Damn it, I might as well fix her properly at the side
of the road!"

I turned back and, propping her up anew, jumped for my
only shelter, a naked wall. Two men crouched on the
hither side.

"Where are you going, digger?" was their greeting.

"The dug-out just beyond the railway."

ital

"Then I should b-------- well get there tout-suite.
He's been pumping hell over this last hour."

to patch

I began to leap like a frog from patch between old
shell-holes. I stumbled choking and sneezing through
the fume and brickdust of a close burst.

2

It was the moment when you feel, "I'm going to be knocked this time---certain." The fields, sky, shell-clouds, grey road, seemed all parts of a menacing scenery staged for death.

The railway spanned a stream-gully, along which I clambered. As I came to the rough bridge, its trestle supports caught the large square pigeon basket strapped on my back. Unfastening this, I saw two men beckon me to join them where they knelt beside an embankment dug-out. "I prefer our own dug-out," I decided; got the basket off and stepped under the bridge.

The beams and the ground shook. Through the arch I saw débris shower down. Clods, stones, sleepers, iron rails, seemed to go on falling around, fountain-like, for several minutes. "A horrible way to get killed," I muttered---"crushed under a bridge."

Nothing happened. I leapt out, ran back for the

3

neglected basket of pigeons, and scraping a way with my
burden along the narrow entrance passage, reached the
sodden clay steps that dropped to the water-logged dug-out
below.   White-faced and panting, I kept repeating to
sheltering gunners my escape as if it was a thing unique.

This was the refilling point where I left pigeons to be pic
picked up by infantrymen from the line.   Another lull
intervening, I was soon off on my undamaged "'bus."

         *   *   *   *   *

Corporal

"Did ye hear tell about Cpl. Green?" I was asked
next morning by Dan, the gritty Irishman in charge of
our refilling point.

"No.   What happened?"

"Killed---yesterday.   In the embankment dug-out when
you came through."

"Dan, that must have been Green who beckoned to me to
go down to him!   Of course---he'd got pigeon baskets."

4

"Poor old Green," I mused.   "The days and days I've
dished out pigeons to him.   Now he's flattened out!   And
I never guessed!"

"And yon mon Littleton with him---ye mind him?---his arm
was blown off.   XXHXXRX A Despatch Rider in the dug-out
was wounded, too.   I never did think much to yon dug-out!"
Dan shook his head with professional disparagement.   "Ye
may think ye're lucky ye came on."

ital.

"I made sure I was going to stop that shell, Dan.   I
don't expect Green felt it coming---he's made the trip
safely so many times---yet it got him.   Curious.   That's
just how it happens."

5.

DIGGING DEFENCE LINES.

BY OSWALD HARCOURT.

[ARTICLE, LENGTH 470 WORDS, by OSWALD H. DAVIS, contributor to
DAILY MAIL, DAILY NEWS, PUNCH, COUNTRY LIFE, ACADEMY, EVERYMAN, ETC.]

ADDRESS: CPL. O.H. DAVIS, 148768, DESPATCH RIDER, X CORPS H.Q. SIGNAL COY, B.E.F.

In the evening we pioneers, girt with
tin hat, box respirator, rifle, shovel and pick,
emerge from our delapidated billets.
Forming into file, we march in sections
to the ground allotted to us under the
defence scheme. "Stop smoking," comes the
order as we approach hostile observation.

The journey is often a long plod and
stumble through the dark across wet and
slippy fields, ploughed soil, muddy tracks,
or down and up over old trenches. Sometimes
only the pale crust of dried mud or dust on
improvised leggings makes visible the guiding

1

DIGGING DEFENCE LINES (JUNE 1918)

form in front. One has to listen carefully
for the leader's warnings:

"Hand wire overhead. Big hole on the left.
Step over here — wire underfoot."

If a serious obstacle is met, a halt is
called by the officer, and he waits till the
message "All closed up" (with the obstacle
behind) comes.

On arrival, ground is marked out by
the officer pacing so many feet to each man.
~~We "argue the toss": will it be ~~ ~~trench~~
~~so ft. deep by 4 ft. wide with a bottom~~
~~soft wide, so they cross to 3 x 2 ft.?~~

It is when working in shrapnel helmets,
with gas masks at the alert and fixed
bayonets handy, that knack and experience
count. The old hand uses a bright clean

2.

shovel, and, first digging a "spit" — a stratum
of soil the length, of his portion of trench
and the full depth of the spade — he throws
the "loose" on the parapet.

<small>and width</small>

Working in pitch dark, the wavering brilliance
of the Verey light is not unwelcome : we
sometimes wait for it to check progress and
correct construction.

If the order comes round, "Go home
by platoons as soon as finished," a zest
is put into our efforts which soon "gets
the job groggy". The sergeant and his
measuring stick are anxiously sought.

"A spit and a scrape, with the sides
trimmed, will do it here, sergeant."

"When you've done that, get up and
clear the berm, and level down the

3

parapet to 9 inches," responds that official impassively. The berm is a 2ft. space between the trench edge and the parapet.

The task completed, the officer inspects the job, and, if satisfied, orders: "Get dressed," and then, "get closed up in the trench."

With the peevish rattle of machine guns and the vindictive thump of shells receding behind us, we eagerly await the permission, "Smoke if you like." If dead beat with toil and tramp, not a syllable passes our lips. If lively, wit and genial abuse fly.

Last of all comes the soothing desire of tea at billets, and when we "get down to it" the early morn is on us. We sleep late, parade for inspection, and the rest of the day till the night spell is our own.

PRESS BUREAU,
Passed as censored

K.W. 4.

DIGGING DEFENCE LINES.

ARTICLE, LENGTH 470 WORDS, by OSWALD HARCOURT [OSWALD H. DAVIS, contributor to DAILY MAIL, DAILY NEWS, PUNCH, COUNTRY LIFE, ACADEMY, EVERY MAN, ETC.]

ADDRESS: CPL. O.H. DAVIS, 145768, DESPATCH RIDER, X CORPS HQ SIGNAL COY, BEF

20/8/15

THE GATES OF LEAVE

~~PAYING TOLL FOR BLIGHTY.~~

Short article, length 1120 words, by Oswald H. Davis.
Address:
Cpl. O.H. Davis, 148768, R.E.
X Corps H.Q. Signal Coy., B.E.F., France.

------

ital.

At last in the little bed-stuffed orderly clerks' room
back of the Épicerie shop the miracle happened for which
the three of us had waited seventeen months.   All our
pay credit of over 100 francs each was handed to us
together with the green paper leave warrant, a medical
certificate of health, a typewritten pass, and a sheet
of leave-conduct instructions.   Our kit donned, we sang
our way to the station in the "quarter-bloke's" ration
lorry.
Our leave smile irradiated the Railway Transport Office.

"What time does the leave train start?   We wanted to
get a posh dinner to celebrate the occasion if there's
a chance."

soldier

"Can't help that," barked the clerk.   "Parade in
the waiting-hall at 1 o'clock.   Next man!"

THE GATES OF LEAVE (AUGUST 1918)

322 | TRIUMPH ON THE WESTERN FRONT

The banquet foregone, our pride of leave yet turned the
slow train ride into a festival of travel. Our seaport
was reached at dusk, "Shall we have the luck to be whisked
magically away to Blighty?" we murmured. "Form up in the
yard," was shouted. The multitude shuffled into fours and
gradually straggled across the quay sidings.

Then, instead of being beckoned shipward and spirited
over the strip of water, the trail of leave pilgrims was led
through the town and up a rough dark hill behind. Men who
had been all morning "flogging" it from the line stumbled
under their gear and kit-bag. After a mile or so we halted
upon a wide space between dim hut-shapes of a camp lit wanly
by electric standards.

"Line up!"

"Fall out warrant officers, staff sergeants and sergeants,"
megaphoned a grizzled S.M. in slacks.

Half an hour's wait while hurricane lamps made swaying
yellow spots in the dark. "You ten men," ordered a voice
suddenly, "D line, last tent. Draw two blankets each from
the store over there. Breakfast at 7."

We puzzled the tent out. A good supper was brought us
ere we had made the cold circle of canvas clean and habitable.

At the warm well-appointed canteen, cheap hot dishes were
to be bought. A ration breakfast of copious tea, ham
and pickles, revived us after a frozen night-doze on the
wind-swept plateau.

Having waited half the morning on parade, we were
marched loosely off. "Down to the boat at last!" we
carolled. But misgivings crept into our morning gaiety
as we detoured over the hills. Sadly we saw the head of
the column right-turn into a large camp, and fall in, line
behind line.

Again the megaphone chant: "Fall out. . . etc. Fall
out all men of ------- Division or attached." (Poor
devils---leave cancelled!) And then a regular church
service of prohibitions, winding up with---"To your left
front are the latrines; right front, the ablution shed". . .
and so on.

After dinner the various huts and canteens closed down.
The wintry cold made it too cheerless for sitting or reading
even under canvas. Before us stretched the length of hours
or days we might have to spend here, a dull void of doing
and seeing nothing, always at the mercy of a possible
recall, while over there, safe in "God's own land", every
one of these wasted minutes could have been touched to
gold by the magic of home. We prowled desolately between
the loathed scenery of huts and tents, and round and round

the barbed wire which, day and night, squared us off from
the rolling freedom of fields and the towm. At last I
understood the intense misery of the jailed.

At 5, through a packed scrimmage in the canteen, we
conquered tea and a seat in the warmth, till suddenly
a voice bawled through the room (instantly departing):

3.

"Réveillé at 3 a.m. Breakfast 6.30, passes stamped at 5."
Delight at the chance of departure tingled our veins,
and we danced through driving rain to our tent.

Before midnight half the tent floor was flooded by a
strong gale. The men stood or crouched good-humouredly
in the chill candlelight till the whistle blew at 3.

In the streaming murk could be seen the usual messroom
queue, huddling patiently as cattle. Waiting, we
noticed elsewhere a vast herd nosing and edgeing, kit-laden,
in a certain direction. By painful inches we worked our way
round vague shapes of tents, after the column of soldiers.
An hour elapsing, we reached a show of movement, a hut door
aglow.

"Hurry up! Leave warrant---back upward. Pass through,"
shouted one of two sergeants seated at a trestle table as he
banged a rubber stamp on the warrant of each man filing by.
"Come on, I've got nowt to do!" chimed the other, waving
his hand for a pass to date. And thus we won a day's
extra leave to compensate for the 24 hours lost by delay

"Rest Camps"

in camp.

"We're off, by God!" The cry spoke truth. Soon we
marched blithely to the harbour and wound slowly in and
out the enclosed dockside. Should we be searched for
shell-noses or letters at the last moment? "Pass on,
pass on! Show only your green warrant, stamped side
uppermost," enjoined the scarlet-banded M.P. Two more
red-caps at the gate and one at the ship side glanced at our
papers. All over! We pranced on board, diving well down
amongst the machinery.

The boat is filled. Officers make every man seek out
and wear cork floats from the lockers. The sea and its
traffic look the *much* same as in peace. A bar of cloud
changes into the creamy front of Blighty. . .

Disembarking, we are shepherded by red-caps to the trains
and away from the prim listless port. We can't realize we're
home. After the robust traffic *activities* of war zones, the countryside seems in a swoon. Victoria! Now we know our leave
is real as we step out to the plash of station traffic,
breathe the savour of London streets, and feel the stinging
beauty of Englishwomen.

      *   *   *   *   *

Victoria again, ~~down~~, a fortnight later. The platform
entrances are a crush of soldiers heaving with quiet purpose to
toward the trains. There is no strife and little noise.
A few low words are passed to accompanying loved ones,
and the men are tragically off.

At sea again, we have no interest now but to slumber
darkly between decks.   In the night we are once more marched
off to a camp and lined up.   Officers, enquiring our unit,
consult their lists and designate our trains, as B rear
or C front.   After taking supper and haversack rations
we parade near midnight and jog down to the drear station
and the crowded unlit trains.   There we lie wearily
in an icy luggage van till the compartment starts to
jolt, screech and crawl to an unknown destination in the
bitter dawn.

PRESS BUREAU,

Passed as censored.

6

THE GATES OF LEAVE

ARTICLE, length 1120 words, by OSWALD HARCOURT
(OSWALD H. DAVIS, contributor to DAILY MAIL, DAILY NEWS,
PUNCH, COUNTRY LIFE, ACADEMY, POETRY REVIEW, ETC.).

ADDRESS: CPL. O.H. DAVIS, 148768, DESPATCH RIDER,
X CORPS H.Q. SIGNAL COY., B.E.F. FRANCE.

Passed by MILITARY CENSOR, PRESS BUREAU, WHITEHALL S.W.I on 16-3-18.

THE GATES OF LEAVE – PAGE 7

CANT ABOUT KHAKI (DECEMBER 1918) – NOT AUTHORISED BY THE PRESS
BUREAU FOR PUBLICATION

AUTHOR'S NOTE.

The OFFICIAL PRESS BUREAU, on December 27th. 1918, refused permission for this article to be published. The Bureau returned the article to me registered as No. 143806.

With the raising of the Censorship there appears to be no reason for the suppression of the MS.

:CANT ABOUT KHAKI.

—Article, length 1900 words, By Oswald Harcourt.

Address: Oswald H. Davis, 578 Coventry Road, Birmingham.

After soldiering, I find myself constrained to agree with
views which, before the war, I thought extreme. One of
the opinions to which I have become a convert is the
conviction that the British public, on the subject of its own
virtues, is guilty of habitual cant.

During war-time such cant finds intensified expression,
because, in praising its soldiers, the nation is subtly
lauding itself for qualities not actually assayed except
by proxy.

From reading normal official speech and conventional
screed about the war, I conclude that a nation which can encourage such widespread delusions about itself in khaki
is a nation born into cant by tradition, and sustained in

1

cant by an organized conspiracy of government and press. Obviously, truth should be more generally told and a shock administered, before the nation's constitution, weak from systematic drugging by flasehood, becomes too enfeebled for reform.

In glorification of our army the press and eminent public men have made continual representations which are seen to be false as soon as they are coldly examined in the light of logic or experience.

The prime, recurrent theme in these effusions is the unfailing courage of our troops. Nay, more than courage, foolhardiness. Men were supposed loudly to repine that owing to an accident of leave or sickness they had "missed a show"--been honourably debarred from deadly battle. The "only regret" of our fleet is reported to have been that "they couldn't have another smack" at the German navy. Put into plain sense, this means that soldiers and sailors have addressed themselves thus: " An unfortunate event (say the Armistice) has robbed me finally of the chance of being dismembered or blown to pulp, unless I decide to

2

hack myself with a cutlass or play with explosives."
Men going over the top have been described as exhilarated
and eager to "do him in", and the cavalry as "keen-faced
for combat", and so forth. Can the bulk of men who are
about to offer their bodies to ghastly mutilation,
poisoning or death, feel aught beforehand but a deadly
sickening which they strive to overcome? Has any war
correspondent been allowed to relate cases of cowardice
in British soldiers? You would infer that panic never
occurs and that men with white livers have suffered
mysterious transfiguration. The whole army, almost
without exception apparently, was cool, resourceful,
audacious--infact superhuman. Before the war there existed certain classes of people hated and abused by press
and public--strikers, crooks, hooligans, etc. These men
enlist and don khaki; straightway one and all become Sir
Galahads, whom, with our lips, we are proud to admire.
 Actually, we know that bravery in the human race is
of a fairly fixed percentage. Roughly speaking, a

3

quarter of any given army are practically fearless; half (the average) are neither of pronounced courage nor pusillanimity, but are capable of either; the remaining quarter are rank cowards. I have seen in the army worse poltroons and more absurd panic than I had ever before imagined possible. On the other hand, an emotion such as loyalty to comrades, or desire of revenge, will sweep like fire over the average half and affect them martially; or such temperaments will allow a gradual development of valour. But the first and last classes rarely alter. As it is with human nature, so it is with us and our soldiers.

In patriotism, civilians excel. The avuncular generation who toiled hard all the week and acted as special constable in their brief leisure, worked harder than the otdinary soldier. That the 1914 volunteers and others were patriotic in the highest sense, is evident. But harshness and unim-

usually / patriotism aginativeness of service treatment soon killed all that.

few Conversing with hundreds, I have met no soldiers who woul

join the colours again except on two grounds: (a) Love o

sensual what is lazy, sensual and irresponsible in the life; (b)

4

Means of gaining a livelihood.   As I write, the men who
"fought for King and Country" are saying:[*]

A corporal: "If they want me again, they'll have to drag me
out of the house with a rope."

An Irishman: "Never again!   The girls can stick white
feathers all over me--they'll come in handy for cleaning
my pipe."

A Scotchman: "Next time they 'need' me I shall 'need'
something--a contract in black and white to keep my wife

and bairns and business decently going while I'm away."

A soldier's bark is worse than his bite: he attributes
fictitious failings to himself.   Make due allowance for this
and you have the truth.

The following are typical news paragraphs of war years.

"The King, during his visit to the front yesterday,

- -

[*] Written December 1918 at a Reception Camp, Menin.
The paucity of voluntary re-enlistments, even in response to
the Churchill bounty scheme and the genuine bait of happy,
indolent days in the Rhine Army, have now proved my words.

5

reviewed the famous ------ Regiment.   It was noticeable
with what proud mien and alert bearing the men carried out
their duties thenceforward.   All day beaming faces were
everywhere."

Again—

"The King took a hand at pushing the truck himself.   The
pioneers were delighted at His Majesty's prowess and deeply
touched by this mark of condescension."

Is kingship then divine, or do British soldiers normally
conduct themselves like swains in love, that they pulse with
ecstasy and pride when a human being who happens to be a hard-
working, modest, likeable monarch passes by at 20 paces,
or exhibits cursory interest in their work?

What soldiers actually say (and I have several spicy
verbatim reports collected on such occasions) would not bear
repeating here.   Men who painfully "posh up" for review,
and then wait stiffly and vacantly on a sodden parade ground
for an hour or so, do not luxuriate in the experience.

The French Army, without fuss, is really democratic.   Their
officers converse freely with the men, and will eat with them.

6

Our army, now as ever, is ruled by caste. One day, the Officer Commanding a Brigade of R.F.A. found himself passing his men as they were seated eating, exposed to his gaze, in an open cookhouse. Thereupon he ordered that the room should be screened off from his view or the cookhouse moved. Such incidents can be multiplied indefinitely.

Our new army contained in its ranks men of wealth, sometimes of title. Do you think those illustrious privates were not fully conscious of their influence, or failed to make it felt? Snobbery, either of brains, money or birth, is rife in the army. It is notorious that influence can secure "cushy" berths for its protégés. It is not in civilian life alone that there is one law for the well-connected and another for the basely born.

Why was it necessary to represent Tommies as always cheerful? Photographed in a sagging ruin, see them, framed by sandbags and a rockery of tin cans, simpering with bliss amid the foetid damp. Their daily pork and beans is a ration they "expectantly await". No "wounded hero" in bandages was complete without a "smiling" or "radiant" face.

7

Ital.

Ital.

Had the photographer spent a few weeks, as a soldier under discipline, on iron rations, with no privacy, uncouth sanitation, insect troubles and other demoralizing discomforts of active service, his own smile would have been somewhat wry.

A well established form of cant is that covered by the idea of casualness in the British soldier. Tommy was pictured as drily smart, saying (on his return from leave), "We've just got to go back and sweep up the mess over there," (I.e. "We're such wonderful creatures that to restore order in a convulsed continent is a mere bagatelle to us.") A battle is a "scrap." "We just side-slipped over and bagged their headquarters and a few batteries," yawns an officer. To pretend that things in reality big are to us small is mere hypocrisy.

Are we a chivalrous race? Undoubtedly. Yet war is war. You do not get vast bodies of men artificially herded together in camps or barracks save at the expense of morals. The soldier's one virtue is that he is brutally frank about the matter. The animal side has been forced to the front:

8

he admits it.   Naturally, his relations with women suffer.
He comes into contact only with certain types, generally
speaking.   If people at home heard the language of our
soldiers before and to women in the average estaminet, they
would refuse to credit their senses.   They would do so because
they are unimaginative and illogical.   They refuse to see
that the price of militarism includes moral degradation
besides blood and gold.   Furthermore, at home, they cloak
sensuality with a decent mantle; and this silken screen
they persist in throwing over khaki.

So universal with us is the habit of make-believe that
it has begun to cover up all true details of the war, as
sandbags disguised the features of a town under fire.   'A
public writer who deems himself the national executioner of
cant once pilloried a clergyman who accused soldiers of
blasphemy in hospital.   I have so far escaped military hos-
pitals, but from what I have heard of corruption and
callousness in many such, I should say they invited khaki
blasphemy, considering that it is the natural thing for
soldiers to curse and take the Lord's name in vain.

9

When, in order to swell the army on paper, the craze was high for pushing everyman into khaki, there was much discussion about artists. Since artists are unduly sensitive, commonsense would say, "They are the last men for the firing line." But no. Press and public cried out: "Never mind art: artists should go the same as other men." Though artists are irreplaceable, let that pass on the understanding that a man, being a man, must fight in the common cause of mankind. Yet what, in practice, do we find? While a Rupert Brooke and his obscurer kin had their steps trenchward unobtrusively accelerated, till death was reached, our professional prizefighters (who should, if any, be able to fight) discovered themselves shunted with equal facility on to home service jobs and made Company Sergeant-Major Instructors. (I may mention that a C. S. M. in the army enjoys power that sultans might envy.) At base stations footballers and cricketers were hung on to like earls, the paramount object being to strengthen their unit in sports prowess.

10

There are many minor manifestations of this practice of cant. Such as fulsome praises from a Parliament and War Staff which call their fighters "deathless heroes who saved Europe", etc. etc. ad nauseam, but take no real steps to ascertain how these admirable Crichtons get treated by the underlings of Military Authority/. The priestly fiction that men "found" religion at the front. That soldiers work with enthusiastic industry. That their diversions are in- nocuous. That our organization is "clockword." That generals idolized by the public are beloved of their troops, or that devotion to officers is a feature of our so- called "democratic" army. Each of the above inventions could be added to in number, or expanded to a paragraph.

But enough has been said to show that the odious tissue of misrepresentation is being continually spun in thicker and wider webs that threaten to enmesh and clog our best activities. In spite of this and other shortcomings we won the war because of a great cause, some virtues, plus a fleet, natural resources and sound allies. But, should we be launched on another war, lacking happy

11

auspices and friends, then the penalty of such inveterate
self-deception will be grave. We should go into the fight
a blindfolded people. On the other hand, if we first learn
the truth, and know and understand ourselves, we can seek
a cure and reform. We have, as soldiers, some remarkable
qualities, so far largely unrecognised, rarely appraised.
Yet these qualities are distinctive, appropriate to a great
nation. On them we could safely found an honest, zealous,
efficient and impressive force, which should make for lasting
peace or help to preserve it in Europe.

12

CANT ABOUT KHAKI.

ARTICLE, length 1900 words, By Oswald Harcourt

(Oswald H. Davis, contributor to Country Life, Academy,
Daily News, Daily Mail, Everyman, etc.).

ADRESS: C.H. Davis, 578 Coventry Road, Small Heath, Birmingham.

END NOTES

1. *Everyman* was created by publisher J. M. Dent in October 1912, but was stopped sometime during the war. The magazine was relaunched in 1929 addressing the subjects of books, drama, music and travel.
2. Unsure of the meaning of this word. Cooper can mean to fix up, so possibly Oswald is saying sarcastically in the negative.
3. This could possibly be a type of Hessian.
4. A book by Arnold Bennet, whose biography Davis later wrote.
5. The Sussex Yeoman was in fact wrong here. Charles I came from the House of Stuart. I think Oswald was being humorously sarcastic here.
6. This is most likely referring to people from Derby, a town sixty miles southeast of Manchester.
7. 'The Dead March' comes from a work *Saul* which is an oratorio in three acts written by George Frideric Handel.
8. Better known as Sergeant Schofield.
9. Unsure what Oswald meant by this.
10. A training scheme i.e. set training drill or procedure.
11. This refers to both the anarchist Peter Piakow of the 1911 Sidney Street Siege and the Mauser pistol that he wielded.
12. 'Flimsies' refers to the thin paper onto which all despatches were triplicated if they were to be carried DR or pigeon.
13. 'Warm' here refers to dangerous.
14. A device used to open an exhaust valve in order to stop an engine or to assist in starting.

[15] Unsure what Oswald meant by this.

[16] Unsure what a Tiffy Shop is.

[17] The word 'crush' is contemporary slang for a unit of chums.

[18] A routine message delivery.

[19] Mauvauts is the name of an estaminet. Later in the diary it is mentioned again and frequented by Oswald.

[20] 'Jute' may be contemporary slang for remanufactured. By 1918 damaged motorcycles were returned to the factories for comprehensive overhaul, but enforced use of unskilled labour meant poorer standards of workmanship than before the war.

[21] All motorcycles at this time depended on magneto ignition.

[22] See Appendix .

[23] See Appendix.

[24] See Appendix.

[25] See Appendix.

[26] Stout, hard-wearing road surface of very large cobbles. Often greasy and difficult for despatch riders to traverse.

[27] See Appendix.

ND - #0190 - 270225 - C0 - 234/156/16 - PB - 9781908487568 - Gloss Lamination